Promoting Competition
in Regulated Markets

p1 -13
p55 -99

Studies in the Regulation of Economic Activity

Promoting Competition in Regulated Markets

ALMARIN PHILLIPS, Editor

The Brookings Institution / Washington, D.C.

300567

Library of Congress Cataloging in Publication Data:
Main entry under title:
Promoting competition in regulated markets.

(Studies in the regulation of economic activity)
Based on papers, except the first chapter of this
book, prepared for a conference of experts in regulatory
affairs held at the Brookings Institution, Oct. 1971.
Includes bibliographical references and index.
1. Industry and state—United States—Addresses,
essays, lectures. 2. Competition—Addresses, essays,
lectures. I. Phillips, Almarin. II. Series.
HD3616.U47P76   338.6'048'0973   74-277
ISBN 0-8157-7052-9

9 8 7 6 5 4 3 2 1

THE BROOKINGS INSTITUTION is an independent organization devoted to nonpartisan research, education, and publication in economics, government, foreign policy, and the social sciences generally. Its principal purposes are to aid in the development of sound public policies and to promote public understanding of issues of national importance.

The Institution was founded on December 8, 1927, to merge the activities of the Institute for Government Research, founded in 1916, the Institute of Economics, founded in 1922, and the Robert Brookings Graduate School of Economics and Government, founded in 1924.

The Board of Trustees is responsible for the general administration of the Institution, while the immediate direction of the policies, program, and staff is vested in the President, assisted by an advisory committee of the officers and staff. The by-laws of the Institution state, "It is the function of the Trustees to make possible the conduct of scientific research, and publication, under the most favorable conditions, and to safeguard the independence of the research staff in the pursuit of their studies and in the publication of the results of such studies. It is not a part of their function to determine, control, or influence the conduct of particular investigations or the conclusions reached."

The President bears final responsibility for the decision to publish a manuscript as a Brookings book or staff paper. In reaching his judgment on the competence, accuracy, and objectivity of each study, the President is advised by the director of the appropriate research program and weighs the views of a panel of expert outside readers who report to him in confidence on the quality of the work. Publication of a work signifies that it is deemed to be a competent treatment worthy of public consideration; such publication does not imply endorsement of conclusions or recommendations contained in the study.

The Institution maintains its position of neutrality on issues of public policy in order to safeguard the intellectual freedom of the staff. Hence interpretations or conclusions in Brookings publications should be understood to be solely those of the author or authors and should not be attributed to the Institution, to its trustees, officers, or other staff members, or to the organizations that support its research.

Foreword

THIS volume is the thirteenth in the Brookings Studies in the Regulation of Economic Activity. The series was planned at a time when only a few had recognized that economic regulation was generating chronic and growing public policy problems. True, it was clear to even the casual observer that the railroads and the Interstate Commerce Commisson were in trouble; but it was not widely perceived that the same general problems were shared by other regulated industries and by regulatory agencies at all levels of government.

The present book appears at a time when the many failures in economic regulation are all too obvious. Recent years have seen increasing criticism of the effects of government regulation on consumers, on regulated firms, and, indeed, on the authority and capacity of the regulatory agencies to deal with the problems of the next several decades. The President, the Congress, state legislatures, and, in some instances, the regulatory agencies themselves are actively considering far-reaching changes. Proposals for reform range from the complete abolition of regulation, through changes in regulatory procedure, to the extension of regulation into new areas.

This book investigates the possibility and desirability of diminishing the scope of regulation. It presents the findings of intensive studies of eight different industries and an appraisal of the practical legal and institutional difficulties likely to be encountered in changing regulatory policy. The following kinds of questions are raised: What aspects of the industry are regulated? What are the goals of regulation? How do various regulatory agencies react to particular problems? Does the public benefit from regulation? Would the substitution of competitive market forces for direct regulation be preferable in some cases? The authors generally agree that competition should play a larger role in regulated industries, but they differ in the degree to which they see such change as being desirable or possible.

George C. Eads considers domestic air service; Thomas Gale Moore, surface transportation; Robert Larner, ocean shipping; Leonard W.

Weiss, electric utilities; Walter J. Primeaux, Jr., the costs of electricity in a competitive situation; Leonard Waverman, the role of the Federal Communications Commission in intercity telecommunications; Dennis E. Smallwood, the automobile insurance industry; H. Michael Mann, the New York Stock Exchange; and Almarin Phillips, depository financial institutions. In addition, Mr. Phillips provides an introduction to the issues, and Edwin Zimmerman gives a legal overview focusing on the problems associated with efforts to expand the scope of competition.

Earlier versions of all but the first chapter of this book were prepared as background papers for a conference of experts in regulatory affairs held at the Brookings Institution in October 1971. The participants in that conference are listed on pages 385–86.

Mr. Phillips and the authors wish to acknowledge especially the help provided by W. Bruce Allen, William O. Bailey, Donald I. Baker, William F. Baxter, Richard S. Bower, Gary Bowman, Samuel B. Chase, Allen Ferguson, Gene Finn, Victor P. Goldberg, William A. Jordan, Paul MacAvoy, Michael D. McCarthy, James W. Meehan, Jr., James C. Miller III, Neil Murphy, Roger G. Noll, William Nordhaus, Richard A. Posner, Robert H. Rasche, Benjamin R. Schenck, Richard Schmalensee, Dean E. Sharp, Robert Stern, Hugh Tobin, Richard F. Walsh, Lawrence White, and John F. Wilson. Thanks are also extended to the anonymous referees, whose comments were helpful in the revision of the papers for publication. Ellen A. Ash edited the manuscript and Evelyn P. Fisher checked the sources and data. Florence Robinson prepared the index.

The Brookings series of Studies in the Regulation of Economic Activity presents the findings of a program of research focused on public policies toward business. The program is supported by a grant from the Ford Foundation and has been directed by Joseph A. Pechman, director of the Brookings Economic Studies program, and Roger G. Noll, professor of economics at the California Institute of Technology and a former Brookings senior fellow.

The views expressed in this book are those of the authors and should not be attributed to the trustees, officers, or staff of the Brookings Institution or to the Ford Foundation.

KERMIT GORDON
President

January 1975
Washington, D.C.

Contents

Figures

CHAPTER ONE

Introduction

ALMARIN PHILLIPS

THE DISTINCTION that has been drawn in law and economics between regulated and unregulated industries is misleading. It is possible, of course, to identify regulatory agencies that have specifically mandated controls over particular types of economic activity. State public utility commissions and federal agencies such as the Interstate Commerce Commission, the Federal Power Commission, the Federal Communications Commission, the Civil Aeronautics Board, and hosts of others fall into this category: regulation is their business. Nonetheless, lumping firms that fall under the jurisdiction of such agencies into the class of "regulated" industries and explicitly or implicitly relegating others to the "unregulated" class creates a distinction that is more artificial than real.

Such a distinction should be avoided for two reasons. First, there are profound differences in rationale and mode of regulation among members of the regulated class.[1] For instance, regulation may be required in the distribution of gas and electricity because of economies of scale and the existence of "natural monopolies"; this surely is not the basis for regulating the price farmers receive for milk. Regulation of radio and television involves licensing and limited control over service quality, but essentially no control over pricing. Regulation of taxi service, on the other hand, involves detailed price regulation as well as licensing in some locales, and little regulation of any kind in others. Second, there are no industries that are totally unregulated. The automobile industry would not ordinarily be considered regulated, yet special laws have been enacted to govern its dealings with distributors and to enforce safety and pollution standards. Is the industry regulated or unregulated? Meat packing and food canning

---

1. For a brief discussion, see Alfred E. Kahn, *The Economics of Regulation: Principles and Institutions* (John Wiley, 1970), vol. 1, pp. 1–19.

1

would typically be classed as unregulated industries, but they are subject to numerous grading, packaging, and health regulations. Regulated or unregulated? What of the pharmaceutical industry? Barbers and beauticians? Operators of private fleets of trucks?

The important issues in the consideration of regulation concern not whether a particular activity is regulated or unregulated, but rather what aspects of the activity are regulated, why they are regulated, and whether or not the public benefits from the regulations.

This book is about the regulation of industry—not just public utility regulation in the traditional sense, but the regulation of markets generally. In contrast to most books dealing with the economics of regulation, little is said here about rate base, allowable return on investment, and other traditional concerns of utility regulation. In the context of this book, the economics of regulation is the economics of "market failure"; that is, it is concerned with failures of the market mechanism to allocate resources properly and with the regulatory devices, including the use of market forces, that may be employed to correct for these failures.

Regulation and Market Failure

Market failures occur for many reasons.[2] It is failure due to structural deficiencies that has received by far the greatest attention in the literature of industrial organization. Here, monopoly, oligopoly, and otherwise imperfectly competitive market structures cause inefficient resource allocation and socially undesirable market performance. Included in this category are market shortcomings arising from the actions of market participants— monopolization, price discrimination, advertising and other forms of non-price rivalry, entry-preventive behavior, and (especially emphasized in recent literature) business conduct directed toward objectives other than profit maximization. In general, antitrust policy and regulation through the creation and maintenance of competitive conditions are the remedies suggested for such market failures, but direct regulation of certain facets of industry behavior—product quality regulation, for example—are not infrequently imposed on ostensibly competitive industries.

Market failure due to "natural monopoly" is a special case of structural failure. Natural monopoly occurs when economies of scale are so extensive

2. For an early and excellent discussion, see Francis M. Bator, "The Anatomy of Market Failure," *Quarterly Journal of Economics*, vol. 72 (August 1958), pp. 351–79.

relative to the size of the market that only one firm can operate efficiently within the bounds of market demand. Remedy by means of the structural modifications intended to create competitive conditions is impossible. Instead, direct regulation, often under the rubric of "public utility" regulation, has been utilized. The character of the regulation differs greatly among the industries in which conditions of natural monopoly may exist, and public utility regulation has often been applied in cases where natural monopoly clearly does not exist.

A second category of market failures includes those due to externalities. Even without inefficiencies caused by structural or conduct deficiencies, the social and economic organization may be such that evaluations of costs and benefits by decision-making units within the market differ from social evaluations. The classic case involves what might be called "Marshallian-Pigouvian" externalities.[3] Failure occurs when real or technological, as contrasted with pecuniary, external economies or diseconomies produce decreasing or increasing industry costs. While each firm in an industry may operate efficiently from its own point of view, none responds to the fact that social cost is below or above private cost. Theoretically, the remedy is the imposition of an appropriate tax (for increasing costs) or the grant of an appropriate subsidy (for decreasing costs) in order to equalize private and social costs. At the policy level, however, this sort of regulation is rare, probably because of the paucity of evidence that externalities present important problems in the real word.

The situation is different, however, where market failure occurs because of other kinds of externalities.[4] If the costs of one firm are affected by the rate of output or other performance characteristics of another firm, externalities in production exist. Air and water pollution are obvious illustrations of such market failure: the costs of some firms are increased because of the waste disposal practices of others. Similarly, if the satis-

---

3. For a theoretical treatment, see Howard S. Ellis and William Fellner, "External Economies and Diseconomies," *American Economic Review*, vol. 33 (September 1943), pp. 493–511. See also Alfred Marshall, *Principles of Economics* (8th ed., Macmillan, 1920), bk. 5, chap. 13.

4. For discussions of externalities and their effects on resource allocation, see, in addition to Bator's "The Anatomy of Market Failure," James M. Buchanan and W. Craig Stubblebine, "Externality," *Economica*, n.s. vol. 29 (November 1962), pp. 371–84; E. J. Mishan, "The Postwar Literature on Externalities: An Interpretative Essay," *Journal of Economic Literature*, vol. 9 (March 1971), pp. 1–28; and Otto A. Davis and Andrew B. Whinston, "Some Notes on Equating Private and Social Cost," *Southern Economic Journal*, vol. 32 (October 1965), pp. 113–26.

faction of one consumer is affected by the consumption behavior of others, externalities in consumption exist. And if the well-being of a consumer is related to the output or other performance characteristics of firms, externalities between consumption and production exist.

Judging from the volume of recent literature on the subject and the number of regulatory devices suggested and used as remedies, market failures due to such externalities must be both ubiquitous and consequential. While structural and conduct remedies analogous to regulation via competition are sometimes suggested,[5] tax-subsidy approaches similar to those indicated for the Marshallian-Pigouvian externalities dominate theoretical literature.[6] In practice, the direct regulation of conduct is by far the more common approach. Thus, because of externalities, conduct regulations abound in the areas of health, education, culture, and safety; and their number is currently growing in the area of environmental qualities of all sorts.

There is a special class of externalities relating to so-called public goods.[7] These are goods which, when provided for one person or group of persons, yield similar benefits to others. Put another way, consumption by one person of a public good does not lessen the quantity of that good available to others. Pure cases of public goods are difficult to find. The provision of national security is the most frequently cited example; whatever its level and regardless of whom the security immediately affects, all derive the benefits (or, perhaps, the social costs). Quantities of it can in no way be assigned to individuals; by definition, individuals cannot choose to take less of a public good in exchange for more of any other good. Problems of collective action thus emerge, with political processes supplanting the market mechanism.

Whether or not pure public goods exist, there are many goods that have similar characteristics. To some extent, police and judicial systems, public art galleries, beautification programs, and parks fall into this category. Samuelson has noted that there are dimensions of television

5. See, in particular, R. H. Coase, "The Problem of Social Cost," *Journal of Law and Economics*, vol. 3 (October 1960), pp. 1–44.

6. For an elementary, but typical, treatment, see Earl R. Rolph and George F. Break, *Public Finance* (Ronald, 1961), p. 375.

7. See Paul A. Samuelson, "The Pure Theory of Public Expenditure," *Review of Economics and Statistics*, vol. 36 (November 1954), pp. 387–89; and idem, "Aspects of Public Expenditure Theories," *Review of Economics and Statistics*, vol. 40 (November 1958), pp. 332–38.

and radio services that are public in character.[8] Market failures attributable to the nature of public goods also require regulation, and publicly operated production facilities and the direct regulation of private facilities are the typical remedies.

Criticisms of Regulation

While there are numerous theoretical rationales for regulation, regulatory activity can also be criticized on both theoretical and practical grounds. It is the theory of second best that provides the most general caveat about regulation aimed at allocative efficiency.[9] In brief, the theory says that Pareto optimal conditions define welfare-maximizing conditions only when they are applicable to *all* economic activities. Should there be a violation of these conditions in *any* activity in the economy—because of monopoly, sumptuary controls, mandatory income distribution constraints, or whatever—the attainment of what otherwise would be optimal conditions in every other sector of the economy is not consistent with the constrained, second-best result. That is, the usual optimal conditions may apply to *some* other sectors, but they cannot apply to *all* other sectors. Moreover, while the second-best conditions are easily defined mathematically, isolation of the sectors in which the usual Pareto conditions apply and those in which other conditions apply requires specification of the social objective function, of the constraints arising from technical causes, and of the "additional" constraints. Without such specification, there can be no assurance that policy aimed at reducing monopoly power in any one market, or creating "ideal" pricing rules in a public utility, will necessarily increase social welfare. This makes decisions about regulation much less straightforward, since good judgment about complicated circumstances rather than formally demonstrable optimal conditions must

8. "Aspects of Public Expenditure Theories." See, however, the controversy on this point beginning with Jora R. Minasian, "Television Pricing and the Theory of Public Goods," *Journal of Law and Economics*, vol. 7 (October 1964), pp. 71–80, and comments and replies by Samuelson, James M. Buchanan, and Minasian in the October 1967 (vol. 10) issue of the *Journal*, pp. 193–207.

9. See R. G. Lipsey and Kelvin Lancaster, "The General Theory of Second Best," *Review of Economic Studies*, vol. 24 (1), no. 63 (1956–57), pp. 11–32, although this was not the first work to consider the problem.

be relied upon in deciding what to regulate, how to regulate, and what the resulting social benefits will be.

At a less general level, but still related to the second-best concept, is the theoretical criticism of rate-of-return utility rate making. If regulation in a natural monopoly case takes the form of requiring "fair" (or competitive) rates of return on investment, it can easily be demonstrated that the price which provides a fair return for a firm with decreasing average costs can never be the socially optimal price. If the firm has increasing average costs, the fair return price may happen to be the socially optimal price, but there is no reason to think that this coincidence would frequently occur. It has also been shown theoretically that rate-of-return rate making leads to a managerial bias resulting in greater capital intensity in the regulated sector than is consistent with efficiency.[10] On the one hand, these criticisms of regulation suggest the need for alternative regulatory techniques. On the other hand, so long as such regulation exists, it is illustrative of exactly the kind of "additional" constraint that prevents the application of efficiency conditions elsewhere in the economy. Given rate-of-return regulation in any sector, it cannot be rigorously shown that competitive conditions in the remainder of the economy will necessarily be ideal.

Regulation has also been criticized for more practical reasons. Regulation long antedates economists' considerations of efficiency, and its development was in fact stimulated by factors other than efficiency.[11] Some regulations, for example, grew out of discontent over income distribution; whatever *popular* support exists for competitive policy may be attributable to this rather than to efficiency grounds. More important illustrations, however, are found in the areas of labor and agricultural market regulations. Here, equity, not efficiency, is the governing concern.

There is also the criticism that regulation, in effect if not in initial design, favors the regulated at the expense of the public.[12] In this view, the Interstate Commerce Commission has operated primarily on behalf of the railroads; the Civil Aeronautics Board, on behalf of the domestic trunk

10. Harvey Averch and Leland L. Johnson, "Behavior of the Firm under Regulatory Constraint," *American Economic Review*, vol. 52 (December 1962), pp. 1052–69; William J. Baumol and Alvin K. Klevorick, "Input Choices and Rate-of-Return Regulation: An Overview of the Discussion," *Bell Journal of Economics and Management Science*, vol. 1 (Autumn 1970), pp. 162–90.

11. For interesting illustrations of early regulatory practices and a strong argument for regulation in the public interest, see the dissent of Justice Louis D. Brandeis in *New State Ice Co.* v. *Liebmann*, 285 U.S. 262 (1931).

12. Aspects of this view appear in Chapters 2, 3, 4, 7, 9, and 10.

airlines; the Federal Communications Commission, on behalf of the Bell System and the established radio and television networks; the Securities and Exchange Commission, on behalf of old-line investment bankers and brokerage firms; the bank regulatory agencies, on behalf of existing banks; and much of the regulatory machinery at the state and local level, on behalf of—or even under the direction of—those who are ostensibly regulated. Even in the somewhat more charitable version of this criticism, regulated firms are seen as adaptively responding to regulations in ways that thwart the achievement of the public benefits intended by the regulators. It has been argued, too, that regulation, as it has evolved under the antitrust laws, is essentially protective of the capitalist establishment.[13]

Little is known of the general effects of regulation on technological progress, but a growing literature appears to be delivering harsh judgments of regulation on this score, also.[14] And, finally, there is the critical impression, based in part on organizational theory and in part on observation, that the typical response of regulatory agencies to failures in regulation is to extend and compound their own regulations. Thus, criticisms of regulation may have the effect of making regulation still more perverse.

Competition and the Regulation of Industry: A Preview

Despite the danger that additional criticism may lead to more, and less efficient, regulation, this volume is intended to have the opposite effect. It contains studies of nine industries and an overview of the legal problems relating to regulation. Behind the work was the idea that better substitutes for present forms of regulation may exist. In particular, attention is focused on whether the elimination of certain forms of direct regulation and the substitution of procompetitive market forces is not preferable in some circumstances. That regulation is required when markets fail is denied in none of the papers; that regulation may in reality have

13. Robert Paul Wolff, "Beyond Tolerance," in Robert Paul Wolff, Barrington Moore, Jr., and Herbert Marcuse, *A Critique of Pure Tolerance* (Beacon, 1969), pp. 46ff. See also Simon Lazarus, "Halfway up from Liberalism: Regulation and Corporate Power," in Ralph Nader and Mark J. Green (eds.), *Corporate Power in America: Ralph Nader's Conference on Corporate Accountability* (Grossman, 1973).

14. William M. Capron (ed.), *Technological Change in Regulated Industries* (Brookings Institution, 1971).

8   ALMARIN PHILLIPS

been misdirected in terms of social welfare is probed in some detail. Thus, both the reasons for regulation and regulatory shortcomings are examined.

In Chapter 2, George Eads presents an analysis of domestic air service. A model of the quality-quantity dimensions of air service is developed, with attention to the time costs of travel, including the probability of there being available point-to-point air transportation when one wishes to travel and the relative costs of alternative means of transportation. Eads also provides an empirical study of U.S. carriers, with some discussion of the intrastate experience in California. The behavior of air carriers under regulatory constraints is considered, especially the complications that arise when attempts are made collectively to lower the quality of service through agreements to restrict flight frequencies. Eads concludes that the existing policies of fixing minimum fares, on the one hand, and fostering competition through parallel route assignments for two or more carriers, on the other, lead to poor results in air carrier markets. In contrast to those who would restrict market entry and foster collusive service restrictions, Eads holds that free entry and uncontrolled fares and service offerings would yield improved quantity-quality service mixes. He acknowledges that, under his proposals, particular route segments may be occupied by single carriers, but he sees the restraints on behavior due to free entry and potential competition as effective in the prevention of abuses of market power. According to Eads, regulation in this industry is more a cause of than a cure for market failure.

Thomas Gale Moore gives an intriguing study of the regulation of surface transportation in Chapter 3. With imaginative methods and perhaps, in some instances, rather bold assumptions, Moore estimates the social losses attributable to the regulation of rail, motor, inland water, and pipeline transportation. Considered in relation to the proportion of the gross national product originating in the surface transportation sector, losses due to transportation regulation appear at least as substantial as those due to the exercise of private monopoly power in the unregulated sectors of the economy. Moore recognizes that perfectly competitive market structures cannot be realized in some of the transportation industries, but raises serious doubts as to whether the gains from deregulation would not more than offset potential losses. Again, regulation is seen as at least one important reason for the failure of the industry to perform in the public interest.

The regulation of ocean shipping is complicated by international factors and, in recent years, by the emergence of containerized vessels and the related freight-handling revolution. Robert Larner studies this industry in Chapter 4, with attention to several proposed changes in shipping conference rules, proposed mergers between U.S. containerized carriers, and relations between U.S. and foreign shipping interests. Larner is not optimistic that either open competition or proposed changes in regulation would yield much improvement. On balance, he sees the need to explore competitive forces more thoroughly in the consideration of mergers among carriers and to avoid the approval of the newly proposed anticompetitive conference rules.

In Chapter 5, Leonard W. Weiss examines the electric utilities industry, including its generation, transmission, and distribution phases. The transmission phase seems to Weiss to have the attributes of a natural monopoly, which makes a competitive structure impossible to achieve. Some form of regulation is required, but not necessarily the form now in use. The same is probably true at the distribution level. In generating, however, Weiss suspects that considerably more competition is possible, particularly if discriminating barriers to the use of transmission and distribution facilities were reduced. Thus, both vertical and horizontal aspects of industry structure are considered. Competition would benefit the public by eliminating or reducing the use of the high-cost facilities that current regulatory practices tend to protect. Weiss gives empirical support for his contentions, and offers a critique of the policies of the Federal Power Commission and state and local utility commissions. He also comments on the recent interests of the Justice Department's Antitrust Division in the industry.

The sixth chapter is a novel investigation of the effects of competition on the costs of electricity. Using a set of largely ignored data from communities where customers have a choice between two suppliers, Walter J. Primeaux, Jr., presents a series of regressions to compare costs per kilowatt hour of municipally owned utilities in the duopoly cities with those of similar companies in monopoly cities. Scale factors, degrees of capacity utilization, differences in fuel use, in the purchase of power, in the characteristics of the distribution systems, and in regulation, are among the aspects of the industry represented by variables in the regressions. Primeaux concludes that there are interaction effects from the duopoly-monopoly classification. The effect on the regression constant is negative, indicating lower costs in the duopoly cases. Nonetheless, the duopoly communities appear to have higher marginal costs, so that as output levels increase, a point is reached where the monopoly utilities have lower costs.

The author discusses possible reasons for his results, including managerial motivations as well as attributes of the technical systems where parallel services exist. Policy conclusions on the basis of the single study are obviously hazardous, but Primeaux is confident that more attention needs to be given to the possibilities for competition in an industry that has historically been accepted as a prime illustration of natural monopoly.

The Federal Communications Commission was, until recent years, firm in its view that intercity telecommunications also constituted a natural monopoly. In Chapter 7, Leonard Waverman recounts the development of FCC policies in this area, including the changes in policy in the past decade that have broadened entry possibilities and weakened the position of the American Telephone and Telegraph Company as the exclusive, regulated monopolist. Theoretical and empirical analyses of scale economies are presented, with attention to changes in scale in links between two nodes and changes in scale in a system of links among many nodes. The arguments that competition leads only to "cream skimming" and reductions in the rate of technical progress are criticized. Waverman also treats the possibility of substituting contractual arrangements between monopoly city distribution systems and competitive, but interrelated, intercity carriers for the present regulated intercity system. On balance, he concludes that the possibilities for achieving significant public benefits from freer entry and more competition are remote, indeed.

Dennis E. Smallwood offers a unique combination of theoretical modeling, empirical investigation, and institutional study in Chapter 8. The subject is the automobile insurance industry, an industry in which natural monopoly seems not to exist and which, despite nationwide markets, is regulated principally by the states. Smallwood develops a model of risk selection by profit-maximizing insurers, showing the behavior of individual firms—their risk surcharge practices and resulting acceptance practices. The industry is then examined in the light of the theory, and the extent to which actual underwriting experience is attributable to variations in regulation by the states is assessed. Differences in performance that might occur under "no-fault" plans are also discussed. Smallwood sees insurance companies as suppliers of a product with a varying quality that depends primarily on their claims policies. A provocative product-quality model emerges, followed by a statistical study of the quality of service provided by a large sample of insurors. No-fault plans are again woven into the context, and Smallwood concludes that, while no-fault may yield many improvements, dissatisfaction with quality would remain even if it were adopted.

Chapter 9 deals with minimum brokerage fees on transactions at the New York Stock Exchange. In it, H. Michael Mann examines arguments for the collective setting of fees, looks at the structure of the industry, and estimates the probable effects on structure if the price fixing were abolished. He concludes unequivocally that, from a public policy point of view, the minimum commission schemes have no justification.

Chapter 10, by Almarin Phillips, considers the regulation of deposit financial institutions. A general model is developed to show that regulation is partially endogenous to the market process. That is, while it is clear that regulation affects market performance, it can also be contended that, over time, regulation is itself influenced by market performance. Phillips traces the history of regulation of commercial banks, savings and loan associations, and mutual savings banks to illustrate the endogenous character of regulation. In its development, regulation has protected financial institutions from both inter- and intraindustry competition, although recent events—particularly periods of tight money and the appearance of new technologies—have increased the degree of both kinds of competition. Moreover, Phillips argues that, while regulators have usually attempted to mitigate rather than foster competitive forces, technological opportunities are making their efforts less effective. New forms of regulation that would re-create the historic protection from competition and preserve the structures of financial industries are seen as both undesirable and impossible to achieve. Thus, some radical restructuring of financial markets is predicted, and regulatory changes that would facilitate an orderly restructuring are suggested.

Finally, despite protestations that regulation is often the formulation of "rules by men" rather than "rules of law," the legal system—laws, delegations of authority, and the judicial process—shapes what regulators are permitted to do and, within such constraints, influences their behavior. In the concluding chapter, Edwin M. Zimmerman provides a legal overview of regulation. He assays the possibilities of new regulatory techniques, especially the increased use of competition as a regulatory device. The many suggestions made in the preceding chapters are reviewed in terms of their efficacy and achievability. Zimmerman concludes with observations similar to some of those expressed in this chapter. Allocative efficiency—understandably the focal consideration of the authors in this volume—has not been the dominant reason for regulatory legislation or the primary concern of regulators. Zimmerman is sympathetic with the view that competition should play a larger role in regulation, but is less than optimistic that substantial reform is probable in the foreseeable future.

CHAPTER TWO

Competition in the Domestic Trunk Airline Industry: Too Much or Too Little?

GEORGE C. EADS

WHETHER COMPETITION produces socially desirable results in the airline industry has been an open question ever since the industry was brought under governmental regulation. One of the original purposes of regulation was to control the "excessive competition" that, it was claimed, was eroding safety standards and driving the industry to the brink of bankruptcy.[1]

Soon after its establishment in 1938, the Civil Aeronautics Authority—in 1940 renamed the Civil Aeronautics Board (CAB)—imposed a total blockade on entry into the trunkline industry that has survived to this day.[2] At the same time, the agency directed a reorganization of the route structures of the existing carriers so that by late 1940, 90 percent of all city-pair markets (accounting for 59 percent of all passenger-miles) were noncompetitive.[3] Following the Second World War, the CAB launched a

1. See Samuel B. Richmond, *Regulation and Competition in Air Transportation* (Columbia University Press, 1961), pp. 10–15.

2. The board defines a trunkline as a carrier operating over "routes serving primarily the larger communities" (Civil Aeronautics Board, *Handbook of Airline Statistics, 1969 Edition* [1970], p. 536).

3. Frederick W. Gill and Gilbert L. Bates, *Airline Competition: A Study of the Effects of Competition on the Quality and Price of Airline Service and the Self-Sufficiency of the United States Domestic Airlines* (Harvard University, Graduate School of Business Administration, Division of Research, 1949), p. 27. A route is arbitrarily considered to be competitive if a second single carrier or two carrier-connecting services account for at least 10 percent of the traffic. For problems associated with the use of such a measure as an index of competition, see Richmond, *Regulation and Competition*, pp. 37–40.

13

Table 2-1. Airline Carrier Competition in Major City Pairs,[a] 1970

Number of effective competitors[b]	Number of city pairs
One	4[c]
Two	90
Three	38
More than three	3
Total	135

Source: U.S. Department of Transportation, "Top City Pairs, 1970" (1971; computer tabulation), tables entitled "Ranking on Passengers" and "Ranking on Passenger Miles."

a. Major city pairs are defined as the combination of the top 100 city pairs ranked in terms of passengers and the top 100 city pairs ranked in terms of passenger-miles in 1970. In that year, these 135 routes accounted for almost half of all airline traffic.

b. Defined by the CAB as a carrier having at least a 10 percent share of the market. The total number of carriers authorized to serve the market is at least the number shown and often greater.

c.

Market	Passenger rank	Passenger-mile rank
Minneapolis–New York	53	49
Dallas–San Antonio	63	123
St. Louis–San Francisco	118	72
Atlanta–San Francisco	122	61

program to extend the routes of the existing trunk carriers and reduce the number of noncompetitive markets. As Table 2-1 shows, there is scarcely a route of importance that is not now served by at least two or three carriers. In making these route awards the board argued that it was fulfilling its legal mandate to authorize "competition to the extent necessary to assure the sound development of an air-transportation system properly adapted to the needs of the foreign and domestic commerce of the United States, of the Postal Service, and of the national defense."[4]

That the board was exceeding its mandate was claimed almost from the outset. The first major study of airline competition was the volume published in 1949 by Gill and Bates. They examined the markets in which the CAB had authorized more than one carrier and concluded that the board's program of competitive route authorizations had even then proceeded too far. In particular, they criticized the board for allowing more than two carriers to serve any route.[5] In certain cases they felt that the addition of even a second carrier had led to higher costs and had not resulted in any significant improvement in service quality.[6]

4. 72 Stat. 740, 49 U.S.C. 1302(d).

5. Gill and Bates, *Airline Competition*, p. 631.

6. See, for example, their analysis of the New York–Boston case, especially p. 394 in ibid.; see also chap. 20.

David Bluestone, writing in 1953 and 1954, was even more direct in his criticism of the CAB's policy toward competition, claiming that "competition among domestic trunk airlines cost at least $84,000,000 in 1953."[7] Bluestone recommended that "serious consideration be given to reducing parallel airline competition and thereby raising the traffic density of the route system."[8] He proposed that the board accomplish this reduction primarily by purchasing routes from competing carriers, and suggested that traffic pooling be tried as an interim measure.

One of the most recent criticisms of the board's attitude toward inter-carrier competition has been expressed by Frederick Thayer, who believes that airlines should be considered as a form of "natural monopoly":

It is time to face the reality that direct competition between airlines on any route is intensely wasteful and indeed irrational. . . . The system of direct competition must go, and it may take an explicit Government-public-industry partnership effort to restructure the entire industry. Haphazard merger applications or multi-company "agreements" will not be enough, especially if key Congressmen and the Justice Department continue to misperceive the problem.[9]

The major competitive "waste" to which these authors refer is the tendency of an air carrier, discouraged by CAB regulation from competing on the basis of price, to apply its competitive energies to service quality, by increasing the number of flights it offers in any given city-pair market. Since rival carriers are unwilling to see their market shares decline, they respond by matching this higher volume of service. Load factors are driven down as the capacity offered outstrips traffic, with, since this capacity must be paid for, both higher air fares and lower airline profits as the result.

The scheduled carriers, who flew the North Atlantic in 1970 with only 55 percent of their seats filled and charged $420 for a round-trip coach fare between New York and London, have been compared unfavorably with the charter carriers, who flew nearly 100 percent full and charged less

7. David W. Bluestone, "The Problem of Competition Among Domestic Trunk Airlines—Part I," *Journal of Air Law and Commerce*, vol. 20 (Autumn 1953), p. 379. In 1953, total domestic trunk operating expenses were $790 million, so Bluestone was claiming that competition raised costs by about 12 percent. Perhaps more significant is the fact that industry operating profit in 1953 was $88 million.

8. Bluestone, "The Problem of Competition Among Domestic Trunk Airlines—Part II," ibid., vol. 21 (Winter 1954), p. 87.

9. Frederick C. Thayer, University of Pittsburgh, letter in the *New York Times*, Business Section, Nov. 15, 1970. See also his *Air Transport Policy and National Security* (University of North Carolina Press, 1965), chap. 11, for an elaboration of his views as they affect international air carriers.

than $200. Persons concerned with protecting the environment observe that half-empty planes mean wasted fuel, while those concerned with air safety and airport congestion point to the sharp reduction in the number of aircraft movements that would be made possible by substantially higher load factors.[10]

All of these forces, plus the pressures generated by the substantial losses and low load factors experienced by the industry after 1970, have spurred interest in methods of limiting service rivalry. This phenomenon, and certain proposals for dealing with it, are the subjects of this chapter. The next section presents a model that focuses on one important form of service rivalry, the level of capacity offered in a city-pair market. The model is used to predict the pattern of capacity that would be offered in ideal markets. Following is a comparison of this predicted pattern with the pattern actually observed. The deviations are explained in the next section. Then, the various proposals for direct limitations on competition aimed at reducing service rivalry are examined, and a proposal is advanced that would produce optimal levels of service rivalry while avoiding some of the undesirable results that seem to be inherent in other proposals. The last section discusses the possibility that adoption of such a proposal would lead to "destructive" competition.

Defining an "Optimal" Level of Service Competition

Determining whether the level of service competition currently engaged in by the scheduled air carriers is "excessive" or "wasteful" requires first a definition of what the level would be in an ideal state in which the industry was either perfectly competitive or regulated in accordance with consumers' preferences. A model recently developed by George Douglas allows the determination of such an optimum level on a given route under an appropriately restrictive set of assumptions.[11] This model abstracts from complications introduced by the need to offer connecting service and the

10. For example, see Robert Fink, "Flying the American Way," *New Republic*, vol. 164 (Feb. 13, 1971), pp. 19–22.

11. For the complete statement of the model, see any of the following: "Testimony of George W. Douglas," CAB Docket 21866-9, Exhibit DOT-T-3; Douglas, "Excess Capacity, Service Quality and the Structure of Airline Fares" (paper delivered before the Transportation Research Forum, October 1971; processed); Douglas, "Excess Capacity: The Cost of Service Quality in Scheduled Air Transportation" (University of North Carolina, 1971; processed).

problems of scheduling aircraft on multiple routes. Nonetheless, it offers extremely useful and generally realistic insights into the problem of defining optimal standards of service quality in actual markets.

The Consumer Viewpoint

Recent studies of the demand for travel have found it useful to abandon the concept that any such thing as the demand for air, auto, or train travel exists as such, and have instead attempted to characterize modal choice as a function of the attributes of the various travel modes and the relative value the consumer places on each.[12] For example, Reuben Gronau sought to explain the variations in choice of travel mode as a function of distance by defining the price of the trip π as the sum of two components, the money costs P and the opportunity costs of the elapsed time KT, where K denotes the value a traveler places on his time and T measures total elapsed trip time. Using actual modal split data and published fares and access times, Gronau determined that the rational person traveling alone would fly rather than drive regardless of the value he placed on his time if his trip was over 590 miles. As distance decreased, the value of time required before the traveler would choose air over private automobile was found to rise rapidly. A value of time of approximately $5 per hour was required if the traveler was to fly on trips of 75 to 100 miles, while the traveler would have to value his time above $14 per hour to fly on a trip of less than 75 miles. Among modes of public transportation, Gronau found that air is preferred to rail transportation for a trip of 150 miles only if the value of personal time exceeds $11.80 per hour. Beyond 176 miles, the choice was found to be between air and bus, with the decisive price being $4.70 per hour. Only a person who valued his time at less than $1 per hour would always choose the bus over the plane.[13]

Gronau's model suffers from his implicit assumption of the instant availability of a vehicle once the traveler decides to make a trip. While this assumption holds true for the private (and, to a lesser degree, the rental)

12. For a survey of some of the more sophisticated methods that have been attempted, see Richard E. Quandt (ed.), *The Demand for Travel: Theory and Measurement* (Heath Lexington, 1970).

13. Reuben Gronau, "The Effect of Traveling Time on the Demand for Transportation," *Journal of Political Economy*, vol. 78 (March–April 1970), pp. 377–94. Money costs include modal access costs, such as the cost of getting to and from the airport. Gronau's model does not take account of differences in comfort or safety among modes.

automobile, other modes of intercity transportation operate on a fixed schedule. On average, therefore, a period of time must elapse between the traveler's desired departure time and the first scheduled departure. Furthermore, the first scheduled departure may be sold out, subjecting the would-be traveler to additional delay. Both these factors obviously have an effect on the expected time the trip will require using various modes, and this will affect modal choice. (Specifically, they increase the "switching distance" for all modes, relative to the automobile, for any given value of time.) The model proposed by Douglas, however, incorporates both of these scheduling factors, termed by him "frequency delay" and "stochastic delay," respectively, and "schedule delay" in sum.[14]

FREQUENCY DELAY. Assume that passengers arrive at a constant rate of p per hour between times t_0 and t_N. The problem is to dispatch F vehicles of fixed capacity S at times $t_1, t_2 \ldots, t_N$, in order to minimize total delay D. Simpson and Neuve Eglise have shown that the optimal dispatch pattern is to distribute departures evenly over the period and have derived a simple expression for average delay per passenger $\bar{D}$.[15] Furthermore, they have shown that in the case of a periodic, deterministic, but nonuniform demand, which is nonzero from t_0 to t_N and where the objective is to minimize a weighted average of delay and dispatch costs, this expression for average delay still largely holds, provided no flight is dispatched at full capacity.[16] If some flights are dispatched fully loaded so that some people arriving prior to departure must wait until the next flight, the average delay will increase.

Douglas arrived at a similar expression for frequency delay by simulation. He transformed the daily pattern of demand observed for a typical set of routes into a discrete frequency distribution. He then developed an algorithm that scheduled F flights during the day such that each flight

---

14. As presented here, this model embodies the assumption that the interval between the desired and actual departure times is entirely wasted. This obviously need not be the case, as Douglas recognizes ("Testimony," p. 13, note 1). Yet it does not seem unrealistic to assume that travelers have certain preferred departure times based upon their work habits, and that any rearrangement of work in order to accommodate travel schedules results in a loss of productivity.

15. $\bar{D} = T_d/2F$, where $T_d = t_N - t_0$. R. W. Simpson and M. J. Neuve Eglise, "A Method for Determination of Optimum Vehicle Size and Frequency of Service for a Short Haul V/STOL Air Transport System," Flight Transportation Laboratory Report R-68-1 (Massachusetts Institute of Technology, May 1968; processed), pp. 4–5.

16. Ibid., pp. 5–10.

faced a demand of equal size. He computed the difference between each traveler's desired and actual departure times, summed their absolute values, and computed an average. The procedure was then repeated for $F + 1$, $F + 2$, and so forth. In this way, a series of observations was generated giving average expected delay and flight frequency. Douglas found that the best estimate of the relationship between expected delay and daily flight frequency was

$$T_f = 92F^{-0.456},$$

where T_f is frequency delay (in minutes).[17]

STOCHASTIC DELAY. Douglas characterized stochastic delay as a queuing phenomenon and described it as a Markov process.[18] He was able to obtain data showing daily passenger traffic on selected routes for February and November 1969. He approximated the frequency distribution of these data as normal distributions with mean N_D and standard deviation σ_{ND}. He assumed that each of F daily flights of identical capacity S faced an identical, independent demand distribution with mean $N_f = N_D/F$ and standard deviation $\sigma_f = F^{-1/2}\sigma_{ND}$. He then defined a Markov process in which the state of the system was defined by a variable Q—the number of passengers desiring space on a given flight—and constructed a one-step transition matrix defined by specification of the parameters of the demand distributions facing each flight and the aircraft size S.[19]

Douglas calculated the steady-state matrix for this system, that is, the probabilities that Q will be of any given size. The probabilities were calculated for each of 360 values of the demand and capacity parameters,

17. "Excess Capacity, Service Quality and the Structure of Airline Fares," app. A, p. 1.

18. The following description follows closely Douglas, "Excess Capacity: The Cost of Service Quality," pp. 11–12; and Douglas, "Excess Capacity, Service Quality and the Structure of Airline Fares," pp. A1–A3. The reader is referred to these sources for examples of the transition matrices and a fuller explanation of the procedure of estimation.

19. The process was generalized by expressing these parameters in a single measure of relative capacity,

$$X = \frac{S - N_f}{\sigma_f}$$

and the ratio of the mean and standard deviation of flight demand,

$$Y = \frac{N_f}{\sigma_f}.$$

Table 2-2. Expected Delays per Passenger, Hypothetical Air Transportation Route[a]

Average load factor	Frequency delay (minutes)	Stochastic delay (minutes)	Schedule delay (minutes)
0.40	23.86	6.90	30.76
0.44	24.92	9.07	33.99
0.48	25.93	11.87	37.80
0.52	26.90	15.54	42.44
0.56	27.82	20.40	48.22
0.60	28.71	26.97	55.68
0.64	29.57	36.05	65.62
0.68	30.40	48.96	79.36
0.72	31.21	68.03	99.24
0.76	31.99	97.60	129.59
0.80	32.74	146.63	179.37

Source: George W. Douglas, "Excess Capacity: The Cost of Service Quality in Scheduled Air Transportation" (University of North Carolina, 1971; processed), table 6.
a. Distance, 600 miles; mean daily passenger demand, 800; aircraft, three-engine turbofan.

and from this the probability that the traveler will face no delay, a delay of one period, a delay of two periods, and so on was calculated. Once computed and appropriately weighted, a series of observations existed showing stochastic delay as a function of capacity and demand parameters. Using these observations, Douglas estimated the following relationship between these parameters and stochastic delay:

$$T_s = 0.455 Y^{-0.645} X^{-1.790} T^*,$$

where T_s is stochastic delay (in minutes) and T^* is the average interval between flights. Douglas tested this expression by comparing actual and predicted load factors for certain representative routes and satisfied himself of its general reasonableness.[20]

SCHEDULE DELAY. Given these expressions for T_f and T_s, Douglas was able to compute schedule delay, $T = T_s + T_f$, as a function of average load factor N_f/S. Table 2-2 shows Douglas's estimates for a market with a mean daily (one-way) demand of 800 passengers, assuming the use of three-engine turbofan equipment.[21] What is particularly striking is how

20. Douglas, "Excess Capacity: The Cost of Service Quality," pp. 12–13.
21. Eight hundred one-way passengers per day represent 584,000 passengers per year exchanged between two cities. In 1968, the two city pairs coming closest to that level of traffic were Buffalo–New York City (534,000 origin-destination passengers) and

Figure 2-1. Load Factor and Probability of at Least One Seat Being Available at Time of Departure, Local Service Air Carriers, 1962

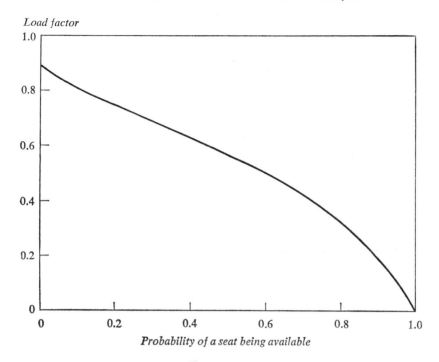

Load factor

Probability of a seat being available

Source: Derived from data showing average passenger loads at departure for all flights of F-27, Convair and Martin aircraft (all of about forty-seat capacity) operated by local service carriers during October 1962 Civil Aeronautics Board, "Airline Subsidy Reduction Program," Report to the President pursuant to Transportation Message of 1962 (June 1963; processed), app. 11.

rapidly stochastic delay rises as the load factor rises, reflecting a decreasing probability of being able to obtain a seat on the most desired flight. This rapid deterioration of service quality as load factor increases is further illustrated in Figure 2-1, which shows the probability that at least one

---

Chicago–Los Angeles (632,000 origin-destination passengers). These cities ranked thirteenth and twelfth, respectively, in terms of passengers generated (CAB, *Handbook of Airline Statistics, 1969 Edition*, p. 389).

According to the CAB's *Aircraft Operating Cost and Performance Report* (August 1969), p. 9, the average seating capacity of three-engine turbofan equipment during 1968 was 105.2. This figure is an average of the two types of three-engine turbofan equipment that were then in general service, the B-727-100 (average capacity 95.7) and the B-727-200 (average capacity 128.6).

seat will be available at departure as a function of the average load factor.[22]

If the average load factor is 0.6, the probability that at least one seat will be available at departure time is approximately 0.4; however, as the average load factor rises to 0.8, this probability falls to 0.1. At load factors above 90 percent, seats are virtually unavailable, or, to use Douglas's terminology, stochastic delay approaches infinity. This finding is consistent with experience. The highest load factor ever obtained by U.S. domestic trunk carriers in scheduled service was 89.4 percent in 1944.[23] At that time, airline seats were subject to rationing, queues were long, and the probability of finding an empty seat on a departing flight was, for all practical purposes, zero.

Given the information in Table 2-2 and an estimate of the value the consumer places on his time, it is possible to calculate the cost to the consumer of the various components of schedule delay and thus to derive the value to him of adding a given increase in load factor.[24] This is shown in columns 4 and 5 of Table 2-3.

The Producer Viewpoint

To complete the model it is necessary to determine the cost to an air carrier of supplying a given improvement in service quality, measured, in

22. The distribution that was fitted to the data represented in the figure allows the probability of at least one seat being available at time of departure to be calculated as

$$Pr = \int_0^S F(x)dx,$$

where S is the size of vehicle used. (In contrast to Douglas, we found that a highly skewed distribution provided the best fit.) The average load factor the carrier would experience was calculated as

$$L = \frac{P}{S},$$

where P is the average passenger load computed as

$$\int_0^P F(x)dx = \int_P^S F(x)dx.$$

23. CAB, *Handbook of Airline Statistics, 1969 Edition*, p. 26. The Big Four carriers (American, Trans World Airlines [TWA], Eastern, and United), flying the denser routes and using slightly larger equipment, obtained an average load factor of 91.3 percent during that year. The other trunks reached only 84.6 percent.

24. Ignoring the possibility that the interval between the actual and desired time of departure may not be entirely nonproductive for the consumer.

Table 2-3. Value to the Passenger and Reduction in Cost to the Airline of Adding a 4 Percentage Point Increase in Average Load Factor, Hypothetical Route[a]

Average load factor (ALF) (1)	Schedule delay per passenger (minutes) (2)	Increase in delay for 4 percentage point increase in ALF (minutes) (3)	Value to passenger of avoiding increased delay		Total economic cost per passenger to airline (dollars) (6)	Reduction in cost associated with a 4 percentage point increase in ALF (dollars) (7)
			Time = $5 per hour (dollars) (4)	Time = $10 per hour (dollars) (5)		
0.40	30.76				43.84	
		3.23	0.27	0.54		2.85
0.44	33.99				40.99	
		3.81	0.32	0.64		2.38
0.48	37.80				38.61	
		4.64	0.39	0.77		2.02
0.52	42.44				36.59	
		5.78	0.48	0.96		1.74
0.56	48.22				34.85	
		7.46	0.62	1.24		1.51
0.60	55.68				33.34	
		9.94	0.83	1.66		1.33
0.64	65.62				32.01	
		13.74	1.14	2.29		1.17
0.68	79.36				30.84	
		19.88	1.65	3.31		1.05
0.72	99.24				29.79	
		30.35	2.52	5.06		0.94
0.76	129.59				28.85	
		49.78	4.13	8.30		0.85
0.80	179.37				28.00	

Source: Derived from George W. Douglas, "Excess Capacity: The Cost of Service Quality in Scheduled Air Transportation" (University of North Carolina, 1971; processed), table 6.

a. Distance, 600 miles; mean daily passenger demand, 800 (for purposes of this example, assumed to be independent of capacity offered); aircraft, three-engine turbofan.

Douglas's model, by a decline in average load factors leading to a reduction in schedule delay. Douglas had at his disposal a cost model developed by the CAB that, when supplied with appropriate inputs, gives the total economic cost (total operating cost plus provision for income taxes and return on investment) as a function of load factor, trip distance, and aircraft type.[25] Douglas acknowledged the limitations inherent in this model and accepted its use only as a "first approximation."[26]

Column 6 of Table 2-3 shows total economic cost per passenger to the airline by average load factor for the route length, aircraft type, and daily traffic. Column 7 shows that while per-passenger cost decreases as load factor rises, reflecting a spreading of certain fixed cost elements associated with providing a flight, this reduction is less than proportional. Thus, the cost to an airline of providing a given increase in service quality through an increase in capacity offered falls, although at a decreasing rate, as the carrier's load factor rises.

The optimal load factor (and its associated optimal level of capacity) for an airline is now defined as the level at which the marginal per-passenger cost of increasing load factor by a given amount equals the associated marginal value the passenger would place on avoiding this increase in schedule delay. Table 2-3 shows that, for a value of time of $5 per hour, the optimal load factor for the route shown is approximately 65 percent, while for a value of time of $10 per hour, the optimal load factor is lower— approximately 57 percent. The traveler who places a higher value on his time is willing to pay the price necessary to provide the higher level of service (lower frequency or stochastic delay, or both) implicit in the lower load factor.

Given the value that various kinds of travelers are assumed to place on their time, optimal load factors can be computed in this manner for routes with various distances, mean daily demands, and type of aircraft. Aircraft operating costs increase with distance (although less than proportionally), so the cost of a given reduction in load factor will increase as distance increases. This means that the optimal load factor should rise with distance, ceteris paribus. Figure 2-2 shows Douglas's composite curve relating optimal load factors to distance for high ($10 per hour) and low ($5 per hour) values of time.[27]

25. For a description of the model, see CAB, "Costing Methodology" (Version Six), Docket 21866-7, Exhibit BC-3999 (August 1970; processed); the required inputs are listed on pages 9 and 10. Examples of output are given in CAB, *Domestic Fare Structure: Costing Tabulations for 1969*, vol. 3, Docket 21866-9, Exhibit 2999 (November 1970).

26. Douglas, "Excess Capacity: The Cost of Service Quality," p. 13.

27. Douglas also shows optimal load factor curves for trips of 600 and 2,200 miles in length as a function of mean daily demand, assuming a value of travel time at $10 per hour ("Testimony," p. 24). Optimal load factor is found to rise with route density because of the nonlinearity of the relationship between frequency delays and flight frequency ("Excess Capacity: The Cost of Service Quality," p. 16).

Figure 2-2. Relation of Optimal Average Load Factor to Trip Distance, by Selected Values of Time

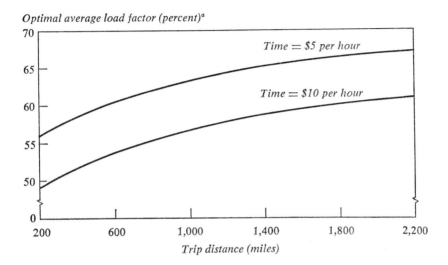

Optimal average load factor (percent)[a]

Trip distance (miles)

Source: "Testimony of George W. Douglas," CAB Docket 21866-9, Exhibit DOT-T-3, p. 19.
a. Mean daily passenger demand, 800.

Empirical Evidence for Load Factors

Data on flight segment load factors are jealously guarded by air carriers, but limited data have recently become available on a delayed basis.[28] Figure 2-3 shows curves hand fitted to the earlier data reported by Fruhan on average load factors by number of competitors for several distance intervals.[29] Fruhan's data are for a "typical carrier and a typical month" during the mid-1960s. In contrast to the standard practice, Fruhan defines

28. These data are now available as part of the CAB's Form 41 reports submitted by the carriers.
29. William E. Fruhan, Jr., *The Fight for Competitive Advantage: A Study of the United States Domestic Trunk Air Carriers* (Harvard University, Graduate School of Business Administration, Division of Research, 1972), p. 54.

Figure 2-3. Load Factors, by Trip Distance and Competition, Typical Domestic Airline Trunk Carrier in an Average Month, Mid-1960s

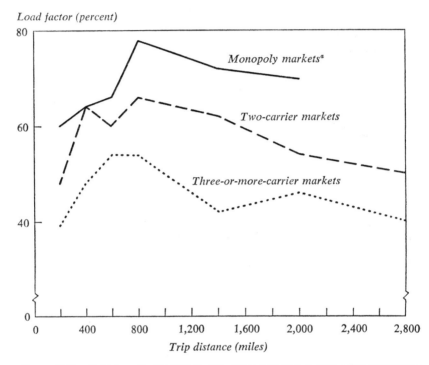

Load factor (percent)

Trip distance (miles)

Source: William E. Fruhan, Jr., *The Fight for Competitive Advantage: A Study of the United States Domestic Trunk Air Carriers* (Harvard University, Graduate School of Business Administration, Division of Research, 1972), p. 54.
a. No monopoly markets were shown for distances over 2,000 miles.

a route as being a monopoly if a single carrier has 80 percent or more of the market.[30] These results show, first, that average load factors decline as the number of competitors increases and, second, that average load factors first rise with distance, as theory suggests, but then fall as distance increases. The latter phenomenon appears to be particularly important in competitive markets.

Table 2-4 presents several regression equations based on 1969 load-factor data for individual carriers in selected city pairs. In each equation

30. Ibid., p. 53, note 4.

load factor is the dependent variable while distance is the independent variable. In general, the results are consistent with Fruhan's, except that they do not indicate a significant decline in load factors with distance for monopoly routes. The difference between equations (2a) and (2b) and between (3a) and (3b) is that each of the "b" equations includes a cubic term for distance. Equations (2b) and (3a) appear to provide a slightly, but inconclusively, better fit to their respective sets of data. A comparison of these results with Fruhan's suggests that the general level of load factors has shifted downward since the mid-1960s. Contrary to conventional wisdom, the trend holds for *each* class of competitors, and cannot be traced entirely to the generous route awards made by the CAB during the late 1960s.[31]

As an examination of the individual carrier constant terms shows, load factors generally decline as the number of carriers serving a route increases. At first glance, this conclusion appears to confirm the criticism, such as that made by Thayer and Bluestone, that airline competition is wasteful and leads to excessive amounts of service rivalry, reduced profits, and higher fares. However, one must be careful to avoid a definition of optimality that makes higher load factors always superior to lower ones. Douglas's model shows that load factors can indeed be too high as well as too low. Further-

31. Douglas's empirical results confirm that load factors decline with an increase in the number of competitors and with distance (Douglas, "Excess Capacity, Service Quality and the Structure of Airline Fares," table 2). Douglas does not test the hypothesis that load factors first rise with distance, but he makes the same qualitative inferences about efficiency as made here.

The inverted U-shaped relationship between load factors and trip distance is confirmed in a 1968 CAB staff study employing 1965 data on load factors (CAB, Bureau of Economics, Rates Division, "A Study of the Domestic Passenger Air Fare Structure" [CAB, 1968; processed], pp. 94–95), though no breakdown by the number of competitors is offered (see Table 2-5 below).

The trend is also supported by evidence contained in testimony submitted by the National Economic Research Associates (NERA) on behalf of TWA in phase 9 of the Domestic Passenger Fare Investigation conducted by the CAB in the early 1970s ("Testimony of National Economic Research Associates, Inc.," CAB Docket 21866-9, Exhibit TW 9-T-B, pp. 11–12). The NERA testimony contains the only evidence against the hypothesis that load factors decline with trip distance. It reports (ibid., p. 26 and table 2) that load factors *increase* with distance once a number of other variables (passenger volume per carrier, growth rate, and number of firms) are taken into account. See, however, the cross-examination testimony of James C. Miller III, which explains the apparent contradiction and asserts that the NERA testimony is actually consistent with the other studies (CAB Docket 21866-9, transcript vol. 17, July 26, 1971, pp. 1934–37).

Table 2-4. Coefficients for Domestic Trunk Airline Load Factors, by Trip Distance and Competition, 1969[a]

Variable or summary statistic	Monopoly[b]		Route competition and equation			
			Two carriers[c]		Three or more carriers[c]	
	(1a)	(1b)	(2a)	(2b)	(3a)	(3b)
Constant[d]	38.72	39.99	43.26	38.46	40.00	37.05
	(9.10)	(8.07)	(13.55)	(9.83)	(9.38)	(7.86)
Distance	...	−0.0011	0.0063	0.026	0.011	0.027
		(0.51)	(1.53)	(2.53)	(2.51)	(2.29)
Distance^2	...	...	−0.0000043	−0.000024	−0.0000054	−0.000023
			(2.55)	(2.51)	(3.08)	(1.88)
Distance^3	...	...	...	0.0000000051	...	0.0000000048
				(2.09)		(1.45)
Carrier dummies						
American	22.25	21.98	10.21	10.47	12.71	12.92
	(3.42)	(3.34)	(3.04)	(3.14)	(2.76)	(2.81)
Braniff	15.47	15.02	9.65	10.20	2.56	2.55
	(3.02)	(2.87)	(2.37)	(2.52)	(0.36)	(0.36)
Continental	24.26	24.19	8.18	8.18	3.00	3.17
	(4.03)	(3.99)	(2.14)	(2.16)	(0.54)	(0.58)
Delta	21.13	21.24	3.56	3.98	8.43	8.48
	(3.70)	(3.69)	(0.91)	(1.02)	(1.65)	(1.66)
Eastern	24.25	24.31	3.13	3.10	−0.62	−0.38
	(4.25)	(4.22)	(0.92)	(0.91)	(0.14)	(0.08)
National	6.74	7.22	3.03	3.30	−2.14	−1.77
	(1.26)	(1.32)	(0.67)	(0.73)	(0.42)	(0.35)

Northeast	7.45	6.48	1.03	1.03	−5.37	−5.19
	(1.31)	(1.11)	(0.18)	(0.18)	(1.03)	(1.00)
Northwest	13.51	13.29	−0.10	1.09	−8.76	−8.60
	(2.46)	(2.39)	(0.03)	(0.31)	(1.64)	(1.61)
Trans World	15.09	15.10	8.61	8.41	0.87	0.88
	(2.75)	(2.73)	(2.49)	(2.45)	(0.19)	(1.90)
United	23.83	22.91	12.16	12.62	6.52	6.57
	(3.67)	(3.37)	(3.99)	(4.17)	(1.41)	(1.42)
Western (omitted)	...	...	...	...	...	...
Summary statistic						
R^2	0.36	0.35	0.17	0.18	0.18	0.19
Standard error of estimate	8.51	8.58	10.28	10.19	11.51	11.47

Source: Based on 1969 load-factor data for selected city pairs, from Civil Aeronautics Board, Docket 21866-6.

a. Load factors are for an individual carrier for an individual city pair. Trip distance is airport-to-airport distance in miles. Numbers in parentheses are t-statistics.

b. A route is considered a monopoly route if one carrier has 90 percent or more of the total city-pair traffic.

c. Two-carrier routes are those in which each of at least two carriers has at least a 10 percent share of the traffic (more than two carriers may be certificated for the city-pair traffic). The same definition applies to three or more carrier routes.

d. The constant terms for the individual carriers are as follows (the numbers in parentheses are the relevant equations):

Carrier	Monopoly (1a)	Two carriers (2b)	Three or more carriers (3a)
American	61	49	53
Braniff	54	49	43
Continental	63	47	43
Delta	60	42	48
Eastern	63	42	39
National	45	42	38

Carrier	Monopoly (1a)	Two carriers (2b)	Three or more carriers (3a)
Northeast	46	39	35
Northwest	52	40	31
Trans World	54	47	41
United	63	51	47
Western	39	38	40
Mean	55	44	42

more, it has been demonstrated that in an industry in which fares are regulated but service quality is not, a monopolist (or a group of firms acting jointly as a monopolist) facing a price fixed by a regulatory agency could increase profits by restricting the quality of service offered—for example, by reducing the number of flights offered—thereby raising load factors.[32] But such load factors would not necessarily be optimal. As is shown below, optimality depends on the fare set by the regulatory agency.

Without additional facts concerning such things as the actual value that travelers place on their time, it is not possible to tell whether the load factors in monopoly markets reflect unacceptably low quality while those in competitive markets reflect unnecessarily high quality. Nevertheless, if Douglas's range of time values ($5–$10 per hour) is reasonable, and Fruhan's data are truly typical, load factors generally, at least in the mid-1960s, were above optimal levels in monopoly markets except for flights of the longest distance; were within the optimal range for short and medium distances but below for longer distances in two-carrier markets; and regularly fell below the optimal range, particularly for longer distances, in markets with three or more carriers. If the 1969 results are considered comparable with Fruhan's, the inference is that during the late 1960s, load factors were below optimal on all but relatively short-haul monopoly routes. However, without further refinement this conclusion is not rigorously demonstrable.

No such qualifications arise in interpreting other findings. The model presented above suggests that load factors should rise with distance. There is evidence, in fact, that load factors *decline* with distance, at least in competitive markets.[33]

32. This argument assumes that the elasticity of demand with respect to increases in flight frequency is less than unity in absolute value over the relevant range. For a demonstration that this must be true in equilibrium, see Arthur De Vany, "The Economics of Quality Competition: Theory and Evidence on Airline Flight Scheduling" (University of California, Los Angeles, Department of Economics, c. 1969; processed). For a formal derivation of these results, see Lawrence J. White, "Quality Variation When Prices Are Regulated," *Bell Journal of Economics and Management Science*, vol. 3 (Autumn 1972), pp. 425–36.

33. The rise of load factors with distance shown in Figure 2-3 and confirmed in Table 2-4 and the CAB staff study appears to be more rapid than suggested by Douglas's model. First, according to Gronau's results, the value of time to the *average* air traveler should fall with trip distance. This means that for short trips the curve representing the average value of time would lie nearer the bottom of Douglas's range, while as trip distance increases the curve would shift toward the top of the range. Second, for reasons of clarity, Douglas's model neglected to consider the problems raised by "tag-end"

Causes of Excessive Service Rivalry
in Competitive Markets

It was suggested above that load factors are lower in competitive markets than in noncompetitive markets and that, given the number of competitors, load factors first rise and then decline with distance. This section presents explanations for the decrease in load factors with competition and the decline in load factors with distance.

Why Are Load Factors Lower on Competitive Routes?

It has already been noted that a monopoly carrier, faced with a constant price, could increase profits by curtailing the frequency of service offered, thereby raising load factors. However, there are other reasons why load factors should be lower on competitive than on noncompetitive routes. In an industry characterized by a relatively homogeneous product for which all firms charge virtually the same price, one would expect the market share of a firm to be closely related to the share of industry output it offered. Studies seeking to explain the market shares of air carriers in individual city-pair markets have found such a relationship.

N. K. Taneja found evidence that the relationship between offerings and market shares is nonlinear.[34] While he tried several functional forms, the most successful appeared to be those that produced an S-shaped relationship of the type shown in Figure 2-4. This relationship implies that a carrier attempting to restrain capacity unilaterally will suffer a more than

---

routes. Suppose many short-haul flight segments are such tag-ends (for instance, the Philadelphia–New York portion of a Los Angeles–Philadelphia–New York flight). The aircraft used on such a flight would be of a size and on a schedule suited to the Los Angeles–Philadelphia segment, so a low load factor would be expected on the Philadelphia–New York segment. No data appear to exist that would allow the quantitative importance of this factor to be determined.

34. "Airline Competition Analysis," FTL Report R-68-2 (Massachusetts Institute of Technology, Flight Transportation Laboratory, September 1968; processed), pp. 16–21. Among other variables important in explaining market share in city pairs, Taneja identified "airline image," the airline's share of all flights departing from a particular terminal (pp. 31–35). Taneja used a carrier's share of the nonstop flights between two cities as the capacity share variable. The share of seats offered might be another possible variable. Unless different airlines employed aircraft of widely differing seating capacity or seating configurations, these two variables would be virtually equivalent.

Figure 2-4. Relationship between Frequency Share and Market Share of Trunk Airlines, by Number of Carriers

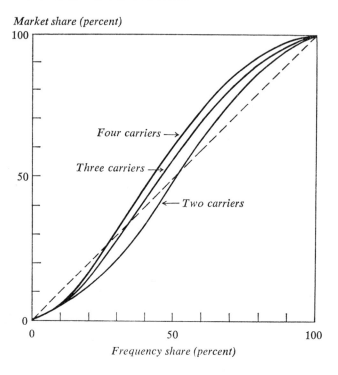

Source: Gilles Renard, "Competition in Air Transportation: An Econometric Approach" (M.S. thesis, Massachusetts Institute of Technology, 1970), p. 36.

proportional loss in market share, while a carrier that can outdo its rivals in service frequency can substantially expand its share.[35] Fruhan, taking Taneja's results as a starting point, has cast the airline scheduling decision

35. The S-shaped relationship between frequency share and market share is widely accepted in the industry. Evidence supporting its existence has also been advanced by Gilles Renard in "Competition in Air Transportation: An Econometric Approach" (M.S. thesis, Massachusetts Institute of Technology, 1970), and in NERA, "Testimony," pp. 13–19 and figs. 1-4. See also the statement by an airline economist quoted in Laurence Doty, "Trunk Loads Plummet for March," *Aviation Week and Space Technology* (hereafter referred to as *Aviation Week*), vol. 94 (April 19, 1971), p. 23, and the statements of industry experts in the load factor phase of the CAB's Domestic Passenger Fare Investigation, Docket 21866-6.

However, John W. Drake has presented results that, while confirming that there is an important relationship between capacity offered and market share, cast doubt on

on competitive routes into an explicit game-theoretic framework.[36] Employing hypothetical examples, he argues that the solution is of the well-known "prisoner's dilemma" type, in which competitors bring about results that none of them wants—in this case, more flights and lower profits. Certain of Fruhan's examples, and testimony submitted by the National Economic Research Associates on behalf of TWA during the CAB's Domestic Passenger Fare Investigation, tend to confirm the implication of the S-shaped relationship that a carrier attempting unilaterally to restrain capacity will suffer substantial financial losses.[37] That such losses will not be typical is argued by Yance, who shows that whether strategy results in profits or losses depends on the elasticity of traffic with respect to frequency of service and the elasticity of market share with respect to relative capacity offered. Yance argues that loss-producing equilibria are unlikely except in markets offering fewer than three or four flights a day.[38]

Taneja's claim that the relationship is of the form shown in Figure 2-4. Drake claims that when several quality-of-service variables are included the nonlinearity disappears. (John W. Drake, "Forecasting Competitors' Market Shares in Local Service Markets" [1970, processed].)

Furthermore, some evidence suggests that price competition loosens the S-shaped relationship between market share and frequency share. Jordan ran regressions using time-series data in which he sought to explain the market share of the intrastate carriers (principally Pacific Southwest Airlines) in the three major California markets by variables such as the share of seats they offered, the price differential between their fare and the intrastate fare offered by the certified carriers (principally United and Western), and other measures of service quality. In two of the three city pairs (Los Angeles–San Francisco and Los Angeles–San Diego), Jordan was able to obtain a high degree of explanation ($R^2 = 0.97$ and 0.90, respectively). In both cases, seat share was highly significant but in neither case was it significantly different from unity. In the Los Angeles–San Francisco market, the coefficient was 1.084 with a standard error of 0.125, while in the Los Angeles–San Diego market, the coefficient was 0.837 with a standard error of 0.151. Average seat share for the 1952–65 period was 28.5 percent in the former case and 39.1 percent in the latter. The regression for the San Diego–San Francisco route was much less satisfactory ($R^2 = 0.36$): the coefficient for seat share was considerably less significant (0.246 with a standard error of 0.121). The average seat share for the intrastate carriers in that market between 1952 and 1965 was 71.9 percent. (William A. Jordan, *Airline Regulation in America: Effects and Imperfections* [Johns Hopkins Press, 1970], pp. 158–77.)

36. Fruhan, *The Fight for Competitive Advantage*, chap. 5 and pp. 166–77.

37. NERA, "Testimony," pp. 16–19, and Fruhan, *The Fight for Competitive Advantage*, table 5.3. However, Fruhan's hypothetical profit matrix (p. 167) does not include any elements showing that an actual loss is the result of any capacity strategy.

38. Joseph V. Yance, "The Possibility of Loss-Producing Equilibria in Air Carrier Markets" (Boston University, Department of Economics, 1971; processed).

In testimony before the board in the Domestic Passenger Fare Investigation, Yance suggested an alternative reason for expecting lower load factors on competitive routes.[39] He observed that in making the decision to add a flight, the number of "new passengers" (that is, the number of passengers the airline is not already carrying aboard its existing flights) is the critical variable, since it determines the revenue gain to the carrier from the addition. On a monopoly route, the only truly "new" passengers attracted by an additional flight are those who were not previously flying at all; the remaining "new" passengers are those lured from the same carrier's other flights. Assuming that in the relevant range the number of new passengers declines as the number of flights increases, the marginal passenger load will lie below the average passenger load. This means that the marginal revenue from adding a flight will be less than the average revenue.

On a competitive route there are two sources of "new" passengers: passengers who are persuaded to fly because of the availability of the additional flight and passengers who desert competitors. Where competitors are numerous, the marginal and average passenger load attracted by an additional flight is virtually identical—almost no passengers are attracted from the carrier's existing flights. If the carriers on the competitive route follow the same decision rule as the carrier on the monopoly route is assumed to follow—add a flight if the marginal revenue is at least as great as the marginal cost—the number of flights on the competitive route obviously will be greater, so average load factors will be lower. Indeed, if the long-run marginal cost of adding a flight is constant, only a normal rate of return will be earned on the competitive route in the long run, while excess profits will be earned on the monopoly route.

If the carriers in a market can agree, either tacitly or overtly, to exercise restraint in scheduling, load factors can be raised and profits improved. Such agreements would be most likely in situations in which there are few competitors, in which they are of approximately equal size and financial strength, and at times when conditions in the industry have been relatively stable. The advent of a new competitor who is unfamiliar with the rules of the game, or unwilling to play by them, is likely to disrupt any tacit agreement that exists. Capacity competition would be expected to be particularly intensive after a major series of route awards, as new carriers attempt to win places in markets and old carriers react to these incursions.

39. Rebuttal testimony of Joseph V. Yance, Domestic Passenger Fare Investigation, CAB Docket 21866-6, Exhibit DOT-RT-1 (July 27, 1970), pp. 6–7.

During such periods, carriers might incur short-run operating losses as they seek to improve their long-run market position.[40]

The past willingness of the CAB to grant fare increases when industry profits were low, regardless of evidence that the problem resulted from scheduling rivalry, has put the board in a position of actually encouraging such rivalry. In terms of the gaming model mentioned above, the board's policy has had the effect of raising all elements of the payoff matrix. The penalties attached to the solution in which all firms adopt aggressive capacity strategies have been lessened relative to the payoff for successful unilateral aggressiveness.[41]

The Decline with Distance

The decline of load factors with distance, except on noncompetitive routes, is a direct result of the interaction of the fare structure policy pursued by the board until very recently and the forces that lead to rivalry over frequency of service in competitive markets. Since much of the cost associated with transporting a passenger between two points is independent of the distance traveled (the costs of ticketing, processing the passenger and his luggage at the terminal, and taking off and landing the aircraft), costs per mile will fall with trip distance. Operating costs also decline, at least to a point, as the number of passengers flying between two points—known as the route density—increases.

Figure 2-5 shows the relationship between costs and fares in 1965–66, as estimated by the CAB staff in its study of the domestic air fare structure. The curve labeled "fares" shows published jet day coach fares as a function of distance. The curve labeled "yields" shows the average revenue per

---

40. A possible example is provided by developments in the Hawaii–U.S. mainland market. See "Can a Hotelman Run an Airline?" *Fortune*, vol. 83 (February 1971), pp. 31–32; Harold D. Watkins, "Hawaii Market Tests Airline Policies," *Aviation Week*, vol. 92 (April 6, 1970), pp. 31–34; "Mainland–Hawaii Market Participation, February 1970," *Aviation Week*, vol. 92 (May 11, 1970), p. 46; "Mainland–Hawaii Market Participation, February 1971," *Aviation Week*, vol. 94 (April 26, 1971), p. 30.

41. Fruhan recognizes this point (see *The Fight for Competitive Advantage*, pp. 170–71). For a discussion of the possible implications of the board's fare policy in this regard, see "Rebuttal Testimony of George W. Douglas," CAB Docket 21866-7, Exhibit DOT-RT-2. The board's acceptance of the principle that load factors should be taken into consideration when setting fares designed to produce a "fair and reasonable rate of return" for the industry is a recognition of the validity of this principle. See the decision of the board in Docket 21866-6B, Domestic Passenger Fare Investigation, Phase 6B—Load Factor (April 9, 1971).

Figure 2-5. Jet Day Coach Fares, Costs, and Yields, 1965–66

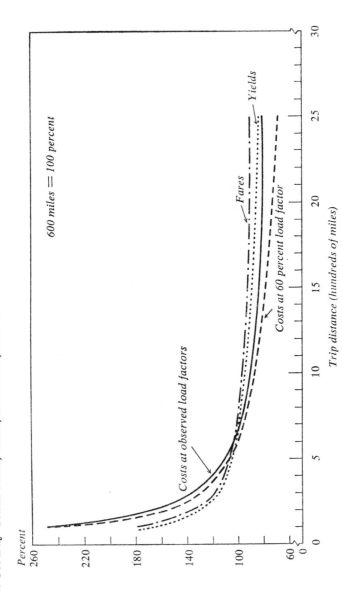

Percent

600 miles = 100 percent

Costs at observed load factors

Fares

Yields

Costs at 60 percent load factor

Trip distance (hundreds of miles)

Sources: CAB, Bureau of Economics, Rates Division, "A Study of the Domestic Passenger Air Fare Structure" (CAB, 1968; processed), p. 142; and author's calculations. Based on a sample of passenger-miles flown in scheduled domestic air service in the year ended Sept. 30, 1965, air fares published in 1966, and cost data reported on CAB Form 41 for the year 1965.

Table 2-5. Jet Day Coach Load Factors, by Revenue Passenger-Miles, 1965

Revenue passenger-miles	Jet day coach load factor (percent)
100	56.0
200	58.5
300	60.5
400	62.0
500	63.0
600	63.5
800	64.5
1,000	64.0
1,300	61.5
1,600	58.0
1,900	55.5
2,200	51.5
2,500	46.0

Source: CAB, Bureau of Economics, Rates Division, "A Study of the Domestic Passenger Air Fare Structure" (CAB, 1968; processed), p. 94.

revenue passenger-mile received by carriers as a function of distance, and diverges from the "fares" line because of the greater availability of discount fares for trips of longer distances.

The curve labeled "costs at observed load factors" shows the total economic cost—including total operating costs and provision for a 10.5 percent rate of return on investment and normal income taxes—per revenue passenger-mile as a function of distance. Since costs are on a revenue passenger-mile basis, they are sensitive to the load factor assumed. The board used load factors (shown in Table 2-5 above) that were considered to be representative for various aircraft types and distances, based upon 1965 experience.[42]

That both fares and yields exceeded costs on long-haul routes and were less than costs on short-haul routes reflects the long-standing CAB policy of cross-subsidization, a policy that economists have vigorously attacked as inefficient and inequitable.[43] However, it is important to note that the

42. For an explanation of the methodology employed in deriving cost, fare, and yield curves, see CAB, "A Study of the Domestic Passenger Air Fare Structure," pp. 78–99.

43. See, for example, Richard E. Caves, *Air Transport and Its Regulators: An Industry Study* (Harvard University Press, 1962), pp. 402–03, 435–36.

decline in fares with distance, generally called the fare "taper," that existed during the mid-1960s was designed to permit the carriers to engage in cross-subsidization and still earn what the board considered to be a "fair and reasonable" return on their investment,[44] and it allowed them to do so even with low load factors. A fare structure more tapered would have produced losses with such load factors, and therefore would have forced carriers to reduce capacity offered, thus raising load factors.

To illustrate this point, the curve labeled "costs at 60 percent load factor" was constructed. The points on this curve were derived using the same methodology employed by the CAB staff, but it was assumed that a 60 percent load factor, a figure roughly in the middle of Douglas's optimal range for longer distances, was achieved for trips of 900 miles or more.[45] The difference between the "cost" curve and the curve for "costs at 60 percent load factor" at any given distance represents the cost to the passenger of the lower load factors that actually prevailed.[46] The board, by establishing the fare and yield taper shown, was validating this higher degree of frequency rivalry.

Given the number of competitors and the market density, there is no basis for concluding that frequency rivalry should be any less vigorous in short-haul than in long-haul markets.[47] The only reasonable explanation for the observed effect of distance on load factors is that it is caused by the fare structure established by the board. For long-haul trips, air transportation exerts some monopoly power, so fares can be maintained at a

44. That is, 10.5 percent. In 1965, the trunklines actually earned a 12.2 percent rate of return on investment (total investment less equipment deposits and capitalized interest), and in 1966 they earned a 10.9 percent rate of return. Both figures exclude the investment tax credit. (CAB, *Handbook of Airline Statistics, 1969 Edition*, pp. 371, 466.)

45. The basic cost data used in constructing this curve are contained in CAB, "A Study of the Domestic Passenger Air Fare Structure," tables 4–7, pp. 84–91, col. BBB in each case. The choice of the type of aircraft to assign to a given distance was made according to tables 11 and 12, pp. 98–99, in ibid.

46. An example may clarify this point. The load factor for trips of 2,500 miles—roughly the distance between New York and Los Angeles—was 46.0 percent in 1965. The total economic cost of providing a trip of this distance (jet coach) was $101.50 (CAB, "A Study of the Domestic Passenger Air Fare Structure," p. 99). The total economic cost of providing the same trip at a 60 percent load factor on the same type of aircraft (four engine turbofan) would have been $85.25 (ibid., p. 84, col. 34BBB: 3.41 cents per mile × 2,500 miles), or $16.25 less. This $16.25 paid for the higher quality of service represented by a 46.0 percent rather than a 60.0 percent load factor.

47. Douglas's load factor regressions include the number of passengers in a city-pair market as an independent variable, yet he still finds that load factors decline with distance (Douglas, "Excess Capacity: The Cost of Service Quality," table 7).

level that will support frequency rivalry. For trips of shorter distance, competition from alternative modes of transportation checks this power somewhat. The point at which this check ceases to be effective cannot be pinpointed precisely. Gronau's results suggest that the automobile remains an effective competitor at distances up to about 600 miles for a single traveler and even further for a group. These switching points would fit in well with the pattern of load factors observed here.[48]

Proposals Designed to Limit Service Rivalry

The evidence suggests that service rivalry, made possible by the fare structure established by the board, drives down load factors and produces a quality of service above that desired by the traveling public, particularly in long-haul markets. The proposals that have been advanced to limit this rivalry fall into two classes: the first would reduce the number of competitors, and the second would explicitly control flight frequencies.

Reduction in the Number of Competitors

A reduction in the number of competitors serving a route could be achieved by decertification, merger, or route purchase. Each raises its own problems of feasibility.

Bluestone examined the power of the CAB to suspend or revoke the certificates of public convenience and necessity that firms must obtain from the CAB before they may begin operating. He observed that while precedent allows indefinite suspension, subject to the requirements of public convenience and necessity, outright revocation can occur only if a carrier intentionally fails to carry out an order of the CAB and ignores a subsequent order directing compliance. Bluestone noted, however, that even the board's suspension power had not been tested thoroughly in the courts.[49]

48. However, in commenting on an earlier version of this paper William Jordan remarked that the California experience indicates that air travel dominates all other modes of travel for trips of over 200 miles in length. This obviously reflects the fact that air fares in the major California markets are approximately one-half to two-thirds those in similar markets elsewhere. If these fares were employed in Gronau's model, the switching points would shift inward markedly.

49. Bluestone, "The Problem of Competition—Part II," pp. 70–72.

In the only court tests, two suits were filed by trunk carriers against the CAB in the early 1950s, alleging that suspending their authority where they were permanently certificated and replacing them with local service carriers constituted taking property without due process of law. The courts found for the board in both cases, but specifically refused to consider the boundaries of the board's suspension powers, contenting themselves with ruling that the board had not exceeded its statutory authority in the cases before them.[50] Should the board undertake to restructure the industry through its suspension powers, numerous legal challenges undoubtedly would arise. Amendment of the Federal Aviation Act to permit their broader use might be required.

The authority of the board to approve carrier-initiated mergers—even those that would substantially lessen competition—is clear. The board also can suggest mergers, but its power to force them upon unwilling carriers is open to question. When the trunk carriers were dependent upon the government for subsidies, the board had a weapon that could have been used to "encourage" mergers. Today, it might threaten to withhold crucial fare increases or to inundate a carrier with competition on important routes, but such actions would be subject to legal challenges. Again, congressional sanction might be necessary.

The CAB's power to approve purchases of one carrier's routes by another seems to be well established. All that is required is the finding that such a transfer would be in the public interest. In 1947, United Air Lines was allowed to purchase Western Air Lines' route from Denver to Los Angeles.[51] The only condition set by the board was that the transaction not result in any net increase in the asset base of the combined carriers, since this would have raised the total dollar profits United could earn under a constant allowed rate of return. It is unlikely, however, that route purchases could bring about any major restructuring of routes that would involve the dismemberment of existing carriers, some of which might be unwilling victims.

Controls over Frequency Competition

Most proposals for reducing intercarrier competition envision not a reduction in the number of carriers competing on any one route but in-

---

50. *Western Air Lines, Inc.* v. *Civil Aeronautics Board*, 196 F.2d 933; *United Air Lines, Inc.* v. *Civil Aeronautics Board*, 198 F.2d 100.

51. United Air Lines, Inc.–Western Air Lines, Inc., Acquisition of Air Carrier Property, *Civic Aeronautics Board Reports*, vol. 8 (April–December 1947), p. 298.

stead direct controls over flight frequencies. Although direct control by the board over service frequency is forbidden by the Federal Aviation Act,[52] other means are available to achieve the same result. Under the plans that have been advanced by the airlines, whenever load factors on any competitive route fall below a certain level (55 percent has been mentioned), carriers flying the route would be authorized to negotiate a program of mutual schedule cutbacks.[53] Presumably, enforcement would depend upon the recognition of mutual interest by the carriers, for no formal enforcement scheme has been proposed.

As experience has shown, such voluntary agreements would be extremely difficult to negotiate and even more difficult to enforce.[54] In late 1970, TWA suggested that carriers be allowed to negotiate schedule cutbacks on certain city pairs. When formal requests for permission were filed early in the spring of 1971, the board issued the necessary approval, and at a meeting of carriers twenty-one "over-served" markets were identified.[55] In eight of the twenty-one, at least one carrier objected even to a discussion of limitations. Therefore, the board approved discussions only for the thirteen markets.[56] In the end, agreement could be reached on a formula for capacity reduction on only four of these routes;[57] the negotiated reductions were to average 29 percent during the winter of 1971 and 14 percent during the summer of 1972. The aim of the agreement was to raise load factors on the four routes to the 52 percent level.

The markets in which an agreement could be reached were those in which the Big Three transcontinental carriers (American, TWA, and United) were the only ones certificated to provide service.[58] The smaller carriers were either unwilling to engage in capacity-limitation talks or

52. 49 U.S.C. 1371(e)(4).

53. "TWA Asks the CAB for Talks on Problem of Excess Capacity," *Wall Street Journal*, Dec. 22, 1970.

54. See F. M. Scherer, *Industrial Market Structure and Economic Performance* (Rand McNally, 1970), pp. 160–61.

55. Laurence Doty, "Opposition May Stall Agreement on Flight Cuts," *Aviation Week*, vol. 94 (March 29, 1971), p. 28.

56. "Eight Airlines Granted Permission to Discuss Joint Flight Cutbacks," *Wall Street Journal*, May 17, 1971, p. 10. These thirteen markets included the top twelve ranked by passenger-miles.

57. On the other nine, the talks broke down over such things as the proper weight to allow wide-bodied jets in the reduction formula. See "Reduction Impasse," *Aviation Week*, vol. 94 (June 28, 1971), p. 15; and "Airlines Sign Pact to Reduce Flights on 4 U.S. Routes," *Wall Street Journal*, June 22, 1971.

58. New York–Newark–Los Angeles, New York–Newark–San Francisco, Chicago–San Francisco, and Washington–Baltimore–Los Angeles.

mistrustful of the motives of the Big Three.[59] In fact, not even the Big Three could agree on a formula in three city pairs in which they were the only competitors.[60]

Such difficulties are not unexpected. Since carriers do not normally compete on the basis of price, frequency of service determines market share to a substantial degree. A carrier with a relatively small share of a market condemns itself to a permanently inferior position if it agrees to a cut in schedules, though such a cut may temporarily raise its profits. It is the carrier with the largest market share that has the most to gain; its share remains secure and its profits increase. Furthermore, if an agreement is reached and load factors rise above the level that automatically triggers a new agreement, a carrier assigned to a smaller number of flights by the agreement would have a strong incentive to initiate a new scheduling war in hopes of improving its position in the next round of negotiations. To assure that such agreements were effective, they would have to be permanent (that is, not initiated by any trigger mechanism), and they would have to be legally enforceable in court, even upon non-signers. Congressional legislation appears necessary to establish these safeguards.

Revenue pooling offers an alternative to attempts to reach an agreement on flight schedules. Under pooling, each carrier bears the cost of operating its own schedules, but revenues are placed in a common pool and divided on an agreed basis. The practice is common among European carriers and, according to Bluestone, is legal under section 412 of the Civil Aeronautics Act.[61] However, except during strikes, the CAB has never permitted it for domestic carriers and has forbidden U.S. international carriers from participating in international pooling agreements. The adoption of pooling would not solve the problem of negotiating an agreement among the participating carriers. It would merely shift the

59. Braniff, Northwest, and Delta opposed the idea of capacity limitations and refused to participate in discussions. Continental was reported as having only a "casual interest" (Doty, "Opposition May Stall"). Northeast balked at the proposed formulae in the Florida markets for which discussions were held ("Reduction Impasse"). See also Laurence Doty, "CAB Control of Scheduling Feared," *Aviation Week*, vol. 95 (Aug. 30, 1971), pp. 19–20.

60. New York–Newark–Chicago, Philadelphia–Los Angeles, and Boston–Los Angeles. This example suggests that a board policy of merging trunkline carriers into two or three large systems that still compete with each other on most routes might be the only way to achieve the recognition of mutual self-interest required to make a policy of "voluntary" capacity agreements work.

61. Bluestone, "The Problem of Competition—Part II," p. 82.

focus from schedules to the division of the pool. As with any cartel agreement, the problems of maintaining a pooling arrangement over time are formidable, and success would likely require legal enforceability.[62] Even Bluestone advocates that pooling be tried only for "temporary" periods.[63]

Effects on Service Quality, Air Fares, and Carrier Profits

Reductions in the number of competitors would lead to a reduction in the number of flights offered and to increases in load factors, according to evidence presented above. Effective agreements among carriers would have the same result. The wider spread between actual and break-even load factors would mean higher industry profits, which *could* be shared with consumers in the form of fare reductions.

That neither of these effects is inevitable is shown by the experience in Europe, where airline competition is limited by pooling arrangements and by restrictions on the number of competitors on any route. As Figure 2-6 shows, intra-European load factors have been more stable than U.S. domestic load factors, and have not declined so sharply over time.[64] Table 2-6 compares fares in a number of U.S. domestic and intra-European routes of similar distances and densities. The European routes shown are subject to capacity agreements and the fares shown are those offered by the carriers participating in the pooling agreements.

The public has not benefited from the higher load factors resulting from these pooling agreements.[65] European carriers have squandered much of the potential cost savings from high and stable load factors by operating inefficiently. Straszheim has developed measures of relative carrier efficiency in matters such as crew, labor, and capital scheduling. He finds that all the major European airlines, with the exception of Alitalia, ranked very low in technical efficiency.[66] British European Airways, a carrier almost all of whose routes are subject to pooling arrangements and which in 1962 experienced a systemwide load factor of a little over 60 percent,

---

62. For an account of European problems, see Richard F. Coburn, "Pooling Runs into Cost, Revenue Share Snags," *Aviation Week*, vol. 91 (Oct. 20, 1969), pp. 204 ff.

63. Bluestone, "The Problem of Competition—Part II," p. 87.

64. See also "Load Factors on Intra-European Routes," *Aviation Week*, vol. 93 (Dec. 14, 1970), p. 31.

65. L. L. Doty, "Frequencies, Fares Emerging as European Growth Bars," *Aviation Week*, vol. 85 (Oct. 31, 1966), p. 32.

66. Mahlon R. Straszheim, *The International Airline Industry* (Brookings Institution, 1969), pp. 167–68.

Figure 2-6. Load Factors of Intra-European and U.S. Domestic Airline Trunk Carriers, 1959–69

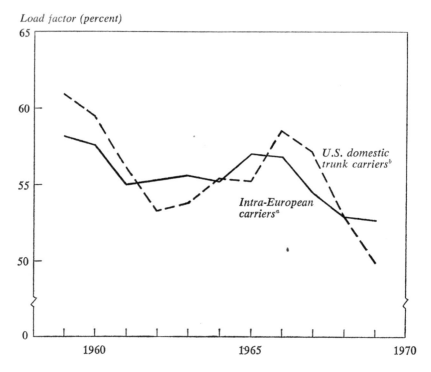

Load factor (percent)

U.S. domestic trunk carriers[b]

Intra-European carriers[a]

Sources: International Air Transport Association, *World Air Transport Statistics* (various issues); CAB, *Handbook of Airline Statistics, 1969 Edition* (1970), p. 108, and *1971 Edition* (1972), p. 26.
a. Includes only members of the European Airlines Research Bureau, made up primarily of flag carriers.
b. A strike occurred July 8 to August 20, 1966.

was singled out by Straszheim as "one of the highest-cost of all carriers serving short hops."[67]

Inefficiency is not the only way in which potential fare reductions resulting from higher load factors could be lost. Where the number of carriers serving a route is maintained, and if agreements to reduce flight frequencies and raise load factors could be negotiated and enforced, other possibilities to increase service quality (and costs) would remain. According to Doty, on the intra-European routes, "inflight service standards are set by pools which keep them at an unusually high level. Some observers have called this kind of service the best in the airline industry."[68]

67. Ibid., p. 168.
68. Doty, "Frequencies, Fares," p. 36.

Table 2-6. Air Fares and Annual Number of Passengers in Selected U.S. Domestic and Intra-European Markets, 1968–71

Route	Distance (miles)	Annual number of passengers (thousands)[a]	Fares[b]			
			Total (dollars)		Per mile (cents)	
			First class	Coach	First class	Coach
London–Paris	216	1,383	45.90	31.00	21.2	14.4
New York– Washington	214	1,853	31.48	24.07[c]	14.7	11.2
London–Geneva	469	268	86.10	59.30	18.4	12.6
Chicago–Pittsburgh	412	269	47.22	36.11	11.5	8.8
London–Rome	898	210	139.00	98.80	15.5	11.0
Chicago–Denver	900	252	85.18	65.74	9.5	7.3
				59.26[d]		6.6[d]
Los Angeles– San Francisco						
Interstate	338	4,807[e]	41.67	32.41	12.3	9.6
				20.37[d]		6.0[d]
Intrastate	338	4,807[e]	32.00	30.56	9.5	9.0
				15.28[d]		4.5[d]

Sources: Civil Aeronautics Board, *Handbook of Airline Statistics, 1969 Edition*, p. 389; California Public Utilities Commission, "Intrastate Passengers of Scheduled Air Carriers, Quarter and Twelve Months Ended December 31, 1969, and 1968," Report 1511.27 (tabulation), p. 2; *The British Airports Authority Annual Report and Accounts for the Year Ended 31 March 1970*, p. 90; *Official Airline Guide, Quick Reference, North American Edition* (Reuben H. Donnelly, May 1971), and *International Edition* (May 1971); mileage, which varies slightly depending upon airport, obtained from the CAB.
a. U.S. data are for 1968; intra-European data are for fiscal 1969–70.
b. One-way fares on jets, excluding tax, as of May 1971.
c. Applies also to air shuttle.
d. Jet economy.
e. Total, inter- and intrastate.

In this country, where formal pooling does not exist, the incentive to resort to these unregulated forms of nonprice competition in the hope of improving market share would remain a factor. "Seat wars," in which the width of coach seats has been the weapon, have occurred. Early in 1971, American Airlines launched a "lounge war" by removing several rows of seats in the rear of the coach section of their 747s and making the area into a large lounge.[69] While some of these "wars" might be ended by

69. "United to Make Skies More Friendly in 747 with 2 Coach Lounges," *Wall Street Journal*, May 19, 1971.

unilateral action, in principle each might be the subject of an intercarrier agreement or board regulation. Whichever course was taken, the board would face the difficult task of ensuring that the resulting service standards were consistent with consumer preferences and not merely set so as to maximize joint carrier profits. The two goals are hardly synonymous.

Further, to see that the cost reductions achieved by carrier agreements were partially passed on to the public in the form of lower fares, the board would have to determine "optimal" levels for all possible dimensions of service quality in every city-pair market. A fare would have to be set to provide a carrier operating at a high level of technical efficiency with revenue just sufficient to provide this optimal quality of service and a normal rate of return. Setting the fare above this level would produce excessive profits, provide revenues to finance excessive levels of service or technical inefficiency, or cover higher-than-market prices for inputs.[70] Setting the fare below this level would impair the long-run financial stability of the carrier or force it to reduce service quality to a level below the optimum.

Douglas's ingenious model may indicate what optimal capacity might be on city pairs of various characteristics; but, as he recognizes, it represents a first approximation and requires considerable refinement before it could be a reliable guide to policy. So the board's explicit recognition of the relationship between fares and the quality of service offered, and its statement that it no longer will continue to grant fare increases if load factors are low—that is, it will not support scheduling rivalry—should be hailed as a triumph of enlightened regulation.[71]

Experience teaches, however, that such triumphs are rare. Given the magnitude of the task, it probably lies beyond the ability of even the most capable, well-financed, and well-intentioned body of regulators to balance public and private interests in this matter. Suppose the board sought to simplify its regulatory load by determining the fare and level of service quality desired by a "typical" air traveler, and established a fare structure to enable the airlines to provide this level of quality. The resulting quality would be too low on short-haul routes and too high on long-haul routes. It would be too low on routes that served primarily passengers with a

70. For more on this point, see below, pp. 51–54.
71. Decision of CAB, Domestic Passenger Fare Investigation, Phase 6B—Load Factor, Docket 21866-6B, and Phase 7—Fare Level, Docket 21866-7, both decided April 9, 1971. For comments on this, see George W. Douglas and James C. Miller III, "The CAB's Domestic Passenger Fare Investigation," *Bell Journal of Economics and Management Science*, vol. 5 (Spring 1974), pp. 205–22.

high time value and too high on routes catering to those with a low time value. Since users of short-haul air travel typically place a high value on their time, they would find service quality to be especially low relative to their preferences. Carriers whose route structure contained a more than proportional share of short-haul routes might find themselves earning less than a normal rate of return, while carriers favored with long hauls might earn rates of return in excess of normal. It is debatable whether this situation could be considered an improvement over the current state of the industry.

A Proposal to Reduce Excessive Service Rivalry by Increasing Competition

Less emphasis on service rivalry among air carriers might well be beneficial to society. The board, however, would face a formidable task in monitoring carrier agreements to reduce service rivalry, and ensuring that reductions in service quality were passed on to the public in lower fares. Nevertheless, the benefits can be achieved without foundering on the difficulties of monitoring. The answer lies in *increasing* rather than restricting competition in the airline industry.

The Role of the CAB

If the board could establish "ideal" fares (as defined above) in each market, carrier agreements on service quality reduction or the reduction of the number of carriers competing on any one route would be unnecessary. Such fares would automatically encourage carriers to provide a structure of service characteristics approaching the optimal—provided that markets were competitive. In fact, the proper policy for the board to pursue would be to open markets to any carrier who chose to serve them and to discourage actively agreements to limit rivalry in any form. Failure to take these steps would invite a quality of service that would be lower than desired, given the fare level. The problem of inducing carriers to supply the quality of service that the board determined to be desirable could be solved by reliance upon market forces.

The problem of determining the desired level of service quality also could be solved, provided one more step were taken. Suppose that the board, in addition to ending control over entry into and exit from both individual city pairs and the airline industry, announced an end to fare regulation. Price competition would develop—if not from one of the carriers currently serving a route, then from another certificated carrier or, more likely, from a newly scheduled carrier. Break-even load factors would rise, pushed by the resulting fare reductions, as participants in the market sought to cut costs in an effort to continue to break even. Curtailment of flight frequencies would be one result, though lower levels of service quality in other dimensions would probably also occur. Also likely would be a trend in many markets for some carriers to drop out as they found it impossible to achieve the higher load factors required, though the low costs of entry into any city-pair market would guarantee that an increased market share for the remaining carriers would not lead to monopoly power.[72] In markets now served by a single carrier, fares might decrease or the quality of service rise as entry, or its threat, restrained existing monopoly power. Finally, in a number of short-haul and low-density markets, fares might rise and service quality fall as cross-subsidization ended. This is because price competition and free entry would dry up the source of funds necessary for cross-subsidization—excess profits earned in long-haul, high-density markets.[73]

The California Experience

The results predicted from increased competition have occurred in the California intrastate markets. The intrastate character of the markets, and the fact that the California Public Utilities Commission chose to regulate price increases only, made price competition possible until 1965 at least.[74] As shown in Table 2-6, competition forced fares in these markets down

72. See Joe S. Bain, *Barriers to New Competition: Their Character and Consequences in Manufacturing Industries* (Harvard University Press, 1956).

73. Service in the short-haul, low-density markets might well be curtailed and perhaps even abandoned by the carriers now serving them, but in many of these markets service might even be improved as short-haul specialists, the descendents of today's air taxis, offered frequent service with aircraft smaller than those currently operated by the trunk airlines. But even if service were eliminated in certain of these markets, little would be lost, for these are precisely the markets in which the airplane has little relative advantage over other modes of transportation and where its artificial encouragement does the most harm to a balanced transportation system. However, if the public interest seemed to call for short-haul, low-density air service, other arrangements could be made to assure it. See George Eads, *The Local Service Airline Experiment* (Brookings Institution, 1972).

74. See Jordan, *Airline Regulation in America*, pp. 2–4. Much of the description that follows is taken from his book.

to roughly two-thirds the level in comparable markets subject to CAB price regulation. As a result, break-even load factors have been pushed up to the 60 or 70 percent range.[75] The leading intrastate carrier, Pacific Southwest Airlines (PSA), has managed consistently to attain load factors high enough not only to break even but to earn an attractive rate of return.[76] The major certificated carriers participating in these markets, United and Western, have seen their combined market share drop to less than 30 percent in the Los Angeles–San Francisco market, the largest in the nation in terms of passengers carried.[77] United, although operating at a 57 percent load factor in early 1970, stated that it was losing money on the route and was reported to be considering abandoning the market to PSA. If it did, and if PSA merged with Air California, as was once contemplated, PSA's share might rise to as much as 92 percent of the market, making it a monopoly under the CAB's definition.[78] However, the threat of entry by other intrastate carriers (assuming authorization by the California Public Utility Commission, since it has recently asserted control over entry) or instant reentry on a massive scale by United would adequately check any attempt by PSA to exploit this quasi-monopolistic situation.

Jordan attributes the success of the intrastate carriers, principally PSA, to their low fares (which have at times been matched by the certificated carriers) and their superior efficiency (which has not), and traces both directly to their freedom from regulation.[79] Jordan finds, for example, that the intrastate carriers have done better in matching capacity offered to

75. William S. Hieronymus, "Local Growth Benefits Pacific Southwest," *Aviation Week*, vol. 92 (May 11, 1970), p. 36. See also Jordan, *Airline Regulation in America*, p. 202.

76. In 1970, PSA earned a 9.2 percent rate of return on stockholder equity, and its net income was $4.9 million. During the same year, the domestic trunk industry as a whole lost $100 million. For PSA's high rates of return from 1957 to 1965, see Jordan, *Airline Regulation in America*, p. 187.

77. According to data for calendar year 1970, PSA had 62 percent of the 5.3-million passenger market, United, 16 percent, and Air California, another intrastate carrier, 14 percent, while Western had ceased to be an effective competitor, its share having fallen below 10 percent. See U.S. Department of Transportation, "Top City Pairs, 1970" (1971; computer tabulation), table entitled "Ranking on Passengers."

78. See note 3, p. 13.

79. In a regression in which he attempts to find an explanation for the intrastate carriers' share in the San Francisco–Los Angeles, San Francisco–San Diego, and San Diego–Los Angeles markets, Jordan finds the fare differential between intrastate and trunk carriers to be a significant explanatory variable only in the first market (*Airline Regulation in America*, p. 167).

peaks in demand. During the period studied, traffic in the California intrastate markets tended to peak on Fridays and Sundays. The certificated carriers offered only about 28.6 percent of their weekly seats on these two days, while the intrastate carriers offered 35.8 percent of their seats on Friday and Sunday in the Los Angeles–San Francisco market, 28.1 percent in the Los Angeles–San Diego market, and 31.2 percent in the San Diego–San Francisco market. Jordan also found that the intrastate carriers changed their schedules more readily to meet shifts in these peaks than did the certificated carriers.[80]

This sort of matching obviously will raise load factors. But it also can raise costs. Several factors appear to explain much of the ability of the intrastate carriers to circumvent this problem. First, since their route structure is much more compact and is simpler than that of the certificated carriers, efficient scheduling of aircraft is easier. The trunks are unable to match equipment to the particular needs of the intra-California market because they optimize their equipment scheduling on a systemwide basis.

A second factor has to do with PSA's relations with its pilots. The pilots of the certificated carriers are paid according to a complex formula negotiated over the years between the carriers and the pilots' unions, principally the Air Line Pilots Association (ALPA).[81] The ALPA has been relatively successful in negotiating guarantees that put a floor under a pilot's pay regardless of how much his services are utilized by the airline, and in gaining control over the scheduling of pilots' flight time.

From the pilot's point of view, the most important impact of the union has been felt on wages. According to Lewis, the ALPA has managed to raise pilots' pay by perhaps as much as 30 percent over what it would be in the absence of the union.[82] From the airlines' point of view, one important effect has been a decline in average pilot utilization, a decline that Baitsell attributes directly to the ALPA.[83] A second effect has been to

---

80. Ibid., pp. 206–09.

81. For an excellent explanation see John M. Baitsell, *Airline Industrial Relations: Pilots and Flight Engineers* (Harvard University, Graduate School of Business Administration, Division of Research, 1966), especially chaps. 4, 5, 7, and 8. Hopkins discusses the lobbying by the ALPA that resulted in the inclusion in the Civil Aeronautics Act (sec. 401[l]) of the basic elements of this pay formula. See also George E. Hopkins, *The Airline Pilots: A Study in Elite Unionization* (Harvard University Press, 1971), chaps. 7–9.

82. H. G. Lewis, *Unionism and Relative Wages in the United States: An Empirical Inquiry* (University of Chicago Press, 1963), pp. 99–105.

83. Baitsell, *Airline Industrial Relations*, pp. 135–36.

transform flight crew pay, representing approximately 10 percent of total operating costs, from a variable into a relatively fixed cost.

PSA's pilots do not belong to the ALPA and, because it is not subject to federal economic regulation, the carrier is not bound by the provisions of section 401(l) of the Civil Aeronautics Act. It has therefore been possible to negotiate a contract whereby pilots are paid according to the number of scheduled miles they fly.[84] This arrangement spurs pilots to boost productivity. It also makes this important component of operating costs much more a variable cost for PSA than it is for the certificated carriers. Thus, the cost of keeping an aircraft on the ground during off-peak periods is lower for PSA than for the certificated carriers.

The California intrastate carriers also have substantially outstripped the certificated carriers in such productivity measures as average annual seat-miles per employee, average annual revenue passenger-miles per employee, and average annual operating revenues per employee.[85] While a relatively low degree of unionization may partially explain PSA's relatively good showing, Jordan lists several other contributing factors and concludes:

It is my own opinion that, in addition to the management policies described in this chapter, the reasons for PSA's greater output per employee lie in its more specialized operation relative to that of the certificated carriers and in its use of price rivalry in addition to service-quality rivalry. PSA specialized in providing one class of service with a single aircraft type (at any point in time) over a homogeneous route structure (which it was free to modify at will). All of this served to increase its width of output. In addition, it was able to concentrate service in high-density markets having large volume characteristics (while, however, being restricted to relatively short-haul markets within the confines of California, thereby reducing the volume aspect of distance). The ability to use price rivalry enabled PSA to ignore high-cost innovations (which the certificated carriers adopted to achieve high service quality) and to delay adopting other technological innovations, thus reducing the cost of their adoption.[86]

If economic regulation of the airlines were eased, the PSA experience would be duplicated in many of the major city-pair markets. In markets such as Los Angeles–New York and New York–Chicago, specialist car-

84. Jordan, *Airline Regulation in America*, p. 222. PSA must abide by FAA rules limiting the total number of hours a pilot can fly.

85. Ibid., pp. 210–20. That PSA does so well by the last measure is surprising in view of its short average passenger haul. Yet, in 1965, the figure was $22,200 for each employee of a certificated trunk carrier and $32,500 for each PSA employee.

86. Ibid., p. 223, note 34. See also Hieronymus, "Local Growth Benefits Pacific Southwest," p. 37.

riers would gain most of the business for the same reasons that PSA has been successful. Another feature of the California experience that might carry over into longer-haul, high-density markets is a single, standardized service offering low fares and high load factors. However, Abbott's work[87] suggests that in such markets, which include both businessmen and pleasure travelers, two distinct types of services might appear—one at premium prices offering frequent flights and relatively low load factors, to the first group (who presumably place a higher value on their time), and the other at low prices offering less frequency and high load factors to the second group. This is what has happened on the North Atlantic route, where charters and scheduled services coexist.

Will Deregulation Lead to "Destructive" Competition?

The opponents of economic deregulation of the airline industry might concede that the argument makes sense in theory, but they would contend that in practice, the result would be cutthroat competition as airlines scrambled to fill seats. This, in turn, would cause carrier bankruptcies and both a loss of vital air services and a deterioration in air safety. While the experience of the California interstate air carriers indicates that deregulation would lead only to lower fares, more efficient operations, and a quality of air service more in line with consumer tastes, and would not cause safety standards to deteriorate,[88] opponents of deregulation are quick to supply reasons why this example is atypical or misleading.[89]

It is true that since the CAB was established, no trunk carrier has been permitted to fail.[90] All exits from the industry have been via merger or acquisition. In contrast, fourteen of the sixteen intrastate carriers that provided service in the California markets at one time or another have terminated operations, in no case via merger.[91] But it seems questionable

87. Lawrence Abbott, *Quality and Competition: An Essay in Economic Theory* (Columbia University Press, 1955).

88. See Jordan, *Airline Regulation in America*, pp. 49–53, for a discussion of the safety record of the California intrastate air carriers.

89. For a partial listing, see Hieronymus, "Local Growth Benefits Pacific Southwest," p. 37.

90. Jordan, *Airline Regulation in America*, pp. 15–17.

91. Ibid., pp. 17–24. In the American-Western merger case, Jordan advanced the proposition that this pattern is explicable because of CAB entry controls. He argued that the primary asset possessed by a carrier is its route certificate; in the California

that public policy should be concerned with the preservation of individual firms as long as their demise does not result in a loss of vital public services. All the available data, both from the California experience and from that of the unregulated commuter air carriers, indicate that the bankruptcy of an air carrier will not by itself result in any such loss.[92] This is hardly surprising, for it would be difficult to find an industry with fewer of the prerequisites for destructive competition outlined by Kahn.[93]

While safety considerations are important, there is no credible evidence in air transportation, or any other industry, linking safety performance to economic regulation. Furthermore, no change in the regulation of safety is being proposed. The FAA would still possess its full powers in this area, powers that could be increased were it necessary. What would be removed would be any incentive the FAA might have to ignore unsafe conditions in order not to injure the economic position of individual certificated airlines.[94]

Conclusions

The airline industry as it exists today suffers from an excessive attention to service rivalry—termed by some "competition." While a reduction in the competitive vigor of the industry through mergers, capacity agreements, regulation of seating configurations and their associated fare differentials, and so on, would reduce service rivalry and offer a *potential* for reduced fares, continual and detailed surveillance of all aspects of air carrier operations by the CAB would be required to assure their realization. This distasteful, costly, and probably futile task could be avoided and the public assured the benefits of lower fares and more appropriate levels of service if the board were to relax substantially its control over fares and entry. The advantages this course of action would have over relying on more regulation have been well stated by Alfred Kahn:

---

case, since entry was free, a certificate had no value. See "Testimony of William A. Jordan," CAB Docket 22916, Exhibit DJ-RT-1, pp. 6–10.

92. See in particular CAB, New England Service Investigation, Docket 22973, "Rebuttal Exhibits of the Bureau of Operating Rights," vol. 2 (1972), Exhibit BOR-R-300 and appendixes.

93. Alfred E. Kahn, *The Economics of Regulation: Principles and Institutions* (John Wiley, 1971), vol. 2, p. 173.

94. Evidence that this may have occurred is contained in Jerry Simandle, "Airline Regulation and the Public Interest" (senior thesis, Princeton University, 1971; processed).

Rivalry in improving service can obviously be just as productive of benefit to the traveling public as in price. How, then, can an economist presume to judge that it has gone too far? He may not, directly. All he can do is ask whether the service improvements have been subjected to the test of a competitive market. That test requires that customers be provided with a sufficient variety of price-quality combinations—consistent with efficient production—so that each can register a free and tolerably well-informed monetary appraisal of the quality differentials that are offered. By this test product inflation could be said to have occurred only if quality competition had operated in such a way as to eliminate, or to fail to develop, lower quality-price combinations that consumers would willingly have purchased in quantities sufficient to cover the cost of producing them. . . .

The objection is not necessarily that airlines have been forced by their competition to incur greater costs for denser schedules, advertising, meals, and in-flight entertainment than they would if they were able to get together and restrict such expenditures to the industry profit-maximizing level. . . . To adopt any such criterion of industry performance would be to take the results of pure monopoly as the ideal: it is precisely the function of competition to force suppliers to do things that are not in their collective interest. The objection is, rather, that these cost-inflating service improvements have not been subjected to the test of having to compete with lower-cost, lower-price alternatives. The defect, in short, has not been the service competition, as such, but the inadequate play of *price* competition along with it.[95]

95. Kahn, *Economics of Regulation*, vol. 2, p. 216. Italics are in the original.

CHAPTER THREE

Deregulating Surface Freight Transportation

THOMAS GALE MOORE

A LARGE and growing body of literature has criticized the Interstate Commerce Commission (ICC) and its regulation of surface freight transportation.[1] Study after study has pointed out the inefficiencies generated by value-of-service rate making, controls on entry, and the regulation of investment and disinvestment. Much of this literature, however, has been qualitative in approach, and what quantitative estimates of the cost of regulation there are have been fragmentary.[2] And, while most studies have suggested policy alternatives that would improve resource allocation,

1. See, for example, Walter Adams, "The Role of Competition in the Regulated Industries," in American Economic Association, *Papers and Proceedings of the Seventieth Annual Meeting, 1957* (*American Economic Review*, vol. 48, May 1958), pp. 527–43; Aaron J. Gellman, "Surface Freight Transportation," in William M. Capron (ed.), *Technological Change in Regulated Industries* (Brookings Institution, 1971); George W. Hilton, *The Transportation Act of 1958: A Decade of Experience* (Indiana University Press, 1969); John R. Meyer and others, *The Economics of Competition in the Transportation Industries* (Harvard University Press, 1959); Robert A. Nelson and William R. Greiner, "The Relevance of the Common Carrier under Modern Economic Conditions," in *Transportation Economics*, A Conference of the Universities–National Bureau Committee for Economic Research (Columbia University Press for the National Bureau of Economic Research, 1965); Merrill J. Roberts, "Transport Costs, Pricing, and Regulation," in *Transportation Economics;* and the studies cited below in notes 2 (Friedlaender), 5, 8, 38, 43, 52, and 58.

2. Ann F. Friedlaender, *The Dilemma of Freight Transport Regulation* (Brookings Institution, 1969); idem, "The Social Costs of Regulating the Railroads," in American Economic Association, *Papers and Proceedings of the Eighty-third Annual Meeting, 1970* (*American Economic Review*, vol. 61, May 1971), pp. 226–34; Robert W. Harbeson, "Toward Better Resource Allocation in Transport," *Journal of Law and Economics*, vol. 12 (October 1969), pp. 321–38.

55

the analysis has tended to focus on existing problems rather than the alternatives. The objective of this chapter is thus two-fold: first, to estimate the order of magnitude of the cost of regulation, and second, to consider proposals for reducing or eliminating regulation and to compare the costs of these alternatives with the present system.

Existing Costs of Regulation

Several kinds of losses can arise from regulation. First, regulation may increase costs within a particular mode. For example, regulation of trucking limits the ability of regulated trucks to secure backhauls, and the legal restrictions on private and agricultural motor carriers force trucks to travel empty a considerable portion of the time. Consequently, costs of motor carriers are increased above what is necessary to carry actual loads. In the railroad industry, prohibitions on the abandonment of uneconomic services have inflated costs. For water carriers, the prohibitions on mixing nonregulated with regulated tows and on having more than three nonregulated tows have also led to higher costs.[3] In other words, regulation has raised the cost of providing a given amount of service.

A second cost to the economy from regulation stems from shifting traffic from low-cost to high-cost modes. For example, if rail rates are raised relative to truck rates, traffic that would be more economically carried by rail will be moved instead by truck. Potentially, regulation could shift traffic among all the modes—rail to water, rail to truck, truck to water, surface to air, all other modes to pipelines, or vice versa.

A third cost of regulation comes from pricing above marginal costs— the traditional welfare triangle.[4] This is the allocative cost caused by the nonshipment of goods due to higher prices.

A fourth loss from regulation is the result of distortions in other sectors of the economy due to locational and product price discrimination. If, for example, the shipping rate for scrap iron is higher relative to cost than the shipping rate for iron ores, there will be less recycling of scrap iron than if rates were based strictly on costs; that is, more iron ore and less scrap will be used. Other distortions result from the general tendency

3. The mixing restriction (P.L. 91-590) was repealed at the end of 1970 (49 U.S.C 903[b]).

4. Harold Hotelling, "The General Welfare in Relation to Problems of Taxation and of Railway and Utility Rates," *Econometrica*, vol. 6 (July 1938), pp. 242–69.

to price shipments of manufactured goods high relative to cost, and raw materials low relative to cost. This induces manufacturers to locate plants near their major customers rather than near the source of raw materials. Besides misallocating resources in terms of private costs, this practice leads to congestion in urban areas, with concomitant external costs.

A fifth—and possibly the largest—loss from regulation is the dynamic loss caused by a reduction in incentives to innovate. If regulatory inertia and pricing umbrellas inhibit innovation, higher costs and a less progressive industry posture are the results.

This chapter does not estimate the regulatory losses caused by the last two factors. Friedlaender has attempted to define the distortion loss and MacAvoy and Sloss[5] have described the dynamic losses due to the inhibition of innovation, but data are inadequate to measure these losses generally.

Costs from Inefficient Provision of Services

Costs of producing a product or service in a noncompetitive situation may significantly exceed the lowest possible cost. Such costs are dead losses to the economy, no matter what other misallocations exist, since it is always desirable to expend as few resources as possible in providing a service. Any saving in resources can generate additional goods and hence is preferable in terms of Paretian optimality. Second-best considerations do not hold here,[6] for, as Mishan has pointed out,[7] it is always desirable to eliminate imperfections that lead to smaller output.

MOTOR COMMON CARRIERS. Regulation, particularly route and commodity restrictions, has forced inefficient practices on common carrier trucking.[8] A 1941 study conducted by the Board of Investigation and Research indicated that commodity restrictions have been narrowly defined: 62 percent of truckers were limited to special commodities and 40 percent of those restricted to one commodity or commodity class, while 88 per-

---

5. Paul W. MacAvoy and James Sloss, *Regulation of Transport Innovation: The ICC and Unit Coal Trains to the East Coast* (Random House, 1967), p. 61.

6. R. G. Lipsey and Kelvin Lancaster, "The General Theory of Second Best," *Review of Economic Studies*, vol. 24 (1), no. 63 (1956–57), pp. 11–32.

7. E. J. Mishan, "Second Thoughts on Second Best," *Oxford Economic Papers*, n.s. vol. 14 (October 1962), pp. 205–17.

8. See for example, James C. Nelson, "The Effects of Entry Control in Surface Transport," in *Transportation Economics*.

cent were restricted to six or fewer commodities.[9] Such limitations impose costs on trucking firms by increasing the difficulty of filling backhauls, so that trucking capacity is underutilized.

About 70 percent of the regular-route common carriers were not authorized to give full service to intermediate points on their routes, and approximately 10 percent had no authority to serve any intermediate point.[10] In addition, they often had to follow circuitous routes and specific highways. Irregular route carriers were generally limited to radial service, which means that their traffic could be picked up from and delivered to only one or more specific points within a geographic region. Many such carriers had to operate through points that they could not legally serve, and thus could not legally pick up and deliver goods within those areas. The board also found that one-third of the intercity truckers had return limitations, with 10 percent having no authority at all to transport traffic on return trips.[11]

In reporting on these restrictions, James C. Nelson concluded that "it is probable that a roughly comparable pattern is in existence today."[12] The ICC acknowledged to a Senate Small Business Committee in 1955 that the same type of restrictions were still in operation,[13] and there is no reason to believe that they have been diminished or abolished since.

Another illustration of the ICC's inattention to efficiency concerns mergers. The ICC requires that merged companies follow the previously authorized routes of each company even though shorter routes may be feasible. Thus to ship from the territory of one firm to that of the other, the trucks must go through the point or points where the territories overlap.

Since ICC regulation makes price competition virtually impossible, motor carriers can engage only in nonprice competition, mainly by increasing their capacity, which, of course, increases costs. Increased capacity permits a trucking firm to offer faster and more convenient service, thus giving it a competitive edge over other firms. While this leads to excess capacity, lower load factors, and added costs, such increases in service

9. *Federal Regulatory Restrictions Upon Motor and Water Carriers*, A Report by the Board of Investigation and Research on Federal Regulatory Restrictions upon Motor and Water Carriers, S. Doc. 78, 79 Cong. 1 sess. (1945), pp. 20–32.

10. Ibid., p. 77.

11. Ibid., p. 126.

12. "Effects of Entry Control," p. 393.

13. Reported in ibid., p. 393.

are not a complete loss to the economy, since there are some gains to the shipper from better service.

A series of court decisions in the mid-1950s held that fresh dressed poultry, frozen poultry, and frozen fruits and vegetables were all exempt commodities under the Interstate Commerce Act and thus not subject to transport regulation.[14] The impact of this deregulation was subsequently studied by the U.S. Department of Agriculture. Transport rates and services for fresh and frozen poultry in 1952 and 1955 (regulated) were compared with those in fiscal 1957 (deregulated); for frozen fruits and vegetables the years compared were 1955 and 1957.[15] After Congress reregulated frozen fruits and vegetables in 1958, the impact of that legislation on rates and services was also examined by the department.[16] These studies showed that rates fell and service improved with deregulation. The rates for fresh poultry fell by 12 to 53 percent (average reduction 33 percent), and those for frozen poultry declined by 16 to 59 percent (average reduction 36 percent). In addition, stopoff charges were reduced or eliminated and the number of stops permitted was increased.[17] For frozen fruits and vegetables the weighted average decline in rates was 19 percent, while rail rates on the same products increased by 6 to 14 percent. Again, stopoff charges were reduced substantially and the number permitted increased.[18]

As part of the study, shippers were asked the advantages and dis-

14. On June 30, 1953, the District Court for the Northern District of Iowa declared that fresh dressed poultry was an exempt commodity as defined by the Motor Carrier Act of 1935 as amended. The U.S. Circuit Court of Appeals affirmed this decision, and the Supreme Court denied review of the case. On April 23, 1956, the Supreme Court affirmed a decision of the District Court for the Southern District of Texas that both fresh and frozen dressed poultry came under the agricultural exemption clause of the Motor Carrier Act. On May 7, 1956, the Federal District Court of the Western District of Washington declared that frozen fruits and vegetables were exempt commodities as defined by the act. The decision was affirmed by the Supreme Court on November 5, 1956.

15. James R. Snitzler and Robert J. Byrne, "Interstate Trucking of Fresh and Frozen Poultry under Agricultural Exemption," U.S. Department of Agriculture, Marketing Research Report 224 (1958; processed); idem, "Interstate Trucking of Frozen Fruits and Vegetables under Agricultural Exemption," U.S. Department of Agriculture, Marketing Research Report 316 (1959; processed).

16. U.S. Department of Agriculture, "Supplement to Interstate Trucking of Frozen Fruits and Vegetables under Agricultural Exemption," Supplement to Marketing Research Report 316 (July 1961; processed).

17. Snitzler and Byrne, "Interstate Trucking of Fresh and Frozen Poultry," pp. 66, 79.

18. Idem, "Interstate Trucking of Frozen Fruits and Vegetables," pp. 1–3, 52–53.

advantages of regulated versus unregulated carriage. Only twenty poultry shippers reported any advantages in shipping by regulated carriage and eighty-five reported disadvantages, while eighty-two found advantages in unregulated carriage and thirty-three reported disadvantages.[19] Since regulation has not improved service in the eyes of shippers, any increase in costs attributable to regulation can be considered a net loss. Since there is no compelling reason to believe that the commodities deregulated by the court decisions were atypical,[20] it can be assumed, following Friedlaender,[21] that rates would fall 20 percent generally if regulation of trucking were eliminated.

In 1968, total truck revenues of class I and class II common carriers were $9.6 billion.[22] On this volume of traffic, a fall of 20 percent in the rates would reduce revenues by $1.92 billion. At this lower level of revenue, the industry would presumably still cover its costs, including a normal profit. Thus, this decline in revenue must reduce monopoly profits and/or costs by a total of $1.92 billion. Any reduction in costs would be a real gain to the economy, while a reduction in monopoly profits would simply mean a transfer of income from trucker to shipper and consumer.

There are several ways to estimate what proportion of the reduction would be cost savings and what proportion would come from monopoly profits. If all trucking firms were continuously being bought and sold and if bookkeeping practices reflected the true value of the firms' certificates, certificate values would equal the present value of the monopoly gains due to regulation. In 1968, the value of intangible property less reserves for amortization of certificates for class I and II motor carriers was $218 million.[23] When a motor carrier purchases a certificate the cost goes into this account. At their discretion, however, carriers can amortize this investment over a five-year period. Figures from class I common carriers (general freight, intercity) suggest that about 20 percent has been set

19. Idem, "Interstate Trucking of Fresh and Frozen Poultry," pp. 47–53.

20. It has been argued that trucking costs for agricultural commodities (although some of these items were frozen, and therefore processed, products) are not typical. Whether or not this is so is irrelevant; the assumption here is that the *mark-up* over marginal cost is typical—that is, average.

21. *Dilemma of Freight Transport Regulation*, p. 74.

22. *84th Annual Report of the Interstate Commerce Commission, Fiscal Year Ended June 30, 1970*, p. 141; U.S. Interstate Commerce Commission, Bureau of Accounts, *Transport Statistics in the United States for the Year Ended December 31, 1968:* pt. 7, *Motor Carriers* (1969), table 37.

23. ICC, *Transport Statistics, 1968: Motor Carriers*, tables 2, 37.

aside in this way. Thus, the gross value of these certificates would be $272 million, although this figure is clearly an underestimate since some of the certificates were purchased long ago and some may never have been sold. If investors in the industry must earn 10 percent before taxes, annual monopoly profits due to regulation would be $27.2 million. Even if investors demanded a higher rate of return—say, 20 percent—before taxes, the annual amount is still fairly negligible. Subtracting either number from $1.92 billion yields the amount by which costs would fall with deregulation. Calculated this way, the *increase* in costs due to regulation of common carrier trucking might be as much as $1.89 billion.

Another way to estimate the amount by which costs are inflated is to look at net profits in 1968. Some of these profits are in fact return on equity capital and so not true monopoly profits. Total assets of class I and II common carriers were $2.42 billion in 1968.[24] If the industry must earn 10 percent before taxes and if it were entirely equity financed, $242 million a year would be required to pay for its investment. Since net operating income was $499 million, $257 million would be the amount of monopoly profits. Subtracting $257 million from $1.92 billion indicates that cost might be inflated by $1.66 billion. If all of the $499 million were monopoly profits and there were no return due on investment, then the minimum estimate of the increase in cost due to regulation would be $1.4 billion

These numbers may strike the reader as surprisingly large. It is possible that some of the gains from regulation go to labor in the form of higher wages,[25] and allegations have indeed been made that teamsters are a major beneficiary of regulation. It is certainly true that regulation causes more truck miles (many unnecessarily empty) to be driven than would be in a free market. The extra truck miles certainly lead to the employment of additional labor and hence an expanded membership for the International Brotherhood of Teamsters. However, if regulation does not lead to higher wages (and there is no convincing economic rationale for the trucking firms sharing monopoly gains with labor), then it is creating a real economic waste.

Annable has shown that trucking labor has received larger wage increases during the postwar period than the rest of the economy. He as-

24. *Annual Report of the Interstate Commerce Commission, 1970*, p. 142; *Transport Statistics, 1968: Motor Carriers*, table 37.
25. I am grateful to Sam Peltzman for pointing out this possibility.

sumes that "the cumulative effect of regulation causes monopoly 'profits' to rise over time."[26] Annable claims that the rise in wages supports his hypothesis that the Teamsters have captured most if not all of the cartel profits.

Theoretically, it seems more likely that cartel profits would decline over time anyway as new substitutes are formed, adjustments are made, and nonprice competition grows. Thus, the evidence that wages in trucking have risen faster than in other sectors appears to be unrelated to the question of whether regulation by itself has raised wages. Moreover, in a number of other sectors—contract construction, for example—wages have also grown faster than in the economy as a whole. This is not to argue that labor in the trucking industry does not reap higher returns than unorganized competitive labor, nor that the Teamsters do not receive substantial benefits in increased membership and employment, but only that such additional labor reflects a waste to the economy, not a transfer of monopoly profits.[27]

Such large losses present compelling incentives to trucking firms to rationalize the system by eliminating the wastes, as, for example, in the merger of motor carriers with complementary certificates.[28] However, such mergers would eliminate union jobs and so would be opposed by the Teamsters. Moreover, trucking firms with balanced certificates could expect stronger competition from such a merged firm and would also oppose such a step. With both labor and other trucking firms opposing a merger, the ICC might be reluctant to authorize the combination. Consequently, it seems quite possible that, although the losses from regulation are quite high, within the context of the conflicting gains and losses, the ICC is unable to rationalize the industry.

PRIVATE TRUCKS. Regulation imposes large costs on private trucking and unregulated farm trucking. Private trucking is in general prohibited

26. James E. Annable, Jr., "The ICC, the IBT, and the Cartelization of the American Trucking Industry," *The Quarterly Review of Economics and Business* (University of Illinois, Bureau of Economic and Business Research), vol. 13 (Summer 1973), p. 42.

27. Actually, if the teamsters union has inflated wages above the competitive level and regulation has led to increased employment, then the amount of the additional wages above the competitive level would constitute a transfer of monopoly profits and not a pure waste. Thus, if regulation has led to an increase in employment of 10 percent and the union has raised wages 20 percent, 2 percent of labor costs would be a transfer of monopoly profits. Since labor costs are about 60 percent of revenue, about 1.2 percent of revenue, or around $115 million, might be labor's monopoly gains.

28. I am grateful to the members of the Industrial Organization Workshop at the University of Chicago for suggesting this point.

Table 3-1. Percentage of Private and Regulated Tractor-Trailer Trucks with Empty Backhauls, and Private Capacity Shortfall, by Body Type, 1969

Body type	Private	Regulated	Private capacity shortfall[a]
Platform	40.9	35.9	7.8
Open-top vans	35.7	20.5	19.1
General-purpose vans	31.4	19.0	15.3
Insulated vans	30.5	21.1	11.9

Source: Edward Miller, "Effects of Regulation on Truck Utilization," *Transportation Journal*, vol. 13 (Fall 1973), pp. 11–12.
a. The percent of private capacity that could be saved if utilization level were the same as for regulated vehicles.

from soliciting traffic on a commercial basis. Since the normal flow of goods for a company is only in one direction, backhauls are normally empty. Similarly, farm trucking brings goods from agricultural areas to consumer areas, but there are few exempt agricultural goods flowing in the opposite direction.

The reduction in capacity achievable in the absence of regulation can be estimated on the basis of a study done by the Department of Transportation that gives the percent of empty backhauls by type of truck and type of carrier (ICC-regulated or private).[29] Only long-haul private trucking could profitably utilize backhaul traffic in an unregulated market, and since tractor-trailer combinations predominate in the long-haul market, only data for this type of rig is presented here (see Table 3-1). Furthermore, all sectors of the economy do not have equal opportunities to solicit backhauls. Manufacturing, trade, agriculture, and forestry would be more able to take advantage of opportunities to compete for backhaul traffic than, say, contract construction and services. Many types of trucks are so specialized that they can haul only particular goods, and this, too, makes it difficult to secure backhauls. Consequently, the analysis has been confined to the four types of trucks generally used: platform trucks, open-top vans, insulated vans, and general-purpose vans. Table 3-1 gives the percent of these trucks that run empty in private and regulated use

29. Edward Miller, "Effects of Regulation on Truck Utilization," *Transportation Journal*, vol. 13 (Fall 1973).

and the percent of truck-miles that could be saved if private trucking achieved the same level of utilization as ICC-regulated vehicles.

The U.S. Bureau of the Census reports the number of truck-miles for each of these types of truck by sector of the economy—agriculture, manufacturing, wholesale and retail trade, forestry, and so forth.[30] A less recent study of line-haul trucking costs shows how cost per vehicle-mile varies with load, and concludes that it costs at least 40 cents per vehicle-mile to move a large truck.[31] Thus, if private trucking in manufacturing, trade, and agriculture could secure the same proportion of backhauls as ICC-regulated trucking, an annual reduction of 390 million vehicle-miles would mean $150 million in annual savings. Likewise the saving for forestry trucks would be about 420 million vehicle-miles, or about $170 million. And if all industries could achieve the average performance of ICC-regulated trucks, the saving in vehicle-miles would be about 2,400 million miles and the dollar saving just under $1 billion.

RAILROADS. Waste due to regulation of railroads is substantial. Railroads are prohibited from abandoning unprofitable routes and services. Furthermore, the rental rates of freight cars are so low as to discourage railroads from purchasing cars, while at the same time providing an incentive to hoard cars in order to offer better service. MacAvoy and Sloss, Gellman, and others have pointed out that regulation has deterred innovations in the railroad industry, resulting in higher costs than without regulation.[32] Passenger losses have also added substantially to the costs of railroads, although quantification of such costs is difficult.

Friedlaender estimated the losses due to the excess capacity caused by regulation at $2.4 billion in 1969.[33] Since her procedure appears faulty,

30. U.S. Bureau of the Census, *Census of Transportation, 1967*, vol. 2: *Truck Inventory and Use Survey* (1970), table 27.

31. Highway Research Board, *Line-Haul Trucking Costs in Relation to Vehicle Gross Weights*, Bulletin 301 (National Academy of Sciences–National Research Council, 1961), figs. 18, 19, 20.

32. MacAvoy and Sloss, *Regulation of Transport Innovation;* Gellman, "Surface Freight Transportation."

33. She estimated ("Social Costs of Regulating the Railroads") both a long-run cost function based on cross-sectional data and a short-run cost function based on time-series data, and from these two cost functions computed long-run and short-run cost elasticities. She shows that

$$E/E^* = \frac{dc/dx}{dc^*/dx} \cdot \frac{c^*}{c},$$

where E is the short-run cost elasticity, c is total cost, x is output, and the long-run

however, a somewhat different technique is used here. First, the average percentage by which rail rates would decline in the absence of regulation is estimated. This decline in rates would produce a comparable decrease in revenue for the same traffic, part of which would reflect lower costs and part lower monopoly profits. Estimating how much rates would fall, however, requires a prediction of the distribution of traffic among modes in the absence of regulation.

There is a general belief that without regulation rails would succeed in capturing some traffic from trucks. Both Friedlaender and Meyer have argued that rail costs are considerably below truck costs for shipments greater than 200 miles, so that much of this long-haul truck traffic would be apt to move to rails. Harbeson's computation of rail and truck costs indicates that, except for the shortest shipments, rail costs are below highway costs.[34]

This proposition seems questionable. First, the major competitive moves by railroads in recent years have been attempts to divert traffic from water carriers rather than from trucks. For example, in the years 1966 to 1970, the ICC reported eleven intermodal cases, eight of which were attempts by railroads to attract traffic from water carriers.[35] Only one was clearly an attempt by railroads to attract traffic from motor carriers and one was an attempt by trucks to attract rail traffic. (The remaining case involved an REA Express attempt to attract pure truck traffic.)

Second, it is widely recognized that regulatory commissions usually develop tendencies to protect the industries they regulate from competition. Since up to 1935 the ICC was concerned primarily with the regulation of railroads, railroad interests could be expected to have prevailed with the commission. Before the regulation of motor carriers in 1935, however, it was the rail companies that most strongly urged controls over them; and it is reasonable to suppose that, while regulation

---

variables are designated by *. Then

$$c^*/c = (E/E^*)(mc^*/mc),$$

where mc is marginal cost. To make this expression operational, Friedlaender assumes that long-run marginal cost equals short-run marginal cost, so that the ratio of the elasticity must equal the ratio of the costs. This assumption is incorrect, however, since if there is excess capacity, short-run marginal cost will be below long-run marginal cost.

34. Friedlaender, *Dilemma of Freight Transport Regulation*, pp. 66–68; Meyer and others, *Economics of Competition*, p. 194; Harbeson, "Toward Better Resource Allocation in Transport," pp. 330–33.

35. *Annual Report of the Interstate Commerce Commission*, issues for 1966–70.

would make the ICC concerned with trucking interests, the commission would not willingly sacrifice rail interests. Without evidence to the contrary, the ICC could be expected to attempt to balance the traffic so that rails and trucks would continue to secure the same share as they would have in the absence of regulation. But, in order to protect the industries and increase profits, both truck and rail rates would be pushed ever higher, thus diverting traffic to the basically unregulated water carriers. Hence, a conservative conclusion is that without regulation railroads would carry at least the same amount of traffic as they do under ICC jurisdiction, albeit a different mixture of traffic. This assumption underlies the estimates of regulatory loss made here.

There have been several studies of the demand for transportation by sector. The best is probably Morton's, which estimates the demand for rail and truck transportation. His study suggests that the price elasticity of demand for rail transportation is close to -1.[36] Consequently, it appears

36. Alexander L. Morton, "A Statistical Sketch of Intercity Freight Demand," *Highway Research Record*, no. 296 (Highway Research Board, 1969), pp. 47–65. See also Eugene D. Perle, *The Demand for Transportation: Regional and Commodity Studies in the United States* (University of Chicago, Department of Geography, 1964). Morton's truck demand function (with *t*-ratios in parentheses) is:

(1) $$\log TK\ VOL = -\underset{(0.343)}{1.841} \log TK\ RATE + \underset{(0.126)}{0.932} \log RR\ RATE$$
$$+ \underset{(0.151)}{2.323} \log GNP.$$

The market cross-elasticity of substitution between goods 1 and 2, n_{12}, can be written

$$n_{12} = n_{12}^* - n_1^I P_1 Q_1 / I,$$

where n_{12}^* is the pure elasticity of substitution, n_1^I is the income elasticity of demand for good 1, $P_1 Q_1$ is total expenditure on good 1, and I is total income. The pure cross-elasticity of substitution between goods 1 and 2 is related to that between goods 2 and 1 by the following expression:

$$P_1 Q_1 n_{12} = P_2 Q_2 n_{21}^*.$$

Consequently, the market cross-elasticity for goods 1 and 2 can be expressed as a function of the other elasticities as follows:

$$P_1 Q_1 n_{12} = P_2 Q_2 n_{21} + n_2^I (P_2 Q_2)_2 / I - n_1^I (P_1 Q_1)_2 / I.$$

Total freight revenues in 1968 for common carrier trucking and railroads were approximately $10 billion each. The following relationship therefore exists:

$$n_{12} = n_{21} + (\$10\ \text{billion}/GNP) \cdot n_1^I - (\$10\ \text{billion}/GNP) \cdot n_2^I.$$

Since the gross national product in 1968 was $864.2 billion, the ratio 10/864.2 is very

that a 20 percent decline in truck prices would necessitate approximately a 20 percent decline in rail prices in order to maintain volume. With railroad freight revenues of about $10 billion, a 20 percent fall in rates for the same volume of traffic would cause total rail revenue to decline to $8 billion. To maintain the same level of profits as earned in 1968 (not an excessive one by any means), railroad costs would have to fall by $2 billion.[37]

It is just possible that much of the value of railroad assets is attributable to capitalized monopoly rents, although this is unlikely since published profit rates have long been very low compared to other sectors. Even if half the asset value of about $27.5 billion reflects the capitalized value of monopoly rents, railroads would have to earn 2.44 percent of $13.8 billion to achieve the same rate of return as in 1968; deducting these capital costs of $337 million from the $8 billion revenue yields costs of $7.663 billion. Actual costs in 1968, figured on the same basis, were $9.329 billion, so costs would have to fall by roughly $1.7 billion to allow railroads the same rate of return as under regulation. This can be considered the low estimate of the amount costs might fall without regulation, in contrast to Friedlaender's high estimate of $2.4 billion.

---

small indeed, and, as a first approximation

$$n_{12} \approx n_{21}.$$

Therefore, with an elasticity of substitution between trucks and rails of 0.93, it can be assumed that the rail-to-truck elasticity is roughly the same—about one. Using Morton's data and fixing the cross-elasticity of demand at one, the demand for rail transportation can be reestimated as:

(2) $\log RR\ VOL = 2.228 - 0.915 \log RR\ RATE + 1.0 \log TK\ RATE$
       (0.356)   (0.200)

       $- 0.097 \log GNP.$
       (0.089)

Under this new formulation, the price elasticity of demand for rail rises to -0.915, and so is not significantly different from -1.

37. Cost savings of this order of magnitude appear large, especially for an industry currently in considerable financial difficulty. Costs might be significantly reduced if the railroads concentrated on moving bulk commodities in unit trains, while handling manufactured products by either piggyback or container. These steps would permit railroads to specialize in the wholesaling of transportation on line-haul trips between major terminals and to abandon a considerable portion of their inefficient equipment and trackage. The Penn Central, for example, has estimated that 90 percent of its traffic is handled on about 60 percent of its trackage (*The Penn Central and Other Railroads*, A Report to the Senate Committee on Commerce, 92 Cong. 2 sess. [1973], p. 217). Significant cost reductions could also be achieved if freight car utilization were improved. On the average, freight cars spend only about 12 percent of their time in line-haul movements and 40 percent in loading and unloading, while about half the time they are either awaiting movement or sitting idle for assignment.

WATER CARRIERS. The ICC proscribes towing regulated and unregulated traffic together. Before 1971, towing more than three types of unregulated commodities by the same barge made the shipment subject to regulation. Until 1967, it was common practice for nonregulated water carriers to put together barges of unregulated commodities, which were then sub-contracted to a regulated carrier operating under the regulated tow rate, thus getting around the mixing rules. In 1967, the Supreme Court upheld an ICC ruling that this practice of mixing regulated and nonregulated barges in the same tow was illegal.

Ruppenthal estimated the impact of this new rule on costs in barge transportation. He studied five large carriers, and, by simulation, computed the costs of operating under the ICC edict. Two estimates of costs per ton-mile were made. One was based on the assumption that an economic tow can be put together with as few as seven barges; the other assumed that eleven barges were needed. For the seven-barge cutoff, he found that the cost per ton-mile would be 3.02 mills, whereas the actual cost in 1967 had been 2.3 mills. With an eleven-barge cutoff, the cost per ton-mile rose to 3.34 mills.[38] The long-run impact of the ruling is thus to add between $207 million and $298 million annually to freight costs (at 1968 levels). Even this is an underestimate of the loss from regulation, since the practice followed before 1967 was presumably not the lowest-cost way to move commodities by water.

PIPELINES. Unfortunately, no data exist that would make possible an estimate of the losses due to regulation of pipelines. Regulation certainly induces the pipeline companies to maintain older pipes, since they go into the rate base and permit larger earnings. However, the extent to which capacity is thereby inflated, thus leading to higher costs, is uncertain.

SUMMARY. As can be seen in Table 3-2, the sheer waste involved in moving existing shipments by existing carriers is monumental. Of national income generated in rail, truck, and water transportation, between 10 and 20 percent is unnecessary to provide the services. These are clear losses to the economy, since they involve using additional resources to provide the same service and not a shift of services from one class to another.

The additional costs would not be pure waste if they reflected improved service, and if regulation causes worse service, the figures underestimate the loss. Deregulation of trucking, where it has occurred, seems to have improved service. Regulation of private trucking and water carriers

38. Karl M. Ruppenthal, "Some Economic Aspects of the Barge Line Mixing Rule," *Transportation Journal*, vol. 9 (Spring 1970), p. 43.

certainly did not improve service. Regulation probably improves rail service only slightly, if at all. Since incentives to innovate and to purchase new freight cars are reduced, and since excess capacity in terms of branch lines must be carried, the improvement in service from regulation is probably negligible and may actually be offset by declines in service due to lack of competitive vigor in the industry.

Losses from Shifting of Traffic

Meyer, Harbeson, and Friedlaender have concluded that considerable traffic travels long distances by truck that would better travel by rail.[39] In a study prepared by the Charles River Associates for the Department of Transportation, an attempt was made to quantify the difference in costs between the two modes, including costs to the shippers. It was found that approximately 26 percent of the approximately 100 billion ton-miles of truck traffic would be more economically moved by rails in the absence of regulation.[40]

Friedlaender estimated the marginal cost of shipping per ton-mile by rail and truck.[41] Except for high-value commodities, marginal cost for shipping over 500 miles is at least one cent per ton-mile cheaper by rail than by truck. At this rate, $1 billion would be saved by shifting modes. Meyer, on the other hand, found the differential for distances over 200 miles to amount to about two cents per ton-mile, or a resource saving of approximately $2 billion.[42]

Peck estimated that in the mid-1960s rails, if deregulated, could attract no more than 10 percent of truck revenue.[43] He argued that shipments of bulk and agricultural commodities provided about 24 percent of regulated motor carriers' revenue, and he guessed that rails could attract no more than half of that. Since rates per ton-mile on bulk commodities tend to be lower than average, his data suggest that something over 10 percent of total common carrier ton-miles would shift. This means that

39. Meyer and others, *Economics of Competition;* Harbeson, "Toward Better Resource Allocation in Transport"; Friedlaender, *Dilemma of Freight Transport Regulation.*

40. Charles River Associates, "Competition between Rail and Truck in Intercity Freight Transportation" (Charles River Associates, Inc., December 1969; processed), p. 45.

41. *Dilemma of Freight Transport Regulation*, table 3.5, p. 51.

42. *Economics of Competition*, table 39, p. 190.

43. Merton J. Peck, "Competitive Policy for Transportation?" in Almarin Phillips (ed.), *Perspectives on Antitrust Policy* (Princeton University Press, 1965).

about 16 billion ton-miles would be attracted to rails, for a net saving of $160 million to $320 million.

In addition, traffic would be attracted from private trucking and from unregulated agricultural commodity carriers. According to the 1967 U.S. Census of Transportation, 29.2 billion ton-miles were moved by private truck.[44] Of this, Peck claims that 5 percent, or about 1.5 billion ton-miles, would shift to rails, producing savings of between $15 million and $30 million. He also claims that 25 percent of revenues for agricultural commodity carriers would shift. If the same ratio of average revenue (1967–69) to ton-miles (1968) is assumed for agricultural commodity carriers as for ICC-regulated trucking, Peck's data predict a shift of 2.84 billion tons to rails, for a saving of $28 million to $57 million. The total saving from shifts to rails would thus range from $203 million to $407 million, according to Peck's analysis.

Harbeson's were the most careful estimates of the costs of shipping by truck rather than rail: he suggests a loss of at least $1.1 billion, and perhaps as high as $2.9 billion.[45] His low figure is approximately the same as the low figure computed on the basis of the Charles River Associates' study.

Table 3-2 presents low, medium, and high estimates of the cost to the economy of the volume of traffic carried by truck rather than rail because of regulation. The low estimate is based on Peck's low figure and is clearly an underestimate; the medium and high figures are taken from Harbeson's study. No measurement of the traffic shift from rails to water carriers was possible, though undoubtedly there has been some shift; no doubt some traffic has shifted to pipelines, as well. Other traffic has been transferred to nonregulated private trucking and, possibly, to air, also; but the net impact of these shifts cannot be measured.

Static Welfare Loss

The last cost to the economy from regulation is the deadweight loss that is the result of some commodities not being shipped because of noncompetitive pricing. Friedlaender estimated this loss at $300–400 million annually. Using Morton's demand equation as reestimated above, a new estimate can be made. Assume, as above, that rail rates would fall sufficiently to maintain rail traffic in the absence of regulation—that is,

---

44. U.S. Bureau of the Census, *Census of Transportation, 1967*, vol. 3: *Commodity Transportation Survey*, pt. 1, *Shipper Groups* (1970), table B, p. 8.

45. Harbeson, "Toward Better Resource Allocation in Transport," p. 332.

Table 3-2. Economic Loss from Regulation of Surface Freight, 1960s

Millions of dollars

	Estimate of loss		
Type of loss	Low	Medium	High
Inefficient use of mode			
Common carrier trucks	1,400	1,660	1,890
Private trucks	100	200	1,000
Rails	1,700	2,000	2,400
Water carriers	200	300	300+
Pipelines	n.e.	n.e.	n.e.
Subtotal	3,400	4,160	5,590+
Traffic shifted to alternate mode			
Trucks to rails	200	1,100	2,900
Water carriers to rails	n.e.	n.e.	n.e.
Pipelines to other modes	n.e.	n.e.	n.e.
Subtotal	200	1,100	2,900
Traffic not carried	175	300	400
Total estimated loss	3,775	5,560	8,890

Sources: The low estimate is based on Merton J. Peck, "Competitive Policy for Transportation?" in Almarin Phillips (ed.), *Perspectives on Antitrust Policy* (Princeton University Press, 1965), pp. 261–65. Medium and high estimates derived from Robert W. Harbeson, "Toward Better Resource Allocation in Transport," *Journal of Law and Economics*, vol. 12 (October 1969), pp. 322–34.
n.e. Not estimated.

rail prices would fall 20 percent as truck rates fell 20 percent. The net impact of these reductions in rates is to increase truck traffic by 18 percent. Since total class I and class II truck revenues were $9.6 billion in 1968, the total change in traffic revenue would be approximately $1.7 billion, and the total welfare loss would be $175 million. This estimate, however, is a conservative one, since it does not allow for any increase in shipments by rail.

Total Losses from Regulation

The low, medium, and high estimates of the total losses from regulation shown in Table 3-2 range from a low of nearly $4 billion to almost $9 billion, and, since a number of important costs are not estimated, it is possible that the loss is as high as $10 billion. To put it another way, as much as one-third of the income generated in surface freight transportation could be pure waste.

It should be cautioned, however, that all the estimates given here are very crude; they are aimed solely at presenting the order of magnitude. Additionally, MacAvoy and Sloss, Gellman, and Nelson and Greiner have argued that regulation retarded major innovations, especially in railroading;[46] though Friedlaender estimated the secondary losses suffered elsewhere at only $12–41 million.[47]

Policy Alternatives

The number of possible alternatives to the present policies is large. Regulation could be modified in a wide variety of ways: more power could be given to the ICC; the commission could be merged with other regulatory agencies such as the CAB and the Federal Maritime Commission; regulatory rules could be relaxed. Or regulation could be abolished. Except for the latter, there is a variety of possible alternatives within each category of change.

It is conceivable that the ICC, if given dictatorial authority over the transportation industries, could achieve an efficient allocation of resources. However, given its record, the imperfections of bureaucratic decision making, and the paucity of information available to decision makers, even dictatorial powers would be unlikely to produce an optimum solution, or even a reasonable second best. Furthermore, many of the costs of regulation are the direct and intentional result of ICC policy. The commission intends to increase empty backhauls of private and agriculture trucking. It encourages the reduction of competition between and within modes. Its limitations on trucking certificates are the cause of obvious wastes. Yet the ICC has the power now to eliminate some of the worst wastes.

If it is the regulatory process itself that is primarily responsible for the wastes outlined above, the remedy would seem to be less regulation. New congressional directives are necessary for moves toward deregulation to be made. It is these alternatives that are considered in the remainder of

---

46. MacAvoy and Sloss, *Regulation of Transport Innovation;* Gellman, "Surface Freight Transportation"; Nelson and Greiner, "Relevance of the Common Carrier."
47. "Social Costs of Regulating the Railroads," p. 227.

this chapter. They range from trivial modifications of ICC regulations to major changes such as abolishing the commission entirely and allowing a completely free market.

Partial Deregulation

There are many methods of partial deregulation that might be used. Here only some of the main alternatives are discussed—removing regulation of minimum rates, repealing the Reed-Bulwinkle Act, and deregulating trucking.

REMOVING MINIMUM RATE REGULATION. One of the suggestions most commonly made for modifying regulation of transportation is to remove minimum rate regulation. In a special message to Congress in 1962, President Kennedy recommended "extending to all . . . carriers the exemption from the approval or prescription of minimum rates" on bulk and agricultural commodities.[48] It is often argued that while maximum rate regulation is necessary to prevent the railroads from exploiting their monopoly power, minimum rate regulations prevent railroads and trucking firms from competing effectively. The problem with this argument is that minimum rate regulation is inseparable from maximum rate regulation.

The courts have upheld, and the law usually requires, adherence to the principle that regulatory commissions should permit regulated firms to earn a fair return on their investment. In fact, if they are to remain in business, it is economically necessary that firms earn at least the cost of capital. In the absence of minimum rate regulation, some prices might be reduced below cost in certain markets, with the result that the earnings of firms could fall below the necessary minimum. The regulatory commission would then have to permit higher rates in other markets. As Averch and Johnson have shown,[49] such policies in regulated markets are not only feasible, but could in fact be profitable. Thus, if there is to be meaningful maximum rate regulation, there has to be some control of minimum rates to insure that the monopolist does not reduce rates in competitive markets, where reduced profits would justify higher rates in the monopoly markets.

48. John F. Kennedy, "Special Message to the Congress on Transportation," April 5, 1962, in *Public Papers of the Presidents of the United States: John F. Kennedy, 1962* (1963), p. 295.

49. Harvey Averch and Leland L. Johnson, "Behavior of the Firm under Regulatory Constraint," *American Economic Review*, vol. 52 (December 1962), pp. 1052–69.

It would probably be better to abolish controls over all rates than over minimum rates only. With no control over rates, there would be no incentive to underprice competitive services in order to achieve higher rates in the monopoly market.

REPEAL OF THE REED-BULWINKLE ACT. The Reed-Bulwinkle Act, a 1948 amendment to the Interstate Commerce Act, authorizes the ICC to approve rate agreements by competing carriers made through bureaus, conferences, or the like. Although such rate making constitutes cartel behavior, repeal of the amendment would not alone improve the situation greatly because the commission itself has traditionally been interested in reducing or eliminating rate competition among carriers. It has used its powers to prevent rate reductions, especially if competing carriers would suffer, to limit entry of competing carriers, and to increase the profitability of firms in the industry. So, even if the Reed-Bulwinkle Act were repealed, the policies of the ICC would still produce empty backhauls, restricted certificates of convenience and necessity, and excess capacity. Repeal thus would not reduce the major losses due to regulation; only if coupled with other measures to permit a more competitive environment would it have a significant impact.

DEREGULATING TRUCKING. A more far-reaching policy proposal is to deregulate the trucking industry. It is widely agreed that the industry could perform in a socially efficient manner in the absence of regulation. Entry costs would be minimal: a used truck, a driver's license, and a rented terminal office are all that would be necessary. The number of trucking firms would be substantial. Meyer concluded that "so-called economies of scale would appear to be equally available to small and large firms."[50] Since the service offered is homogeneous, all the necessary conditions for a highly competitive industry exist.

More than theory suggests that the trucking industry could perform well if deregulated: it has been tried elsewhere and has worked well. The industry was deregulated in Australia in 1954–55; by 1964, it was reported that the industry was free of the "instability" and "destructive and wasteful competition" so frequently forecast as the probable outcome of deregulation.[51] Canada has relied primarily on provincial regulation of trucking; this has ranged from virtually no regulation in some provinces to fairly strict regulation in others. The best evidence suggests that the

50. *Economics of Competition*, p. 97.
51. Stewart Joy, "Unregulated Road Haulage: The Australian Experience," *Oxford Economic Papers*, n.s. vol. 16 (July 1964), p. 275.

trucking industry has had lower rates—by about 0.87 cent per ton-mile—in the unregulated provinces than in the regulated ones.[52]

The agricultural exemption in the United States shows that unregulated trucking can perform well. Farmers, the principal shippers by unregulated agricultural trucking, have consistently opposed bringing farm trucking under ICC regulation. Their objection is based on the supposition that regulation would increase their costs or lead to worse service, or both. Department of Agriculture reports have indicated that unregulated rates generally reflect costs and that there has been ample capital investment to provide a growing capacity and more efficient equipment.[53] The best proof of the viability of unregulated haulage is the beneficial effect of court decisions deregulating the transport of poultry and frozen fruits and vegetables. Moreover, after Congress reimposed controls on frozen fruits and vegetables in 1958, increases in rates occurred, and many shippers reported declines in the quality of service.[54]

Deregulating trucking is thus a feasible alternative. Nevertheless, it is conceivable that deregulation could lead to a different misallocation of resources and to new costs to the economy. If motor carrier rates declined relative to rail rates, freight that could be moved by rail at lower costs might be shipped by truck. Offsetting such losses would be rationalization of the trucking industry. Inefficiencies costing between $1.5 and $2.9 billion annually would be eliminated: trucks would no longer be confined to carrying only specific commodities between specific points along specific routes; backhauls would be filled if traffic could be secured; and so forth.

An estimate of the amount of traffic that might be diverted from rail to truck can be computed from equation (2), above. If truck prices fell by an average of 20 percent and rail rates remained constant, the demand equation indicates that 20 percent of the 756.8 billion ton-miles of commodities shipped by rail in 1968[55] would shift from rails to trucks—approximately 150 billion ton-miles.

52. James Sloss, "Regulation of Motor Freight Transportation: A Quantitative Evaluation of Policy," *Bell Journal of Economics and Management Science*, vol. 1 (Autumn 1970), pp. 331, 347.

53. For a description of unregulated motor carrier hauling, see Mildred R. DeWolfe, "For-Hire Motor Carriers Hauling Exempt Agricultural Commodities: Nature and Extent of Operations," Marketing Research Report 585 (U.S. Department of Agriculture, 1963; processed).

54. USDA, Supplement to Marketing Research Report 316.

55. *Annual Report of the Interstate Commerce Commission, 1970*, p. 78.

In 1968, the average freight revenue per intercity ton-mile was $0.06927.[56] With a 20 percent decline in truck rates, it is estimated that average revenue will also decline by 20 percent. At equal rates for truck and rail, some shippers will have no modal preference. When truck rates are 20 percent lower, those who were modally indifferent at the higher rate would now ship by truck, while others would now be indifferent. If the distribution of shippers who would shift from rail to truck is linear over the decline in rates, the average cost of shipping by truck rather than rail would equal half the reduction in price. The average cost would thus be $0.006927 per ton-mile. For a total shift of 150 billion ton-miles, this amounts to roughly $1 billion.

As noted above, the cost of regulation in terms of higher costs of operation was, at a minimum, $1.5 billion. Consequently, there would be a net gain of $0.5 billion from deregulating only trucking. Moreover, the ICC would be likely to permit rails to reduce their rates in the face of a decline in trucking rates in order for the industry to maintain its competitive position. If rails were not permitted to reduce rates, they would suffer a 20 percent loss of business. Given their large fixed costs and weak profit position, a 20 percent loss would put most railroads in the same financial straits as the Penn Central. With lower rail rates, the net effect of deregulation of trucking would be more positive for the economy, and any loss due to shift of traffic would be small.

Total Deregulation

Policymakers and economists have also discussed total deregulation as a possible solution. How feasible and effective would open competition be in the various transportation industries?

Deregulation of water carriers would present few problems, since only 7.3 percent of the ton-miles that they currently bear is regulated,[57] and since water transportation, like trucking, appears to have the characteristics of a workably competitive industry. Freight forwarders are also regulated by the ICC, but entry standards, at least until recently, have been lenient. In Canada, where freight forwarders are unregulated, the industry operates efficiently, so there would seem to be no bar to its deregulation. Pipelines, on the other hand, have the characteristics of a natural monopoly, so industry has little potential for direct competition

56. ICC, *Transport Statistics, 1968: Motor Carriers*, table 16.
57. *Annual Report of the Interstate Commerce Commission, 1970*, p. 78.

(aside from some interregional and intermodal competition). However, the regulation of oil pipelines could be treated separately. They could be continued under ICC jurisdiction, transferred to the Federal Power Commission, or deregulated.

When railroads were first subjected to federal control in 1887, it was claimed that, at least in some areas, they had a natural monopoly. It was also claimed that they had excess capacity and were subject to large economies of scale. Competitive behavior was, therefore, thought to be impossible. However, historical research has shown that the railroads themselves supported regulation in an effort to stabilize cartel price-fixing agreements.[58] Furthermore, there is no evidence that at the time of regulation there were any substantial economies of scale beyond those already exploited by the large railroads in the nineteenth century.[59] Before 1920, the major monopoly power of the railroads lay solely in their exclusive control over short-haul shipments. In the shipment of bulk, low-cost commodities over long distances, competition was vigorous, not only among railroads operating over the same route, but also with roads operating elsewhere. Wheat, for example, shipped from one region to a particular consuming center could compete with wheat shipped by other railroads from other regions to the same center.

Any monopoly power that railroads possessed in the nineteenth century is considerably less today. In today's short-haul market trucking is a viable alternative. Rails are now a superior choice only for bulk, low-cost commodities shipped long distances. And even for these commodities, rails have little advantage where water transportation is available.

Table 3-3 shows the market structure in railroad freight transportation between regions of the country. For most regions, there are three or more railroads competing for the traffic to most other regions. In some major pairs of producing and marketing areas, such as the Midwest-South, ten to twelve railroads compete. There are a few routes—principally from the north mountain states (Idaho, Wyoming, and Montana) to the south mountain states (Utah, Colorado, and Nevada)—where there are only two railroads in direct competition and no water transportation available.

58. Gabriel Kolko, *Railroads and Regulation, 1877–1916* (Princeton University Press, 1965); Paul W. MacAvoy, *The Economic Effects of Regulation: The Trunk-Line Railroad Cartels and the Interstate Commerce Commission before 1900* (M.I.T. Press, 1965).

59. Robert M. Spann and Edward W. Erickson, "The Economics of Railroading: The Beginning of Cartelization and Regulation," *Bell Journal of Economics and Management Science*, vol. 1 (Autumn 1970), pp. 227–44.

Table 3-3. Market Structure in Surface Freight Shipments, by Region, Early 1970s

Regions of origin and destination	Number of railroads serving route	Water transportation available?
From *New England* (Maine, New Hampshire, Vermont, Massachusetts, Connecticut, Rhode Island) to:		
North Atlantic	3	yes
From *North Atlantic* (New York, New Jersey, Pennsylvania) to:		
South	3	yes
West	4	some
From *Mid-Atlantic* (Virginia, Maryland, Delaware, West Virginia) to:		
North	4	yes
South	3	yes
West	6	no
Southwest	6	no
From *South Atlantic* (South Carolina, Georgia, Florida) to:		
North	3	yes
West	5	yes
From *Midwest* (Michigan, Ohio, Indiana, Illinois, Wisconsin) to:		
Southeast	5	no
Northeast	4	some
South	10	yes
Northwest	7	some
Southwest	12	some
From *East-South-Central* (Kentucky, Tennessee, Alabama, Mississippi) to:		
North	10	yes
South	6	yes
East	6	no
Southeast	5	no
Southwest	6	yes
Northwest	10	some
From *North-Central* (North Dakota, South Dakota, Minnesota) to:		
East	7	some
South	5	some
West	5	no

Table 3-3. Continued

Regions of origin and destination	Number of railroads serving route	Water transportation available?
From *Midcentral* (Nebraska, Iowa, Missouri, Kansas) to:		
North	4	yes
East	12	no
South	8	yes
West	6	no
Southeast	8	no
Northwest	4	no
From *West-South-Central* (Oklahoma, Arkansas, Louisiana, Texas) to:		
North	9	yes
West	6	no
East	6	yes
From *North-Mountain* (Idaho, Wyoming, Montana) to:		
Northeast	5	no
South	2	no
West	4	no
Southeast (Nebraska)	3	no
From *South-Mountain* (Nevada, Utah, Colorado, Arizona, New Mexico) to:		
North	2	no
Southeast	5	no
Northeast	6	no
West	4	no
Northwest	1	no
From *Oregon and Washington* to:		
East	3	no
South	2	yes
Southeast	2	no
From *California* to:		
North	2	yes
East	4	no

Sources: *Moody's Transportation Manual* (Moody's Investors Service, Inc., 1971); D. Philip Locklin, *Economics of Transportation* (6th ed., Richard D. Irwin, 1966), p. 716.

However, there is very little traffic between these areas; most commodities mined or grown there are shipped west or east to consuming areas.

The data presented in Table 3-3 would thus seem to indicate that while the railroad industry in itself can certainly not be characterized as purely competitive, it is probably no more concentrated than a number of manufacturing industries. With the availability of water competition in a number of markets and with the ubiquity of trucks, an unregulated railroad industry would probably be workably competitive.[60]

Having answered the question whether deregulation would be feasible, it must now be asked whether it would cause severe problems for the economy. It is often claimed that deregulation, especially of railroads, would lead to predatory pricing, price discrimination, and intermodal ownership.

PREDATORY PRICING. Railroads might use predatory pricing among themselves or against other modes. There is little danger that railroads would use it against trucks or barges, since entry in these industries is easy and inexpensive. If a railroad tried to eliminate truck or barge competition by cutting prices below its own marginal costs, it would lose money. Even if it succeeded in eliminating the competition, as soon as its price returned to a profitable level, competition would reappear if costs were as low for trucks and barges as for the railroads. On the other hand, if a railroad has a cost advantage, pricing below truck and barge costs would not be a predatory practice, and costs in the other modes would set an upper limit on the railroad's prices.

Canadian experience bears out this argument. In Canada, railroads are free to reduce rates as long as charges cover the variable cost of the movement, yet no charges of predatory pricing against trucks or barges have been upheld. Moreover, the Canadian trucking industry is thriving and apparently competes vigorously for traffic.

Predatory pricing among railroads, on the other hand, would be potentially more profitable and probably more difficult to detect than that against other modes. Unlike the barge or truck industry, railroads virtually bar new entry. Without the power of eminent domain, it is inconceivable that a new company would be able to put together the right-of-way for new tracks; and, unless the case for the new entrant were overwhelming, it is unlikely that either state or federal government would grant it such power. With entry effectively barred (and unless there are substantial diseconomies of scale), the value of competing railroads on a route would be greatest if they combined on one road. Combined, the railroads could operate as a monopoly without the fear of new entry.

60. A series of models that estimates the extent of economies of scale in the railroad industry are presented in the Appendix to this chapter.

Separately, they would have to compete with each other, and there is a tendency in even the most well-ordered cartel to cheat and to spend additional resources on nonprice competition.

If demand is contracting in the railroad industry, which in a relative sense it appears to be, it may become uneconomic in some regions to have two railroads vying for the same traffic. In the absence of regulation or strong collusion, the railroads would tend to drive short-run marginal costs down to a level below long-run marginal costs. Thus, during a period of contraction, losses would continue until one railroad bought out the other.

How can this situation be distinguished from deliberate predatory pricing? No railroad will admit to predatory pricing; it will claim, rather, that its lowered prices are at or above costs and designed to attract a larger share of the market. If public policy permits the merger of failing railroads, predatory pricing will be rewarded by eventual monopoly. If public policy bans mergers, redundant capacity will be maintained long after it should be abandoned, and existing firms will continue to suffer losses. In other words, in the absence of regulation, policymakers would have to determine when losses stem from inadequate traffic for the existing roads and when they stem from predatory pricing.

PRICE DISCRIMINATION. Before formation of the ICC, a major complaint was that the railroads practiced price discrimination. Some shippers received low rates; others were charged much higher rates. Some geographic areas received lower rates for shipping the same commodities the same or longer distances than other areas. Past efforts to reduce regulation have foundered on the fear that the railroads would again discriminate among areas and customers.

In a highly competitive market, there is no opportunity for discrimination. A firm that charged higher prices to one customer than another would lose the former. It must be recognized, however, that even in highly competitive markets, prices can fluctuate considerably by time of the day and season of the year. For example, during peak demand periods in resort areas, prices usually are considerably higher than during off-peak periods. Peak-load pricing, however, is *not* price discrimination, and it allows an efficient utilization of resources.

At least some of the allegations of price discrimination leveled at the railroads must have been due to a confusion between peak pricing and true price discrimination. Thus, during the nineteenth century, commodities tended to flow from the Midwest to the East Coast, with little traffic flowing in the opposite direction, so that rates were often low on west-bound traffic and considerably higher on east-bound traffic.

Railroads in certain markets today may have some monopoly power, allowing them to charge a few customers more than others. In addition, where railroads have established rates above marginal cost, large shippers may be in a position to secure special low rates. This has occurred in the past, and there is no reason to believe that an unregulated railroad industry would not be subject to similar pressure today. Large shippers, however, could not force prices below *short-run* marginal cost, and in the long run could do no more than absorb a portion of the railroad's monopoly profit.

In other markets, railroads might have the power to charge higher rates to special classes of shippers. For example, farmers in isolated areas serviced by only one railroad might be charged considerably higher rates than similar shippers in areas serviced by several roads. But, since rail-roads would not want to charge so high a price as to drive shippers out of business, their monopoly power would be limited. Normally, a railroad cannot affect the market price for a shipped good, so that its rate cannot be greater than the difference between the market price and the opportunity cost of producing the product. In effect, the most railroads can do is to absorb the rents involved in the locational decisions of shippers.

As these examples suggest, the primary discrimination problem is not with manufactured goods, but with the shipment of agriculture and raw materials. Proximity to market, fertility of the soil, and climate all provide farmers with rents that could be absorbed by monopolistic railroads. Even though, in terms of efficiency, this has little long-run allocative effect, higher rates to such farmers make them poorer, a result that is likely to be politically unacceptable.

As was pointed out above, railroads no longer have monopoly power in the short-haul market because trucks can compete on prices and service for all but a few bulk commodities. Inasmuch as goods shipped from one region must compete with goods shipped from elsewhere, the monopoly power of railroads is limited in the long-haul market as well. Consequently, there are few, if any, products shipped between any markets over which railroads would have much monopoly power.

In the absence of regulation, railroads would raise prices on those products where they had unexploited monopoly power and lower them where competition so dictated. There is some evidence, however, that railroads are already charging what the market can bear. Friedlaender has shown that in areas where the railroads have no water competition, rates for shipping the same commodities approximately the same distances tend to be higher than where water competition exists.[61] It would be surprising, in fact, if the railroads were not already exploiting their monopoly power to the fullest. For years the ICC has been concerned about the very poor earnings of the industry, so any railroad filing higher rates for a particular commodity would probably be supported by the ICC against shippers' objections. In May 1967, most railroads in the country petitioned for the first general rate increase in six years. Even though the industry had for the fifth straight year "exhibited considerable improvement in most respects during 1966," the ICC granted the increase promptly.[62] Individual rate changes for a particular commodity are usually even easier to secure. For example, of the 45,160 tariffs received from railroads by the ICC during fiscal 1967, only 158 were rejected; no doubt, a considerable number of those were rejected for lower rates. Deregulation might well, therefore, cause no, or very few, rate increases, and there would likely be considerable reductions in many areas. Still, rates on any products that are now carried at below marginal cost would clearly rise.

Friedlaender and Meyer have both pointed out that a number of commodities are carried at below the out-of-pocket costs measured by the ICC. The ICC measure, however, has little relationship to true marginal cost. It says that out-of-pocket costs "include 80 percent of freight operating expenses, rents and taxes (excluding Federal income taxes) plus a return of 4 percent after Federal income taxes on 50 percent of the road property and 100 percent of the equipment used in freight service."[63] Since this sum has nothing to do with the concept of marginal cost, it is impossible to say whether marginal costs would be higher or lower than out-of-pocket costs.

Price discrimination under deregulation could occur in any of three areas: between commodities, between shippers, and between geographic regions. Even under ICC regulation, commodity discrimination is not uncommon. If out-of-pocket costs as measured by the ICC are at least an index of *relative* marginal costs, the relationship of rates to costs differs greatly among commodities. Table 3-4 shows the contribution to the revenues of class I railroads, relative to out-of-pocket costs, of a number

61. *Dilemma of Freight Transport Regulation*, table 3.8.

62. The statistics in this paragraph are from *81st Annual Report of the Interstate Commerce Commission, Fiscal Year Ended June 30, 1967*, pp. 17, 19, 112. The quotation is from p. 57.

63. Interstate Commerce Commission, Bureau of Accounts, "Rail Carload Cost Scales by Territories for the Year 1968" (1970; processed), p. 4.

Table 3-4. Contribution of Selected Commodity Groups to Class I Railroad Burden and Ratio of Revenue to Out-Of-Pocket Cost, 1966

Dollar amounts in millions

Commodity group	Revenue	Out-of-pocket cost	Contribution to burden	Ratio of revenue to out-of-pocket cost
Farm products	870.8	700.7	170.1	1.24
Forest products	13.1	6.0	7.1	2.17
Fresh fish	2.6	2.5	0.1	1.05
Metallic ores[a]	278.1	308.3	−30.2	0.90
Coal[a]	972.3	961.1	11.2	1.01
Crude petroleum, natural gas, and natural gasoline	4.9	5.1	−0.2	0.97
Nonmetallic ores	305.5	301.6	3.9	1.01
Ordnance and accessories	45.7	12.5	33.2	3.65
Food and allied products	948.1	868.5	79.5	1.09
Tobacco products	13.9	7.6	6.3	1.83
Basic textiles	29.6	16.8	12.8	1.76
Lumber and wood products	634.0	609.7	24.2	1.04
Furniture and fixtures	72.7	55.0	17.6	1.32
Pulp, paper, and allied products	486.5	308.7	177.8	1.58
Printed matter	20.3	13.9	6.3	1.46
Chemicals and allied products	762.0	488.6	273.4	1.56
Petroleum and coal products	192.2	181.1	11.1	1.06
Rubber and miscellaneous plastic products	65.5	41.9	23.6	1.56
Leather and leather products	1.6	1.2	0.4	1.32
Stone, clay and glass products	432.0	309.0	123.1	1.40
Primary metal products	680.8	432.5	248.3	1.57
Fabricated metal products	185.8	123.0	62.8	1.51
Machinery	133.5	68.7	64.8	1.94
Electrical machinery, etc.	120.6	78.8	41.8	1.53
Transportation equipment	587.4	284.7	302.8	2.06

Table 3-4. Continued

Commodity group	Revenue	Out-of-pocket cost	Contribution to burden	Ratio of revenue to out-of-pocket cost
Waste and scrap materials	184.2	122.1	62.1	1.51
Total carload traffic[b]	8,365.0	6,461.6	1,903.4	1.29

Sources: Computed by the U.S. Department of Agriculture from the 1966 regular sample of 1 percent of the weighbills, and Rail Form A (furnished to the author at his request). Loss and damage payments for commodity groups in 1965 are incorporated in the data. Calculations are made from data before rounding.

a. Computed in accordance with Rail Form A rather than by the method used by the ICC in burden studies; this grossly overstates costs because it does not take into account the lower cost per unit for unit trains.

b. Computed from total cost and total revenue information rather than from sums of commodity groups.

of commodity classes in 1966. The revenue-cost ratio varies from 3.65 for ordnance and accessories to 0.97 for crude oil—an almost four-fold difference.[64]

In the absence of regulation, as rates move closer to costs because of competition, such discrimination would be reduced. Where motor carriers were competitive, rail rates would at least approximate trucking costs. But there is little political gain from reduced discrimination, and there may be little allocative gain as well. To the extent that discrimination affects noncompetitive groups of commodities, the allocative effect would be small, perhaps no more than the $12–41 million estimated by Friedlaender.

A second form of price discrimination is between shippers. Total deregulation would presumably permit a railroad to discriminate between shippers on the basis of differences in their demand elasticities. Where shippers have good alternatives to rails, rates will be lower; where shippers are largely restricted to a single carrier, a railroad can extract a monopoly profit. Personal discrimination, banned by the Interstate Commerce Act (part 1, sections 2 and 3),[65] may also arise as conditions change. In the face of excess capacity, railroads might offer reduced rates in order to attract a particular load. Such practices are common in other sectors and are largely a reflection of the workings of a marketplace economy.

64. The ratio for metallic ores is lower, but, as explained in the table, the method used in the computation overstates the costs.

65. 24 Stat. 379, 380 as amended; 49 U.S.C. 2, 3.

But, since motor carriers are much more efficient at hauling small loads than large ones, the small-shipment market would be highly competitive, thus reducing the possibility of unilateral action by the railroads. Large shippers would not be in danger of exploitation, either, since they could divide their shipments into smaller lots. Consequently, discrimination between shippers would probably be no larger a problem in an unregulated transportation market than it is in manufacturing—perhaps less of one because of the potentially high degree of competition in the motor carrier market.

Geographical discrimination has several dimensions. It may involve charging more for one part of a route than for others, or for the whole route. It may involve discriminating between shipping regions or points of destination.

The short-haul provision of the Interstate Commerce Act (part 1, section 4) was designed to deal with the first dimension by prohibiting higher rates for short hauls than for long hauls. But, again the competitive advantage of trucks in the short-haul market means that rails are no longer in a position to practice this sort of discrimination.

Discrimination between areas has been common in the past and still is, as railroads have tended to benefit from the geographical competition of markets by charging higher rates to the more advantaged areas.[66] For example, rail rates relative to out-of-pocket costs (1961) for oranges and grapefruit are higher for shipments from Florida to East Coast markets than from California to the East.[67] While this differential has permitted California citrus fruit to compete on price, it has reduced the earnings of Florida growers and transferred to eastern railroads some of the gains they would otherwise have received from their proximity to major consuming markets.

Geographical discrimination between points of destination also exists today. For example, export freight rates are identical to Boston and to Baltimore from such originating points as Pittsburgh, Cleveland, and Buffalo, even though the distance to the two ports is substantially different. Unless competition were sufficiently vigorous to drive rates down to costs, such discrimination would continue in the absence of regulation. Railroads on the longest routes would be willing to drop rates to marginal

66. D. Philip Locklin, *Economics of Transportation* (6th ed., Richard D. Irwin, 1966), pp. 490–511.

67. Interstate Commerce Commission, Bureau of Accounts, "Distribution of the Rail Revenue Contribution by Commodity Groups—1961" (1964; processed), p. 34.

costs in order to preserve or secure part of the export market. Only if rails servicing the nearer ports dropped their rates so drastically that other roads could not compete—which truck competition might force them to do—would such discrimination be eliminated.

Deregulation would certainly cause changes in prices and new claims of discrimination. Commodity discrimination would no doubt be reduced; true personal discrimination would probably occur more frequently; and geographic discrimination would probably diminish as competitive pressures forced rates toward costs. In any case, some change in prices could be expected, and any change in the price structure will impose costs on shippers, some of whom will gain, others lose. Even if all price changes were downward, shippers that received the smallest or no decreases would actually be worse off if their competitors were granted greater reductions.

Many of the costs imposed on shippers would be only transitory, and over time it would be possible to mitigate or avoid their effects. For example, rates on manufactured goods tend to be high relative to those on raw materials. If, as might be expected, deregulation reduced rates for manufactured goods, firms would find that their plants were located too close to major consuming markets and not close enough to raw supplies for minimum-cost operation. Relocation, with its attendant costs, would thus be inevitable.

In addition, factories located in areas served by uneconomic railroad branch lines would have to either use truck services or relocate if railroads were free to abandon unprofitable service. Major shipping ports might experience changes in their relative competitive positions because of freight rate adjustments that more accurately reflected costs (although this change is likely to have much less impact than containerization). While all these effects of deregulation are in the long-run interest of a more efficient use of resources, it is true that all change is costly, and the transition from regulation to an unregulated industry should be very carefully planned indeed.

Aside from the problems of railroad deregulation, there is little basis for fear of price discrimination by unregulated motor or water carriers. Competition would be vigorous, so that firms attempting to set higher prices to one class of customers than another would lose business to their more eager competitors. On the other side of the coin, large shippers are not in a position to force prices down below marginal costs, which is where rates would tend to settle in the absence of regulation.

INTERMODAL OWNERSHIP. Deregulation of transportation would create new issues in antitrust policy. How to handle the problem of mergers between competing railroads would be one. It would also force the development of a policy on intermodal integration. Railroads have long chafed at restrictions on their rights to form transportation companies. They have claimed that by owning several modes of transportation they could combine their services to offer savings and better service to shippers. However, other modes have opposed their entry, and the Antitrust Division of the Department of Justice has viewed such integration as likely to lead to a reduction in competition.[68]

Any benefits from intermodal ownership would probably be small. If markets worked costlessly, there could be no gains, since if joint services offered cost savings, independent companies would make arrangements to offer them. The only problem would be to divide up the joint profits. Many of the reasons why markets would not, in fact, operate costlessly, and why intermodal ownership might produce savings were set out by Williamson.[69] He points out that uncertainty as to future conditions may make long-term contracts difficult, and the continuous renegotiation of arrangements can be expensive. If expensive equipment is needed to facilitate intermodal transfers, common ownership may be the only practical market organization.

A major objection to intermodal ownership is that nonintegrated firms might be excluded from the market and competition thus diminished. It is claimed that if railroads were free to enter the trucking and water carrier industries, independent truckers and barge owners would be excluded from joint traffic. Would railroads actually monopolize intermodal carriage for their own subsidiaries, and if they did so would it be harmful?

Consider Figure 3-1, which shows a railroad with a monopoly between points A and B, facing independent competitive trucking firms. Let the marginal cost of carrying a piggyback trailer from A to B be \$20. Also shown in Figure 3-1 are points C, C', C'', and D, D', D'', with the marginal costs of shipping from these points to other points and to the railheads

68. See, for example, the testimony of James F. Fort, Counsel, American Trucking Associations, Inc., in *Transportation Diversification*, Hearings before a Subcommittee of the House Committee on Interstate and Foreign Commerce, 86 Cong. 2 sess. (1960), pp. 244–54.

69. Oliver E. Williamson, "The Vertical Integration of Production: Market Failure Considerations," in American Economic Association, *Papers and Proceedings of the Eighty-third Annual Meeting, 1970* (*American Economic Review*, vol. 61, May 1971), pp. 112–23.

Figure 3-1. Marginal Costs of Shipping for Owners of Rail and Truck Transportation[a]

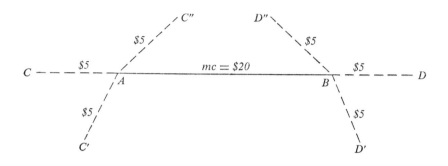

	Marginal costs (mc) of shipping	
Itinerary	Truck	Piggyback rail
C to D	$100	$30
C' to D'	50	30
C'' to D''	31	30

a. See discussion in the text of results of multimodal ownership.

A and B (excluding loading costs). A shipment from C to D carried entirely by truck has a marginal cost of $100, while carrying the same load by piggyback costs $30. A monopoly railroad could charge up to $90 for the carriage from A to B and still attract the load. A truck haul from C' to D', however, would have a marginal cost of $50, and to secure that business the railroad could charge no more than $40 for the A-to-B trip. If the railroad reduced its rate to $39 to attract the C'-to-D' traffic, it would forgo about $50 per trip on the C-to-D route. Whether it would be wise to do so would depend on the relative traffic between the areas. Since it has a $1 marginal cost advantage, the railroad could also compete for the C''-to-D'' traffic, but it probably would not do so because it would have to forgo the monopoly profits on other trips. In other words, the railroad, not being capable of perfect price discrimination, would forgo some traffic for which it is the low-cost carrier.

However, if the railroad owned its own trucks and carried only its own trailers, it could set prices at $89 from C to D, $49 from C' to D', and $30 from C'' to D'' and still secure all the business. This would constitute foreclosure, but, from an allocative point of view, it would be preferable to the situation where the railroad could establish only a single monopoly rate between A and B. Foreclosure would allow the railroad to discriminate perfectly and to capture all the traffic for which the joint truck-rail-truck shipment is the low-cost alternative. To the extent that it resulted in higher rates to some markets it would reduce shipments, with consequent allocative losses. But unless demand were very elastic, these losses would probably be smaller than the misallocation caused by a single monopoly rate. Theoretically, therefore, there would seem to be no objection to permitting railroads to own other modes of transport.

The Canadian experience gives some idea of the effects of a more permissive stance toward intermodal ownership. In Canada, where railroads are permitted to own other modes of transport, Canadian Pacific and Canadian National each operates a large railroad system, one of Canada's largest trucking firms, an international airline, and a major steamship line. No attempts at foreclosure or monopolization have occurred.[70] That the trucks of one of the major railroads carry less than 10 percent of its piggyback traffic is evidence of this situation.[71] Furthermore, railroads own less than 10 percent of the whole trucking industry.[72] Although these data do not appear to be consistent with the model presented above, it must be remembered that the latter dealt with a situation where one railroad has a monopoly. In Canada neither road is in a position to monopolize, and neither can gain much from attempting to practice price discrimination by restricting traffic to its own trucks.

Some of the advantages of intermodal ownership are demonstrated by the large-scale introduction of piggyback service in Canada and by the fact that the first integrated multimodal shipments on the continent were established in 1947 on the White-Pass and Yukon route using truck bodies carried by truck, water carrier, and rail. While the advantages of unified ownership have probably been exaggerated, the drawbacks have, too. It would seem on balance that the net gains would outweigh any

70. Harvey M. Romoff, "Multi-Modal Transportation, Some Comments Based on the Canadian Experience," in Transportation Research Forum, *Papers—Eleventh Annual Meeting, 1970* (TRF, 1970), p. 179.

71. Confidential data furnished to the author.

72. Romoff, "Multi-Modal Transportation," p. 179.

losses and that if regulation were relaxed on entry and rates, it should also be relaxed on multimodal ownership.

Modified Deregulation

In terms of allocation of resources, it is probably true that complete deregulation is desirable. Certainly it would be a vast improvement over the existing situation; much of the waste engendered by ICC regulation would disappear. On the other hand, deregulation might raise rates on certain noncompetitive routes and predatory pricing between railroads might occur. Excess capacity could tempt railroads into pricing at short-run marginal cost levels that were considerably below long-run marginal cost, with the result that rates would be unstable until the excess capacity was eliminated. Although pricing at short-run marginal cost levels and the elimination of excess capacity are desirable in terms of efficiency, such a situation would be costly to the railroads and possibly to other forms of transportation. At a minimum, it would engender considerable political opposition.

Despite the obvious need for change in the current regulatory system (obvious to everyone except those with vested interests, that is), complete deregulation remains unlikely. The political process tends to work to preserve existing income distributions and vested rights, and those who would be adversely affected by deregulation are vocal and knowledgeable. Those who would gain from deregulation are less knowledgeable, less vocal, and less politically organized.

Is it possible to construct a legal framework that would produce most of the gains from deregulation but reduce the likelihood of monopolized markets, personal price discrimination, and predatory pricing? The Canadian legislation governing the regulation of transportation provides a possible model. To prevent predatory pricing, Canada prohibits rates set at less than variable cost of the haul, with the method of determining variable cost defined by law. The Canadian act also allows the setting of maximum rates where a shipper has "no alternative, effective and competitive service by a common carrier other than another" carrier or a combination of carriers of the same mode.[73] In such a case, a shipper can apply to the regulatory commission for a rate not higher than 250 percent of the variable cost of the movement. A shipper whose rate is so fixed must utilize it for all his relevant goods or be obliged to pay damages.

73. Revised Statutes of Canada, 1970, vol. 5, chap. N-17, secs. 33, 40.

One of the virtues of the Canadian legislation is that it limits maximum rate regulation to monopoly situations. Since it was enacted in 1967, there have been only two complaints under the captive shipper clause, both of which are pending before the regulatory commission. No minimum rate protests have been upheld to date. All rates must be filed and published, with a thirty-day notice for increases. Rebates are prohibited. Publishing rates limits the potential for personal price discrimination, but at the same time makes implicit collusion between railroads easier.

A major problem with following the Canadian pattern is the difficulty of measuring costs. Clearly, an ongoing cost analysis of the transportation industry is one of the most important steps that could be taken to improve the allocation of resources. A serious effort should be made to measure carefully long-run and short-run costs for a wide variety of product classifications, and these figures should thereafter be updated regularly. Such data will make it possible to distinguish predatory pricing from simple response to the forces of the marketplace.

The Canadian system seems to work well, permitting the railroads considerable price discretion yet restraining them from either predatory pricing or excessive monopoly pricing. U.S. legislation along the same lines could reduce the political costs of deregulating transportation while still permitting genuine competition between and within modes in the industry.[74]

Conclusions

Only a hardened free-market advocate would claim that deregulating transportation does not present any problems. Without regulation, there would be some residual monopoly situations where railroads might price significantly above costs, some potential for personal price discrimination, and some predatory pricing between railroads. On the other side of the ledger, however, monopoly situations would be rare and of no greater consequence than such situations in manufacturing. Nor is price discrimination likely to lead to greater problems in transportation than in

74. On November 5, 1971, one week after the Brookings conference at which this paper was discussed, the administration sent to Congress the Transportation Regulatory Modernization Act, S. 2842, which provided for regulatory constraints over prices and entry, both of which, however, were still to be under ICC jurisdiction. Some of the features of the Canadian legislation were adopted in the bill, although it did not reduce the degree of regulation to the Canadian level. The bill was not acted upon by Congress, and as of 1974 no similar legislation had been passed.

other sectors of the economy. For a few products and between a few markets, railroad concentration may approach the structure of such industries as aluminum, copper, and automobiles; more often, concentration would be much less and competition more vigorous.

Some minimal regulation may be politically desirable to appease those fearful of railroad monopoly power and could, in fact, be justified on economic grounds. The available evidence supports the proposition that there are no substantial economies of scale in any of the major modes of transportation, with the possible exception of pipelines, and, with the same exception, a substantially unregulated industry could be a major improvement over the existing situation. An investigation of the costs of regulation suggests that they are not only substantial, but monumental. It is a matter of urgent concern that steps be taken to eliminate or reduce significantly the regulation of surface freight transportation.

Appendix: A Model of Economies of Scale in the Railroad Industry

Whether railroad competition is viable today hinges on the extent of economies of scale in the industry. Several studies on this subject have used a variety of techniques. Klein found modest but statistically significant economies of scale based on 1936 data.[75] Borts estimated cost as a function of output by size of railroad and by region of country.[76] He found no appreciable economies of scale generally, and none at all for the large railroads. He concluded that "increasing costs apparently prevail in the East."[77] Griliches also estimated cost functions, and concluded that if there are any decreasing costs, they are not prevalent in the East or among the bigger railroads.[78] Friedlaender fit a Cobb-Douglas production function to cross-sectional data on thirty-three railroads and found that the sum of the coefficients was equal to 0.97.[79] Miller found

75. Lawrence R. Klein, *A Textbook of Econometrics* (Row, Peterson, 1953), pp. 226–36.

76. George H. Borts, "Increasing Returns in the Railway Industry," *Journal of Political Economy*, vol. 62 (August 1954), pp. 316–33; idem, "Production Relations in the Railway Industry," *Econometrica*, vol. 20 (January 1952), pp. 71–79; idem, "The Estimation of Rail Cost Functions," *Econometrica*, vol. 28 (January 1960), pp. 108–31.

77. "Estimation of Rail Cost Functions," p. 128.

78. Zvi Griliches, "Cost Allocation in Railroad Regulation," *Bell Journal of Economics and Management Science*, vol. 3 (Spring 1972), p. 40.

79. "Social Costs of Regulating the Railroads," p. 233.

that when various elements of cost are regressed on traffic per mile, decreasing costs do appear.[80] His study, however, used only class I railroads, including many small lines for which economies of scale may well exist. Moreover, his data are basically concerned with intensity of use and suggest that excess capacity may be common, a conclusion supported by numerous other studies.

An analysis of additional evidence tends to confirm the absence of scale economies among the larger railroads in recent years. The sample on which this analysis is based includes data for the eighteen largest railroads in 1968, except the Penn Central.[81] The basic model (model [1] in Table 3-5) utilizes one Cobb-Douglas production for freight and another for passenger service. Cobb-Douglas functions are particularly useful here because the sum of the coefficients measures the degree of homogeneity of the production function and, therefore, the degree of economies of scale, if any. Some of the factors in the freight production function also appear in the passenger service function, while others are particular to freight or passengers. The model assumes that the ICC establishes rates, and hence output, and that the price of inputs is exogenous. Consequently, railroads are assumed to minimize cost, given output and input prices. The model can be written as follows:

$$(3) \qquad F = aK_f^{\alpha 1}K_o^{\alpha 2}L_f^{\alpha 3}L_o^{\alpha 4}e^v$$

$$(4) \qquad P = bK_p^{\beta 1}K_o^{\beta 2}L_p^{\beta 3}L_o^{\beta 4}e^w,$$

where F is ton-miles of freight shipped (revenue and nonrevenue), P is passenger-miles moved, K_f is the freight-specific capital, K_o is capital used in moving both freight and passengers, L_f is freight-specific labor, L_o is labor used jointly, K_p is passenger-specific capital, L_p is passenger-specific labor, e^v and e^w are random variables (with $Ev = 0$ and $Ew = 0$, where E is expected value, and with constant variances σ_v^2 and σ_w^2), and a, b, α_1 through α_4, and β_1 through β_4 are constants. The railroad's cost C can be written as

$$(5) \qquad C = r_fK_f + r_oK_o + r_pK_p + w_fL_f + w_oL_o + w_pL_p,$$

where r and w are input prices. The railroad, therefore, attempts to mini-

---

80. Edward Miller, "Economies of Scale in Railroading," in Transportation Research Forum, *Proceedings, Fourteenth Annual Meeting, 1973* (TRF, 1973), pp. 683–701.

81. The Penn Central was excluded primarily because the data on it had been stolen from the ICC's files. However, since it is so much larger than the other railroads, data on it might have biased the results and probably would have been excluded in any case.

mize equation (5), subject to satisfying equations (3) and (4). The necessary conditions for this maximization are given in equations (6) through (13), where λ is the Lagrange multiplier.

(6) $$r_f - \lambda_1\alpha_1(F/K_f)e^v = 0$$
(7) $$r_p - \lambda_2\beta_1(P/K_p)e^w = 0$$
(8) $$r_o - \lambda_1\alpha_2(F/K_o)e^v - \lambda_2\beta_2(P/K_o)e^w = 0$$
(9) $$w_f - \lambda_1\alpha_3(F/L_f)e^v = 0$$
(10) $$w_p - \lambda_2\beta_3(P/L_p)e^w = 0$$
(11) $$w_o - \lambda_1\alpha_4(F/L_o)e^v - \lambda_2\beta_4(P/L_o)e^w = 0$$
(12) $$F - aK_f^{\alpha_1}K_o^{\alpha_2}L_f^{\alpha_3}L_o^{\alpha_4}e^v = 0$$
(13) $$P - bK_p^{\beta_1}K_o^{\beta_2}L_p^{\beta_3}L_o^{\beta_4}e^w = 0.$$

The pure exogenous variables in this model are F, P, and the input prices r_f, r_o, r_p, w_f, w_o, w_p. However, some of the inputs are determined solely by the production function they are embedded in, and some are jointly determined. The jointly determined variables, as shown in equations (8) and (11), are L_o and K_o. All the other variables are determined by the purely exogenous variables in their own production functions, and therefore are not interdependent.

A major difficulty in estimating the coefficients is that there is considerable intercorrelation among the variables. Simple correlation coefficients between the variables are generally above 0.9. Thus, the standard deviations of the regression coefficients are increased and the reliability of the estimates is diminished. For example, the simple, naive approach of model (1) regresses net freight ton-miles, revenue and nonrevenue, on capital and labor. The sum of the coefficients is 1.018, not significantly different from one. The coefficient for labor, however, is small, and not significantly different from zero. If railroads are paying labor the value of its marginal product, model (1) predicts that wages should be 8 percent of the total receipts of railroads. In fact, they are considerably higher. The estimates of individual coefficients thus do not appear to be particularly reliable, although the coefficients in total do sum to approximately one.

To solve the simultaneous equation system, a two-stage least squares model (model [2] in Table 3-5) was constructed to estimate the coefficients of K_o and L_o, the two endogenous variables. The results were not greatly different from those of model (1), with the sum of the coefficients still close to one.

A useful way to avoid the multicollinearity problem is to make independent estimates of the value of some of the coefficients. The basic

Table 3-5. Estimates of Railroad Production Functions, 1968[a]

| Model number[b] | Type of equation | Variables | | | | | Sum of coefficients | R^2 | F |
		Freight-specific capital, K_f	Total labor, L_{tot}	Freight-specific labor, L_f	Joint freight-passenger capital, K_o	Joint labor, L_o			
(1)	Ordinary least squares	0.936 (0.141)	0.082 (0.160)	...	...	...	1.018 (0.212)	0.965	207.9
(2)	Two-stage least squares	0.904 (0.179)	0.121 (0.208)	...	...	...	1.025 (0.272)	0.965	208.9
(3)	Ordinary least squares	0.932 (0.050)	...	0.081[c] (0.008)	...	...	1.013 (0.051)	0.961	199.2
(4)	Two-stage least squares	0.176[c] (0.061)	...	0.081[c] (0.008)	0.700 (0.082)	...	0.957 (0.103)	0.895	45.3
(5)	Two-stage least squares	0.176[c] (0.061)	...	0.081[c] (0.008)	0.172 (0.167)	0.678 (0.198)	1.107 (0.264)	0.941	59.8

Sources: Derived from data for the eighteen largest railroads in 1968, excluding the Penn Central (see note 81 in the text), from U.S. Interstate Commerce Commission, Bureau of Accounts, *Transport Statistics in the United States for the Year Ended December 31, 1968*: pt. 1, *Railroads* (1969); ICC records; and Association of American Railroads records.

a. The numbers in parentheses are standard errors.
b. See the text for a discussion of the models.
c. Computed independently of the regression.

model hypothesizes that rates are set by the regulatory commission and input prices fixed. Rewriting equation (6),

$$r_f \cdot K_f = \alpha_1 \lambda_1 F e^v$$

or

$$\frac{r_f \cdot K_f}{\lambda_1 F} = \alpha_1 e^v,$$

where $E\alpha_1 e^v = \alpha_1$. The Lagrange multiplier, λ_1, is the marginal revenue from additional shipments. Given the above assumptions, marginal revenue equals price, so

$$(14) \qquad E \frac{r_{f'} K_f}{TR_f} = \alpha_1,$$

where TR_f is total freight revenue. In other words, the expected value of the ratio of expenditure on freight-specific capital to total freight revenue equals the α_2 coefficient.

A similar procedure can be followed for labor. From the ICC data,[82] ratios of freight-specific labor expenditures to total freight revenue were computed and averaged. The average ratio was 0.081, with a standard error of 0.008; this value was assumed for α_3, the coefficient for freight-specific labor (model [5], Table 3-5).

The cost of freight-specific capital was set at the $3.271 average rental rate per mile on freight cars in 1968 furnished by the Association of American Railroads. This was converted to the rate per mile on the basis of the average miles per day traveled by a freight car.[83] The resulting average rental rate per mile r_f is then $0.0531. Total expenditure on freight cars was taken to be $0.0531 times the number of freight-car-miles. Dividing this by freight revenue and averaging over all roads yields the expected value of α_1, 0.1758.

Table 3-5 pulls together the results for five models. Models (1) and (3) ignore the simultaneous equation problem and estimate the freight production function directly. However, in equation (3), α_3 was determined before estimating the other coefficients. For models (2), (4), and (5), two-stage least squares were used to get unbiased estimates of the coefficients for L_{tot}, K_o, and L_o. In models (4) and (5), predetermined values of α_1 and α_3 were substituted in the equation before estimating the other coefficients.

82. U.S. Interstate Commerce Commission, Bureau of Accounts, *Transport Statistics in the United States for the Year Ended December 31, 1968:* pt. 1, *Railroads* (1969).
83. Ibid., tables 162, 163.

The results for each model are summarized in the "sum of coefficients" column, and it can be seen that all sums are roughly one. No sum is significantly different from one, though all except one are slightly greater than unity, suggesting, if anything, that there may be mild economies of scale.

Given the small size of the sample, the fact that data from only one year were used, and the possibility of misspecification of the model, not too much confidence should be put in the absolute value of specific coefficients. But the sum of the coefficients is a more robust statistic and helps to confirm the findings of other studies that economies of scale for large railroads are negligible.

CHAPTER FOUR

Public Policy in the Ocean Freight Industry

ROBERT LARNER

THIS CHAPTER EXAMINES the effects of containerization on competition among ocean freight carriers and its implications for public policy toward the industry. More specifically, the desirability of a policy shift toward less regulation and a larger role for competitive forces, supplemented by application of the antitrust laws, is assessed.

The History of Regulation

United States regulation of the ocean freight industry began in 1916,[1] principally in response to shippers' complaints of rate discrimination, arbitrary actions of shipping conferences, and the conferences' use of monopolistic devices like deferred rebates and "fighting ships."

Shipping conferences are cartels of ocean carriers that offer liner services on a trade route.[2] The conferences make rates, allocate sailings, police the practices of their members, and handle the complaints of shippers. Deferred rebates were used to tie shippers to conference members

1. Shipping Act of 1916, 39 Stat. 728.
2. There are three types of ocean shipping services: liner services, provided by common carriers sailing on a regular schedule between designated ports; tramp services, provided by contract carriers, available for hire or charter to transport such cargo between such ports as the charterer may decide; and industrial services, provided by private carriers moving proprietary cargoes. Only liners are subject to regulation by the Federal Maritime Commission.

and to ward off competition by independent (that is, nonconference) liners and by tramps. The rebates—usually equal to 5 or 10 percent of the established rate—were earned by a shipper for a specified period—typically three, six, or twelve months—of exclusive patronage of conference ships, but were paid only after an additional period, generally six months, of continued exclusive patronage of conference lines. Deferred rebates, therefore, increased substantially the cost of "disloyalty" to the conference, since a shipper risked losing not only a rebate for the current period but also one previously earned. Shippers that required regular service also complained that conference lines sometimes punished disloyalty by refusing to accept future shipments even at the full conference rates. Another device used by conferences was using fighting ships to compete against nonconference vessels. The fighting ships would meet or undercut the rates of the nonconference ships until the latter were induced to leave the market or to join the conference and observe its rates and policies.

The Alexander Report

In 1911, the Department of Justice brought suit against three conferences, charging violation of the Sherman Antitrust Act through agreements and practices in restraint of trade. In *United States* v. *Hamburg-Amerika S.S. Line*,[3] the Antitrust Division charged the conference lines with allocating steerage passengers and using fighting ships. In *United States* v. *American-Asiatic Steamship Co.* and *United States* v. *Prince Line, Ltd.*,[4] the charges were agreement on rates, on the number of vessels operating in the trade, and on the schedule of sailings; the use of deferred rebates and fighting ships; and the refusal of accommodations to shippers when space was available as a punishment for past use of nonconference ships and as a deterrent to future use. The appeals court, in reviewing the second case, declared the use of fighting ships and the refusal of accommodations to be unreasonable and unlawful restraints of trade, but also ruled that rate-fixing agreements, division of markets, and the use of deferred rebates were not unreasonable and therefore not in violation of the Sherman Act. The court noted that the deferred rebates were uniform and open to all shippers and that, by assuring more regular cargoes and enabling carriers to anticipate the needs of the trade, they reduced

3. 239 U.S. 466 and 216 Fed. Rep. 971.
4. 242 U.S. 537 and 220 Fed. Rep. 230.

the carriers' costs and promoted stability in sailings and service to the benefit of the shippers.[5]

By the time the two cases reached the Supreme Court, the First World War had broken out in Europe, and the conference agreements, involving British and German lines, among others, had been dissolved. The Supreme Court held the questions raised in the cases to be moot and dismissed the charges without prejudice to the government.[6]

Nonetheless, at least partially in response to the antitrust cases, the House of Representatives in 1912 directed its Committee on the Merchant Marine and Fisheries, chaired by Joshua W. Alexander of Missouri, to undertake an extensive investigation of shipping combinations and their practices. The committee issued a comprehensive report in 1914,[7] which became the basis of the regulatory policy embodied in the Shipping Act of 1916.

The Alexander Report weighed the advantages and disadvantages of the conference system and concluded that conferences were a necessary evil that should be allowed to continue, but only under the close supervision of public regulation. In the committee's words:

It is the view of the Committee that open competition can not be assured for any length of time by ordering existing agreements terminated. The entire history of steamship agreements shows that in ocean commerce there is no happy medium between war and peace when several lines engage in the same trade. Most of the numerous agreements and conference arrangements discussed in the foregoing report were the outcome of rate wars, and represent a truce between the contending lines. To terminate existing agreements would necessarily bring about one of two results: the lines would either engage in rate wars which would mean the elimination of the weak and the survival of the strong, or, to avoid a costly struggle, they would consolidate through common ownership. Neither result can be prevented by legislation, and either would mean a monopoly fully as effective, and it is believed more so, than can exist by virtue of an agreement.[8]

Thus, the committee saw as alternatives to a monopoly approved and unilaterally regulated by the U.S. government either a monopoly achieved

---

5. 220 Fed. Rep. 230. No quantitative estimates of the claimed cost reduction were made, however.

6. 239 U.S. 466 and 242 U.S. 537.

7. *Report on Steamship Agreements and Affiliations in the American Foreign and Domestic Trade*, Proceedings of the House Committee on the Merchant Marine and Fisheries in the Investigation of Shipping Combinations, 63 Cong. (1914), vol. 4 (hereafter cited as the Alexander Report).

8. Ibid., p. 416.

by the strongest firms after a protracted price war or a monopoly achieved by merger. Further, the committee regarded the antitrust laws as an ineffective instrument for establishing and maintaining competition.[9]

The committee's view was in accord with that held by most observers since the last quarter of the nineteenth century. According to this view, the ocean freight industry has been characterized by chronic excess capacity interrupted by intervals of high (usually war-related) demand.[10] It is true that since the introduction of steamships, oceangoing vessels have had a life of twenty years or more and their size has been increasing steadily as technology advances. This has caused capacity adjustments, particularly reductions, to lag behind shifts in demand.[11]

The Alexander Report attributed a number of advantages to the conference system: greater regularity and frequency of service, stability and uniformity of rates, economy in the cost of service, better distribution of sailings, maintenance of parity in American and European rates to foreign markets, and equal treatment of shippers through the elimination of secret arrangements and rate discrimination.[12]

A conference line can provide regular and frequent service by coordinating the sailings of its vessels, whereas a single independent line, having a smaller number of ships, can offer less frequent sailings, and a group of independent lines tends to cluster its sailings around a few peak times.[13] This regular and frequent service enables shippers to hold smaller inventories and facilitates their making forward contracts for delivery of goods at a definite date. The committee also believed that, because of the

9. The report does not explain why the committee considered the antitrust laws useless for preventing monopoly. The Sherman Act had already been used successfully to attack monopoly achieved by merger in a 1904 case, *United States* v. *Northern Securities Co.* (120 F. 721, aff. 24 S. Ct. 436), and monopoly achieved by (among other tactics) predatory pricing in two 1911 cases, *Standard Oil Co.* v. *United States* (221 U.S. 1) and *United States* v. *American Tobacco Co.* (221 U.S. 106).

10. John B. Lansing, *Transportation and Economic Policy* (Free Press, 1966), p. 343.

11. The issue of overtonnaging is discussed in the section on containerization below.

12. Alexander Report, p. 416.

13. Peter O. Steiner has noted, in a study of television broadcasting, that a monopolist of a small number of channels (where the number of channels that can serve a given population is limited) has stronger incentives to offer a more varied choice of programs and to avoid program duplication than a group of oligopolists, each owning one of the channels. See his "Monopoly and Competition in Television: Some Policy Issues," in Paul W. MacAvoy (ed.), *The Crisis of the Regulatory Commissions: An Introduction to a Current Issue of Public Policy* (W. W. Norton, 1970), pp. 103–16. Similarly, the domestic airlines, which can collude on price but not on service, tend to cluster flights at peak hours.

greater security given to capital invested in the steamship business by the near monopoly power of the conferences, shipowners could supply an adequate number of vessels of a higher quality and greater speed than the ordinary tramp.

But the most important advantages of the conference system, if it were "honestly and fairly conducted," were the stability and uniformity of rates it could provide. The committee found that shippers regarded as essential a stable selling price in foreign markets for their commodities, and that stable freight rates over a long period of time eliminated part of the speculative risk in selling goods for future delivery and making forward contracts for the carriage of freight. The committee did not consider the allocative function of prices: that is, if a market economy uses changes in relative prices to allocate resources efficiently, then prolonged stability of any price is undesirable. And, to the extent that the more flexible prices that would prevail in the absence of conferences would stimulate the development of a futures market for ocean shipping services, freight rates and selling prices would be stable as well as lower.

Rate uniformity, in the committee's view, was even more desirable than rate stability. The principal complaints of shippers were rate discrimination (as opposed to unduly high rates) and arbitrary treatment at the hands of the ocean carriers and their conferences. The committee feared that uncontrolled monopoly would lead not only to a monopoly rate level, but also to extensive price discrimination in favor of the larger shippers, who would then have a competitive advantage, perhaps even a monopoly, in the foreign trade of the commodities they carried.

The committee also found serious disadvantages with the existing conference system. It noted that:

All monopolies are liable to abuse, and in our foreign carrying trade the monopoly obtained by the conference lines has not been subjected to any legal control. While carriers by land are supervised and must conform to statutory requirements in the matter of rates and treatment of shippers, steamship companies, through private arrangements, have secured for themselves monopolistic powers as effective in many instances as though they were statutory. Even granting the advantages claimed for steamship conferences and agreements, all may be withdrawn in the absence of supervisory control without the shippers having any redress or protection. The lines are under no legal obligation to continue these advantages. They exercise their powers as private combinations and are apt to abuse the same unless brought under effective governmental control.[14]

The monopolistic abuses of the conferences cited by the committee

14. Alexander Report, p. 304.

included: "excessive" rates; rate discrimination, and the lack of published tariffs and classifications; deferred rebates, objectionable on the grounds that they placed the shipper in a state of continual dependence and were unnecessary to secure excellence and regularity of service; indifference to the landing of freight in good condition and arbitrary treatment in the settlement of claims; and the secrecy of conference agreements, which prevented the shippers from knowing whether the conditions that the conferences claimed necessitated such agreements were true or not.

The committee concluded that "the disadvantages and abuses connected with steamship agreements and conferences as now conducted are inherent, and can only be eliminated by effective government control; and it is such control that the Committee recommends as the means of preserving to American exporters and importers the advantages enumerated, and of preventing the abuses complained of."[15] The committee noted that the shippers who testified before it were overwhelmingly in favor of some form of government regulation. Representatives of steamship lines who appeared as witnesses were nearly unanimous in declaring themselves not opposed to "reasonable" government supervision, to be limited to the requirement of full publicity for and approval of all agreements or arrangements that lines may enter into with other carriers or with shippers.

The Alexander Report recommended specifically that the rates and practices of ocean carriers engaged in the foreign trade of the United States be brought under the supervision of the Interstate Commerce Commission (ICC),[16] and that such carriers be required to file for approval with the ICC all agreements, understandings, and conference arrangements with other shipping companies engaged in the American trade, or with American shippers, railroads, or other transportation companies. The ICC would be empowered to investigate complaints charging unreasonable or unfair rates, and to order such rates changed if they were found to be unreasonably high, discriminatory between shippers or ports, or between American exporters and their foreign competitors. The commission could also order restitution to shippers of all sums collected in excess of reasonable rates. Finally, the committee recommended that the use of deferred rebates and fighting ships be prohibited in foreign trade, and that all carriers be

15. Ibid., p. 418.
16. The committee had considered recommending a separate commission to regulate ocean shipping, but decided that the close relations between rail and water transportation would make it preferable to entrust the supervisory control to the ICC.

prohibited from refusing space accommodations to shippers who patronized an independent line or filed a charge of unfair treatment.[17]

The Shipping Act of 1916

The Shipping Act of 1916 embodied the major recommendations of the Alexander Report and remains, as amended, the basic statute regulating ocean transportation. The act established the United States Shipping Board to supervise common carriers operating on regular routes in U.S. foreign commerce. Section 14 of the act prohibits lines from giving deferred rebates, using fighting ships, retaliating against a shipper for any reason by refusing or threatening to refuse space accommodations, and making unfair or unjustly discriminatory contracts with shippers. As subsequently amended, the secretary of commerce was empowered to refuse entry into American ports to any foreign carrier determined by the Shipping Board to have violated these provisions or to be a party to any agreement or understanding that denies an American line admission to a conference on equal terms with all other parties.[18]

Section 15 requires carriers to file with the regulatory agency all agreements, understandings, and conference arrangements, and modifications and cancellations thereof, that fix or regulate rates or control, prevent, or destroy competition. The regulatory agency can disapprove, cancel, or modify any agreement it finds to be unjustly discriminatory to carriers, shippers, or ports, or to American exporters vis-à-vis their foreign competitors, or to operate to the detriment of U.S. commerce. All agreements approved by the agency are granted immunity from the antitrust laws.

Under the original section 18 of the Shipping Act, only domestic water carriers were required to publish and adhere to tariffs and to file maximum rates with the regulatory agency. Although the Shipping Board and its successor were given no specific authority to pass upon the reasonableness of conference rates, its power to disapprove conference agreements constituted a means of influencing rates. In 1935, the United States Shipping Board Bureau held that where a conference rate was so high as to be detrimental to the nation's commerce, the bureau would require its reduction to a reasonable level, even withdrawing approval of the conference

17. Alexander Report, pp. 419–21.
18. 41 Stat. 996.

agreement if necessary.[19] But actual and potential competition from independent liners, tramps, and conferences serving alternate trade routes (in addition to the bargaining power of shippers) were the main forces relied upon to prevent rates from reaching the monopoly level.

How Effective Has Regulation Been?

The Shipping Act of 1916 reflects the attitude that still dominates regulatory policy in the ocean freight industry—some monopoly power, vested in the conference system, is necessary, but it must be closely supervised by a government agency to prevent abuses. Has regulation been effective in achieving the alleged advantages of the conference system while curbing its potential for monopolistic abuse? To what extent has regulation corrected for the market failures that originally prompted it and stimulated the kind of performance that competitive markets are expected to yield?[20]

The Celler Report

In 1962, the Antitrust Subcommittee of the House Judiciary Committee, chaired by Emanuel Celler of New York, issued the results of a comprehensive three-year study of competitive and regulatory problems in the ocean freight industry.[21] It described as "unparalleled" the record of regulatory neglect by the Federal Maritime Board and its predecessors, and stated that "for a period of almost 45 years, lethargy and indifference have characterized its attitude, laxity and inefficiency its procedures, and frustration and ineffectiveness its administration of the regulatory features

19. United States Maritime Commission, *Decisions of the United States Shipping Board, Department of Commerce United States Shipping Board Bureau, and United States Maritime Commission*, vol. 1 (November 1919–November 1938), p. 398.

20. Alfred E. Kahn has observed that "the single most widely accepted rule for the governance of the regulated industries is regulate them in such a way as to produce the same results as would be produced by effective competition, if it were feasible" (*The Economics of Regulation: Principles and Institutions* [John Wiley, 1970], vol. 1, p. 17). Similarly, Roger G. Noll judges the performance of regulatory agencies "by the extent to which their actions correct for the market failures that were the motivation for establishing regulation" (*Reforming Regulation: An Evaluation of the Ash Council Proposals* [Brookings Institution, 1971], pp. 15–16).

21. *The Ocean Freight Industry*, H. Rept. 1419, 87 Cong. 2 sess. (1962) (hereafter cited as the Celler Report).

of the shipping acts."[22] Investigations by the subcommittee's staff disclosed numerous unfiled agreements, particularly "gentlemen's agreements," in violation of section 15 of the Shipping Act, which the Federal Maritime Board had not only failed to approve, but of whose very existence the agency was ignorant.

Despite its scathing indictment of the record, the Celler Report concluded that national shipping policy, including qualified acceptance of the conference system, was "basically sound,"[23] and blamed the failure of regulation on faulty legislation and deficient performance by the regulatory agency. Thus, the proposed remedy was new legislation and improved performance in administering and enforcing the Shipping Act and its amendments.

The same charge of ineffective regulation was reiterated four years later in a report of the Joint Economic Committee on discriminatory ocean freight rates. The report, submitted by Senator Paul H. Douglas, chairman of the committee, found that:

Although the Shipping Act, which provides for conference regulation, was adopted almost 50 years ago, the regulation of steamship conferences has never been carried out in the manner intended by Congress. Extensive investigations by House committees over the last 5 years have established that the abuses intended to be remedied by the act, including even the deferred rebate, still permeate American trade routes. The statutory powers are ample and have been strengthened as recently as 1961, but their enforcement has been grossly inadequate. . . . It was admitted to the Joint Economic Committee in June of 1963 that the [Federal Maritime] Commission had not investigated the level of freight rates, the conference system of ratemaking, the relationship between rates and trade movement, and the effects on the balance of payments of present ocean transportation practices. It was further admitted that the Federal Maritime Commission had rarely disapproved a conference agreement and had never subjected a freight rate to the statutory test of reasonableness.[24]

The primary reasons for the ineffectiveness of the regulatory agency have been the combination of promotional and regulatory functions in the same agency, and the international character of the ocean shipping industry. Public policy toward ocean shipping has always had the dual aims of promotion and regulation, and until 1961 both of these responsibilities were vested in the same agency, without any statement articulating

22. Ibid., pp. 359–60.
23. Ibid., p. 382.
24. *Discriminatory Ocean Freight Rates and the Balance of Payments*, Report of the Joint Economic Committee, S. Rept. 1, 89 Cong. 1 sess. (1965), p. 5.

the relationship between the two goals.[25] In fact, whenever the two aims have conflicted, regulation has been subordinated to promotion.

The introduction to the Shipping Act of 1916 illustrates this priority of promotion over regulation: "An Act to establish a United States Shipping Board for the purpose of encouraging, developing, and creating a naval auxiliary and naval reserve and a merchant marine to meet the requirements of the commerce of the United States with its Territories and possessions and with foreign countries; to regulate carriers by water engaged in the foreign and interstate commerce of the United States, and for other purposes."[26] The Celler Report noted that, in March 1961, only 52 out of a total of 2,765 employees of the Federal Maritime Board and the Maritime Administration were assigned exclusively to regulatory duties.[27] Military and political objectives, not economic ones, have been the principal determinants of public policy toward ocean shipping. The U.S. merchant marine has been assigned the role of a naval or military auxiliary, of carrying the nation's strategic trade in civilian goods during wars or national emergencies, of serving as a training and proving ground for maritime personnel and equipment, and of maintaining the nation's freedom of action in international crises.[28] Government policy has supported the conference system as an instrument for developing a U.S. merchant marine. To the extent that the system permits American shipping firms to earn larger profits than they would in the absence of a cartel, direct government subsidies could be smaller and the budgetary costs (if not the social costs) of the promotional program reduced.

The Antitrust Subcommittee found that the Federal Maritime Board had been lax in monitoring the activities and practices of conferences and had virtually ignored several of its information-gathering duties with respect to conference activities. Furthermore, the agency, instead of independently investigating a shipper's grievance brought to its attention, forwarded the complaint directly to the conference involved to get its

25. All four predecessor agencies to the Federal Maritime Commission (FMC)—U.S. Shipping Board, Shipping Board Bureau, Maritime Commission, and Federal Maritime Board—had promotional as well as regulatory responsibilities. President Kennedy's Reorganization Plan Number 7 of 1961, which established the FMC, transferred full responsibility for maritime promotional and subsidy programs to the Maritime Administration and the Maritime Subsidy Board in the Department of Commerce.

26. 39 Stat. 728.

27. Celler Report, p. 396.

28. See Samuel A. Lawrence, *United States Merchant Shipping Policies and Politics* (Brookings Institution, 1966), pp. 22–27.

side of the story—a practice with an understandably chilling effect on the shippers. The Celler Report concluded that "as a practical matter, the Board tended to emphasize the promotional aspects of its functions at the expense of the regulatory features of its obligations. . . . Rather than face the unpleasant task of attempting to perform inconsistent functions, the Board chose to turn its back on one and devote its energies to the other."[29]

Dual-Rate Contracts

In 1958, the Supreme Court's *Isbrandtsen* decision[30] declared that the dual-rate contracts used by conferences to hinder competition from independent lines were a resort to discriminatory or unfair tactics in violation of section 14 of the 1916 Shipping Act, which, in the Court's view, permitted conferences to regulate competition among members but not to stifle the competition of independent liners. Dual-rate contracts are agreements between individual shippers and all the members of a conference, in which the shipper contracts to make shipments of all commodities on a trade route exclusively on conference vessels, in return for a schedule of rates (the contract rates) lower than the schedule applying to nonsigners (the noncontract rates). The system of dual rates differs from deferred rebates in that the shipper realizes the savings from exclusive patronage immediately upon each shipment. The contracts contain a provision for a penalty—liquidated damage payments—in the event that the shipper uses nonconference vessels when conference vessels are available. These damages, like the deferred rebates, are designed to raise the cost to shippers of patronizing independent lines or tramps by imposing payments to the conference greater than the savings from the lower freight rates offered by nonconference vessels. Both schemes have the effect of increasing the scale of entry into a trade route, since an interloping independent line must be able to offer regular service to a large number of shippers if it is to compete effectively. Deferred rebates are more advantageous to the conference lines, however, because the burden of claiming

29. Celler Report, p. 379. The Ash Council Report also recognized the inherent conflict between promotional responsibilities and regulatory activities in the same agency, and recommended that the two functions be placed in separate agencies (see President's Advisory Council on Executive Organization, *A New Regulatory Framework: Report on Selected Independent Regulatory Agencies* [1971], pp. 79–81).

30. *Federal Maritime Board* v. *Isbrandtsen Company, Inc.*, 356 U.S. 481.

rebates and verifying continued loyalty is on the shipper, while the conference itself must prove a violation of dual-rate contracts and sue for damages.

The *Isbrandtsen* decision was viewed by many as undermining the very foundation of the conference system. Congress hurriedly legislated temporary validation of the dual-rate contracts already in existence, while its committees investigated both the conference system and government regulation of ocean shipping. In 1961, amendments to the 1916 Shipping Act were enacted in Public Law 87-346 that permitted dual-rate contracts while providing some additional safeguards to shippers, and President Kennedy's reorganization plan established the FMC.

Public Law 87-346 imposed several limits to the effectiveness of dual-rate contracts as a restrictive device. The FMC may approve only dual-rate contracts that are equally available to all shippers and are not detrimental to U.S. commerce, contrary to the public interest, or unjustly discriminatory or unfair. Dual-rate contracts must also contain the following provisions: the spread between contract and noncontract rates must be reasonable, in no case more than 15 percent; shipments can be made on nonconference vessels if no conference vessel is available on reasonable notice; shippers must receive 90 days' notice of rate increases; shippers must be able to terminate the contract on 90 days' notice; and damages cannot be punitive, but must be equal to the line's actual loss— the contract rate minus handling costs.

Less than two months before Public Law 87-346 went into effect, the FMC had been vested with the regulatory authority and responsibility provided in the shipping laws. The commission was given the following powers with respect to ocean freight rates:

(1) All rates, inbound or outbound, charged by common ocean carriers and conferences operating in the foreign trade of the United States, as well as the rules and regulations governing the application of rates, must be filed with the FMC, and no carrier can charge rates different from those filed:

(2) Rate increases and new rates must be filed 30 days before the effective date, unless the FMC grants special permission for a rate increase on less than statutory notice. Rate decreases, however, become effective upon filing.

(3) The FMC must disapprove any rate or change in rates that, after hearing, it finds to be so unreasonably high or low as to be detrimental to the commerce of the United States.

Section 15 of the Shipping Act of 1916 was also amended to provide explicitly that no conference agreement should be approved unless conference membership is open on equal terms to any carrier with the intention and ability to provide regular liner service in the trade.

The International Character of Ocean Shipping

The most intractable problem confronting the United States in its attempts to regulate ocean shipping, and the major reason for the relative ineffectiveness of past policies, is the international character of the industry. In 1968, U.S. liners carried only 24 percent of the liner tonnage in the U.S. oceanborne foreign trade; the share was 40 percent in 1956.[31] Over three-fourths of the total liner tonnage was carried in the vessels of the dozen or so major (noncommunist) maritime nations, with no one flag predominating.

The United States is alone among the world's maritime nations in attempting the statutory regulation of ocean shipping conferences, and the attempt has evoked strong and repeated protests from virtually every other maritime nation. Foreign shipowners and their governments have alleged that the United States seeks unilaterally to regulate an international industry, and thereby creates conflicts of jurisdiction and infringes upon the sovereignty of other nations. Furthermore, U.S. regulation is said to protect the interests of the United States to the detriment of foreign interests. Other maritime nations have manifested little concern with the potential or actual monopoly abuses of the conference system, and have generally relied upon negotiations between shippers, either as individuals or jointly in shippers' councils, and conferences to prevent such abuses.[32]

The FMC's administration of the provisions of Public Law 87-346 has elicited further foreign protests. When in 1961 the FMC issued proposed regulations for filing freight tariffs and proposed rules regarding self-policing provisions in conference agreements, ten European governments and Japan filed formal protests. There followed a series of meetings in Paris and London, involving shipping officials of the governments of Great Britain, Belgium, Denmark, France, West Germany, Greece, Italy, Norway, the Netherlands, and Sweden, for the stated purpose of taking collective action against provisions of the law. In addition to their political

31. "Value in Tonnage of Commercial Cargo Carried in U.S. Oceanborne Foreign Trade" (computer printouts of the Maritime Administration, 1957, 1969).

32. See R. O. Goss, *Studies in Maritime Economics* (London: Cambridge University Press, 1968), pp. 20–24.

objections, the foreign governments claimed that the proposed regulations imposed heavy administrative expenses upon shipowners and obstructed their operations.

Foreign hostility to U.S. regulation reached a peak in the mid-sixties, when the FMC ordered foreign lines that were alleged to have violated U.S. shipping statutes to produce documents located outside the United States. In 1963, the FMC directed sixteen conferences to furnish data and documents it considered relevant to its study of the disparity between inbound and outbound freight rates in the U.S. foreign trade. Foreign governments vehemently protested, and review suits were brought in U.S. courts of appeals. As a consequence, the FMC first postponed the compliance date for its orders and later reached voluntary agreement with fourteen maritime nations on furnishing the information. By July 1965, the FMC had received all the information that foreign lines had agreed to furnish. Between 1963 and 1968, however, a majority of European governments enacted legislation or issued decrees forbidding their shipping lines from producing before the FMC or U.S. courts any documents located outside the United States. These prohibitions were sometimes accompanied by stiff penalties for violations.

Some of the legal issues surrounding the controversy were settled by the Second Circuit Court of Appeals decision in the 1966 *Ludlow* case.[33] In this case, the FMC had ordered the members of the Calcutta conference to produce revenue and cost data in connection with an investigation of whether certain of the conference's rates on jute products were so unreasonably high as to be detrimental to U.S. commerce. The court upheld the FMC's subpoena power, contained in section 27 of the Shipping Act of 1916, to compel the production of evidence located outside the borders of the United States and relevant to an FMC investigation. The court was aware, however, of the problems its decision could create, since foreign laws prohibited the defendants from producing the documents. Thus, when the case was returned to the district court, the lower court decided not to impose contempt penalties for noncompliance with the FMC's order. The matter of noncompliance was referred to the commission, which found that the conference members, by not complying with section 27 of the 1916 Shipping Act, had not fulfilled the requirements of section 15. The FMC therefore ordered the conference agreements canceled.[34]

33. *Federal Maritime Commission and Ludlow Corp.* v. *A. T. DeSmedt et al.*, 366 F.2d 464 (1966); later in the same year the Supreme Court denied certiorari (385 U.S. 974).

34. FMC Docket 67-33, order served Sept. 13, 1967.

In 1968, however, the court of appeals set aside the FMC's order and remanded the proceeding to the FMC for further consideration.[35] The court held that cancellation of a conference agreement, while necessary in some kinds of investigative proceedings, was too drastic a response to the refusal of some conference members to provide information in a rate complaint hearing. The commission was directed to proceed with its hearing on Ludlow's rate complaint and told that if it found itself unable to reach a rational determination because of the withholding of relevant data, it could always use the available sanction of disapproving the rate increases.[36] Before the FMC acted, however, Ludlow and the Calcutta conference reached a settlement on the contested rates and the proceeding was discontinued.

The inability of the FMC to obtain documents located outside the United States has seriously impaired the effectiveness of its regulatory efforts. If foreign lines carrying the imports and exports of the United States do not have to produce such documents, they acquire, in effect, a partial immunity to regulation. This means not only that the FMC would be unable to obtain sufficient evidence to determine whether or not the Shipping Act was violated, but also that U.S. lines would be subject to much stricter regulation than their foreign competitors—a situation not likely to be viewed with equanimity by Congress. Even if Congress or the courts should confer jurisdiction on the FMC, the agency would still have no means of enforcement other than the ultimate weapon of disapproving or canceling conference agreements—in effect, forbidding the conference to operate. Such action would be likely to provoke retaliation against American lines by foreign governments, thus worsening diplomatic relations and perhaps reducing U.S. foreign trade.

The "Container Revolution"

Containerization—the shipping of cargo as a unit in large aluminum or steel boxes from point of origin to point of destination—began in the U.S. domestic trade in 1955, when the Pan Atlantic Corporation, a pred-

35. 399 F.2d 994 (1968).
36. The court noted that in 1961 Congress was asked to make approval of conference agreements contingent upon a commitment by each member of the conference to furnish all records requested by the FMC, regardless of where they were located. The Senate, however, rejected this approach, the State Department having strongly represented that such legislation would be severely detrimental to the conduct of United States foreign policy.

ecessor of Sea-Land Service, Inc., carried cargo in experimental containers on a tanker sailing between New York and Houston. A large shore crane was used to load and unload the containers. After only three months of container operations, cargo handling costs had been reduced from $5.83 a ton to only 15 cents a ton.

Spurred by the success of this experiment, Sea-Land began service with specially designed containerships between New York and Puerto Rico, and was able to reduce port handling costs to less than 5 percent of costs in conventional shipping, and to cut port turnaround time from seven days to fifteen hours. At about the same time, the Matson Line introduced containership service between the West Coast and Hawaii. By the mid-1960s, Sea-Land had launched container vessels on its transatlantic routes, a move that was quickly copied by other established lines on the routes.[37] In 1970, there were nearly 400 full or partial containerships sailing on the major trade routes of the world. American firms owned or operated 78 of the 166 full containerships and 112 of the 232 partial containerships.[38] In addition, another 131 full containerships and 185 ships with partial capacities for containers were under construction or on order.[39]

The economic advantages of containerization can be highlighted by contrasting container shipping with conventional, or break-bulk, shipping, where cargo shipments are not unitized in any way. With break-bulk shipping, each parcel of cargo—whether it is a small carton of pins or a several-ton shipment of machine tools or automobile parts—undergoes many separate handlings on its way from the manufacturer to the buyer overseas. First, the shipment must be specially packed for export to protect it against loss, damage, and theft. The cost of export pack is significant, averaging about 8 percent of total shipment value.[40] Each parcel then moves by truck or rail to a pier, where it is stacked and checked before being put

37. For a summary of the early history of containership operations, see the supplement to the Sept. 14, 1968, issue of *The Economist*, p. x. The entire supplement is devoted to the "container revolution."

38. U.S. Department of Commerce, Maritime Administration, "Containerships, as of June 30, 1970" (Maritime Administration, Division of Statistics, n.d.; processed), pp. 1, 12.

39. Maritime Administration, "Containerships under Construction and on Order (Including Conversions) in United States and Foreign Shipyards: Oceangoing Ships of 1,000 Gross Tons and Over, as of June 30, 1970" (Maritime Administration, Division of Statistics, 1970; processed), pp. 1, 10.

40. This estimate is given in *Inland and Maritime Transportation of Unitized Cargo*, prepared by the Maritime Cargo Transportation Conference of the National Academy of Sciences–National Research Council (Washington, D.C.: NAS–NRC, 1963), p. 34.

into a sling and deposited in the ship's hold. In the hold, each parcel must be carefully stowed to prevent damage from the ship's motion. After the voyage, each parcel is lifted from the hold and stacked at the pier or nearby warehouse to await customs inspection and claim by the buyer. Each of these separate handlings takes time and labor, and requires considerable paperwork, as well, since shipping documents must be prepared for each mode of transportation. Finally, insurance rates for high-value cargo shipped in small parcels are high because of the risk of damage or theft.

Containerization consists of stowing large amounts of cargo in strongly constructed, standard-sized boxes or vans, either at the manufacturer's plant or at a nearby consolidating station, and then shipping the entire vanload of cargo as a single unit to its ultimate destination. From the time the container is locked and sealed, the cargo is untouched until it reaches the consignee or a customs inspection station. The container is loaded aboard trucks, rail cars, and ships by mechanical devices that shorten the shipping process and substantially reduce overall labor costs.

The economic advantages of container shipping are substantial.[41] First, there are extensive savings in packaging and claims costs. Since the container itself serves as a warehouse for the cargo while it is being transported, lower-cost domestic pack can be used instead of export pack, reducing packaging cost by an average of 38 percent,[42] and by much more in the case of high-value commodities that are particularly susceptible to damage or theft. Similarly, the reduced risk of damage, loss, or pilferage of cargo is expected to lower cargo insurance rates, although few premium reductions have yet occurred.

A much greater cost saving of containerization comes in the loading and discharging of cargo. In the United States, where cargo handling costs are the highest in the world, between 60 and 70 percent of the operating costs of a conventional cargo liner are incurred in port; by contrast, the figure for Britain and Europe is about 40 percent. The tonnage of containerized cargo loaded or discharged per ship-hour is four to eight times as great as the tonnage handled in break-bulk operation. It has been estimated that pier-to-pier costs of unit load systems, which include palletized as well as containerized cargo, are only 43 to 48 percent of the

41. The impact of containerization on labor relations is not considered here. It is assumed that the port productivity pacts negotiated between longshoremen's unions and the shipping lines and port operators allow the cost savings of containerization to be realized at a price that does not entirely dissipate the economic advantages of container shipping.

42. *Inland and Maritime Transportation of Unitized Cargo*, p. 35.

costs of break-bulk operations, with the major share of this difference accounted for by lower stevedoring and other cargo costs.[43] The stevedoring costs of unit load systems are estimated to be only 15 to 20 percent of those of break-bulk operations; and in the break-bulk system, stevedoring and associated cargo costs comprise 58 percent of pier-to-pier costs.

Finally, ship operating and ownership costs and port charges per ton of cargo are lower for containerships because of their shorter turnaround time due to faster cargo handling. Containerships have a much higher ratio of sea time to port time than conventional vessels, and the less time a liner spends in port loading and discharging cargo, the more voyages it can make per year and the greater are its annual carrying and revenue-earning capacities. One witness in the FMC hearing on the proposed merger between Sea-Land and United States Lines testified that a full containership could achieve a ratio of 80 percent sea time to 20 percent port time, while other vessels found it difficult to achieve better than a 50–50 ratio.[44] A study of the United Kingdom–New Zealand trade found that with conventional ships and dockside handling equipment about 60 percent of total ship time is spent in port, and that cargo is actually being worked during only 15 percent of that time, so that the ship is completely nonproductive a large proportion of the time.[45] In the past, moreover, the long turnaround time caused by inefficient methods of cargo handling in ports has constrained the size of general-cargo liners and limited the achievement of economies of scale. The shorter turnaround time of containerships makes it economical for them to have larger carrying capacities than conventional ships. All of these cost savings stemming from faster turnaround decline as voyage lengths increase, but they remain substantial for even the longest voyages. The faster delivery time with container shipping also means less capital tied up in goods en route, and hence lower inventory costs for shippers. Shippers are assured of a more regular flow of goods, components, and materials, and in turn can offer more reliable estimates or guarantees of delivery time to customers.

Containerization reduces the costs of other modes of transportation, as well. Truck loading and unloading charges at the pier fall, since the container becomes the truck's body after it is hoisted out of the ship's hold. Containerization also eliminates the hours trucks lose waiting in

43. Ibid., p. 10.
44. Cited in FMC Docket 69-56, Brief for the United States, June 9, 1970, pp. 10–11.
45. K. M. Johnson and H. C. Garnett, *The Economics of Containerisation* (London: George Allen and Unwin, 1971), p. 37.

long lines outside piers to pick up or deliver small parcels of cargo, and reduces the amount of lighterage and other port services required by railroads.

Even with a large capital investment in containerships, containers, terminals, and supporting equipment, container shipping has significantly lower costs per ton of cargo transported than conventional, break-bulk shipping. The required capital investment is large in absolute amount, however, and may pose a significant barrier to entry. Containerships are larger and more costly than conventional vessels (although because of the faster turnaround not as many ships are needed to transport a given annual volume of cargo), and require a full supporting system of equipment and services. This support system includes containers, truck chassis, gantry cranes, terminal space, feeder vessels, and sophisticated computers and computer technology.

Testimony presented during the FMC hearings on the containership charter agreement between Sea-Land and United States Lines indicated the high cost of containership operations. An executive of U.S. Lines estimated that an American-flag line would have to invest between $120 and $200 million to provide basic container service (defined as one or two sailings a week to the major ports on each side of the ocean) on a single important trade route between the United States and either Europe or Japan.[46] Another witness estimated that a full containership by itself costs upward of $30 million, compared to $10 to $15 million for a typical break-bulk vessel of the C-4 type, and that the inventory of containers for a single ship costs approximately $6 to $9 million.[47]

The large capital requirements have limited the number of firms able to finance entry into containership operations and led to the formation of several containership consortia among foreign lines. For instance, of the three largest foreign lines operating on the North Atlantic trades, two (Atlantic Container Line and Dart Containerline) are consortia, and the

46. FMC Docket 69-56, Exhibit 91, Verified Statement of Edward J. Heine, Jr., submitted Dec. 4, 1969, pp. 6–7. Heine estimated that basic container service would require six to ten large containerships of the Lancer or Mariner type, costing roughly $20 million per ship; 3,000 containers per ship, costing at least $2,000 each; and shoreside cranes, costing $10 to $20 million ($2 million apiece for two cranes at each terminal, with five to ten terminals). The cost of other supporting equipment was not estimated.

47. FMC Docket 69-56, Statement of Nathan S. Simat, Exhibit 423, pp. II-2, II-3. Simat noted that the lowest bid for each of the six 26-knot, 1,600-container-capacity ships originally planned by American Export Isbrandtsen Lines was $30 million, and that Sea-Land's SL-7 containerships were then being built in West Germany and the Netherlands at a cost of approximately $32 million each.

third (Hapag-Lloyd) is a joint venture of two lines.[48] The two lines that dominate the United Kingdom–Australia trade are also consortia.

Policy Issues Raised by Containerization

The innovation of container shipping and its rapid growth on the U.S. Atlantic and Pacific trade routes[49] have brought three major policy issues before the FMC and the Congress. First, the commission is being asked to approve a North Atlantic Pool Agreement.[50] This agreement, a comprehensive revenue-pooling arrangement among the largest container lines on the North Atlantic trade route, is designed to control or eliminate competition among containerships sailing on the same or neighboring routes. Second, the two largest American containership operators, Sea-Land Service and United States Lines, have sought FMC approval of a merger agreement under which the R. J. Reynolds Tobacco Company and its subsidiary Sea-Land would acquire U.S. Lines, including its fleet of sixteen containerships and related equipment.[51] Third, Congress, the ICC, and the FMC have been asked to extend antitrust immunity to joint through-rates for international intermodal transportation.

The North Atlantic Pool Agreement

The background to the agreement lies in one of the most significant consequences of container shipping—the emergence of new traffic patterns due to the increase in the number of possible routes from a given origin to a given destination. Existing trade routes, each of which serves as the geographic area for which a conference is organized, consist of a range of

48. The participants in the Atlantic Container Line consortium are: French Line, Holland-America Line, Swedish American Line, Swedish Transatlantic Line, Cunard Steamship Co. Ltd., and Wallenius Line. The Dart consortium is composed of Belgian Line, Clarke Traffic Services of Canada, and Bristol City Line of the United Kingdom. Two German lines, Hamburg-Amerika and North German Lloyd, sell their services jointly under the name of Hapag-Lloyd. *Business Week*, no. 2226 (April 29, 1972), p. 50.

49. On the four U.S. North Atlantic/United Kingdom–European Continent trade routes, commercial containerized cargo accounted for 71 percent of the total commercial liner traffic in 1971. On the U.S. Pacific/Far East trade route it accounted for 33 percent. See Maritime Administration, *Foreign Oceanborne Trade of the United States: Containerized Cargo on Selected Trade Routes, Calendar Year 1971* (1973), pp. 5, 7, 36, 43.

50. FMC Agreement 10,000, dated Nov. 29, 1971.

51. FMC Docket 70-51 (1970).

ports on each of two sides of an ocean. With conventional break-bulk shipping, a shipper normally sends his cargo to the closest port for loading and has it discharged at the port nearest its destination to minimize the number of times the cargo is handled. For example, Italian sewing machines made in Milan and exported to the United States would move only through the northern Italian port of Genoa on the westbound U.S. North Atlantic/Mediterranean trade route. In containers, however, they can be transported overland by rail or truck to such northern European ports as Antwerp, Rotterdam, or Hamburg, and there quickly and efficiently transferred to a ship for carriage to a U.S. North Atlantic port over a different trade route.

Thus, ports that possess more of the resources necessary for container shipping and, at least in the short run, ports that have gotten a head start in constructing facilities for handling containerized cargo shipments have expanded their market areas at the expense of ports with fewer resources and facilities.[52] As a consequence, carriers operating on different trade routes have found themselves in competition for cargo that formerly was carried primarily over only one route. This increased competition has induced some conferences to cut certain rates in order to capture containerized cargo that would otherwise be shipped on another route. For instance, the Continental North Atlantic Westbound Freight Conference, covering a range of ports in Western Europe, set a freight rate of $276.50 per 1,000 kilograms for leather shoes valued at from $1,500 to $2,000 per 1,000 kilograms, but put a special rate of $150 per 1,000 kilos for leather shoes of *Italian* origin valued at up to $2,000 per 1,000 kilos.[53] In this way, the conference has been able to divert a significant amount of Italian-made goods to western European ports and thus to put strong pressure on the rates of the Mediterranean conference. Similarly, there has been intense competition for traffic between western European and Baltic ports.

It was in response to this change in competitive relationships and market areas that the largest lines operating containerships on the North Atlantic routes filed two agreements with the FMC for approval. One is aimed at establishing a single conference encompassing all the U.S. North Atlantic–Europe trade routes, and the second creates a revenue pool and

52. For a brief, but excellent, analysis of the determinants of market areas, see C. D. Hyson and W. P. Hyson, "The Economic Law of Market Areas," *Quarterly Journal of Economics*, vol. 64 (May 1950), pp. 319–27.

53. Testimony of M. J. Kelly at FMC hearing, In the Matter of FMC Agreement 9813—Transatlantic Freight Conference, May 28, 1970, pp. 154–59 of transcript.

rationalizes capacity and sailings. The Transatlantic Freight Conference Agreement,[54] which was subsequently withdrawn from FMC consideration after the intervention of the Justice Department, had as a principal purpose the maintenance of effective conference control over competition and rate structures. Diversion of cargo from its "natural routing" was discouraged by a provision that whenever there was transshipment of cargo from a port on one trade route to a port on another, the freight rates in effect for the port that would "normally serve" the origin or destination points would apply.[55] In addition, members of the conference were prohibited from absorbing any inland freight costs between the point of origin or destination and the transshipment port.[56] Thus, an Italian shoe producer would pay the same rate for shipping shoes from Milan to New York, whether the shoes were routed through Genoa, Rotterdam, or Hamburg. The intent was to eliminate actual and potential competition between carriers operating in different port ranges.

The North Atlantic Pool Agreement,[57] whose signatories are the seven largest containership operators on the North Atlantic, would create a comprehensive revenue pool covering nearly all the nonmilitary general cargo carried by its members on the North Atlantic trade routes.[58] The agreement specifies penalty payments for undercarrying or overearning by a member line to discourage cheating, and provides a mechanism for the participants to agree on their service obligations in order to reduce costly service rivalry.

54. FMC Agreement 9813, Transatlantic Freight Conference, Dated August 28, 1969. The eight original signatories of the Transatlantic Freight Conference Agreement were American Export Isbrandtsen Lines, Atlantic Container Line, Dart Containerline, Hamburg-Amerika Line, Moore-McCormack Lines, Norddeutscher Lloyd, Sea-Land Service, and United States Lines. Seatrain Lines later signed the agreement, and Moore-McCormack subsequently withdrew from the North Atlantic trade and hence from the agreement.

55. The phrase "normally serve" and the corresponding concept of "naturally tributary" were not explicitly defined in the agreement or in testimony during the FMC hearing, but they seem to have reference to the port located nearest the shipper or consignee. See the Statement of M. J. Kelly (undated) given at the FMC hearing on Agreement 9813, pp. 19–22. Mr. Kelly, a vice president of Moore-McCormack Lines, was chairman of the New York committee of the carriers who were parties to the agreement.

56. FMC Agreement 9813, Transatlantic Freight Conference, article 6(b).

57. FMC Agreement 10,000, North Atlantic Pool Agreement, Dated November 17, 1971. See FMC Docket 72-17, Exhibit 5, Sept. 11, 1972.

58. The seven member lines and their allocated market shares are American Export Isbrandtsen Lines (8.75 percent), Atlantic Container Line (20.25 percent), Dart Containerline Co. (10.575 percent), Hapag-Lloyd Aktiengesellschaft (14.175 percent), Sea-Land Service (17 percent), Seatrain Lines (11.25 percent), and U.S. Lines (18 percent).

The agreements establishing the Transatlantic Freight Conference and the North Atlantic Pool have presented the FMC with two major competitive issues. Should conferences be permitted to widen their control of competition among ocean carriers by enlarging their geographical boundaries to coincide with the larger geographical dimensions of markets created by technological change? Given what is often described as a situation of overtonnaging and "ruinous competition" on the North Atlantic trade routes,[59] are additional restraints on competition desirable, and, if so, what form should these added restraints take?

The parties to the Transatlantic Freight Agreement argued that, since the primary purpose of the conference system is to enable member lines to control competition among themselves, and since container shipping has made direct competitors of ocean carriers formerly operating in different markets, it is only logical to broaden the conference boundaries to control this new competition, also.[60] Within the context of traditional public policy toward the ocean freight industry, a strong case can be made for a "superconference" such as the Transatlantic Freight Conference would be. If rate competition among carriers is indeed destructive or ruinous, must not this competition be carefully controlled wherever it might appear? Conversely, questioning the desirability of superconferences leads to questioning the desirability of the restraints on trade that are permitted under the existing conference system.

The principal argument made by proponents of ocean shipping cartels is that the size and durability of oceangoing vessels, particularly containerships, give the industry an inherent tendency to overtonnaging or excess capacity—that is, supply tends to overshoot its equilibrium level in responding to changes in demand. This overtonnaging generates downward pressures on rates, as carriers seek to utilize capacity fully in order to cover their large fixed costs. Because of inelastic demand for shipping services and low variable costs in supplying them, however, rates tend to fall below average total costs, eventually forcing exit from the industry and creating a shortage of capacity. Thus, unrestrained price competition is pictured as escalating into "ruinous" or "destructive" competition, leading to alternating periods of overtonnaging and shortages.

It is not the purpose of this chapter to evaluate the overall validity of this argument. Instead, this section will address two more fundamental issues: Has containerization indeed produced overtonnaging on the

59. For example, see "Cooling the Rate War on the North Atlantic," *Business Week* (April 29, 1972), pp. 48–52.
60. Statement of M. J. Kelly, pp. 9–10.

North Atlantic trade? If so, what should the response of public policy be?

There are several conceptual and empirical difficulties in ascertaining whether excess capacity exists on an ocean shipping route. First, optimal capacity is consistent with a utilization rate of substantially less than 100 percent because of directional imbalances (that is, U.S. imports exceed U.S. exports) and seasonal or yearly variations in trade. Second, excess capacity is less likely to develop in ocean shipping than in land transportation such as railroads, since the investment of shipowners is more mobile than that in railroads. For instance, an ocean carrier does not have to construct its own right-of-way, and freedom of the seas is a centuries-old principle of international law. Furthermore, harbors and ports are constructed by governments, not shipowners; and although user charges are imposed on carriers, they probably amount to less than the cost of providing the facilities.[61] The cost of these facilities, while fixed to society in the short run, are thus made variable to carriers. Ocean shipping can also be more responsive to regional shifts in demand than industries in which the plant is tied to a fixed physical location, since vessels may be moved with relative ease from one part of the world where trade is slack or declining to another part where trade is active.[62]

Finally, several phenomena often attributed to overtonnaging, such as declining rates and low levels of capacity utilization, may be explained by other factors, while other phenomena, such as negative profits and exit from the trade, may not demonstrably exist at all. Proponents of the pool agreement point out, for instance, that published conference rates have risen by less than prices generally in recent years, and that, because of malpractices and illegal rebates, actual rates have been considerably lower than published rates. While these facts are consistent with the overtonnaging hypothesis, they are more easily explained by the superior efficiency of containerships over break-bulk vessels.

Likewise, an alternative explanation of the low level of capacity utilization, in addition to the directional imbalance and seasonal variations

---

61. The author was unable to find any data bearing on the relation between the costs of harbor and port development and improvement and user charges. Meyer, however, while recognizing the complexities of constructing user-cost taxation schemes, found that user taxes in effect in 1959 did not cover the costs of inland waterway operations (John R. Meyer and others, *The Economics of Competition in the Transportation Industries* [Harvard University Press, 1959], pp. 122–23).

62. Worldwide overtonnaging does not appear to be a likely possibility with containerships, since containerization has been introduced on trade routes sequentially, depending upon the volume of trade carried on a route, rather than simultaneously.

in trade mentioned above, is that it is caused by the suppression of price competition by the conferences. To the extent that conference lines agree not to use rates as an allocative device, more emphasis is given to such nonprice forms of competition as service rivalry, particularly the use by each line of more vessels and a more frequent schedule of sailings.[63] The greater service to shippers may or may not be worth the additional cost of the increased capacity, but it is clear that it is caused by the restraint of price competition. In addition to increasing the capacity of its members, if a conference, through its pricing policies, earns supernormal profits, more liners and tramps will be attracted to the trade, thus further increasing capacity on the route. Further, if overtonnaging exists, it would be expected to lead to a withdrawal of capacity. Instead, at least two containerships for the North Atlantic trade are now being constructed (the decision to build them having been made in 1970, one year after the alleged overtonnaging was generally identified as a problem), and the pool members are expected to have over 40 percent more container capacity in 1975 than they had in 1970.[64]

Unfortunately, the most important data relevant to the question of overtonnaging—the profitability of shipping activities on the North Atlantic trade—is unavailable, since the finances of the individual shipping lines have been excluded from consideration in the pool hearings. What can be concluded, however, is that the signers of the pool agreement, who do have access to the relevant data, have not made a convincing case that overtonnaging does exist. In fact, an examination of the oil tanker industry, which shares many characteristics with the ocean liner industry, suggests that overtonnaging and ruinous competition are not the inevitable fate of the ocean liner industry.[65] Like the containerized North Atlantic trade, the oil tanker industry has experienced rapid technological change. The industry is capital intensive, fixed costs are two-thirds of total costs, efficient tankers are costly and durable, and both demand and rates have been unstable. Yet concentration is low (the four largest firms account

63. The North Atlantic Pool Agreement seeks to control capacity and service rivalry by penalties for "overearning," or exceeding allotted market share. The domestic airline industry is perhaps the most frequently cited example of how lack of price competition can induce excessive service and capacity rivalry (see Chapter 2).

64. See Docket 72-17, Exhibit 81, Direct Testimony of Allen R. Ferguson on Behalf of the Department of Justice in Agreement No. 10,000, North Atlantic Pool Agreement, p. 13.

65. See Docket 72-17, Exhibit 82, Direct Testimony of Morris A. Adelman on Behalf of the Department of Justice in Agreement No. 10,000, pp. 7–9.

for less than 20 percent of the business), the real cost of tanker services has declined by roughly 73 percent since 1945, the world tanker fleet has increased by a factor of eighteen since the Second World War, and the record of innovation has been impressive—all this without a single conference or pool agreement.

Even if it is assumed, for the sake of argument, that there is overtonnaging on the North Atlantic trade, a pair of questions remain to be answered: Will the excess capacity be chronic, and what ought public policy to do about it? There is reason to believe that excess capacity in a containerized trade will not become chronic. As indicated above, capital requirements for the operation of containerships are great enough to limit severely the number of firms or consortia able to enter the market. In addition to the dollar cost, the time required for entry is significant. The president of Sea-Land has estimated that building an effective containership operation takes two to three years.[66] Given the difficulty of entry into containership operations, any tendency to overtonnaging and ruinous competition should disappear after one "round," and so not be a long-run problem. The industry's high concentration and its conditions of entry can thus be expected to serve as a restraint on actual and potential competition.

If excess capacity is not likely to be a chronic problem on the North Atlantic trade routes, what, if anything, ought public policy to do about excess capacity if it exists now? In this connection, it is important to distinguish between the social and private costs of excess capacity in an industry.[67] Excess capacity involves social waste because scarce resources have been used to construct new capacity whose output is unable to earn enough revenue to recover its cost of production. The social loss from excess capacity is incurred at the time the redundant capacity is constructed, and from then on represents a sunk cost to society. That is, once the investment of resources has occurred, there is no way for society to recapture its loss, and the relevant question then narrows to the efficient use of the excess capacity.

Excess capacity is used efficiently when it is employed as fully as possible, so long as the revenue earned by its output exceeds or equals the variable costs of producing the output. Thus, if there is overtonnaging on a shipping trade route, for instance, the socially efficient use of the excess ca-

66. FMC Docket 69-56, Transcript, p. 2190.

67. This discussion follows the reasoning of Allen Ferguson in his Direct Testimony, cited above.

pacity is to transfer it to another route where it will be profitable, or to continue its use on the unprofitable route, but at lower rates and with greater service in order to stimulate increased utilization. This socially efficient use of excess capacity, however, imposes financial losses on the owners of the excess capacity, since they do not recover the cost of their investment.[68] Some firms may even go into bankruptcy, although their capacity and other physical assets remain in existence for further use. The financial losses to entrepreneurs are real, but they are different from the social waste of excess capacity. Society may decide to prevent financial losses to the owners of excess capacity or to compensate them for the losses, but there can be no recovery of the social waste from excess capacity. In fact, to the extent that public policy acts to discourage full utilization of excess capacity, the social loss is increased.[69]

The Sea-Land–U.S. Lines Merger

In October 1969, Sea-Land Service, Inc., and United States Lines, Inc., filed with the FMC for approval a charter agreement[70] under which Sea-Land would lease for a period of twenty years U.S. Lines' entire containership fleet of sixteen vessels and related equipment. At the expiration of the charter, Sea-Land would have the option of purchasing the containerships and equipment. In November 1970, the R. J. Reynolds Tobacco Company, Sea-Land's parent, entered into an agreement with Walter J. Kidde & Company, U.S. Lines' parent, under which Reynolds would acquire, through a subsidiary, sole ownership and control of U.S. Lines, subject to the prior approval of the FMC.[71] The Antitrust Division of the Department of Justice intervened in the FMC hearings on the two agreements and, challenging the FMC's jurisdiction over mergers between ocean carriers, also filed a suit against the merger, contending that

68. These financial losses result, of course, from mistaken investment decisions made by the owners themselves. If there is overtonnaging of containerships on the North Atlantic trades, it is because the containership lines overestimated demand or underestimated productivity.

69. After this chapter was written, an FMC administrative law judge found the North Atlantic Pool Agreement to be in the public interest and concluded that it should be accepted in principle, subject to certain conditions, for a trial period of three years.

70. FMC Docket 69-56, vol. 5, Agreement No. 9827, dated October 29, 1969, pp. 1–7.

71. FMC Docket 70-51, vol. 8, Agreement of Merger No. 9827-1, p. 9. The agreement provided for the automatic cancellation of both the merger and the previously filed charter agreement if the merger agreement failed to win the approval of the FMC, the ICC, or the Maritime Administration.

it would eliminate actual and potential competition between Sea-Land and U.S. Lines and raise concentration and barriers to entry on the various U.S. Atlantic and Pacific trade routes.[72]

If a merger with the same characteristics as the Sea-Land–U.S. Lines combination were to occur in an unregulated industry, it would almost certainly be found to violate section 7 of the Clayton Act. Given the criteria for determining relevant markets and submarkets set forth by the Supreme Court in the *Brown Shoe* case,[73] the relevant product markets found to be affected by the Sea-Land–U.S. Lines merger are likely to be the services of U.S.-flag full containership systems and all-flag full containership systems. The services of containerships and their supporting systems would likely constitute a relevant submarket under section 7 because of their distinct cost and revenue advantages to operators and their distinct service advantages to shippers. The services of U.S.-flag containerships would also constitute a relevant submarket because the United States' cargo preference laws require that all military cargo shipped by the Department of Defense and at least half the cargo shipped by other agencies of the government in foreign commerce be carried in U.S.-flag bottoms.

On all the U.S. Atlantic and Pacific trade routes taken together, Sea-Land and U.S. Lines are the two largest containership lines, apparently accounting for 57 percent of U.S.-flag full containership capacity (four carriers account for 90 percent) and 36 percent of all-flag full containership capacity (four carriers account for 59 percent).[74] On the North Atlantic trades alone, Sea-Land and U.S. Lines carried 88 percent of all U.S.-flag container cargo and 55 percent of total commercial container cargo during the first half of 1969, and it has been estimated that by 1974, the two companies after merger would have 71 percent of U.S.-flag container capacity and 36 percent of all-flag container capacity.[75]

72. The district court ruled that Congress did not grant the FMC authority over merger agreements when it enacted the Shipping Act of 1916, and denied the FMC's motion to stay the court's proceedings or to dismiss the complaint. See Opinion in *United States* v. *R. J. Reynolds Tobacco Co.*, United States District Court for the District of New Jersey, filed April 7, 1971, 325 F. Supp. 656. The Supreme Court has agreed to review the Pacific Far East Line case, in which the FMC's jurisdiction over merger agreements between ocean carriers is also at issue.

73. 370 U.S. 294.

74. Complaint filed by the United States on December 15, 1970, in the U.S. District Court for the District of New Jersey in *United States* v. *R. J. Reynolds Tobacco Co.*, pp. 9–10.

75. FMC Docket 70-51, vol. 2, Initial Decision of Clarence W. Robinson, Presiding Examiner, dated October 21, 1971, p. 44.

Even in the context of the regulated ocean shipping industry, it is by no means clear that this merger is consistent with established public policy. The Supreme Court in a maritime case has held that "once an antitrust violation is established, this alone will normally constitute substantial evidence that the agreement is 'contrary to the public interest,' unless other evidence in the record fairly detracts from the weight of this factor."[76] Sea-Land, in an effort to show that the merger passes the test set forth in the *Svenska* decision, claimed that the merger would enable it to integrate U.S. Lines' fleet of fast, modern containerships with its own highly efficient system for collecting cargo from and delivering it to points in the interior and in the vicinity of ports through use of its pioneering feeder-ship and relay system. Such integration, according to Sea-Land, would provide extraordinary benefits to shippers and, ultimately, to consumers. Internal expansion, as an alternative to merger, was represented as nonviable because of the delay involved in constructing new containerships and the competitive pressures from foreign lines, whose containership capacity is expected to expand significantly in the 1970s. Sea-Land further argued that, without the merger, U.S. Lines could not continue as a viable operation.

In an initial decision, the FMC ruled that the proposed merger was anticompetitive and not "required by serious transportation need, necessary to secure important public benefits or in furtherance of a valid regulatory purpose of the Shipping Act." It also found that the merger was not necessary to maintain a viable U.S. Lines.[77]

In its final decision, the commission approved the merger on the condition that U.S. Lines be operated as a separate, competing company, independent of Sea-Land.[78] The FMC found U.S. Lines to have fundamental financial problems and Walter Kidde, its parent, to be anxious to dispose of the line. The only alternatives, according to the FMC, were merger with Sea-Land or dismemberment. The conditions attached to approval of the merger agreement, the FMC stated, would prevent the anticompetitive effects attributed to the merger, while still enabling U.S. Lines to receive the financial assistance essential to its viability that only Sea-Land's parent could provide. In its decision, the FMC announced its continuing surveillance of the parties to the agreement to ensure compliance with the conditions set and to watch for the emergence of any anti-

76. *Federal Maritime Commission* v. *Aktiebolaget Svenska Amerika Linien* (*Swedish-American Line*), 390 U.S. 238, 245–46 (1968).

77. See Docket 70-51, Initial Decision of C. W. Robinson, especially p. 43.

78. FMC Report in Dockets 69-56 and 70-51, vol. 4, dated February 12, 1973.

competitive effects. Significantly, the commission noted that "we find that our decision herein is required by our overriding duty to protect the foreign waterborne commerce of the United States; and a very important tool in the implementation of that responsibility is an American merchant marine which is permitted to have active companies as strong financially as the commercially or governmentally mandated conglomerates of foreign merchant marines."[79]

Joint Rates

A third competitive issue raised by containerization involves the legality of joint rates. A joint rate is a single charge established by agreement between two or more carriers operating in different modes of transportation for through service between inland points in the United States and ports or inland points in a foreign country. Containerization has made joint rates practicable because the cumbersome loading, unloading, and reloading necessary for the intermediate transfer of break-bulk cargo has been replaced by the swift transfer of containers from one carrier to another.

Joint rates have become a significant issue because there are now no explicit statutory provisions regarding the filing, approval by a regulatory agency, and antitrust exemption of rate agreements between a conference or group of ocean carriers and a rate bureau or group of domestic surface carriers. The prevailing view is that such rate agreements between groups of carriers subject to the jurisdiction of the FMC and the ICC, respectively, would violate the antitrust laws.[80] Two efforts, one involving express statutory authorization and the other involving extension of the ICC's and FMC's regulatory jurisdiction within existing legislation, have been made to confer antitrust immunity on such approved rate agreements.

The Department of Transportation submitted to Congress a proposed bill, entitled the Trade Simplification Act of 1969, that would permit common carriers engaged in international transportation to enter into agreements to offer joint rates, to issue single bills of lading for through movements, and to interchange or pool equipment and facilities. These agreements would be subject to the approval of each regulatory agency (the ICC, the FMC, and the Civil Aeronautics Board) having jurisdiction

---

79. Ibid., p. 9.
80. "Legal and Regulatory Aspects of the Container Revolution," *Georgetown Law Journal*, vol. 57 (February 1969), pp. 537–44.

over a common carrier that is a party to the agreement, and each agency would have jurisdiction only over that part of the joint rate relating to a carrier ordinarily subject to its jurisdiction. The agencies could also specify in the agreement a division of revenues among the carriers. The proposed bill would not, however, authorize pooling of traffic, services, or earnings. Agreements would be permitted between single carriers in different modes of transportation and between a group of carriers in one mode and a single carrier or group of carriers in another mode. No agreement could prevent any participating carrier from entering into similar arrangements with other carriers. Approved agreements would receive antitrust immunity. The Ninety-first Congress took no action on the bill, however, and the Department of Transportation did not submit a similar bill to the Ninety-second Congress.

In 1969, the FMC and ICC also instituted new rules to facilitate the use of joint and through rates.[81] The FMC amended regulations to require specifically that carriers subject to its jurisdiction file their through-rates for the through transportation of cargo between ports or points in the United States and ports or points in foreign countries, and that a memorandum of every joint rate agreement to which such carriers were a party be filed concurrently with the through-rate tariff. The ICC, under its proposed new rule, would require the filing of tariffs covering international rates offered jointly by a domestic surface carrier subject to ICC jurisdiction and an ocean carrier. Partly because of objections by the FMC, however, the ICC withdrew this proposal.

Through service and the accompanying through or joint rates encourage international trade by enabling shippers to contract with one carrier for the movement of cargo all the way to its destination at a total rate published in a single tariff. Through service and joint rates also facilitate the use of simplified documentation in international intermodal transportation, and stimulate carriers in different modes to provide for efficient coordination and integration of intermodal transportation. It is not clear, however, that an antitrust exemption for rate agreements between shipping conferences and rate bureaus is either necessary or desirable in promoting joint-rate arrangements.

The existing statutory framework presents no legal impediments to agreements between *individual* ocean and inland carriers to offer through service and joint rates; in fact, both are already rather widely available in

---

81. FMC Docket 69-53; ICC Ex Parte 261.

U.S. foreign commerce. Of the more than 500 companies that responded to the shipper questionnaire prepared by the Study Group on Legal Aspects of Intermodal Transportation, 45 percent of the exporting companies and more than one-third of the importing companies reported that they used predominantly single-factor (that is, a rate stated as one amount) through and joint rates.[82] In addition, shippers can now be quoted a total rate for transporting containerized cargo from point of origin to point of delivery by a carrier that has itself purchased from carriers in other modes the services it cannot supply. Ocean carriers are at a disadvantage relative to land carriers or freight forwarders with such an arrangement, however, since the latter are able to extend their transportation networks overseas, being regarded by the FMC as non-vessel-operating common carriers for the water leg of the route. Entry by ocean carriers into domestic surface transportation, on the other hand, is prevented by the certification requirements of the Interstate Commerce Commission.

Public policy ought to encourage, through both legislation and regulatory action, joint-rate agreements between individual carriers in different transportation modes, while at the same time explicitly prohibiting such agreements between groups or conferences of carriers. Competition among pairs of individual carriers is more likely to set joint rates at levels that reflect the economies of containerization and the cost savings of more efficient coordination of intermodal transportation than intergroup rate making, the object of which is invariably to set rates as close as possible to the monopoly level.[83] Where a carrier has significant market power in its own mode, public policy can prevent anticompetitive uses or consequences of joint-rate agreements by prohibiting exclusive dealing, tie-in, and reciprocity arrangements.

Conclusions

The impact of containerization on ocean shipping has brought public policy toward the industry to a crossroads. Containerization has enlarged the geographic dimensions of shipping markets and upset the carriers'

82. Maritime Transportation Research Board, Study Group on Legal Aspects of Intermodal Transportation, *Legal Impediments to International Intermodal Transportation: Selected Problems, Options, and Recommended Solutions* (Washington: National Academy of Sciences, 1971), p. 139.

83. The FMC has only limited control over the rates set by shipping conferences because of dual national sovereignty over transportation in foreign trade.

tight control of competition by means of the conference system. It has also made entry into the major trade routes more difficult by raising substantially the capital costs of providing ocean transportation services. In this context, the FMC and the Congress have been asked to enlarge the regulatory apparatus by approving a more extensive conference covering all North Atlantic trade routes, by approving a comprehensive pool agreement for the North Atlantic trades, by allowing a merger between the two largest U.S.-flag containership lines, and by extending antitrust immunity to joint-rate agreements between groups of carriers in different transportation modes. What is proposed is thus a maintenance of the existing regulatory structure, while improving its effectiveness through changes in the organization, statutory authority, and policy decisions of the regulatory agency. This is only one of the possible options for public policy, however. Two alternatives are briefly discussed here: deregulation, either moderate or extensive, within the framework of the conference system; and a weakened, though still operative, conference system through withdrawal of the American lines.

As was pointed out earlier, if the primary goal of regulatory policy is to correct for the market imperfections that are offered as the initial rationale for regulation, regulatory policy in the ocean shipping industry must be judged to have fallen short of its goal. The close governmental supervision of shipping conferences and their activities, which the Alexander Report saw as the safeguard against the abuse of monopoly power, has simply never become a reality. Indeed, the periodic congressional examinations of the regulatory record prompt the question whether the performance of the industry would have been very different if there had never been any regulation at all.

Part of the explanation of this unsatisfactory record can no doubt be found in organizational defects of the regulatory agency, particularly those found by the Ash Council to exist quite generally: the agency's isolation from the political system and its lack of accountability to Congress or the President; its collegial form and inefficient administrative procedures; the difficulty of attracting and keeping highly qualified commissioners and staff; and the inherent conflict between its dual responsibilities (either legislated or perceived) of promotion and regulation.[84] Ideally, these defects could be corrected through organizational reforms, but compelling evidence is accumulating that they are inherent in all regu-

84. President's Advisory Council on Executive Organization, *A New Regulatory Framework*, pp. 4–7.

lation because of the political environment in which regulatory laws are enacted and regulatory agencies function.[85]

In addition to deficiencies in regulatory performance and in regulatory organization, the efforts of the U.S. government to supervise effectively shipping conferences and their practices have been frustrated by the international character of ocean shipping. Unilateral regulation of the industry necessarily infringes upon the sovereignty of other nations; and an international regulatory effort would be unlikely to succeed because the other major maritime nations do not share the traditional American distrust of cartels and the corollary conviction that they must be closely regulated by a government agency to prevent abuses of their power. Furthermore, shipping interests in those nations exert a stronger influence on governmental policy than their counterparts in the United States, and they can be counted on to use their influence to oppose stricter regulation.

If past regulation of the ocean shipping industry has had little effect on performance, and if even an improved regulatory system offers little promise of significantly changing performance in the future, perhaps the answer lies in the other direction—to rely less on the behavioral constraints imposed by regulation and more on the forces of the market to shape the performance of the industry. One alternative is to begin the process of deregulation with the FMC's refusal to approve superconferences or pool agreements among containership firms. This first step does not require legislation and does not represent a reversal of existing policy, but would signify a determination not to extend further the monopoly power of the conferences.

As a second step, Congress might prohibit dual-rate contracts in order to encourage the entry of and greater competition from independent lines. It might also bring mergers between ocean carriers explicitly within the scope of the Clayton Act, so that such mergers would be subject to the same careful scrutiny for possible anticompetitive effects as those in the industrial sector of the economy. At present, the FMC judges merger agreements between ocean carriers according to the standards of public interest expressed in the Shipping Act of 1916, not according to the provisions of the Clayton Act, and therefore is not as sensitive to the issue of concentration as the courts are. Furthermore, the FMC has no authority to enforce the Clayton Act or to determine violations of it, and past decisions have reflected the commission's discomfort at reconciling evi-

85. For a summary of the evidence, see Noll, *Reforming Regulation: An Evaluation of the Ash Council Proposals.*

dence of potential anticompetitive abuses with its belief that other effects of a merger will produce important public benefits.[86]

Finally, Congress and the regulatory commissions might refuse to confer new antitrust immunities upon the conduct of ocean carriers, particularly upon rate agreements between groups of carriers in different modes of transportation or between an individual carrier in one mode and a group of carriers in another.

A second alternative to the current system—and one that could be carried out simultaneously with the program outlined above—is to continue regulation and the conference system for foreign carriers, but to prohibit U.S. carriers from joining the conferences or abiding by conference agreements. By retaining the conference system, the United States would avoid (or at least minimize) a bitter fight with the governments of the major maritime nations, a fight that would be extremely troublesome for foreign relations in general.

The effect of this stimulus to competition cannot be determined a priori. On the one hand, ocean shipping markets will still be concentrated, and the long history of cooperation between American and foreign shipping lines may have formed attitudes and habits that would enable them to collude tacitly to the same effect as their overt collusion under the existing conference system. Even in this extreme case, however, the performance of the ocean freight industry can be no worse than it is now, and the experience of other industries suggests that persistent monopoly performance is less likely with tacit collusion than with open, formally enforced collusion.

On the other hand, U.S. firms have pioneered the development of container shipping and its related technology, so, since labor costs are a smaller proportion of total costs in container shipping than in break-bulk shipping, the cost disadvantage of U.S.-flag carriers relative to foreign-flag carriers is lessened. This could spur the American firms to take the competitive initiative through innovation and lower freight rates, forcing the foreign lines to follow suit. If the American firms are thus stimulated to compete vigorously, the monopoly power of the conferences would be limited, if not altogether dissipated, and the need for regulation would be correspondingly diminished.

The prospects for attaining a workably competitive market in the ocean shipping industry are not bright, regardless of the policy alter-

86. See especially the initial decision of Chief Hearing Examiner Paul D. Page, Jr., in FMC Docket 69-56, vol. 6, July 28, 1970, pp. 19–34.

native chosen. The industry's structural conditions are not favorable, and its international character largely thwarts efforts to change structure or performance by direct governmental action, either regulatory or anti-trust. A policy aimed at allowing market forces to work their full effects, however, seems more likely to lead to an acceptable outcome than a policy that assists ocean carriers in controlling the forces of competition.

CHAPTER FIVE

Antitrust in the Electric Power Industry

LEONARD W. WEISS

ELECTRIC POWER is often pictured as a "natural monopoly." Yet some competition exists in the industry today, and the possibility of more competition might well be enhanced if the structure of the industry were changed. In recent years, the Antitrust Division of the Department of Justice has adopted an active policy toward the industry. This chapter evaluates the possibilities both for more competition and for various types of antitrust action.

The Potential Role of Competition

The electric power industry is conventionally subdivided into generation, transmission, and distribution components. Generation accounts for about 53 percent of the total costs of the industry, transmission about 12 percent, and distribution about 35 percent.[1] The possibilities for competition vary among the three sectors.

1. Derived from Federal Power Commission, *Statistics of Privately Owned Electric Utilities in the United States, 1968: Classes A and B Companies* (1969), tables 17 and 20 (hereafter referred to as *Statistics of Privately Owned Electric Utilities*). Administration and general expenses and general plant are excluded in these calculations. Depreciation, taxes, interest, and return on equity are estimated at 13 percent of the utility plant assigned to the three sectors. These capital charges are then added to operating, maintenance, and other expenses assigned to these functions and the sums are divided by the total for the three to arrive at these percentages. Customer and sales expenses are assigned to distribution.

Generation

Most important regions could support enough generating plants to permit extensive competition if the plants were under separate ownership and had equal access to transmission and distribution. The physical limits on the size of the market are set by transmission costs, which vary approximately in proportion to distance and inversely with the square of transmission voltages. As the power load has grown, extra-high-voltage transmission (currently 230 to 765 kilovolts) has become profitable, thus greatly reducing the impediment to long-distance transmission.[2] One result has been such spectacular developments as the 850-mile, 750-kilovolt Pacific Northwest–Pacific Southwest intertie, connecting the Columbia River with Los Angeles, and the 600-mile, 500-kilovolt line running from the Four Corners site in New Mexico to Los Angeles. In the more populous parts of the country, the possibility of high-voltage networks makes it technologically feasible for plants anywhere in a wide region to supply any consuming center connected with the network, though costs will still vary with the supplier's location. Much of the new capacity intended to supply the largest load centers is, in fact, being constructed at points more than 100 miles away in order to use local fuel supplies and to reduce air pollution in the more congested areas.

Table 5-1 gives estimates of concentration among bulk-power producers within 100 or 200 miles of ten of the thirteen largest load centers.[3] Although there are at least two bulk-power producers within 100 miles, and several within 200 miles, of each of these cities, the markets are highly concentrated. Their oligopolistic character is reinforced by the present regulatory blockade to entry by large, private bulk-power producers.

Some features of bulk-power transactions, however, tend to make

2. Transmission costs per 100 miles are estimated at 0.66 to 0.90 mill per kilowatt-hour on a 200-kilovolt line, 0.48 to 0.66 on 345 kv, 0.36 to 0.48 on 500 kv, and 0.3 to 0.36 on 700 kv. These estimates are for point-to-point transmission and probably overstate costs where transmission by displacement on an integrated network is possible. At prevailing generation heat rates, the 0.3–0.36–mill cost at 700 kv is competitive with oil or coal by shuttle train, but not with barges or oil or gas pipelines (Federal Power Commission, *The 1970 National Power Survey* [1970], pt. 3, p. 118). In comparison, the national average generation cost is about 8.0 mills per kwh.

3. Seattle-Tacoma, Portland, Oregon, and Knoxville–Oak Ridge, Tennessee, are excluded because the predominance of federal power in those areas makes concentration measures unrepresentative.

Table 5-1. Estimated Concentration in Electric Generating Capacity within 100 and 200 Miles of Ten Major Load Centers, 1968[a]

Load center	Within 100 miles			Within 200 miles		
	Number of firms with greater than 100-megawatt capacity	Share of largest firm (percent)	Share of four largest firms (percent)	Number of firms with greater than 100-megawatt capacity	Share of largest firm (percent)	Share of four largest firms (percent)
New York	12	29	75	18	21	57
Chicago	7	61	93	17	43	67
Los Angeles	6	67	97	8	55	93
San Francisco	2	97	100	8	76	89
Detroit[b]	8	48	90	13	30	75
Philadelphia	9	29	79	19	21	57
Houston	2	79	100	7	44	81
St. Louis	5	52	94	15	24	59
Washington	8	38	79	11	16	57
Boston	6	26	79	14	32	65

Sources: For firms that operate entirely within the market specified, total capacity is from Federal Power Commission, *Statistics of Privately Owned Electric Utilities in the United States, 1968: Classes A and B Companies* (1969), and FPC, *Statistics of Publicly Owned Electric Utilities in the United States, 1968* (1969). Where only part of a firm's capacity is within the market, only the capacities reported in FPC, *Steam-Electric Plant Construction Cost and Annual Production Expenses, Twenty-First Annual Supplement—1968* (1969), and FPC, *Hydroelectric Plant Construction Cost and Annual Production Expenses, Twelfth Annual Supplement, 1968* (1970), are included. Ontario capacities are from Hydro-Electric Power Commission of Ontario, *Annual Report, 1968.*

a. All members of a holding company are treated as a single firm, but members of pools are treated as separate firms. Where data are available, joint ventures are allocated among owners within the specific market in the proportions reported; on an equal-shares basis otherwise. The portion of joint ventures within a market owned by firms otherwise outside the market is considered a single firm. All federal capacity and individual municipals in a market are also treated as owned by a single firm.

b. Includes Hydro-Electric Power Commission of Ontario.

tacit collusion difficult. Sales among bulk-power producers or to distribution utilities or large industrial users (that is, customers that can receive power at high voltage) are often for large blocks of power over long periods of time, and the transactions are very diverse in character. They include long-term sales of blocks of capacity from particular units; long-term sales of blocks of firm power from the supplying system as a whole; sales of interruptible energy; spot sales of "economy" energy arising from the allocation of a region's load among units on the basis of short-run marginal costs; exchanges of "diversity" power to take advantage of different peaks; and sales or exchanges of emergency assistance, with varying limits on the sellers' commitments. Marginal costs vary among the types of transactions, among producers for any given type of transaction, and even within a firm according to the size, timing, and duration of the transaction. Since these sales are large (some in the hundreds of megawatts) and individually negotiated, substantial price competition seems possible in many of the load centers shown in Table 5-1, where regulatory and ownership conditions permit.

In practice, competition among generating companies is impeded by the ownership of transmission and distribution systems by individual generating firms. Transactions involving "wheeling" do occur, but they are voluntary and of minor importance at present.[4] If the owners of transmission lines or systems were treated as common carriers, the generating firms of a region could compete for the loads of independent distribution systems and, conceivably, large industrial users throughout the region.[5] Where generation costs and environmental considerations are similar throughout a region, plants would still tend to supply neighboring load centers, but generating companies would have only limited local monopoly because of potential competition from more distant plants whose costs would exceed theirs by only the extra transmission expense.

The possibility of competition in supplying distribution systems is slight where generation-transmission companies own the distribution systems they serve. An unregulated, profit-maximizing firm is influenced by its potential suppliers even if it is actually integrated; that is, it chooses to make or buy inputs according to the expected effect on its costs, unless integration also enhances its market power. A regulated utility faced with

4. Wheeling refers to transmission by one firm of energy generated by another firm and delivered to a third party—that is, the generating company inputs energy into the transmission system of the intermediate utility, which delivers the same amount of energy to the third firm. The generating company is paid by the customer for the power, and the intermediate firm receives a wheeling charge for the use of its transmission lines. Wheeling differs from a sale of power to and resale by the intermediate firm in that it is the generating company that controls the price. Although the FPC requires voluntary wheeling agreements to be filed with it, it has never regulated wheeling charges. In 1968, privately owned utilities generated 1,022 billion kilowatt-hours, sold 175 billion for resale, and wheeled 33 billion (*Statistics of Privately Owned Utilities, 1968*, p. XLIII).

5. The Supreme Court's interpretation of the interstate commerce clause in *Public Utilities Commission of Rhode Island* v. *Attleboro Steam and Electric Co.*, 273 U.S. 83 (1927), together with the jurisdiction assigned to the FPC in the Federal Power Act of 1935 (16 U.S.C.A. 824[b]-[d]), seem to place sales for resale beyond the reach of state territorial allocation, or "antipirating," laws; but sales to large industrial consumers are retail transactions, and as such would be limited by many states even if wheeling were required by the FPC.

the same choice might tend to favor integration because of the larger rate base that results.

In 1968, privately owned utilities accounted for 77 percent of all energy generated and 75 percent of the energy sold to ultimate customers. Of the 212 Class A and B private electric utilities, only six were pure distribution systems with no generation capacity, and together these accounted for only 0.1 percent of the energy sold to ultimate customers.[6] A more important group of systems purchased a large part of their power while retaining some generating capacity. All Class A and B utilities together purchased about 8 percent of their energy from sources other than affiliated firms and sold about 8 percent to nonaffiliates for resale.[7] It would appear, then, that about 92 percent of *private* sales to ultimate customers, or about 69 percent of *all* sales to ultimate customers, are on a privately owned, vertically integrated basis. Wholesale competition can have only a peripheral effect on this large segment of energy sales.

Bulk-power producers, unless they are combination utilities, also face intermodal competition from other fuels, especially gas. Most studies show a significant positive cross-elasticity of residential demand for electricity with respect to gas, and this seems to increase as electric rates fall and to reach high levels where such appliances as water heaters and electric space heaters are involved.[8] The technical possibilities for inter-

6. *Statistics of Privately Owned Electric Utilities, 1968*, sec. 7. The other pure distribution companies listed there are subsidiaries of other firms with generating capacity (see Moody's Investors Service, *Moody's Public Utility Manual, 1968*).

7. In 1967, privately owned Class A and B utilities generated or received a total of 1,088.6 billion kwh, of which 158.0 billion were purchased and 155.7 billion were sold for resale (*Statistics of Privately Owned Electric Utilities, 1968*, p. XLIII). Their resales were 55.2 billion kwh to affiliated companies, 23.9 billion to nonaffiliated private firms, 23.4 billion to municipalities, and 18.7 billion to cooperatives, for a total of 121.2 billion kwh (FPC, *Sales of Firm Electric Power for Resale, 1965–1967, by Private Electric Utilities, by Federal Projects* [1969], p. 1). If it is assumed that the 34-billion-kwh sales not included in this breakdown involved interruptible energy that was distributed among customer classes in the same proportion as firm power, the estimated total sales to nonaffiliates would be 85 billion kwh, or 7.8 percent of the energy generated or received. Using the same calculations, 71 billion of the 158 billion kwh purchased would be from affiliates, 31 billion from other Class A and B utilities, and 56 billion from other sources (mainly in the form of interruptible energy from federal projects). The estimated purchases from nonaffiliates add up to 87 billion kwh, or 8.0 percent of the energy produced or received. Purchases by privately owned utilities are slightly understated in these calculations because of the exclusion of firms smaller than Class B utilities.

8. The most comprehensive study is John W. Wilson, "Residential and Industrial Demand for Electricity: An Empirical Analysis" (Ph.D. thesis, Cornell University, 1969). His cross-elasticities, estimated in single-equation, cross-section regressions

modal competition are likely to increase with the development of gas air conditioning, which can be integrated into the heating system and thus offer the gas company a much more stable seasonal load curve, and with the expansion of electric heat systems offering similar advantages to consumers and power companies in warmer parts of the country. At the industrial and commercial levels, additional competition may arise from the development of "total-energy" installations, where consumers can profitably produce their own power if they have use for the resulting waste heat. Even at the household level, the fuel cell could conceivably offer a total-energy alternative to electric utility service in the future.

Intermodal competition ordinarily involves duopolistic rivalry, with a competitive fringe occupied by suppliers of other fuels. This may well have an effect on prices, in view of the differing cost functions and seasonal peaks of electricity and gas and of the widespread use by both of disguised promotional price concessions. The prospect of gas shortages or rising prices should mean less pressure on electric rates from intermodal competition in the future.

If intermodal competition does have an effect, one would expect to find combination utilities charging higher rates, unless they can realize economies great enough to offset the effect of any monopoly gain. Most studies confirm that combination utilities do charge higher rates and sell less power per customer than straight electric utilities, though much of this may be due to systematic differences in costs, demand, and regional characteristics. Straight electrics have distinctly higher promotion expense, much of which is really disguised price concessions in the form of free or

---

using electric rates, gas rates, median incomes, degree days, and mean housing unit size as other variables, ranged from 0.18 in a sample of cities with high electric prices to 0.55 in low-price cities. Cross-elasticities seem to be as high as 1.3–1.9 for water heaters and 0.9–1.8 for space heaters. The elasticities of residential demand for electric power are generally more than one and rise with the cross-elasticity, reaching such striking levels as 2.4 for ranges, 3.9 for water heaters, and 6.5 for space heaters. (Wilson, pp. 64–66 and 70.) Other studies that have yielded significant positive effects of gas prices on electric demand are Thomas G. Moore, "The Effectiveness of Regulation of Electric Utility Prices," *Southern Economic Journal*, vol. 36 (April 1970), p. 372; Franklin M. Fisher and Carl Kaysen, *A Study in Econometrics: The Demand for Electricity in the United States* (North-Holland, 1962), pp. 109–10; J. B. Vermetten and Joh. Plantinga, "The Elasticity of Substitution of Gas with Respect to Other Fuels in the United States," *Review of Economics and Statistics*, vol. 35 (May 1953), pp. 140–43; John R. Felton, "Competition in the Energy Market Between Gas and Electricity," *Nebraska Journal of Economics and Business*, vol. 4 (Autumn 1965), pp. 3–12; and unpublished regressions run by the author.

below-cost services. Their relative prices are lowest for high-volume customers, where competition with gas seems most likely.[9] Gas rates of combination companies probably do not differ very significantly from those of straight gas companies,[10] possibly because gas faces more com-

9. See Franklin H. Cook, "Comparative Price Economies of Combination Utilities," *Public Utilities Fortnightly*, vol. 79 (Jan. 19, 1967), pp. 31–39; National Economic Research Associates, *Combination Companies, A Comparative Study* (New York: NERA, 1968); W. A. Collins, "The Social Desirability of Combination Gas-Electric Utilities" (FPC, July 1970; processed); Regina E. Herzlinger, Testimony in *Combination Utility Companies*, Hearings before the Subcommittee on Antitrust and Monopoly of the Senate Committee on the Judiciary, 92 Cong. 1 sess. (1971), pp. 365–69 (reporting on studies made at the FPC in 1966–67); Bruce M. Owen, "Monopoly Pricing in Combined Gas and Electric Utilities," *Antitrust Bulletin*, vol. 15 (Winter 1970), pp. 713–26; Paul S. Brandon, "The Electric Side of Combination Gas-Electric Utilities," *Bell Journal of Economics and Management Science*, vol. 2 (Autumn 1971), pp. 688–703; J. Landon, "Electric and Gas Combination and Economic Performance," Working Paper 28 (Case Western Reserve University, 1971); and J. D. Pace, statement submitted to the Senate Subcommittee on Antitrust and Monopoly (Aug. 27, 1971; processed). The first six studies all show higher residential rates and lower per capita consumption for combination utilities. The first four compare means for various performance variables taken one at a time. Owen, Landon, and Pace all use single-equation, multiple regression models, controlling for various demographic and cost variables, and Brandon uses a simultaneous equation model.

Landon and Pace found that combination had no significant effect on average residential revenue once demographic, climate, and cost variables were controlled for, though Landon showed that combinations have significantly lower selling costs and profit rates. Pace also worked with typical electric bills, finding that straight electric customers had nonsignificantly higher bills at the 250 kilowatt-hour level, but lower bills at 500, 750, and 1,000 kilowatt-hours. The difference between combination and straight electrics was greater, the larger the monthly usage, but even at 1,000 kilowatt-hours was only marginally significant. Both Landon and Pace explain rate levels in part with endogenous variables such as volume, fuel prices, and tax per kilowatt-hour or per dollar of revenue. If combination companies are less prone to price promotionally, if they are able to attain lower fuel (especially gas) prices, and if they maintain more plant per kilowatt-hour (and therefore pay more property tax), they might still display higher rates in a complete, simultaneous equation model. Brandon did find a mild tendency for combinations to have higher average residential revenues and lower average residential demand in a simultaneous system that included cost, average revenue, and demand equations, though significance levels were very low. Owen, Landon, and Pace all introduce regional variables. Since straight electrics are heavily concentrated in the South and combinations in the North, it is difficult to distinguish the effect of region from that of combination.

10. The NERA study shows slightly lower gas revenue per million cubic feet for combination companies; Herzlinger found higher overall average rates but lower rates in individual consumer classes; and Owen shows a positive but not significant effect. Collins merely reports that the effect of combination on gas rates, costs, and sales was not significant. In general, the data on gas are poorer than those on electric power, and the samples used differed greatly among the four studies.

petition from other fuels than does electricity, so that a combination company is inclined to discriminate in favor of gas customers.[11]

An additional effect of combination utilities may be to encourage the off-peak consumption of gas as boiler fuel. The marginal off-peak cost of gas to a combination utility is equal to the pipeline commodity charge, whereas a straight electric utility will commonly have to buy from a gas distribution utility at a price that more completely exploits the distributor's monopoly. The available evidence does show a tendency for combinations to burn more gas.

A sample of forty-five straight electric companies and thirty-nine combination companies was examined.[12] Gas accounted for almost the same percentage of total British thermal units consumed for both; but both figures were inflated by the utilities in gas-exporting states that burn mostly gas. If these are excluded, the straight electric companies burn 8.7 percent (with a standard error of 3.2) and the combination companies, 25.3 percent (standard error, 5.3).[13] The following regression can be estimated from the data (the numbers in parentheses are t-statistics):

$$PCT\ GAS = 23.6 + 12.1\ COMB + 78.7\ GX - 0.012\ M$$
$$\quad\quad\quad\ (2.85)\quad (2.17)\quad\quad\quad (8.59)\quad (-1.70)$$

$$\bar{R}^2 = 0.61;\ \text{degrees of freedom} = 84 - 4 = 80,$$

where $PCT\ GAS$ is percentage of Btus by gas, $COMB$ is a dummy with a value of one if the firm is a combination utility, GX is a dummy with a

11. Suggested in John H. Landon and John W. Wilson, "An Economic Analysis of Combination Utilities," *Antitrust Bulletin*, vol. 17 (Spring 1972), pp. 237–68.

12. The sample consisted of all companies listed in the NERA study (*Combination Companies*), except Idaho Power, Puget Sound Power and Light, and Washington Water Power, none of which had any important fossil fuel plants. The reported percentages were based on the amounts of fuels used and the British thermal unit (Btu) per unit reported in FPC, *Steam-Electric Plant Construction Cost and Annual Production Expenses, Twenty-First Annual Supplement—1968* (1969), and exclude some of the smaller plants of the reporting firms and a good deal of their peaking capacity.

13. The gas-exporting states excluded are Texas, Oklahoma, Louisiana, Kansas, and New Mexico, plus Montana Power Company, a combination utility that supplies its plants with gas from its own wells and gas imported from Canada. A case might be made for excluding the California utilities, also, since they had to burn gas for environmental reasons during much of 1968; the percentages would then be 6.6 percent (standard error, 2.3) for the straight utilities and 23.5 percent (standard error, 5.1) for the combinations.

value of one for gas-exporting states, and M is the number of miles from Wichita Falls, Texas.

If field prices of gas accurately reflected its social value, the greater use of gas as boiler fuel by combination utilities might be considered a virtue, but if field prices are uneconomically low, combination utilities are burning excessive amounts of this fuel.

In addition to the limited direct competition at the wholesale level and the intermodal competition faced by straight electric utilities, there is active, though indirect, rate competition for industrial load. Although electric power is a small part of total costs for most manufacturing industries, the industries in which it is important account for about half of the total industrial load.[14] These heavy industrial users pay very low rates, partly because they choose low-rate locations and partly because of the special rates set for high-load customers. Estimates of the elasticity of industrial demand are quite high, especially for such industries as chemicals and primary metals, where electric power costs are important.

In his thorough study of industrial demand, Wilson,[15] using single-equation, cross-section regressions, found that electric rates had significant effects on industrial electric consumption in at least nine of the fourteen two-digit industries he examined. He estimated elasticities to be in the neighborhood of 1.3–1.5, controlling for value added and, in some cases, for fuel prices, capital intensity, and growth. It is possible that Wilson's results depend on his single-equation estimation method, and that the elasticities he found are caused by declining costs in electric power production. As a check on this possibility, a seven-equation model was constructed by Klein in which residential, commercial, and industrial rates depended on volume and appropriate exogenous variables and where each type of demand depended on the relevant rates for a sample of thirty-two utilities. Wilson's high elasticities held up in this model, the tentative overall elasticity of industrial demand being 1.42.[16]

14. In 1962, the seventeen four-digit manufacturing industries whose electricity purchases exceeded 3 percent of the value of shipments accounted for 48 percent of all kilowatt-hours purchased by manufacturers (U.S. Bureau of the Census, *Census of Manufactures, 1963*, vol. 1, *Summary and Subject Statistics* (1966), chap 7, table 2); Bureau of the Census, *Annual Survey of Manufactures, 1962*, chap. 2, table 1.

15. In "Residential and Industrial Demand for Electricity," using the logarithmic regressions in tables 4 and 5.

16. J. Douglass Klein, "Single Equation versus Simultaneous Equation Estimation of the Demand for Electric Power" (paper prepared for a seminar, University of Wisconsin, 1971; processed).

Other estimates yielding high elasticities of industrial demand have
been made by Fisher and Kaysen, and Peltzman.[17] Both studies are based
on single-equation, cross-section estimates. Their elasticity estimates may
partially reflect the declining block pattern of rates, since they used industrial electric revenue per kilowatt-hour as their price variable, but many of
Wilson's estimates are based on typical electric bills for industrial users
at uniform levels of demand, thus avoiding the danger of bias.[18]

From the point of view of a utility, demand may be even more responsive than these estimates suggest, since heavy industrial load is likely to
carry with it additional employment, and hence increased residential and
commercial demand, as well. Indirect competition, however, is naturally
less likely to be important in areas such as the Northeast that have high
electric rates.

Transmission and Distribution

There seem to be sharply increasing returns to scale in transmission,
at least within the range of voltage now in use.[19] It follows that additional
transmission lines beyond the number needed for reliability would normally be undesirable. Additional transmission capacity is, of course,
required as demand grows; but, due to the increasing difficulty of acquiring additional right-of-way, it is often created by the replacement of
existing lines with others of higher voltage rather than by the construction
of parallel lines. As a result, it is unlikely that much competition in transmission can be expected through the construction of additional facilities
in the way that additional pipelines have sometimes served to permit
competition in the transmission of natural gas. In short, transmission
qualifies as a classic "natural monopoly."

The ownership of transmission lines can be used to impose more
monopoly in generation or more vertical integration on the power in-

17. Fisher and Kaysen, *A Study in Econometrics*, pp. 120–42; Sam Peltzman,
"Pricing in Public and Private Enterprises: Electric Utilities in the United States,"
Journal of Law and Economics, vol. 14 (April 1971), p. 139.

18. R. E. Baxter and R. Rees, in "Analysis of the Industrial Demand for Electricity," *Economic Journal*, vol. 78 (June 1968), pp. 277–98, did find less elastic demands
in a number of industries, but their work is based on time series data and so cannot
reflect the effect of interregional competition within the power industry.

19. Transmission capacity increases as the square of voltage, while cost of construction is about proportional to voltage for extra-high-voltage installations (FPC,
1970 National Power Survey, p. I-14-5).

dustry, or both, than is technically necessary. How transmission lines are owned can thus be crucial in determining the competitive possibilities of the industry. Perhaps the most competitive organization of the industry would be public ownership of transmission lines such as occurred in Britain in the interwar years.[20] If, as seems probable, transmission remains in private hands, competition at the generating level could be inhibited unless line owners are required to interconnect with and wheel power for other generating and distribution companies. While the FPC can require interconnection, it has ruled that it does not have the power to require wheeling,[21] and, indeed, does not now regulate wheeling charges.

It is widely believed that interutility competition in distribution would involve excessive costs due to duplicate distribution plants.[22] If so, this would rule out direct competition for most residential, commercial, and small industrial loads at the local level. Economies in distribution seem to arise from increased load densities and are little affected by the absolute size of distribution systems, as the following regression demonstrates. A sample of thirty privately owned utilities was randomly chosen, except that utilities serving standard metropolitan statistical areas with more than one million population were excluded to avoid the effect of extensive underground distribution in large cities. Distribution and sales costs *DC* per kilowatt-hour *kwh* were found to be closely correlated with load density but not significantly affected by number of customers served *C* (the numbers in parentheses are *t*-statistics):

$$\frac{DC}{kwh} = 1.15 - \underset{(-6.1)}{0.000029} \frac{kwh}{C} - \underset{(-0.8)}{0.00000008} \ C.$$

$$\bar{R}^2 = 0.58, \text{ degrees of freedom} = 27.[23]$$

20. William G. Shepherd, *Economic Performance Under Public Ownership* (Yale University Press, 1965), p. 6. Harold Demsetz suggests public ownership of distribution systems as a means of facilitating competitive bidding by utilities ("Why Regulate Utilities?" *Journal of Law and Economics*, vol. 11 [April 1968], p. 63).

21. *City of Paris, Kentucky* v. *Kentucky Utilities Company, Public Utility Reports*, vol. 70, 3d series (1967), p. 475; ibid., vol. 80, 3d series (1969), p. 331. The ruling applied specifically to municipal utilities and did not address the issue of wheeling to privately owned distribution utilities. See the discussion of the *Otter Tail* case below.

22. Although see Chapter 6, where Primeaux presents evidence that duopoly does not systematically increase unit costs for smaller municipal utilities.

23. Firms reported in *Statistics of Privately Owned Electric Utilities, 1968. DC* included distribution, customer accounts, and sales expenses reported in sec. 5, plus 13 percent of the distribution plant costs shown in sec. 6. Total number of customers and kilowatt-hour sales are both from sec. 4.

The addition of C^2 to the equation adds nothing to its explanatory value and, in fact, reduces $\bar{R}^2$.

There would thus seem to be no technical barrier to the existence of many geographically small distribution systems in an area. Some direct competition at the retail level may be possible (if not prevented by state territorial assignments or antipirating laws) for larger industrial loads that are close enough to service area boundaries to make the extension of transmission lines across such boundaries feasible or where open land between distribution utilities is being developed. However, the main sources of retail competition will remain intermodal competition, competition to attract new industrial load, and possibly "yardstick competition" in dealings with regulatory agencies. Both of the latter would be enhanced by the presence of many distribution utilities within a region, each with access to the various generation sources of the region on a competitive basis.

The Costs of Competition

Would the net effect of increased competition in the electric power industry be beneficial? This section examines various dimensions of the industry to attempt to answer this question.

Economies of Scale and Pooling

A number of independent bulk-power producers large enough to assure competition within a region may or may not be consistent with the attainment of the greatest possible economies of scale in generation. Optimal capacity for boiler-generator units is large and has grown faster than demand in the post–Second World War years.[24] But whether optimal scale will continue to increase at such a pace in the future is doubtful. Increases in the frontier unit scales regularly brought improvements in

---

24. The largest single unit was 208 megawatts in 1950 and 1,028 megawatts in 1965 (FPC, *National Power Survey, 1964* [1964], pt. 1, p. 14; FPC, *1970 Fiftieth Annual Report*, p. 19). Excluding these two cases, maximum new unit size rose from 200 megawatts in 1952 to 950 megawatts in 1967 (FPC, *1952 Annual Report*, p. 126; FPC, *Steam-Electric Plant Construction Cost—1967*, list of plants by state, notes). These approximately five-fold increases in scale were accompanied by a little greater than three-fold growth in generation from 1950 through 1965.

heat rates and capital savings in the last two decades,[25] but the gains in thermal efficiency virtually ended by 1966, as pressures stopped rising.[26] They will undoubtedly fall as nuclear units become more important. Moreover, the capital economies of large units seem to be at least partially offset by their declining reliability. Low reliability is to be expected from the first few units of a newly attained scale, but the high forced outage rates for units over 200 megawatts (far short of the frontier) have persisted throughout the 1960s and seem to have become, if anything, more severe.[27]

Present forecasts show unit sizes growing no faster than demand in the future, and probably more slowly. The maximum scales of the FPC's projected new units increase from 1,028 megawatts for 1965–69 to 1,300 megawatts for 1972–79.[28] Since load doubles in the space of about a decade, maximum unit size should grow more slowly than demand through the period covered by already planned additions. Over the longer range, less concrete projections indicate increases in scale through 1990 that are proportionately much smaller than expected increases in demand.[29] If these expectations are fulfilled, the large increase in optimal scale relative to demand in the 1950s and 1960s will turn out to be a one-time change rather than a trend.

Much of the capacity installed to date has involved unit sizes far inside the frontier scale. Firms that have built such plants may now begin to increase unit sizes faster than frontier growth rate. Moreover, the growing shortage of suitable sites may result in larger, multiunit plants, particularly in tidewater areas where cooling water capacity is not a limiting factor.

---

25. William R. Hughes, "Scale Frontiers in Electric Power," in William M. Capron (ed.), *Technological Change in Regulated Industries* (Brookings Institution, 1971), pp. 60–67.

26. FPC, *Steam-Electric Plant Construction Cost—1969*, table 9.

27. Edison Electric Institute, *Report on Equipment Availability for the Nine-Year Period 1960–1968* (EEI, 1969), and *Report on Equipment Availability for the Ten-Year Period 1960–1969* (EEI, 1970). See also C. C. Boone, "Financial Impact of Outages" (paper presented at American Electric Power Conference, 1969; processed). Paul MacAvoy and Stephen Breyer report that industry sources attribute the higher forced outage rates to a decline in the quality of new equipment generally rather than increased scales.

28. *1970 Annual Report; Steam-Electric Plant Construction Cost—1969*, table 7.

29. FPC, *1970 National Power Survey*, pt. 2, p. II-2-73. These predictions suggest that maximum unit capacities will grow to 1.5 to 2.5 times present maxima over the two decades, while total load will roughly quadruple.

An increase in plant concentration is unlikely to be forced by changing optimal unit sizes as it was during the 1950s and 1960s, but some increase may still occur as smaller systems adjust to changes in optimal scale and as plant sites are used more intensively.

There are extensive multiplant economies in generation. Large systems can attain economies because of large units, reduced need for reserves relative to system load, and greater diversity of load. Such gains continue almost indefinitely as system size increases, but they become marginally very small in the largest systems. One estimate suggests economies for systems up to 25,000 megawatts or beyond in 1980.[30] Engineering estimates show *some* economies with larger scale coordination almost indefinitely, but they do not take into account most of the variables that can yield increasing costs. In contrast, the two available empirical studies of economies of scale for firms, as opposed to plants, show distinct minimum efficient scales beyond which unit costs are about constant or may even increase.[31] Given expected growth between 1968 and 1980 and diseconomies ignored in engineering estimates, minimum efficient system size in densely populated areas might have been 5,000 or 10,000 megawatts in 1968. If all generating companies were of this size, the opportunities for competition would be quite limited. Half the load centers shown in Table 5-1 were too small to support two 5,000-megawatt firms within a 100-mile radius, and only New York, Chicago, and Philadelphia could support more than two; within a 200-mile radius, only Chicago and the four East Coast cities could have supported more than one 10,000-megawatt firm.

There are two main alternatives to huge multiunit firms: closely co-

30. G. C. Hurlbert, "Power Generation in the 1970's," in *1969 Future Power Forum: Perspective for the 70s* (Westinghouse, 1969), p. 78. This roughly agrees with Hughes's "benchmark standard" of twenty to thirty major planning units for the United States ("Scale Frontiers in Electric Power," p. 76). Hurlbert sees "dramatic" savings up to about 15,000 megawatts and greatly diminished ones beyond the 25,000 mark.

31. J. Johnston, *Statistical Cost Analysis* (McGraw-Hill, 1960), pp. 72–73; Marc Nerlove, "Returns to Scale in Electricity Supply," in Carl F. Christ and others, *Measurement in Economics: Studies in Mathematical Economics and Econometrics in Memory of Yehuda Grunfeld* (Stanford University Press, 1963), pp. 175–83. Nerlove may have understated the economies of system scale by treating members of holding companies as independent firms, but the economies of scale in even his middle-size classes were not very great. He found increasing unit costs in his largest-size class. Suilin Ling, in *Economies of Scale in the Steam-Electric Power Generating Industry: An Analytical Approach* (North-Holland, 1964), also deals with firms, but his is mainly an ex ante engineering study and ignores transmission costs.

ordinated pools, or widespread individual contracts among independent but strongly interconnected utilities for firm power, emergency assistance, and exchanges of diversity power and economy energy.

The closely coordinated pools developed over the last decade commonly involve joint projections of demand, joint planning of capacity on a joint-venture or staggered-construction basis, and shared reserves. A few have established joint dispatching, and virtually all provide for sale of economy energy on predetermined terms. Whether such pools are adequate substitutes for common ownership depends on the ability of the partners to reach optimal agreements about timing, location, scale, and technology of new capacity and how it is to be shared among the members; about the level of reserves—what firm is to carry them and how it is to be compensated; and about the terms and conditions for sales of economy energy. Conventional terms for the exchange of economy energy involve the short-run incremental costs of the supplying utility plus half the difference between its incremental cost and the buyer's decremental costs. This rule offers savings to both parties and should result in an efficient allocation of output among existing power sources. At least some of the newest and most complex pools (the New York Pool and the New England Power Pool) have been able to establish joint dispatching early in their histories, although even without it, firms can attain most of the same economies by daily, or even more frequent, "shopping" among their pool neighbors.[32]

The most crucial decisions are probably those about new capacity and reserves. Compensation terms that produce efficient decisions seem feasible, but the bargaining process could result in suboptimal agreements. The success of voluntary pooling agreements might be expected to depend on the number of pool members and their relative sizes: many members tend to make agreement more difficult, and a firm that is much larger than its partners would have relatively little to gain from sharing reserves and new capacity and thus little incentive to reach economically efficient agreements.

For example, if the cost of a new unit is allocated in proportion to the amounts of firm power taken by the participants, the large partner would have little to gain over building new capacity himself, while the

32. William R. Hughes, "Short-Run Efficiency and the Organization of the Electric Power Industry," *Quarterly Journal of Economics*, vol. 76 (November 1962), pp. 592–612.

small firm would realize large economies. If the gains from pooling were shared on some other basis, the large firm might have more incentive to participate, but accounting costs to individual firms would then differ from true long-run marginal costs, so that uneconomic decisions could result. The division of gains from reserve sharing raises similar problems. Large firms tend to prefer reserve requirements equal to fixed percentages of the participants' largest units, while small firms seek rules by which members maintain reserves of a specific percentage of their loads or pay penalties to their partners for reserve deficiencies.

Voluntary pooling thus seems most likely to be successful if the pool contains only a few members of roughly the same size. The feasibility of individually negotiated contracts for reserves and new capacity, however, is even more dependent on firms of roughly comparable size. It follows that the case for mergers among small bulk-power producers in an area is good, while mergers that would increase the size of larger firms in a region would make effective pooling more difficult.

The regressions shown in Table 5-2 represent an attempt to evaluate existing pools in terms of the unit sizes installed. The dependent variable in each case was the capacity of new steam units installed in 1967–69 or for which plans were announced by 1969 for pools and nonpool companies. Unit capacity was regressed on trend, on a dummy with a value of one if the unit was nuclear, on either 1968 pool capacity (equations [1] and [3]) or 1968 firm capacity (equations [2] and [4]), and on a separate dummy for each pool. Equations (1) and (2) show results for all large units installed in or planned for 1967 through 1979. But, since many pools were organized only in the late 1960s, equations (3) and (4) show units planned for 1972 or later.

In equations (1) and (3), the "pool capacity" variable was the 1968 capacity of the relevant pool for units installed by members five years or more after the pool was formed, and the capacity of the installing firm otherwise. If capacity planning is as well coordinated in a pool as in a holding company of the same size, the coefficient for an individual pool's dummy should be zero. That is, one would not expect a pool to build units any larger than those installed by a single firm of the same size, so the test is whether the dummy coefficients fall significantly below zero. Such a one-tailed test indicates that for 1972–79, only MOKAN, CAPCO, CCD, INTERPOOL, the Wisconsin Pool, and perhaps the Michigan Pool did not plan units significantly smaller than nonpool firms of the same size; but members of the other thirteen pools built or planned significantly smaller units than would have been predicted from their pool sizes.[33]

In equations (2) and (4), unit capacities were regressed on firm sizes for pool members and nonpool companies alike. One would not expect pool members to build smaller units than nonpool firms of the same size, so the test here is whether the coefficients for the individual pool dummies are significantly greater than zero. Using a one-tailed test reveals that MOKAN, CAPCO, CCD, INTERPOOL, CARVA, the Michigan Pool, the Florida Interconnected System, PJM, and CALPP do build units larger than those built by nonpool firms of the same size, but that members of the other ten pools do not build significantly larger units.

These regressions probably understate the accomplishments of pools. Some of the nonpool firms with which pool members were compared have close interconnections with nearby firms and can install units that depend in part on transactions with those neighbors. Moreover, in the case of joint ventures, the firm capacity used is that of the largest participant; for example, the joint venture units installed by the WEST group are treated as built by Southern California Edison, and the various New England "Yankees" are treated as built by Northeast Utilities. These joint venture units are much larger than what some of the smaller participants could build individually.

Altogether, several of the pools seem about as well coordinated as firms of the same size, and about half offer some increase in scale to their largest members.[34] Probably most offer increased scale to their smaller members. In addition to larger scale, pools can offer their members greater reliability and economies from reserve sharing, diversity, and

33. The largest pools (NYPOOL, CALPP, and especially the WEST group and PJM) are considerably larger than the largest firm, the Tennessee Valley Authority. It may well be that units of the scale projected by a linear regression for these pools were not available or were not yet economical at the date of observation.

34. The regressions shown in Table 5-2 were also run with the expected percentage growth in load from 1970 to 1980 for the power supply areas in the region of the new unit (as reported in *The 1970 National Power Survey*). This growth variable always had a negative coefficient, significantly so in equation (4). This unexpected result seems to be due to a mild negative correlation between region growth and pool strength. With growth included, the results for individual pools were about the same as those shown in the table. A log-log form of the same regressions was also attempted, with similar results, but the coefficients for the Michigan Pool, CALPP, and the Florida Interconnected System then become statistically insignificant in equations corresponding to (2) and (4) in the table.

Table 5-2. Coefficients Relating Steam Unit Sizes Installed or Planned, 1967–79, to Electric Power Pool or Firm Sizes and to Particular Pools[a]

Variable or summary statistic	1967–79 installations		1972–79 installations	
	Equation (1) Controlling for pool capacity	Equation (2) Controlling for firm capacity	Equation (3) Controlling for pool capacity	Equation (4) Controlling for firm capacity
Variable				
Constant	475.9[b]	386.0[b]	388.2[b]	311.8[b]
	(13.9)	(11.8)	(5.0)	(4.6)
Trend (t–1967)	19.2[c]	19.8[c]	26.6[c]	24.0[c]
	(5.2)	(6.0)	(3.6)	(3.5)
Nuclear unit dummy	128.1[b]	120.7[b]	139.0[b]	138.9[b]
	(6.0)	(6.2)	(4.9)	(5.5)
1968 pool capacity	0.023[b]	...	0.028[b]	...
	(7.1)		(5.7)	
1968 firm capacity	...	0.033[b]	...	0.037[b]
		(10.7)		(8.3)
Pool dummies[d]				
Missouri-Kansas Pool	3.2	170.8	55.6	253.0
(MOKAN)	(0.04)	(2.4)	(0.6)	(2.6)
Central Area Power Coordination group	−26.3	115.6	−100.2	130.4
(CAPCO)	(−0.5)	(2.2)	(−1.3)	(1.7)
Cincinnati, Columbus, Dayton Pool	−27.4	96.9	−14.0	129.1
(CCD)	(−0.5)	(1.7)	(−0.2)	(1.6)
Intercompany Pool	−37.1	77.9	−49.4	87.1
(INTERPOOL)	(−0.6)	(1.3)	(−0.6)	(1.1)
Carolinas-Virginia Power Pool	−126.1	106.2	−191.9	130.4
(CARVA)	(−3.4)	(2.9)	(−4.1)	(2.5)
Wisconsin Power Pool	−16.5	29.8	−11.8	42.6
	(−0.2)	(0.5)	(−0.1)	(0.5)
Michigan Pool	−71.8	69.7	−73.9	103.9
	(−1.5)	(1.5)	(−1.0)	(1.4)
Florida Interconnected System	−116.0	68.0	−105.3	117.7
	(−2.2)	(1.3)	(−1.4)	(1.6)
Pennsylvania–New Jersey–Maryland Interconnection (PJM)	−319.9	166.7	−403.3	186.7
	(−6.1)	(5.3)	(−5.6)	(3.9)
California Power Pool	−173.9	68.7	−228.1	76.6
(CALPP)	(−2.8)	(1.4)	(−3.0)	(1.3)
Illinois-Missouri Pool	−142.6	10.7	−165.1	25.7
(ILL-MO)	(−3.2)	(0.2)	(−2.4)	(0.4)

Table 5-2. Continued

Variable or summary statistic	1967–79 installations		1972–79 installations	
	Equation (1) Controlling for pool capacity	Equation (2) Controlling for firm capacity	Equation (3) Controlling for pool capacity	Equation (4) Controlling for firm capacity
Kentucky-Indiana Power Pool (KIP)	−159.5 (−2.3)	−33.2 (−0.5)	−153.8 (−1.7)	−1.7 (−0.02)
New England Power Pool (NEPOOL)	−258.9 (−5.3)	24.8 (0.5)	−273.1 (−2.9)	58.7 (0.6)
South Central Electric Companies (SCEC)	−256.4 (−6.4)	16.0 (0.4)	−288.4 (−5.5)	43.5 (0.8)
Upper Mississippi Valley Power Pool (UMVPP)	−186.3 (−5.3)	−31.0 (−0.4)	−366.3 (−3.2)	−145.3 (−1.3)
Iowa Pool	−206.7 (−2.0)	−84.5 (−0.9)	−191.6 (−1.6)	−53.0 (−0.5)
Western Energy Supply and Transmission Associates (WEST)	−339.5 (−4.6)	−28.7 (−0.5)	−463.3 (−4.1)	−69.1 (−0.8)
New York Power Pool (NYPOOL)	−337.6 (−6.4)	−41.7 (−1.0)	−408.4 (−5.8)	−26.1 (−0.4)
Texas Interconnected System (TIS)	−328.5 (−6.8)	−63.9 (−1.7)	−423.1 (−5.7)	−100.6 (−1.6)
Summary statistic				
$\bar{R}^2$	0.5245	0.6085	0.5116	0.5960
Degrees of freedom	244	244	147	147

Sources: FPC, *Steam-Electric Plant Construction Cost—1967, 1968*, and *1969*, notes to data sheets for individual plants, and ibid., *1969*, table 7. Pool memberships were determined from descriptions in FPC, *The 1970 National Power Survey* (1971), pts. 2 and 3.

a. Each unit was a separate observation, and only units of 500 megawatts or larger were included because planned fossil-fuel units of smaller capacity are not reported in the source. Units planned were those planned as of 1969 for 1972–79. All units installed by pool members five years or more after the pool began were assigned to the pool. All capacity of a holding company is treated as that of a single firm. The Tennessee Valley Authority, the Nebraska state system, and individual municipal utilities or cooperative associations were also treated as firms. Joint venture units were assigned to the largest participating firm. Southern California Edison and San Diego Gas and Electric were treated as members of the CALPP except for units explicitly planned with the WEST group. Units installed before 1971 by members of the old Upstate Interconnected Systems and the Southeastern New York Power Pool were assigned the NYPOOL dummy and given pool capacities equal to the 1968 capacities of the members of the older pools. The numbers in parentheses are *t*-statistics.

b. Megawatts.

c. Megawatts per year.

d. The coefficients for all the pool dummies are in megawatts.

exchanges of economy energy. Even the seemingly weakest pools in Table 5-2 are probably useful undertakings, all things considered. Since the majority of the pools are still quite young, it is likely that more will attain full pool-sized units in the future. On the other hand, even pool-sized units may be suboptimal if the pool is small; the Wisconsin (1,845 megawatts in 1971) and Iowa (2,614 megawatts in 1968) Pools, for instance, seem too small to win all the economies of scale without transactions outside the pool. A compensating virtue of pools is that they can be more easily rearranged than mergers if it appears that changes are required.

As an alternative to pools or large firms, many of the economies of scale might be attained through individually negotiated contracts for firm power, unit power, diversity exchange, economy energy, and emergency power. The administration of such contracts would involve continuous coordination of operations among the contracting firms, but the basic negotiations for each contract could still be conducted separately. There has been little experience with such bilateral contracts among interconnected systems that are not affiliated with pools. Some firms with strong interconnections but no formal pool agreement have built units that were much larger than their own loads would have permitted, presumably because they were able to buy and sell capacity and share reserves with other firms. This is true of the newest units installed or planned by the New England Gas and Electric Association, which buys and sells capacity and reserves with other unaffiliated New England systems; those of Northern Indiana Public Service and of Central Illinois Electric and Gas (before its acquisition by Commonwealth Edison), both of which benefited from close interconnections with Commonwealth Edison; those of the Sacramento Municipal Utility District because of its interconnection with Pacific Gas and Electric; and those of Florida Power and the Orlando and Jacksonville municipal utilities due to their access to the Florida Interconnected System.[35]

Economies of Combination and Integration

There are probably some economies to be gained from combining gas and electric systems, but they do not appear to be large. The most likely sources of such economies are customer costs (meter reading and billing),

35. Both the New England and Florida interconnections are treated as pools in Table 5-2, but neither is described as a closely coordinated pool in the *National Power Survey* or in interviews at the FPC. In each case, the utility's largest unit had a capacity of more than one-third of the utility's own load when installed. The dissolution of the CARVA pool in 1970 does not seem to have resulted in any reduction in unit sizes installed. Its former members have continued to announce "pool-sized" units.

sales (the avoidance of mutually offsetting promotion), some regulatory activities (right-of-way and service extension matters), possibly fuel prices (off-peak gas), and some administrative personnel. The last can offer only small gains at best, since all but the top personnel are specialized. The gain from promotion is also small, because sales constitute only 1.7 percent of total operating revenues and because some of the expenses involved benefit consumers through education or as disguised price reductions in the form of low-cost services. The fuel price advantages might be characterized as a pecuniary rather than a real economy, since they may induce uneconomic use of gas because of other distortions in gas prices. The most concrete economies might be expected in customer accounting, but, again, this cost category accounts for only a small part (2.5 percent) of total electric revenues.[36]

The divestitures of gas subsidiaries under sections 8 and 11 of the Public Utility Act of 1935 involved a good deal of litigation concerning whether combinations yielded "substantial" economies. For 1942 through 1968, the economies due to combination were estimated at from 0.4 percent to 5.8 percent of gas revenues (mean of 3.0 percent) in fourteen cases, and at 1.8 percent to 11.0 percent of gas revenue deductions (mean of 5.75 percent) in eight cases.[37] The petitioners in all these cases had a vested interest in showing large economies, and in a majority of them, the Securities and Exchange Commission (SEC) held that the savings claimed had not been proven. Since the estimated gains from combination seemed to be assigned primarily to the gas operations, the overall economies from combination utilities must have been small, indeed.

Some attempts to compare combination and straight electric or gas utilities examine costs as well as outputs.[38] They fairly consistently show that, with the exception of selling costs, combination utilities have, if anything, higher, not lower, costs per kilowatt-hour, though straight gas companies may have a somewhat higher unit cost. Herzlinger, for example, found combination utilities to have per-kilowatt-hour total costs ranging from 25.6 percent higher in the large-scale class to 15.2 percent higher for small utilities. Collins found that, although most individual expenses per kilowatt-hour were not significantly higher in combinations,

36. Percentages derived from *Statistics of Privately Owned Electric Utilities, 1968*, tables 15, 17, pp. xxxiii, xxxvi.

37. Derived from lists (duplications eliminated) in *New England Electric System* v. *Securities and Exchange Commission*, 376 F.2d 107 (1967), and Securities and Exchange Commission, *Decisions and Reports*, vol. 41 (June 1, 1962, to May 31, 1964), p. 905.

38. See note 9, p. 141, for full citations of studies in this paragraph.

distribution expense per kilowatt-hour was, though that is the very area in which most of the economies might be expected. Her results showed that only selling expense per kilowatt-hour was significantly lower in combinations. The NERA study covers costs in less detail than Collins but yields similar results: distribution expense per customer is somewhat lower in combination utilities, but distribution expense per kilowatt-hour is lower for straight electrics. The NERA study does show higher costs in straight gas companies, but the small gas sample and lack of statistical tests make reliability difficult to judge. Brandon found that the overall effect of combination (using a reduced-form equation) was to increase average costs, though the direct effect (using a structural equation) was negative. In other words, the direct cost savings were more than offset by the cost-increasing effects of lower sales per customer in combinations.

While no study has been made of the economies of vertical integration between generation-transmission companies and distribution utilities, it is difficult to envision many direct economies other than the conventional ones in purchasing and administration. And neither of these seems likely to be large, because distribution and production-transmission involve quite different equipment and staff. A nonintegrated industry where generating companies competed for the business of independent distribution utilities might involve greater risks for individual generating companies than the present system. However, because of the rapid growth and cyclical stability of demand for electricity and the long-term character of contracts for firm power, they would still be in quite a secure position compared with typical manufacturing firms.

If transaction costs are not large, and if the owners of transmission lines are required to wheel at reasonable charges, contract terminations would be unlikely to result in the premature obsolescence of transmission lines since it would generally be cheaper for a new supplier to let previous suppliers wheel power to the new customer than to build new lines. If competition should lead to the replacement of transmission or generation plants, the abandoned equipment would probably have been economically obsolete anyway, since the new supplier must cover his long-run marginal costs to make the additional sale profitable while the old supplier would find it worthwhile to continue service as long as he at least covers short-run marginal costs.

Perhaps some gain in planning could be achieved by vertical integration, but demand and capacity statistics and projections are already remarkably complete in the power industry. Moreover, any errors in investment decisions made by independent generation-transmission companies should be relatively easy to correct, given contracts that require several years' notice for termination and the rapidly growing demand that characterizes electric power. Vertical integration, itself, could cause suboptimal plant decisions since it would permit small or poorly located generating plants to supply their captive distribution utilities. The integrated utility might opt for such suboptimal decisions because of the greater rate base available when it generates rather than buys power.

In general, the economies of vertical integration seem unlikely to be great, but no final judgment can be made until the possibilities have been thoroughly explored.

Municipals and Cooperatives

Among the main beneficiaries from increased competition at the generating level would be the municipal and Rural Electrification Administration (REA) cooperative utilities. These utilities have received substantial subsidies in the form of reduced interest costs due to the federal income tax exemption for municipal bonds and, until recently, the 2 percent interest charged the cooperatives by the REA.[39] In addition, both types of utilities are exempt from federal income taxes and have preferential access to low-cost, federally generated power, although the exhaustion of hydro sites means that such access will be a smaller advantage in the future.

The growth of municipal and REA cooperative distribution systems has been limited by their restricted access to low-cost power outside of the areas supplied by federal projects. An increase in competition could be expected to bring their purchased-power costs closer to the incremental costs of integrated utilities, with the possible result of some geographical misallocation due to the expansion of service by the subsidized systems. On the other hand, unrealistically low capital costs and high costs of purchased power encourage cooperatives to build suboptimal generating

39. The 2 percent REA loans were discontinued in favor of guaranteed and insured loans in 1973 (P.L. 93-32). The standard rate for insured loans is now 5 percent, though a special 2 percent rate is available for low-density or low-revenue areas and for hardship cases.

plants, so more competition in bulk-power supply should reduce the incentive for these firms to generate their own power.[40]

Altogether, it seems unlikely that the efficiency effects of the subsidies now available to municipals and cooperatives would be intensified by greater competition at the generating level. There probably would be a redistribution of generating costs in favor of the customers of municipals and cooperatives and some growth in the share of distribution undertaken by such systems. This growth would itself increase competition by reducing the extent of vertical integration and by limiting, through the threat of municipalization, the retail rates that integrated firms can charge.

Other Effects of Competition

Increased competition would have a mixed effect on the extent of rate discrimination. More competition for industrial load would presumably lead to lower industrial rates relative to residential rates; this could mean higher, lower, or unchanged residential rates, depending on whether long-run marginal generation and transmission costs are respectively increasing, decreasing, or constant. If residential rates were limited by regulation, the Averch-Johnson argument would imply higher residential rates as industrial demand became more elastic.[41] However, if, as Moore suggests, residential rates are set at approximately profit-maximizing levels already,[42] any further Averch-Johnson effect would be nil. In any event, since competition for large industrial load is already intense, further reductions in industrial rates relative to residential rates would be limited. The major effect of procompetitive policy on discrimination is thus likely to be simply to preserve the opportunities for competition that already exist.

Intermodal competition would lead to discrimination in favor of uses of electricity that compete closely with gas. While such discrimination

40. If owners of transmission lines had common carrier status so that all sellers had access to all wholesale customers, the generating firms with access to interest subsidies might become the low-cost sources of power, thus producing a mislocation of generation. Such a threat seems remote today, but if it should become a reality, the appropriate response would be a reduction or elimination of the subsidies rather than trade restrictions aimed at preventing their effect.

41. See Harvey Averch and Leland L. Johnson, "Behavior of the Firm under Regulatory Constraint," *American Economic Review*, vol. 52 (December 1962), pp. 1052–69.

42. "Effectiveness of Regulation," p. 372.

at the residential level could cause Averch-Johnson rate increases on the inelastic elements of demand, the main effects of intermodal competition would be to make large segments of residential demand more elastic, thus reducing the opportunity to discriminate between industrial and residential customers, and to make discrimination between gas and electric customers impossible.

Increased competition for the load of distribution utilities might result in some uneconomic geographic rate differences, but the main effect would be to reduce residential rates generally.

There could be conflict between the effects of increased competition and the goals of environmental protection. Intermodal competition and competition for industrial load encourage the increased use of energy, while some environmentalists have proposed flat or even inverted rate structures to discourage it. There would be no conflict between flatter block rates and competition among generation companies for the loads of distribution utilities, however, and a system of effluent charges would be fully consistent with all forms of competition in the power industry. The shift of generating facilities away from densely populated areas for environmental reasons would, in fact, increase the possibilities for competition.

If the separation of generation and distribution functions caused widespread bilateral monopoly, the result could conceivably be wholesale rates above the internal marginal generating and transmission costs of an integrated company, with higher retail rates as the ultimate effect.[43] A competitive wholesale market would prevent such a development. For vertical disintegration to be unequivocally beneficial to consumers, it should be accompanied by free access to interconnection and wheeling and by the absence of mergers that greatly increase regional concentration.

The classic concern about "cream skimming" receives little attention today in the electric power industry, but it might well become a problem if regionwide competition for industrial and retail utilities' loads should develop. It could be argued that the capture of large industrial loads by more distant bulk-power suppliers would result in high costs and hence higher residential rates in the service area of the original supplier. But, because of the transmission costs involved, such a result is likely only where the distant utility has a large cost advantage. In that case, the high-cost utility could reduce costs by buying power to supply its own load,

---

43. See Fritz Machlup and Martha Taber, "Bilateral Monopoly, Successive Monopoly, and Vertical Integration," *Economica*, n.s. (May 1960), pp. 101–19.

an option that would be available to it in a competitive market. If generation and distribution utilities were separate, the high-cost generating company would also be forced into some such adjustment. Even with no vertical divestiture, the generator would still be under pressure to adjust because of the threatened loss of bulk-power customers and the conceivable loss of retail business caused by the formation of new municipals. Cream skimming would therefore seem to be a minor problem at worst, and might even have beneficial effects in encouraging vertical disintegration and a more rational geographic rate pattern.

Summary

The question posed at the beginning of this section—what would be the net effects of increased competition?—can now be tentatively answered. The economies of gas and electric combination are probably small. Those of vertical integration have not been investigated thoroughly but are also likely to be small. Any net losses from increased competition due to the advantages won by municipals and REA cooperatives, to discrimination, successive monopoly, or cream skimming are problematical. The net effects of these changes might, in fact, be socially useful in and of themselves. The main concern about the effect of competition on the power industry's performance must thus be the conventional one—the industry's ability to attain economies of scale. The crucial question is whether pools or contracts among independent firms can achieve such economies as efficiently as the multiunit firm. Experience with pooling or bilateral contracting where there is extensive high-voltage interconnection among independent firms has been too brief and incomplete, however, to warrant a final assessment at present of the desirability of large-scale horizontal mergers.

Antitrust and Related Issues in the Industry

Until the late 1960s, the role of antitrust in the electric power industry was a minor one, but the new possibilities of competition created by increasing transmission voltages and the new application of antitrust law to regulated fields after the *El Paso Natural Gas* and *Philadelphia National Bank* cases[44] have led to a series of antitrust actions.

44. *El Paso Natural Gas Company* case of 1962 (28 FPC 688); *United States* v. *Philadelphia National Bank*, 374 U.S. 321 (1963).

Eliminating Impediments to Wholesale Competition

Market-sharing agreements among bulk-power suppliers were attacked in the *Florida Power* case.[45] An explicit agreement allocating territories for wholesale power sales between Florida Power and Tampa Electric had been filed with and approved by the Florida Public Service Commission. The Justice Department sued, charging that the agreement constituted illegal collusion under section 1 of the Sherman Act and that approval of sales for resale were beyond the jurisdiction of the state commission. The case was settled in a consent decree requiring the elimination of the market-sharing agreements.

If such settlements become common, competition for the business of retail utilities would be facilitated, but this by itself may have little real effect for several reasons. First, the bulk-power company whose territory contains a retail utility may refuse to wheel power from a rival firm (though see the *Otter Tail* case discussed below). Second, state regulations that specify service areas or state antipirating laws that prevent competition for existing loads of other utilities might still impede wholesale competition, even though the federal government's ruling makes such laws unenforceable. Finally, tacit collusion among bulk-power producers could have the same effect as formal agreements. This seems especially likely where the customer is a municipal or a cooperative. Competition for industrial load is also subject to state restrictions that have not been attacked under the Sherman Act.

The prohibition of market sharing was reinforced by another antitrust suit, the *Otter Tail* case.[46] Otter Tail, a Minnesota, North Dakota, and South Dakota utility, refused to sell power at wholesale or to wheel power to Elbow Lake, Minnesota, when that community substituted a municipal utility for Otter Tail's local franchise. The Antitrust Division sued Otter Tail, charging that the company's actions, coupled with harassment through intensive litigation, amounted to monopolization under the Sherman Act. The district court ruled in favor of the government, and the Supreme Court's affirmation represents a step toward eliminating refusals to wheel as a barrier to competition. Though, in view of the other elements

45. *United States* v. *Florida Power Corp. and Tampa Electric Co.*, U.S.D.C., Middle District of Florida, Tampa Division, Civil No. 68-297-T.; settled in a consent decree, *1971 Trade Cases*, ¶73, 637 (August 19, 1971).

46. *Otter Tail Power Company* v. *United States*, 331 F. Supp. 54 (1971), affirmed 410 U.S. 366 (1973).

of Otter Tail's actions to isolate Elbow Lake, considerably more is needed to establish that owners of transmission lines are unequivocally common carriers, *Otter Tail* could usefully be followed by further suits with broader applicability. The power of the FPC to order interconnection will then become increasingly important.

Government successes in such cases might open up a wider range of electric power issues to antitrust consideration, either by further Antitrust Division actions, by private suits, or by regulatory commission actions. One such issue is the propriety of the pooling agreements and related joint ventures themselves. Such agreements necessarily involve extensive interfirm coordination that almost inevitably results in less active competition among pool members than would be possible if they acted independently.

If closely coordinated pooling offers the only realistic alternative to merger as a means of attaining economies of scale, market-sharing agreements may be unavoidable. It would be unfortunate if the courts were to impose a per se prohibition on such agreements without considering their potential benefits. Yet some aspects of pooling contracts may be more restrictive than necessary and might reasonably be the subject of antitrust investigation. For example, some pools are reported to have agreements about wholesale rates in transactions among their members; it is worth investigating whether such agreements are inevitable. The construction of new capacity on a joint venture basis so that most of a region's output would ultimately derive from a commonly owned set of plants would produce less competition than staggered construction, with pool members attaining economies of scale by selling blocks of power to one another.

Perhaps because of its long isolation from antitrust action, the electric power industry seems to engage fairly commonly in practices that would be of doubtful legality elsewhere. Wholesale contracts often contain provisions preventing purchasers from reselling except at retail, from supplying certain classes of industrial customers, or even from interconnecting with or wheeling for third parties. Some agreements involve long-term requirement contracts.[47] Support of these restrictions would

47. The Justice Department cites a number of such restrictions in contracts of Consumers Power Company and of Southern California Edison in its advisory letters on Midland Plant Units 1 and 2, AEC Dockets 50-329A and 50-339A (June 28, 1971), and on San Onofre Units 2 and 3, AEC Dockets 50-361A and 50-361B (July 12, 1971). Alex Radin, general manager of the American Public Power Association, listed other

not be consistent with the positions taken by the Supreme Court in *Standard Oil, Schwinn*, or *Topco*,[48] and it would surely be hard to portray the power companies as "newcomers" or "failing firms," or the markets in which the provisions were negotiated as so competitive that the courts might wish to make an exception.[49] Again, the joint owners of transmission systems have sometimes refused to admit small utilities to ownership or to permit them direct connection even though such systems can reasonably be classified as essential bottlenecks in the same sense as terminal railroads or the Associated Press, where the courts have required access for all competing firms.[50] In general, the removal of these restrictions seems to be within the scope of present law and would enhance competition in the power industry while having few, if any, harmful side effects.

Much of the antitrust activity in the area of bulk-power supply has been aimed at assuring access for small utilities, usually municipals and cooperatives, to the low-cost power produced by pooling agreements and joint ventures. Small utilities have been excluded from voluntary pools or joint ventures because they offer little additional gain for the larger firms while attaining large economies themselves. Typically, pool participants have been willing to supply the smaller utilities on a wholesale basis at average cost, but not at the incremental costs they realize from the pool. Both the FPC and the Antitrust Division have sought to bring small utilities into such agreements. An FPC order that was supported by the Supreme Court required a large utility to interconnect with a municipality and provide it with emergency power on the same terms on which it shared reserves with neighboring privately owned utilities.[51]

The issue has also been forced by the licensing of nuclear units by the Atomic Energy Commission (AEC) and the supervision by the SEC of

---

restrictive contracts in testimony before the Subcommittee on Antitrust and Monopoly in 1970 (*Competitive Aspects of the Energy Industry*, Hearings before the Subcommittee on Antitrust and Monopoly of the Senate Committee on the Judiciary, 91 Cong. 2 sess. [1970], pt. 2, pp. 417–25).

48. *Standard Oil Company of California* v. *United States*, 337 U.S. 293 (1949); *United States* v. *Arnold, Schwinn and Co.*, 388 U.S. 365 (1967); and *United States* v. *Topco Associates, Inc.*, 405 U.S. 596 (1972).

49. As in *Tampa Electric Co.* v. *Nashville Coal Co.*, 365 U.S. 320 (1961); *White Motor Co.* v. *United States*, 372 U.S. 253 (1963); see also American Bar Association, *Antitrust Developments, 1955–1968* (ABA, 1968), p. 18.

50. *United States* v. *Terminal Railroad Association of St. Louis*, 224 U.S. 383 (1912); *Associated Press* v. *United States*, 326 U.S. 1 (1945).

51. *Gainesville Utilities Department* v. *Florida Power Corp.*, 402 U.S. 515 (1971).

joint venture corporations that build and operate new plants. The Atomic Energy Act of 1954 explicitly requires a consideration of whether a proposed commercial license "would tend to create or maintain a situation inconsistent with the antitrust laws,"[52] and the Court has instructed the SEC to consider the effect of the exclusion of municipals from a joint venture nuclear plant, and indicated that the commission had the power to require that they be included.[53] Under a 1970 amendment to the Atomic Energy Act, the AEC is required to seek the advice of the Justice Department about the competitive effect of each new license. This has resulted in requests by the Antitrust Division for hearings on antitrust issues concerning not only participation by municipals in nuclear projects but also their access to high-voltage transmission systems and coordinated bulk-power development.[54] Faced with the prospect of extensive litigation in connection with the licensing of new nuclear plants, a number of utilities have agreed to interconnect with small utilities, share reserves with them, and wheel power for them. In some cases, municipals have been permitted to participate in new nuclear units. Occasionally, participants have even agreed to staggered development instead of joint ventures.

The efforts to remove barriers to competition among bulk-power producers by preventing refusals to wheel, territorial allocations, and contract provisions that are more restrictive than necessary go some way toward creating a competitive wholesale power industry, especially if there is less vertical integration in the future. The effort to win access to low-cost bulk power for municipals and cooperatives may also be procompetitive in that it would produce lower concentration, but it could also increase vertical integration by promoting municipal participation in joint generation ventures. Moreover, such participation may discourage privately owned utilities from participating in the joint ventures, or even from pooling at all. Thus, if pooling is the only alternative to merger as a means of attaining the requisite economies of scale, the requirement that municipals and cooperatives participate in pools may be counterproductive.

The emphasis on municipals and cooperatives in antitrust policy is

52. 68 Stat. 938, sec. 105c.

53. *Municipal Electric Association of Massachusetts* v. *Securities and Exchange Commission*, 413 F.2d 1052 (1969).

54. See, for example, the data in the AEC dockets on the Midland Plant and San Onofre units, which were among the first utilities reviewed by the Antitrust Division.

perhaps inevitable because of the near absence of privately owned distribution utilities and the reluctance of many private utilities to bring antitrust suits. However, this emphasis tends to confuse the issue by raising the emotion-laden public-private power question, and it would be better if such important general issues as free access to wheeling could be settled on their own merits without the influence of such red herrings. To the extent that antitrust in electric power becomes a campaign to save municipals and cooperatives per se, it is apt to be diverted to secondary issues.

The wisdom of the well-established government commitment to pooling also seems open to question. From a competitive point of view, the optimal situation would be independent utilities that buy and sell power among themselves on the basis of separately negotiated contracts. There has been only limited experience with such arrangements where modern, high-voltage interconnections exist, and no experience at all where free access to wheeling and less vertical integration generates competitive pressures. What is clear at this point, however, is that pooling and monopoly should not be the only possible arrangements considered.

Mergers

The 1950s and 60s were marked by a great many mergers that reduced the number of privately owned electric utilities from 581 in 1955 to 472 in 1965.[55] About 150 municipals were acquired during the same period.[56] Some of these mergers, especially horizontal ones among small utilities, are uncontroversial, but horizontal acquisitions by the largest utilities and the continuing acquisition of small distribution utilities by bulk-power producers could have serious anticompetitive effects. Acquisitions by some of the largest power systems—Commonwealth Edison, Southern California Edison, and American Electric Power—were approved during the 1960s, but the policy behind such approvals may now be changing.

Two major mergers have been challenged by the SEC staff and the Antitrust Division: the acquisition of Columbus and Southern Ohio Electric (CSOE) by the American Electric Power System (AEP), and the combination of Boston Edison with the New England Electric System and Eastern

---

55. U.S. Bureau of the Census, *Statistical Abstract of the United States, 1969* (1969), p. 512.

56. Testimony of David S. Schwartz, assistant chief, Office of Economics, FPC, in *Competitive Aspects of the Energy Industry*, pt. 2, p. 563.

Utilities Associates to form Eastern Electric Energy System (EEES).[57] The first case involves the acquisition by the largest (in terms of generation) American bulk-power system of a good-sized (1,171 megawatts in 1968) operating company that is one of three partners in the closely coordinated Cincinnati-Columbus-Dayton pool. If approved, this merger would probably break up a successful pool and might well lead to the formation of a second holding company as large as AEP that would include all the other privately owned bulk power producers in Ohio.[58] If the merger is prevented, a precedent would be set that might limit further horizontal mergers by the top six or eight corporate power systems.[59]

In the other case, the proposed combination of the second, third, and seventh largest (measured by generating capacity) power systems in New England would create a single firm with 36 percent of the generating capacity in New England and 52 percent of the capacity within 100 miles of Boston.[60] While the Antitrust Division said that it would not oppose mergers among the smaller utilities of New England, it argued that this combination would have serious anticompetitive effects in increased concentration, probable impediment to joint development with smaller New England utilities, and further mergers.

Smaller mergers among electric utilities, especially among pooling partners, have been regularly approved by the FPC and the SEC. With the possible exception of the EEES case discussed above, this policy would seem to permit the conversion of many pools into holding companies. Even if economies of scale should turn out to require common ownership, however, it is questionable whether further acquisitions by a firm the size of AEP is necessary. At expected growth rates, it should come close to 25,000-megawatt capacity within its own system by 1980, the date for which

57. SEC file 3-1476, *In the Matter of American Electric Power Company, Inc.*, and SEC file 3-1698, *In the Matter of New England Electric System, Eastern Utilities Associates, Boston Edison Company, Eastern Electric Energy System* (70-4663). Both cases are SEC administrative proceedings under the Public Utility Act of 1935.

58. A holding company agreement is under negotiation, pending completion of the AEP-CSOE proceeding, that would combine the other two pooling partners, Cincinnati Gas and Electric and Dayton Power and Light, with the five CAPCO pool members (see the annual reports of the companies that would form the proposed holding company in Moody's Investors Service, *Moody's Public Utility Manual, 1970*).

59. Operating company mergers are subject to FPC rather than SEC approval, and it is not certain that SEC decisions would affect FPC merger policies. However, since in many jurisdictions interstate power systems must be organized as holding companies to permit separate corporations to exist in each state, the SEC decision will have wide application.

60. Derived as for Table 5-1.

that high estimate of optimal pool scale was indicated. The EEES merger case is more controversial, especially because of the widely held view that it is the large number of small utilities in New England that account for the high cost of power in the region.[61] If merger is the only effective route to realization of optimal economies of scale, then the EEES merger would be too small, if anything. But if pooling or a series of bilateral contracts are adequate alternatives, a firm such as EEES might impede the attainment of economies because of its reduced incentive to pool or contract with smaller firms. Since merger is largely irreversible, a case could be made for the suspension of merger proposals involving or creating predominant bulk-power suppliers such as AEP and EEES. If, however, transmission costs were to fall sharply in the future, and if regulatory and ownership restrictions on competition were removed, the geographic extent of markets for bulk power could conceivably be so increased that a generating industry composed even of AEPs could be acceptably competitive.

The merger of pools into holding companies is also a permanent change that would eliminate whatever competition there exists among pool members and is less reversible than pooling agreements if individual contracts should become desirable. On the other hand, mergers among smaller firms of a region might be beneficial if the combined firms were better able to negotiate with their pooling partners or with other utilities in individual contracts.

Intermodal Competition

Large-scale divestiture of gas utilities by electric holding companies was accomplished by the SEC in its administration of the Public Utility Act of 1935. Some of the most efficient electric systems and gas distribution companies were created in the process. The agency continues to require the separation of gas properties when it approves mergers if the gas and electric

61. William D. Shipman, *An Inquiry into the High Cost of Electricity in New England* (Wesleyan University Press, 1962), pp. 189–205. Since 1962, the major bulk-power producers of New England have been interconnected by extra-high-voltage transmission lines, several regionwide joint venture nuclear plants have been initiated, and some large generating units based on long-term power sales among independent power systems have been installed. However, it is still questionable whether the present structure of the New England power industry can attain the economies of which the region is capable (H. Zinder and Associates, Inc., and others, "A Study of the Electric Power Situation in New England for the New England Regional Commission" [1970; processed], pp. 60–67).

utilities are combined through a holding company. This policy has been thoroughly supported by judicial interpretation of the legislation.[62] The FPC is less consistent on mergers involving combination utilities, and has recently questioned its authority to require such divestiture at all.[63] Close to half of retail electric sales remain in the hands of combination utilities, however, and these will not be affected by present policies unless they merge.

A monopolization suit might be a useful tool in this respect. Unlike most dissolution suits, a case against one of the large combinations, such as Pacific Gas and Electric or Public Service Electric and Gas, would have great value as a precedent. The case would have to be primarily structural in character, but the presence of monopoly power by the demanding criteria suggested in *Alcoa*[64] should be easy to show, and the respondents would be unable to argue that monopoly was "thrust upon them."

Somewhat less significant antitrust issues have been raised by the promotional practices of certain utilities faced with interfuel competition. It is common for electric companies to offer free installation of underground cable to developers building "all-electric" homes. Such practices have been attacked in private suits charging that they constitute unlawful tie-ins under section 1 of the Sherman Act and section 3 of the Clayton Act. The Supreme Court has refused to review court of appeals rulings that state regulatory approval exempts such promotions from federal antitrust action.[65]

In a well-operating market with informed buyers, such contracts would amount to a form of (possibly discriminatory) price cutting. That the price cuts are disguised and often individually negotiated may facilitate more price competition than would otherwise occur in a duopoly. Yet if house-buyers are poorly informed about alternative heating systems and if prices on the new housing market respond imperfectly to differences in costs and demand, some customers who might choose differently otherwise will choose all-electric appliances. The suits are certainly consistent with other

62. *Securities and Exchange Commission* v. *New England Electric System*, 390 U.S. 207 (1968).

63. FPC Docket Nos. E-7494, CP 70-73, Opinion 590, *In the Matter of Iowa Power and Light Company and Iowa Illinois Gas and Electric Company*, December 24, 1970, pp. 2–3.

64. 148 F.2d 416 (1945).

65. *Washington Gas Light Co.* v. *Virginia Electric and Power Company*, 438 F.2d 248 (1971), and *Gas Light Co. of Columbus* v. *Georgia Power Co.*, 440 F.2d 1135 (1971), certiorari denied 404 U.S. 1062 (1971).

interpretations of tie-ins in antitrust law.[66] They may be mildly procompetitive, but if so they would work by reducing consumer confusion.

The cable contracts are only one of a large number of promotional practices in situations of intermodal competition that have received attention in the last few years.[67] Other forms of payments to builders, either directly negotiated or made at announced rates to all builders in a class, could have effects similar to the cable contracts. But it is unlikely that direct payments to consumers, special services rendered to them, or low prices on appliances sold by the utility could produce as much consumer confusion as payments to builders.

An Evaluation of Competitive Policy Alternatives

Given the costs and consequences of increased competition explored above, and the implications of various antitrust positions toward the industry, what ought public policy toward the electric power industry to be?

Maximum Competition

Maximum competition consistent with low costs, though possibly an unattainable ideal, would require a restructuring of the power industry to include: (1) the separation of generation-transmission companies from distribution companies; (2) the dissolution of combination utilities; (3) the elimination of public and private territorial restrictions on sales to distributors or large industrial customers; (4) a general requirement of interconnection and wheeling at reasonable charges; (5) the elimination of

66. FTC consent order, Proceeding Docket C-1251, *On the Matter of General Electric Co.* (June 30, 1967) (concerned ties attached to promotional payments on all-electric houses); *Fortner Enterprises, Inc.* v. *United States Steel Corp.*, 394 U.S. 495 (1969).

67. See, for example, *Promotional Practices by Public Utilities and Their Effect upon Small Business*, A Report of Subcommittee No. 5 to the Select Committee on Small Business, H. Rept. 1984, 90 Cong. 2 sess. (1968), passim. Many of the complaints reported by the subcommittee are transparent requests from gas companies and appliance dealers for protection against price competition. At least some of the alleged discrimination is really off-peak pricing, such as the efforts of gas companies to promote gas air conditioning and of electric utilities with summer peaks to promote electric heating.

preferential access to federal power and preferential tax and capital-cost treatment for municipals and cooperatives; (6) the elimination of legal restrictions on entry into bulk power; and (7) the limitation of horizontal mergers among generation-transmission companies to cases where the partners are too small to negotiate effectively with other bulk-power producers of a region. The last of these stipulations is the least certain. As more information accumulates, large-scale mergers may be needed to attain reasonable economies of scale. On the other hand, in a more competitive setting bilateral contracts by unaffiliated firms or less restrictive pooling agreements may offer the same economies as either large single-owner systems or closely coordinated pools.

Modified Competition

Such a thorough restructuring of the industry may not be practically or politically possible in the foreseeable future. A more limited policy goal that may be more nearly attainable would involve (1) the elimination of private and public territorial restrictions on sales for resale, and possibly private restrictions on sales to large industrial customers, as well; (2) a general requirement of interconnection and wheeling; (3) control of horizontal and vertical mergers; and (4) at least some divestiture of gas properties in connection with further mergers. These changes would effect a further reduction in vertical integration because of the increased access of municipals and cooperatives to power at competitive prices and the increased competitive pressure on small utilities that are presently integrated. If such policies resulted in a large-scale expansion of municipals, political circumstances might allow the elimination of some of their special advantages, as well. A more general dissolution of combination utilities, under section 2 of the Sherman Act, may also be within the range of possibility; the country has once, after all, accepted such a change for a large part of the industry.

Under these second-best policies, the public could still benefit from increased wholesale competition and, to the extent that combination utilities could be dissolved, intermodal competition. The increase in wholesale competition might be substantial or minor, depending on whether economies of scale are attainable short of large-scale merger, or, even better, short of closely coordinated pooling. Since complete elimination of the special advantages of municipals and cooperatives seems unlikely, industry reorganization might lead to some uneconomic expansion by such utilities, and probably would bring about a redistribution in favor of their customers. On the other hand, municipals and cooperatives would probably be less prone to invest in suboptimal capacity than they are now.

In spite of these substantial changes, the industry's performance would probably be much less significantly changed by the second-best set of policies than under the more thorough restructuring outlined first, because the largest part of demand would still be served through distribution utilities owned by bulk-power producers and would therefore be little affected by increased wholesale competition. This is perhaps the main stumbling block to the procompetitive policies envisioned today. Perhaps the barriers to large-scale vertical divestiture have been overestimated merely through lack of familiarity with the results. It is certainly difficult to identify any technical gains from vertical integration in this industry; separation of bulk-power supply and distribution in the Pacific Northwest and the Tennessee Valley, for example, seems to have presented few disadvantages. A recent proposal for the reform of the New England power industry had as one of its main elements the acquisition of all bulk-power supply in the region by a publicly owned power authority, leaving the existing utilities as pure distribution firms. While this proposal, in contrast to the alternatives presented here, would substitute public ownership for competition at the wholesale level, it does indicate that vertical integration is seen by at least one group of investigators as being far from inevitable.[68]

Even if many of the procompetitive policy goals turn out to be unattainable, most of the elements of the program outlined above would still be economically desirable. If private or, more likely, public limits on territorial competition and wheeling remain intact, wholesale competition would be much less than it might be, but the public would still benefit from intermodal and indirect competition. However, the case for eliminating the special advantages of municipals and cooperatives would then be weaker and the case for vertical divestiture stronger. The retention of present restrictions on direct wholesale competition may make voluntary pooling easier, since pool members would not have to share their advantages with smaller firms, but it would leave firms under less pressure to

68. Zinder and Associates, "Study of the Electric Power Situation," pp. 18–20. Another advocate of regional generation and transmission companies that are separate from distribution companies is S. David Freeman of the U.S. Office of Science and Technology (see his testimony in *Competitive Aspects of the Energy Industry*, pt.1, pp. 94–132).

attain low costs by pooling or bilateral contracting. A policy of requiring coordination with small utilities would thus seem more desirable if present restrictions are retained.

If large regional mergers are permitted so that most market areas have only one or a few bulk-power suppliers, wholesale competition would be reduced, but the removal of territorial and wheeling restrictions (and vertical divestiture, if attainable) would still enhance what competition there was. The need for the dissolution of combination utilities would then seem even more pressing; but the resulting intermodal competition could not have the same effect as direct competition at wholesale because of (1) the substantial segment of demand where gas and electricity are not interchangeable, (2) the duopolistic nature of intermodal competition, and (3) the probable rise in gas prices.

Finally, failure to dissolve combination companies would leave the industry less competitive than otherwise, but none of the effects of the other policies outlined above would seem to be seriously altered.

The Role of Regulation

Even with the most thorough reorganization of the industry, regulation would still have a role. Transmission would continue to be a monopoly, so the requirement of interconnection and wheeling and the regulation of wheeling charges would be essential. The determination of reasonable wheeling charges could be a difficult problem because the decreasing costs of transmission result in marginal costs that are below average costs. How effective regulation of these charges would be is not certain, but it is to be hoped that the FPC could at least prevent charges that were designed to be prohibitive.

Retail distribution would also remain monopolistic, except perhaps for large industrial loads and under intermodal competition, so conventional state regulation of retail rates would still be in order. Such regulation might well be more effective than it is now because pure distribution utilities would be less complex and thus easier to regulate, and because intermodal competition and competition for industrial load would reinforce regulatory controls in important areas.

If territorial and wheeling restrictions were removed, vertical integration eliminated, and substantial numbers of firms maintained at the generation level, much of the need for regulation at wholesale would be obviated. Since this falls under FPC jurisdiction, a national policy of partial deregulation would seem appropriate. Controls over interconnections and wheeling charges would still be necessary, and the industry would still be subject to public actions with respect to environmental matters, but entry and rate questions could be left to the marketplace. If regulation were retained (as might happen if large mergers are permitted), the increased competition should serve to reinforce rather than weaken its impact.

The continuation of widespread integration between retail and generation utilities seems likely under present policies. If so, competition will continue to have only a peripheral effect on a large part of bulk-power supply, and widespread regulation at both retail and wholesale levels will still be necessary. Even under those conditions, however, a procompetitive policy would probably help to offset some of the manifest imperfections in regulation.

This discussion has largely ignored the environmental issues that seem certain to play a growing role in the power industry. There is clearly room for interaction between environmental and competitive policies. The removal of generating plants from the immediate vicinity of load centers would probably enhance direct wholesale competition. There seems to be no conflict between the use of effluent charges and increased competition.

The history of antitrust in other regulated industries suggests that a successful and widely effective procompetitive policy might well stimulate new legislation exempting many aspects of the electric power industry from antitrust action. Such legislation has in fact been proposed by the FPC.[69] An electric power bill on the model of the Reed-Bulwinkle Act[70] would seem to be an everpresent danger, and may ultimately prove to be a greater impediment to competition in the industry than any of the alleged economies of scale.

69. For instance, S. 3136, 89th Congress (1966) and S. 1934 and H.R. 10727, 90th Congress (1968). The FPC continues to make the same proposal (see FPC, *1970 Annual Report*, pp. 7–8).
70. P.L. 80-662, 80 Cong. 2 sess. (1948) (62 Stat. 472).

CHAPTER SIX

A Reexamination of the Monopoly Market Structure for Electric Utilities

WALTER J. PRIMEAUX, JR.

MONOPOLY in the local electric utility industry is so taken for granted that it is almost forgotten that competition ever existed. That competition fails to function effectively among electric firms serving the same market is a matter of record; the industry is a textbook illustration of structural conditions that make competition unworkable. However, it may not be the structural conditions faced by such firms that served as the rationale for regulation in the first place. That is, when in the late 1800s electric services first became technically feasible, the institutions necessary to organize them as public services were unavailable, but the corporation was highly developed and capable of absorbing the new technology. Thus, it was a disparity in institutional development that was a decisive factor in the emergence of private monopoly as the dominant form of organization in public service industries.[1]

Although the regulation of electric utilities has been far from satisfactory,[2] the proposed remedies usually stop short at suggesting changes in

1. See Walter Adams and Horace M. Gray, *Monopoly in America: The Government as Promoter* (Macmillan, 1955), pp. 186–87. Essentially the same argument was presented by Richard T. Ely, "The Future of Corporations," *Harper's New Monthly Magazine*, vol. 75 (July 1887), pp. 259–66.

2. Its many critics have included John Bauer, "Electric Power and Light Utilities—Discussion," in American Economic Association, *Papers and Proceedings of the Forty-first Annual Meeting, 1928* (*American Economic Review*, vol. 19, March 1929), Supplement, pp. 219–25; Walter Adams, "The Role of Competition in the Regulated Industries," in idem, *Papers and Proceedings of the Seventieth Annual Meeting, 1957* (*American*

the regulatory mechanism, rather than calling for a modification of the structure of the industry to place more reliance on the market mechanism.[3] The objective of this chapter is to fill this critical lack by examining the feasibility of encouraging more competition in the local electric utility industry. The procedure used is an empirical test of the hypothesis that electric utility firms facing competition operate at lower costs than they would in the absence of competition. If the hypothesis is borne out, the basic argument for monopoly loses its force. That is, if resource costs are found to be lower in a nonmonopoly market structure, competition would yield social benefits through increased outputs of other goods and, possibly, lower prices for electricity. If, on the other hand, higher resource costs result from competition, regulated monopoly would be vindicated as the most efficient market structure for electric utilities.[4]

Theory traditionally assumes that all firms seek to maximize profits, with output produced at minimum costs; in this context, there is no reason to expect competition to lower operating costs below the monopoly level. An alternative to the profit maximization model is assumed here. The cost savings that would accrue from competition are assigned to the "X-efficiency" concept.[5] That is, where competitive pressures are few, the disutility of greater effort, search, and control of other firms' activities is traded by managers for the utility of less pressure and better interfirm relations. Where competitive pressures are great, the costs of such trades are high, since there is little utility to be gained from freedom from pres-

---

Economic Review, vol. 48, May 1958), p. 528; Richard A. Posner, "Natural Monopoly and Its Regulation," Stanford Law Review, vol. 21 (February 1969), pp. 548–643; and Henry Kohn, "A Re-examination of Competition in Gas and Electric Utilities," Yale Law Journal, vol. 50 (March 1941), pp. 875–79.

3. An exception is Kohn ("A Re-examination of Competition"), who argues that competition could enhance the effectiveness of regulation.

4. The idea that a single electric utility firm operates at lower costs than it would if other firms existed permeates the public utility literature; however, such a view is based more on opinion than on confirmed evidence. John Stuart Mill (Principles of Political Economy [London, 1848], pp. 171–72) and Henry C. Adams (Relation of the State to Industrial Action, Publications of the American Economic Association, vol. 1, no. 6 [1887], pp. 55, 59–60) were instrumental in generating this idea, yet adequate cost data were obviously unavailable to them for empirical examination. Furthermore, until the income tax law went into effect, detailed records of capital asset items did not exist (Warren G. Bailey and D. E. Knowles, Accounting Procedures for Public Utilities, with Special Reference to Electric Light, Gas, Water, and Electric Railway Utility Companies (A. W. Shaw, 1926).

Harvey Leibenstein, "Allocative Efficiency vs. 'X-Efficiency'," American ew, vol. 56 (June 1966), pp. 408–13.

sures. Competitive pressures thus induce efforts toward cost reduction, and costs tend to rise in the absence of such pressures.

Methodology

This chapter presents data on cities with competing electric utility firms,[6] to allow an evaluation of the impact of competition on cost levels. Virtually no discussion of such electric utility duopolies has appeared in the literature. In most of the cities studied, a privately owned electric firm competed with a municipally owned firm, and the duplication of facilities was such that the consumer had a choice of being served by one firm or the other. In the Texas and Missouri cities, for example, a customer could switch from one firm to the other at will. In Portland, Oregon, on the other hand, customers could not switch from one firm to the other once service had been established. Cities where territories are allocated and duplication of facilities does not exist were not included.

Although individual statistical reports of privately owned firms are compiled in an annual report of the Federal Power Commission (FPC),[7] the cost data, unfortunately, are not useful, basically because the report does not require costs to be allocated to individual cities for firms that operate in more than one city. This makes cost comparisons within a particular city impossible. Neither do the reports required by the public service commissions of most states allocate costs to individual cities. Likewise, although municipally owned firms are required by law[8] to file cost and revenue information with the FPC, many do not do so. The FPC's annual statistical reports[9] are thus incomplete.

Because of this paucity of information, this study is confined to municipally owned firms. Cost data for as many municipally owned firms facing competition as possible were gathered from FPC reports; this subset of firms was used to indicate cost levels in a duopolistically competitive environment. For purposes of comparison, another subset of firms, consisting

6. In a letter to the author (July 29, 1969), F. Stewart Brown, then chief of the Bureau of Power of the Federal Power Commission, revealed that as of January 1, 1966, direct competition between two electric utility firms existed in forty-nine cities with a population of 2,500 or larger.

7. Federal Power Commission, *Statistics of Privately Owned Electric Utilities in the United States.*

8. Federal Power Act (49 Stat. 859), sec. 311. The FPC apparently has no authority, however, to levy any sort of penalty for failure to file.

9. FPC, *Statistics of Publicly Owned Electric Utilities in the United States.*

of those not facing competition, was selected from the same reports. In general, a "matched" firm without competition was selected for every firm with competition. The cities with competition, the matched cities, and their sizes measured by kilowatt-hour sales in 1968 are shown in Table 6-1.

The criteria used to select the matched pairs were as follows. First, to the extent possible, the matched firm should be from the same state as its counterpart. Second, the matched firm should be approximately the same size as the firm with which it would be paired; if no such firm existed in the relevant state, a larger firm was accepted. In no case, however, was a competitive firm matched with a smaller firm. Third, also to the extent possible, types of power sources should be identical for both firms. These criteria were designed to accomplish several objectives. First, they should reduce heteroscedasticity and the variance in the error term in the regressions. Second, if the matched firm was in the same state as the firm with competition, some interstate cost differences not picked up by the estimating equations might be eliminated. Third, if the matched firm was at least as large as the competitive firm, any cost differences due to scale effects not picked up by the estimating equations would tend to bias the results of the analysis in favor of the monopoly cities. This assures that the results are on the conservative side. Fourth, matching the types of power sources for the competing and noncompeting firms should eliminate any cost differences due to supply characteristics not picked up by the estimating equations.

It was not possible to adhere to these guidelines in all cases. Lincoln, Nebraska, for instance, is included, although it was not one of the competitive cities mentioned by the FPC in its 1969 communication. In this case, data for 1964–65 only were used for comparison, since competition did not exist in 1966–68. In the case of Hagerstown, Maryland, 1968 data are included even though customers were prevented in the fall of 1967 from switching to the competitive firm. The decision to use that data was based on the fact that duplication had not been completely eliminated at that time, so that any downward influence on costs in 1964–67 would probably persist during 1968.

Furthermore, some cities with competition were excluded from the analysis because data considered by the FPC too incomplete for publication would have been used. Data for the prospective matched noncompetitive firms in these cases were retained, however, which accounts for some of the unmatched data in Table 6-1; the remainder is explained in the notes to the table. Where it was not possible to select matched firms from

the same state as the firm with competition, firms situated in states geographically near to the competing firms were chosen. Cost adjustments
used to compensate for this difficulty are discussed below.

**Table 6-1. Cities with Monopoly or Duopoly Municipally
Owned Electric Utilities, by Kilowatt-Hours Sold, Fiscal Year 1968[a]**

Thousands

Cities with competition	Kilowatt-hour sales	Matched cities without competition	Kilowatt-hour sales
Bessemer, Alabama	108,838	Florence, Alabama	447,181
Tarrant City, Alabama	56,573	Scottsboro, Alabama	98,280
Anchorage, Alaska	189,357	. . .[b]	. . .
Fort Wayne, Indiana	330,383	Richmond, Indiana	390,824
Maquoketa, Iowa	17,528	Algona, Iowa	28,186
Hagerstown, Maryland	106,089	Bristol, Virginia[c]	211,763
Allegan, Michigan	15,775[d]	Niles, Michigan	56,974
Bay City, Michigan	95,484	Wyandotte, Michigan	126,265
Dowagiac, Michigan	21,090	Hillsdale, Michigan	64,971
Ferrysburg, Michigan[e]	128,774	Lansing, Michigan	1,300,318
Traverse City, Michigan	67,299	Sturgis, Michigan	73,527
Zeeland, Michigan	26,952	Petoskey, Michigan	30,612
. . .	. . .	Carthage, Missouri	55,181
Kennett, Missouri	34,915	Rolla, Missouri	52,427
Poplar Bluff, Missouri	67,197	Columbia, Missouri	189,737
Trenton, Missouri	25,451	Marshall, Missouri	36,730
Lincoln, Nebraska	124,026[f]	Omaha, Nebraska	2,343,826[f]
Cleveland, Ohio	546,707	Springfield, Illinois[e]	692,543
Columbus, Ohio	166,771	Anderson, Indiana[e]	318,606
Piqua, Ohio	119,715	Logansport, Indiana[e]	130,236
Springfield, Oregon	166,707	Eugene, Oregon	1,185,032
Greer, South Carolina	47,727	Greenwood, South Carolina	77,747
Sioux Falls, South Dakota	23,526	Watertown, South Dakota	57,659
. . .	. . .	Springfield, Missouri	585,954
Garland, Texas	337,562	San Antonio, Texas	3,325,771

Sources: Federal Power Commission, *Statistics of Publicly Owned Electric Utilities in the United States,
1968* (1969), and *1965* (1967) and *1967* (1969) issues.
a. This table, which presents data for 1968, except where noted, shows the relative size of the firms used
in the regression model discussed in this chapter. In the model, data were used for the five-year period
1964–68, except in the cases of Maquoketa and Algona, Iowa, for which 1964 data were not available;
Greer, South Carolina, for which 1964–65 data were not available; Allegan, Michigan, for which 1964–67
data were used, as there was no competition in 1968; and Lincoln, Nebraska, which had competition in 1964
and 1965 only. The fiscal year varies among the firms, generally ending either June 30 or December 31.
b. No suitable matched city could be found in Alaska.
c. Matched cities could not be found within the competitive firm's state. Some cost adjustments were
made to compensate for state differences.
d. 1967 data; competition did not exist in 1968.
e. This city is served by both the city of Grand Haven Board of Light and Power and the Consumers
Power Company.
f. 1965 data; competition did not exist in 1966–68.

A pooling of cross-section and time series data was used to strengthen and give depth to the available statistics.[10] Data for the five-year period 1964 through 1968 were used in most cases; note *a* to Table 6-1 indicates the cities for which fewer years were used. The table also shows the relative sizes of the firms in terms of kilowatt-hour sales. The crucial test here is thus the comparative sales volumes of competitive and noncompetitive firms.[11]

The Variables

Multiple regression analysis was used to examine the relative cost levels of competitive and noncompetitive electric firms. This section discusses the variables used for specification of the regression model.[12]

Scale Factors. Cost advantages to a firm as it increases in size have two possible sources. First, there are savings associated with the size of the sales volume, because it is more economical per kilowatt-hour to *distribute* power as more power is sold.

These distribution economies should be reflected in a variable X_1 constructed from the volume of electricity sold by each firm to all customer classifications.

Second, there are savings associated with economies of scale from generating facilities that are the result of a lower average cost of production as more electricity is *generated*. These economies accrue partly because of an inherent characteristic of electric generators that, within limits, causes larger generators to function at lower average cost than smaller generators. The variable to reflect generating economies, X_2, consists of the size of the individual generating stations of the utility firm. A simple average size would not reflect the fact that a utility tends to generate most of its power with its larger plants. Therefore, station capacities were summed in descend-

10. Following Klein, who acknowledges that "the pooling principle is [a means] of enlarging our sources of basic information" (Lawrence R. Klein, *A Textbook of Econometrics* [Row, Peterson, 1956], p. 237).

11. The question of sample bias may be raised, since the sample does contain firms with very high sales levels. However, as explained in note 32 below, elimination of the largest observations does not change the results of the equation.

12. Some of the algorithms used in constructing variables follow closely procedures used by William Iulo in *Electric Utilities—Costs and Performance: A Study of Inter-Utility Differences in the Unit Electric Costs of Privately Owned Electric Utilities* (Washington State University, 1961), pp. 37–82.

ing order of size until at least half the total generating capacity of the firm was accounted for.[13] Generating size was taken as the average of these larger stations.

Capacity Utilization. The rate of capacity utilization should also affect costs.[14] The total installed generating capacity for each firm was multiplied by 8,760 (the number of hours in a 365-day year): the product is the potential number of kilowatt-hours that each firm could have provided during a year if its capacity had been fully utilized, without down time for repairs or maintenance and with no consideration of particular demand conditions. To ascertain the extent to which the potential capacity was actually utilized, total potential capacity was divided into the number of kilowatts actually generated by each firm. The resulting variable is represented by X_3. Since there are costs associated with providing the potential capacity, whether or not it is extensively used, a higher rate of capacity utilization would be expected to reduce average total costs.

Steam-Electric Fuel Costs. Following Iulo,[15] composite fuel costs—represented by X_4—for all firms within a given state for each year were computed.[16] These figures were adjusted for burning efficiency by applying factors taken from Kent's *Engineers' Handbook* for power.[17] The products were then weighted by the proportionate utilization of steam-electric generation and total electric generation. An exception to this procedure was made where the matched city was in a different state than the competitive firm. To avoid firm cost differences due to the wide variation in fuel costs among states, the steam-electric fuel costs used for the matched firm were those for the competitive firm's state and not the state in which the firm was actually situated.

Hydroelectric Fuel Costs. This variable, X_5, was constructed by weighting the total hydroelectric production investment per kilowatt of hydroelectric generating capacity by the proportion of total generation accounted for by hydroelectric generation.[18]

13. This procedure generally parallels Iulo, *Electric Utilities—Costs and Performance*, pp. 44–45.

14. The construction of this variable is identical to that by Iulo, ibid., pp. 60–61. The computations were made for each firm for each year and then pooled.

15. Ibid., pp. 68–72.

16. *Steam Electric Plant Factors* (National Coal Association, various years).

17. William Kent, *Mechanical Engineers' Handbook*, vol. 1, *Power*, ed. J. Kenneth Salisbury (12th ed., John Wiley, 1950), pp. 2–14

18. Iulo, *Electric Utilities—Costs and Performance*, pp. 75–76.

Internal Combustion Fuel Costs. This variable, X_6, was constructed by dividing total internal combustion production investment by internal combustion generating capacity in kilowatts. The results were then weighted by the proportion of internal combustion generation to total generation. Although this measure is somewhat imperfect, it should still reflect the *relative* level of internal combustion fuel costs for the firms.

Distribution among Customer Classifications. This variable, X_7, used to reflect the effect on costs of serving residential customers, consists of the ratio of total kilowatt-hour sales to residential customers to total kilowatt-hour sales for each utility for each year.[19]

Consumption per Commercial and Industrial Customer. This measure differs from the preceding one in that the latter reflects a *proportionate* distribution while this variable, X_8, is the *actual* average annual consumption of commercial and industrial customers of each utility for each year.[20]

Consumption per Residential Customer. This variable, X_9, is another that reflects the density of residential consumption. The measure employed was the actual average annual consumption of power per residential customer.[21]

Cost of Purchased Power. Another factor that affects the costs of an electric utility firm is the cost of purchased power. The variable used, X_{10}, was the proportion of purchased kilowatt-hours of power to total kilowatt-hour sales.

Market Density Factor. In addition to the two other consumption density variables, costs of an electric utility firm should be affected by the number of customers of all types served by the firm in a given area.[22] The X_{11} variable was constructed by dividing the number of square miles in each city into the number of customers of all classes served by the utility.[23]

Dummy Variables. Dummy variables were employed to take into con-

19. Iulo (ibid., pp. 76–77) found that it was the *proportion* of residential to total sales that affected costs.

20. See ibid., p. 82.

21. Ibid.

22. High consumer density per mile of line has been cited as an important source of economies on the distribution side (FPC, *National Power Survey, 1964,* pt. 1 [1964], p. 272). Since data on number of miles of line were unavailable, it was thought that the number of customers per square mile would be a satisfactory surrogate.

23. Land area in square miles was taken from U.S. Department of Commerce, *Area Measurement Reports,* various years; these data are in turn based on the 1960 Census of Population of the U.S. Bureau of the Census.

sideration other factors that might affect costs.[24] One variable, $DCOM$, was used to indicate whether a firm faced competition; it took a value of one if competition existed and zero if not. Another variable, DX_3, was used to indicate whether a firm had generating facilities; it had a value of one if the firm generated electricity and a value of zero otherwise.

A dummy variable, DX_4, was also employed to isolate the effects on costs of the presence or absence of steam-electric generation by a firm; it had a value of one for firms having steam-electric generation and a value of zero for the others. Similarly, a variable DX_5 reflected the presence of hydroelectric generation. Here, however, the variable reflects the proportion of hydroelectric generation to total electric generation.

Another zero-one dummy variable, DX_{10}, was used to reflect the relative cost levels of firms that purchased power; it had a value of one for firms that purchased any quantity of power and zero otherwise. The DX_6 variable indicated whether a firm produced any amount of electricity by internal combustion generation. Its value was one for firms that did, zero otherwise.

Dummy variables were used for the years 1967, 1966, 1965, and 1964 to measure the effect of time on cost levels. 1968 was used as the reference year, with D_{64}, D_{65}, D_{66}, and D_{67} designating the others.

Dummy variables were also used for the individual states in which the firms were located. The dummy variable for Alabama, for example, had a value of one for a firm located in that state and zero for a firm located in another. The same procedure was followed for Indiana, Iowa, Maryland, Michigan, Missouri, Ohio, Oregon, South Carolina, South Dakota, Texas, Nebraska, and Alaska. Michigan was arbitrarily selected as the state omitted from the equations. A D plus a two-letter abbreviation of the states' names represents these variables.

Public Finance. There is no variable in the model to take into account the cost and benefits of public finance, although it could well be an important factor, especially if comparisons were to be made between privately owned and municipally owned utility firms. However, comparisons of prices between firms would be meaningless in this regard, since some cities use their utility operations as a means of tax collection (by charging high

24. Most of the dummy variables were used at various times instead of one of the economic variables discussed above. The distinction between those that were employed to reflect unique characteristics and those that were sometimes substituted for other variables should be obvious.

rates for services). This is one reason why costs of operation instead of relative prices were used to assess the effect of competition.[25]

Another facet of the public finance question had to be considered in constructing the model. Municipal governments do not all have the same tax rate, and some municipally owned firms pay no taxes or tax equivalent. The problem this created in cost comparisons was overcome by eliminating all tax and tax-equivalent charges from the cost data. Municipally owned firms may also enjoy lower capital costs than privately owned firms because of lower external interest costs and capital contributions from the municipality. The first benefit was of no consequence to the analysis since only municipally owned firms were included. The impact of the second element is difficult to assess. Municipally owned utilities will be disinclined to rely on capital contributions from the city if they seriously wish to tie costs to the users of their services. Furthermore, there is no reason to believe that the benefit of such capital contributions accrued to the competitive subset of firms more than to the other. It was therefore assumed that the effect, if any, was distributed randomly among competitive and noncompetitive firms.

The Model

The multiple regression estimating technique used was ordinary least squares, with equations of the form

$$\hat{Y} = A + B_1X_1 + B_2X_2 + B_3X_3 + \cdots + B_nX_n,$$

where $\hat{Y}$ is the estimated average cost for the firm.[26] Linear equations were regressed, using pooled data for firms. Certain variables were eliminated from early equations, either because of insignificant t-statistics or because

25. In addition, price competition is only one element in a multifirm market. A previous study made by the author of competing electric utility firms in Sikeston, Missouri, revealed that nonprice competition was very important indeed to consumers. Utility firms in that city attempted to attract customers by such additional services as tree removal without charge, electric poles for television antenna installation, and electrician services. This sort of superior service and a long and satisfactory relationship, in addition to price, were found to be important factors in a customer's decision to buy from one electric firm or the other.

26. Values for $\hat{Y}$ were computed by dividing total costs of the firm, excluding taxes and tax equivalents, by annual sales in thousands of kilowatt-hours.

of the high correlation between them and other variables that gave a better fit.

Table 6-2 presents the first results. It includes all state dummy variables, even those with insignificant t-values. The t-statistics and the signs of the regression coefficients are all consistent with prior expectations, and the signs are consistent with those in Iulo's study for the common variables.

The significant t-statistic and the negative sign on the coefficient of X_1 (millions of kilowatt-hours sold to all customers by the utility) reveal that there are some scale effects that cause per-unit costs of the utility to decline as sales increase. These effects accrue from the ability of the firm to use its plant, including generating and distributing facilities, at a rate that tends to lower the average cost of production below that of smaller levels of output.[27]

The market density factor X_{11} measures the effect on costs of the number of customers per square mile. Its sign shows that as distribution costs of serving customers are spread over more customers in a given area, average cost per unit of electricity sold is lowered.

The coefficient of X_{10} (cost of purchased power) was significant and the sign was consistently negative. This implies that as the percentage of purchased power of an electric utility increases, average costs tend to decline. The sign may at first appear to be perverse, but other studies have shown that it may be more economical for a firm to purchase power than to generate its own.[28]

The coefficient of DX_6 (dummy variable for internal combustion generation) was positive and statistically significant. The dummy variable was used in the equations instead of the internal combustion fuel variable because this substitution improved the fit of the whole equation. This result is consistent with expectations, since internal combustion generation is considered a high-cost generating method.

The state dummy variables reveal that there were important cost differences between firms in different states. These can be partially explained by the interstate difference in input prices. The algorithm for computing steam-electric fuel costs was designed to eliminate cost differences between firms because of location, but virtually all other costs could be affected by

27. It was originally thought that X_1 would pick up the scale effects of distribution and X_2 the scale effects from generating power. The high correlation between the two variables, however, revealed that the X_1 explained a large proportion of X_2, and vice versa.

28. Iulo, *Electric Utilities—Costs and Performance*, pp. 99–100; FPC, *National Power Survey, 1964*, pt. 1, p. 273.

Table 6-2. Effect of Competition on Costs of Electric Utility Firms, Using Basic Equation[a]

Variable or summary statistic		Partial regression coefficient	t-statistic	Conformance of coefficient to expectation
Variable				
X_1	Sales of electricity (millions of kilowatt-hours)	−0.0014	−4.3923*	Yes
X_3	Generating capacity utilization	−0.0806	−5.3267*	Yes
X_4	Steam-electric fuel cost	0.0519	2.6526*	Yes
X_6	Hydroelectric fuel cost	0.0056	2.8776*	Yes
X_8	Consumption per commercial and industrial customer	−0.0291	−9.4084*	Yes
X_9	Consumption per residential customer	−0.4053	−7.0091*	Yes
X_{10}	Cost of purchased power	−0.0197	−3.4451*	Yes
X_{11}	Market density factor	−0.7583	−3.8121*	Yes
DX_6	Internal combustion generation dummy	1.2752	3.3614*	Yes
DAL	Alabama dummy	−5.7932	−9.7784*	...[b]
DIN	Indiana dummy	−0.9975	−1.5519	...
DIO	Iowa dummy	−2.4449	−3.5664*	...
DML	Maryland dummy	−2.6242	−4.2759*	...
DMO	Missouri dummy	−2.3100	−6.1223*	...
DOH	Ohio dummy	−0.5714	−1.3150	...
DOR	Oregon dummy	−0.9133	−0.9533	...
DSC	South Carolina dummy	−3.1664	−4.5550*	...
DSD	South Dakota dummy	−3.5351	−5.0183*	...
DTX	Texas dummy	−3.8965	−6.6138*	...
DNB	Nebraska dummy	−0.0884	−0.0943	...
DAK	Alaska dummy	1.5373	1.9428†	...
$DCOM$	Competition dummy	−0.7954	−2.5799*	...

Summary statistic
N (degrees of freedom plus number of variables) 224
$\bar{R}^2$ 0.8373
Constant 23.4814 (mills)
Standard error of estimate 1.6053 (mills)

Source: Derived from pooled data for the competitive and noncompetitive utilities in Table 6-1. A detailed explanation of the variables is given in the text, along with specific sources that describe their construction and sources for the basic data. Also see the Table 6-1 source.
* Significant at the 1 percent level.
† Significant at the 5 percent level.
a. A linear multiple regression equation was fitted to 1964–68 data, with exceptions as explained in Table 6-1, note a.
b. There is no a priori basis for predicting the direction of the sign of the coefficient for this and the following dummy variables.

geography.[29] For statistical reasons, the dummy variable for Michigan was excluded from the equations; it appears that, all other things being equal, electric utility firms in Michigan operated at higher costs than those in all other states except Alaska.

Some of the cost differences among firms in different states may be due to secondary effects of electric utility regulation. This possibility could not be rigorously tested, but its logic is quite straightforward. The firms in this study were all municipally owned and therefore not subject to direct regulation by any state agency. Nevertheless, it is likely that the pressures on firms to operate efficiently and at lower costs would differ from state to state, depending upon the vigor of the public body regulating the privately owned firms in the same state. That is, where the regulatory body is lenient with respect to the costs it allows privately owned firms to include for rate making, and where the regulator is generous in allowing privately owned firms to increase rates enough to cover all costs and provide a fair return on investment, municipally owned firms will be less powerfully motivated to lower costs.

Table 6-2 reveals the competition dummy variable $DCOM$ to have a statistically significant negative coefficient. The equation indicates that competition between electric firms causes downward pressure on average costs in the magnitude of 0.7954 per thousand kilowatt-hours—approximately $\frac{8}{10}$ of a mill.

The pooled cross-section and time series data gave a good statistical fit and appeared to estimate cost levels satisfactorily. To ascertain whether it was statistically justified to pool the time series data, however, it was necessary to determine whether the parameters had shifted during the five-year period covered by the data. The statistical procedure involved computing a separate regression for each of the five years and then applying an analysis of variance test (Chow test). As indicated in Table 6-3, the hypothesis of unshifted parameters cannot be rejected, since the calculated F-value of 0.74298 is less than the F-table-value for 111 degrees of freedom in the denominator and 23 degrees of freedom in the numerator. These results reveal that each year can be treated as a separate observation.

29. Iulo (ibid., pp. 126–28) failed to find any significant regional effect when he segmented his universe into eight geographical areas. He explains, however, that the geographic effect may already have been reflected by other independent variables in his analysis, or that the factors associated with location may simply have counteracted each other's influence.

Table 6-3. F-Test Statistics of Annual Pooled Cross-Section and Time Series Electric Utilities' Data, 1964–68

Regression	Standard error of estimate	Degrees of freedom df	Number of variables k	df + k	Mean squared error	Sum of squared residuals
Pooled	1.6053	201	23	224	2.5769	517.9569
1964	1.8928	22	22	44	3.5826	78.8172
1965	1.8935	23	23	46	3.5853	82.4619
1966	1.9058	23	22	45	3.6320	83.5360
1967	2.2780	23	22	45	5.1892	119.3516
1968	1.9620	22	22	44	3.8494	84.6878

$$F_c = 0.74298 < F_{111}^{23}(0.01) \approx 2.00$$

Source: See Table 6-2.

The next step in the analysis involved estimating the full impact of competition. The basic equation of Table 6-2 determined that there was a downward shift of the cost curve due to competition, but it did not reflect the effect, if any, that competition may have had on the slope coefficients of the individual variables. To estimate these interaction effects, a variable was constructed for each economic variable by multiplying each by the competition dummy variable. The results are presented in Table 6-4. The manipulation lowered the t-statistics of several variables compared with those in Table 6-2, primarily because of collinearity among the interaction terms and the original variables. All the interaction variables proved to be statistically insignificant, except that for X_1. This suggests that competition not only shifts the total cost curve downward but causes it to become steeper, implying that competition causes marginal costs to increase above the noncompetitive level.[30]

Table 6-5 presents the statistics necessary to test the hypothesis that all coefficients of the interaction variables in Table 6-4 were zero, except the variable for X_1. The results show that the hypothesis cannot be rejected (that is, the calculated F-value of 0.5781 is less than the F-table-value for 192 degrees of freedom in the denominator and 8 degrees of freedom in the numerator). Thus, it was necessary to modify the basic estimating equation

30. The linear average cost function implies a quadratic total cost function, which will rise initially as long as the intercept of the average cost function is positive, and will continue rising to a peak at $-\alpha_0/2\alpha_1$, where α_0 is the intercept and α_1 is the coefficient of X_1 (the volume of electricity sold). Hence, the total cost function is parabolic.

Table 6-4. Interaction Effects of Competition on Variables in the Electric Utilities' Cost Equation

Variable or summary statistic		Partial regression coefficient	t-statistic	Conformance of coefficient to expectation
Variable				
X_1	Sales of electricity (millions of kilowatt-hours)	−0.0013	−3.8869*	Yes
X_3	Generating capacity utilization	−0.0843	−3.9750*	Yes
X_4	Steam-electric fuel cost	0.0535	1.6642†	Yes
X_5	Hydroelectric fuel cost	0.0059	2.2822†	Yes
X_8	Consumption per commercial and industrial customer	−0.0333	−5.6157*	Yes
X_9	Consumption per residential customer	−0.4346	−6.5355*	Yes
X_{10}	Cost of purchased power	−0.0189	−2.1067†	Yes
X_{11}	Market density factor	−0.5916	−2.2979†	Yes
DX_6	Internal combustion generation dummy	1.8160	3.0451*	Yes
DAL	Alabama dummy	−5.7572	−9.2613*	...[a]
DIN	Indiana dummy	−1.1991	−1.7819†	...
DIO	Iowa dummy	−2.3706	−3.2082*	...
DML	Maryland dummy	−2.5534	−3.7474*	...
DMO	Missouri dummy	−2.1804	−5.3446*	...
DOH	Ohio dummy	−1.2904	−2.6356*	...
DOR	Oregon dummy	−0.7629	−0.7147	...
DSC	South Carolina dummy	−3.4316	−4.5036*	...
DSD	South Dakota dummy	−3.2658	−4.0751*	...
DTX	Texas dummy	−4.2251	−6.2203*	...
DNB	Nebraska dummy	0.2217	0.2375	...
DAK	Alaska dummy	1.5996	1.8241†	...
$DCOM$	Competition dummy	−0.7537	−0.4806	...
$X_1 \cdot CD^b$	$X_1 \cdot DCOM$	0.0063	3.4205*	...
$X_9 \cdot CD$	$X_9 \cdot DCOM$	−0.0940	−0.6466	...
$X_4 \cdot CD$	$X_4 \cdot DCOM$	−0.0310	−0.7379	...
$DX_6 \cdot CD$	$DX_6 \cdot DCOM$	−1.0543	−1.3472	...
$X_8 \cdot CD$	$X_8 \cdot DCOM$	0.0092	1.1208	...
$X_{11} \cdot CD$	$X_{11} \cdot DCOM$	0.0003	0.8122	...
$X_3 \cdot CD$	$X_3 \cdot DCOM$	−0.0053	−0.1715	...
$X_5 \cdot CD$	$X_5 \cdot DCOM$	0.0045	0.4853	...
$X_{10} \cdot CD$	$X_{10} \cdot DCOM$	−0.0090	−0.8262	...

Summary statistic
N (degrees of freedom plus number of variables) 224
$\bar{R}^2$ 0.8466
Constant 23.6241 (mills)
Standard error of estimate 1.5588 (mills)

Source: See sources and notes for Tables 6-1 and 6-2.
* Significant at the 1 percent level.
† Significant at the 5 percent level.
a. There is no a priori basis for predicting the direction of the sign of the coefficient for this and the following variables.
b. This and the following interaction variables were constructed by multiplying an economic variable by the competition dummy variable.

Table 6-5. F-Test Statistics of Annual Pooled Cross-Section and Time Series Electric Utilities' Data with Interaction Variables in the Equation

Regression	Standard error	Degrees of freedom	Mean squared error	Sum of squared residuals
Equation in Table 6-4, including all interaction variables	1.5588	192	2.4298	466.5216
Equation in Table 6-6, including only $X_1 \cdot DCOM$ interaction	1.5456	200	2.3888	477.7600
Difference	. . .	8	. . .	11.2384

$$F_c = 0.5781 < F_{192}^8(0.01) \approx 1.98$$

Source: Derived from Tables 6-4 and 6-6.

only by adding the $X_1 \cdot DCOM$ interaction variable to reflect the effects on costs of competition.

Table 6-6 presents the basic equation but including the competitive dummy variable as well as the $X_1 \cdot DCOM$ interaction variable. After eliminating the other interaction variables, the t-statistics of the coefficients of the variables remaining in the equation increased in significance; the adjusted coefficient of multiple determination ($\bar{R}^2$) increased slightly from 0.8466 to 0.8492, and the standard error of estimate was reduced from 1.5588 to 1.5456. As one would expect, the t-value of the competitive dummy variable was increased.

The effect of competition on costs of electric utility firms can now be inferred from the equation. Competition causes the average cost curve to shift downward by approximately 1.5155 mills, and at the same time causes the slope of the total cost curve to increase so that average costs increase by approximately 0.0068 mill for each increase of one million kilowatt-hours of electricity sold. These results and their implications for public policy are explored further in the last section of the chapter.

The first analysis indicated that competition causes costs to be lower within some output range. It was important, however, to determine whether the average cost curve turned upward at some point and so whether what was being compared was the low segment of the competitive firms' cost curve and the high or rising segment of the noncompetitive firms'

Table 6-6. Effects of Competition on Costs of Electric Utility Firms, Using Equation Adjusted for Interaction of the Variables

Variable or summary statistic		Partial regression coefficient	t-statistic	Conformance of coefficient to expectation
Variable				
X_1	Sales of electricity (millions of kilowatt-hours)	−0.0015	−4.6930*	Yes
X_3	Generating capacity utilization	−0.0888	−6.0424*	Yes
X_4	Steam-electric fuel cost	0.0361	1.8779†	Yes
X_5	Hydroelectric fuel cost	0.0063	3.3568*	Yes
X_8	Consumption per commercial and industrial customer	−0.0284	−9.5253*	Yes
X_9	Consumption per residential customer	−0.4422	−7.8396*	Yes
X_{10}	Cost of purchased power	−0.0236	−4.2153*	Yes
X_{11}	Market density factor	−0.5731	−2.9117*	Yes
DX_6	Internal combustion generation dummy	1.2530	3.4299*	Yes
DAL	Alabama dummy	−5.7759	−10.1253*	...[a]
DIN	Indiana dummy	−1.4657	−2.3290*	...
DIO	Iowa dummy	−2.4631	−3.7314*	...
DML	Maryland dummy	−2.7507	−4.6486*	...
DMO	Missouri dummy	−2.3280	−6.4078*	...
DOH	Ohio dummy	−1.3135	−2.8804*	...
DOR	Oregon dummy	−1.0679	−1.1568	...
DSC	South Carolina dummy	−3.3227	−4.9562*	...
DSD	South Dakota dummy	−3.1876	−4.6633*	...
DTX	Texas dummy	−4.3475	−7.5233*	...
DNB	Nebraska dummy	−0.0549	−0.0609	...
DAK	Alaska dummy	1.0971	1.4258	...
$DCOM$	Competition dummy	−1.5155	−4.3910*	...
$X_1 \cdot CD$	$X_1 \cdot DCOM$	0.0068	4.0896*	...

Summary statistic
N (degrees of freedom plus number of variables) 224
$\bar{R}^2$ 0.8492
Constant 24.0888 (mills)
Standard error of estimate 1.5456 (mills)

Source: See sources and notes for Tables 6-1 and 6-2.
* Significant at the 1 percent level.
† Significant at the 5 percent level.
a. There is no a priori basis for predicting the direction of the sign of the coefficient for this and the following variables.

cost curve. This was accomplished by regressing the basic equation in quadratic form. The squared output variable, X_1^2, was found to be statistically insignificant, indicating that the linear equations were valid.[31]

Interpretation of the Data

Table 6-6 shows that competition caused electric utility firms to operate at lower *average* cost levels than they would otherwise. However, the effect was reduced to the extent that the marginal cost of competing firms was higher than the marginal cost of noncompeting firms, thus causing the *total* cost curve to become steeper with competition. Figure 6-1 shows that, at annual sales of 222 million kilowatt-hours, the net effect of competition on average costs is zero. Estimations of the point where the two cost curves cross, however, can be only roughly approximated. For one thing, the competitive subset contained only a few firms that achieved such a large level of output, and the noncompetitive subset contained a number of firms with a larger output. For another, since the crossover point is affected by both the estimated slope and estimated intercept of two functions, their equality can be used only as a very rough approximation of the point where competition ceases to lower costs.

At larger outputs, a competitive firm would tend to have higher costs because the effects of economies of scale would overwhelm the effects of efficiency. The data show that the average cost curve for a competing firm has a positive slope throughout the relevant range of output, rising very slightly, at the rate of 0.0053 mill per million kilowatt-hours sold, as output is increased. At the same time, the noncompeting firms have decreasing costs, falling at the rate of 0.0015 mill per million kilowatt-hours sold.[32]

There are at least two credible explanations of the tendency for costs of competitive electric utility firms to rise as output increases. The first has to do with diseconomies of scale. The technology of electric utilities is such

31. Log equations were also tried, but linear equations appeared to give a better fit to the data. This is in agreement with Iulo's conclusions (*Electric Utilities—Costs and Performance*, p. 109).

32. To ensure that this result was not caused by the inclusion of very large firms not facing competition, the equation was reestimated excluding them; no important differences appeared. The average cost function of the competitive firms continued to have a positive slope, and the output level at which competitive and noncompetitive firms' average costs were equal was only slightly different—225 million kilowatt-hours in annual sales instead of 222 million.

Figure 6-1. Average Cost Curves of Competing and Noncompeting Electric Utility Firms

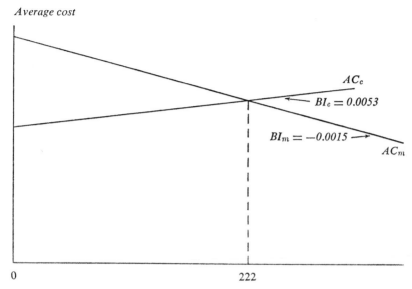

Average cost

0   222

Annual sales of electricity (millions of kilowatt-hours)

AC_c, AC_m = average cost curve of competing and noncompeting electric utility firms, respectively

BI_c, BI_m = rate of change in cost, in mills per million kilowatt-hours sold by competing and noncompeting firms, respectively

Source: The statistics are from the equation in Table 6-6.

that complex networks of transmission lines, distribution lines, transformers, power plants, and so forth, are so situated as to provide power to serve a particular area. The larger the area involved, the more complex the interaction within the networks must be, and competition merely compounds the complexity. Moreover, management in a competitive environment must plan, coordinate, and control firms that are operating in the face of more unknowns than monopoly firms, and these managerial problems are increased in larger cities. The combination of managerial and technological problems could tend to cause average costs to rise in a competitive environment.[33]

33. This explanation was developed partially through consultation with an electrical engineer, and the problems identified were acknowledged by electric utility managers facing competition. Similar explanations for diseconomies of scale in a nonutility environment are discussed in C. E. Ferguson, *Microeconomic Theory* (Richard D. Irwin, 1966), pp. 182–83.

Another explanation for the upward-sloping average cost curve for competitive firms has to do with the "X-efficiency" concept. Given the nature of the competitive situation, it is likely that the X-efficiency effect is more significant for small firms than for larger ones. To the extent that smaller firms face competition from larger rivals, the relative lack of power due to size will force them to operate more efficiently than they would in the absence of competition. In the case of larger firms, their size provides them with a relatively secure position compared with their smaller rivals, so there is less necessity to be efficient. As the firms become larger, the X-efficiency effect would be neutralized, and finally the unfavorable effects on costs of competition will overwhelm the X-efficiency effect so that competitive firms end by operating at higher costs than monopolists.

Whatever the explanation, the significant fact is that there appear to be circumstances in which competitive electric utility firms produce at lower average costs than monopolies, at least within certain size limits.

Public Policy Implications

The findings reported above have important implications for what public policy toward electric utilities should be. Generally speaking, the tendency for many years has been to grant a monopoly to electric utilities and to prevent entry. Although it has long been asserted that competition could not work, competition has, in fact, existed in some cities for over half a century (and this in the atmosphere of a public policy hostile to electric utility competition). To the extent that competition can exist, and to the extent that it causes firms to operate more efficiently, fundamental changes in policy are indicated. Most important, perhaps, is the conclusion that if viable competition can exist in a public utility market, its downward pressure on prices could generate significant favorable effects. Such an effect would provide an excellent complement to maximum rate regulations.

It might be argued that Figure 6-1 also shows that the merger of smaller firms would continue to be beneficial until their aggregated output exceeded 222 million kilowatt-hours per year. After that, monopoly market structure would yield even lower costs than a duopoly. Increased concentration, however, is not a policy recommendation of this study. From a practical point of view, it is more likely that future public policy would aim at creating a climate conducive to admitting competition rather than, by edict, making it impossible for small municipal firms to enter the market. Cities would undoubtedly be more receptive to a policy change that would encourage them to admit rivals than one that would prevent them from entering the market or force them to leave the market because a nearby city could supply electricity at lower costs. Moreover, even though a higher concentration level could lead to lower costs, the lower costs need not result in lower prices if electric rates continue to be set as they are now. Competition, on the other hand, would have a favorable effect on rates and is, therefore, a more desirable policy alternative.

It is important to remember that many electric utility systems have annual sales well below the 222-million-kilowatt-hour level. Table 6-7 shows that in 1962 3,190 systems had annual sales of 100 million kilowatt-hours or less. Furthermore, many of the 427 systems with annual sales of over 100 million kilowatt-hours must still have been below the 222-million mark. Looking at the relative sizes of systems allows the distortion caused by the present policy of restricting entry to be estimated. Based on the data in Table 6-7, it is evident that approximately 92 percent of publicly owned systems are too small to reap the scale benefits of monopoly; these firms, if subjected to competition, would operate at lower average costs. Similarly, the data show that approximately 60 percent of the investor-owned systems had annual outputs of less than 100 million kilowatt-hours, and therefore would also operate at lower costs if subjected to competition. These percentages are very conservative estimates, even allowing for growth in electric systems since the data were compiled. It must be pointed out, however, that while the number of firms small enough to be favorably affected by the cost economies of competition is large, the size of these firms with respect to the total amount of electricity sold per year is less impressive; they account for only about 15 percent of total nationwide retail sales of electricity.[34]

The major objections to competition in electric utility markets have always hinged upon the supposed cost advantages of a monopoly over other types of market structure. While it is perhaps correct that monopoly firms *could*, ceteris paribus, produce at lower costs than competitive firms, the present data show that they sometimes fail actually to do so. Public policy measures have in the past been predicated upon the belief that

34. This does not mean that a competitive policy would not have important effects, only that it would not affect the whole of the electric utility system. It should also be noted that the output definition of a small firm used here is a conservative one; and the proportion of firms that would benefit from competition would be much larger if the output level of 222 million kilowatt-hours were used.

Table 6-7. Number of Electric Utility Systems by Size, Geographic Distribution, and Type of Ownership, as of December 31, 1962[a]

Federal Power Commission statistical region	Number of principal electric utility systems[b]				Number of small electric utility systems[b]				Total number of systems
	Investor-owned	Publicly owned	Cooper-atives	Total	Investor-owned	Publicly owned	Cooper-atives	Total	
Northeast	47	9	1	57	70	188	27	285	342
East central	24	10	3	37	23	261	106	390	427
Southeast	17	61	29	107	18	272	166	456	563
North central	34	8	10	52	52	478	195	725	777
South central	32	22	11	65	51	370	209	630	695
West central	13	8	7	28	21	298	117	436	464
Northwest	15	27	3	45	21	94	70	185	230
Southwest	9	26	1	36	33	36	14	83	119
Total	191	171	65	427	289	1,997	904	3,190	3,617

Source: Federal Power Commission, National Power Survey, 1964, pt. 1 (1964), p. 267.
a. Excludes Alaska and Hawaii.
b. Principal systems are those with net energy output of more than 100 million kilowatt-hours per year, or those with either net energy for system or net energy for load or net generation of more than 100 million kilowatt-hours per year. All other systems are assigned to the "small" category.

monopoly firms *would* operate at the least cost.[35] To the extent that competition results in a net cost advantage over monopoly within some output
range, however, policy must be based on *actual* rather than *possible* cost
levels.

Other arguments against competition have been based on the supposed
inconvenience it would cause consumers.[36] The unsightly appearance of
and greater number of repairs (with consequent traffic obstruction) on
multiple utility lines are included in this broad objection to competition.
In neither Sikeston nor Poplar Bluff, Missouri, however, where the author
engaged in extensive research concerning competition between utility firms,
was any inconvenience from duplication of electric utility facilities mentioned. This does not necessarily mean that competition involved no greater
social cost than monopoly, but only that the citizens considered the
external social costs of competition to be low.[37] In fact, quick repair service
was cited as a *benefit* that accrued from competition. Moreover, it is likely
that monopolists in most cities will retain unsightly overhead electric lines
far into the future, where competition might even help to alleviate the visual
pollution caused by electric lines. This is exactly what happened in a city
with two competing electric companies, where, after the municipal power
company began installing underground cable, the private power company
followed suit.[38]

The FPC acknowledges that there is a strong trend toward installing
underground rather than overhead distribution lines, as well as toward
the development of techniques for improving the appearance of overhead
lines by the selection of materials, structural shapes, and colors that are in
harmony with the environment.[39] In 1968, about 20 percent of the new lines
built in the country were underground, and it is estimated that this per-

35. See Leonard W. Weiss, *Economics and American Industry* (John Wiley, 1961),
pp. 238–39, who discusses conditions that *could* cause a firm to operate at higher than
its minimum average total cost, especially in a regulated environment.

36. Richard Caves, in *American Industry: Structure, Conduct, Performance* (Prentice-
Hall, 1967), pp. 69–72, is among the authors who include with the assumed cost advantages of monopolists the deterrent to competition caused by its presumed inconvenience to customers.

37. External social costs are those costs not incorporated by private industry into
its pricing system but instead shifted to society. The calculations in this chapter exclude
such costs.

38. See Lubbock Power and Light, *51st Annual Report* (Lubbock, Texas: Lubbock
Power and Light, 1967), p. 5

39. FPC, *The Distribution of Electric Power*, Report to the Federal Power Commission Prepared by the Distribution Technical Advisory Committee for the National
Power Survey (FPC, June 1969), pp. 7–8.

centage will increase to about 70 percent by 1975 and 90 percent by 1990.[40] The cost difference between underground and overhead lines has been reduced in the last decade by the development of new materials and installation techniques, particularly for lines serving new residential sub-divisions. The cost difference is expected to be reduced even further, but there will continue to be lower costs for overhead construction.[41]

It thus appears that the fear of a multiplicity of overhead lines if more than one electric firm operates in a city is not a realistic one. Moreover, a public policy change in the direction of more competition could provide for the sharing of poles between competing firms. Pole sharing is already being used in some cities, and it significantly reduces the problems of environmental pollution caused by electric utility competition.[42] Concern for the environment, therefore, need not be a deterrent to more competition.

Another objection to electric utility competition is that, since the product is a necessity, firms should be shielded from competition. The current attitude of most states toward the regulation of public utilities probably follows closely the philosophy expressed by the state of Arizona: "The dual nature of a public utility, a monopoly, but also a provider of essential services, requires that the commission be far more than just a substitute for the competitive market place. The market often forces a financially unstable firm out of business. The Commission, however, must insure that utilities remain financially secure, able to expand their services so that there be no interruption in their provision of the necessities of life."[43] Actually, more reliance on the market system would probably make electric firms operate more efficiently, and produce fewer social costs than policies that protect the interests of inefficient utility firms to the detriment of consumers.

The question of the type and number of firms that should be permitted to compete in a given city is a pertinent one. Although the data in this study show that more cost benefits accrue from duopolies than monopolies in

40. FPC, *The 1970 National Power Survey* (1971), pt. 1, p. I-14–6.

41. In a personal conversation, a professor of city planning has argued that when overhead maintenance costs from windstorms, tornadoes, hurricanes, and so forth, are taken into consideration, the cost of *new* underground service may not be substantially higher than overhead services. This argument has yet to be proved or disproved.

42. The nature of the data made it impossible to assess the impact of rental of rights-of-way where privately owned firms compete with municipally owned firms. Pole sharing or a similar device, however, should not put privately owned firms at a disadvantage.

43. *Arizona Corporation Commission, Annual Report, 58th Fiscal Year, July 1, 1969 to June 30, 1970*, p. 11.

cities with small annual sales, there is no basis for arguing that a larger number of firms would lower costs even more. In fact, three firms may increase costs above the monopoly level, but this possibility cannot be tested since there are no cities with more than two electric firms in direct competition. A duopoly market structure would thus be indicated for cities where competition appears feasible; to help assure competitive vigor, one firm should perhaps be municipally owned and the other either a cooperative or privately owned.

The policy recommendation that competition should be permitted in cities with annual sales of less than 222 million kilowatt-hours per year should now be qualified somewhat. Even if entry were allowed, price competition might not always occur where it would be desirable in lowering costs. It is also possible that a firm could attempt to compete in a system that is already producing at a level where economies of scale offset any prospective competitive benefits. In such cases, public policy should be to prohibit entry. Further, where a market could tolerate competition because annual output is under 222 million kilowatt-hours per year yet where no firm desires to enter, public policy should be to refrain from inducing competition. Merely the threat of competition should tend to make the monopoly perform well, and, should the benefits appear attractive, it is likely that eventually a new firm would wish to enter. This would certainly be true when utility firms realized that they were no longer protected from competition. The minimum policy prescription to cover all cases is essentially this: given a monopoly market with annual sales small enough to offset the cost benefits of competition, a potential rival should not be barred from entry merely to protect the monopoly status of the existing firm.

The question of who should approve or disapprove a firm's entry, given conditions favorable to duopoly, is a matter to be worked out in the governmental structure of each state and will not be explored here. The present attitude of state regulatory commissions toward permitting competition between electric utility firms is illustrated by answers to a questionnaire sent to the regulatory commissions of the fifty states, the District of Columbia, Puerto Rico, and the Virgin Islands. Only a small number of states responding to the questionnaire said they would permit competition between electric utilities, and many offered the classical objection that wasteful duplication and higher costs result from competition.

Despite such present views of regulators, in cities where competition becomes a reality, more reliance could well be placed on letting the market establish price rather than setting price exclusively by regulation. The discipline of the market should induce firms to attract business by maintaining reasonable price levels, help to avoid excessive profits, and probably improve service quality.

Some would argue that such a policy would open the door to rate wars and other attempts by one firm to drive the other out of business. But antitrust laws, along with the utility regulatory authorities that would continue to exist, should protect competitive firms from predatory practices of rivals. Similarly, there should be no problem of price discrimination that could not be regulated by these agencies.

It thus appears that significant social benefits would be gained from a change in policy toward competition between electric utilities. Those in a position to affect public policy should give careful consideration to removing the shield that protects most of the electric utility firms, thus permitting the public to reap the benefits that could accrue from competition.

CHAPTER SEVEN

The Regulation
of Intercity
Telecommunications

LEONARD WAVERMAN

THIS CHAPTER assesses the impact of the policies of the Federal Communications Commission (FCC) on the growth of intercity telecommunications—that is, the transmittal of messages from one local distribution network to another—in the United States. Special emphasis is given to microwave technology, which was introduced in the 1940s and is responsible for the increased demand for competition in the industry. First is a brief history of regulation in the postwar period, particularly as it relates to the potential for competition. The next section discusses the problems involved in determining whether a regulated utility has the attributes of a natural monopoly. In the third section, the attributes of the communications industry in general are examined, and cost statistics for a number of microwave installations are analyzed to determine the scale economies attainable when two points are joined. The economies of scale in operating a system of more than two points are also discussed, as are those available from combining a number of services within a single firm. The final section considers the feasibility of more competition in intercity communications, including the contracting costs that would be involved. Some justification is found for the FCC's monopoly grants in the 1940s as well as for the increased emphasis on competition today. A radical restructuring of the industry is outlined but not recommended, largely because of the probable high cost of contracting among many firms.

The History of Regulation

The Communications Act of 1934 was created "for the purpose of regulating interstate and foreign commerce in communication by wire and radio so as to make available, so far as possible, to all the people of the United States a rapid, efficient, Nation-wide, and world-wide wire and radio communication service with adequate facilities at reasonable charges, for the purpose of the national defense...."[1] Nowhere does the act refer to the need for competition, although it does specify that no one licensed under it may acquire any communication system if the purpose or effect is to "lessen competition" (sec. 314). Earlier court cases involving the 1920 Transportation Act had used the concept of a "public necessity" to show the advantages of competition along a route rather than to prove that competition should be prevented.[2] But an early judicial decision in the telecommunications sector[3] appears to have accepted the notion that monopoly was in the public interest unless proven otherwise, so that the role of competition was never really tested.[4]

So, although no explicit statement was made by legislature or courts on the need to suppress competition in communications, severe barriers to entry were in fact erected, including the FCC's refusal to allow private noncommunications firms to build their own in-plant communications links. And, early in 1945, the FCC in essence granted a monopoly of the frequency spectrum usable for microwave transmission to common carriers.[5] Subsequently, the FCC gave the American Telephone and Telegraph Company (AT&T) a virtual monopoly of the use of microwave by refusing to force AT&T to interconnect with private systems and by not

1. 48 Stat. 1064, sec. 1.

2. The relevant decisions were *Texas & Pacific Railway Company* v. *Gulf, Colorado & Santa Fe Railway Company*, 270 U.S. 266 (1926), and *New York Central Securities Corporation* v. *United States*, 287 U.S. 12 (1932).

3. *Federal Radio Commission* v. *Nelson Brothers Bond & Mortgage Co.*, 289 U.S. 266, 285 (1933).

4. The FCC itself has stated (*Notice of Inquiry to Formulate Policy, Notice of Proposed Rule Making and Order*, Docket 18920 [July 15, 1970], p. 17) that before 1969 "the Commission had no occasion to consider applications for competitive service in this area." Competition had, however, been accepted in intercountry communications as early as 1953 (see *Federal Communications Commission* v. *RCA Communications, Inc.*, 346 U.S. 86 [1953]).

5. See Pike and Fischer, *Radio Regulation, Reports*, vol. 1, pt. 3, pp. 91:57–91:72.

allowing another carrier—Western Union Telegraph Company—to inter-connect with Bell System Companies.[6]

In later years, however, the FCC attempted to diminish the monopoly it had itself granted. In 1959, noting the low rate of increase in private microwave systems, the commission broadened the range of industries in which individual firms could build their own systems, and by 1965, few additional private systems having been constructed, the number of industries that could acquire frequencies was again enlarged, and, in addition, firms were allowed to share microwave systems. After its 1969 decision authorizing a private-for-hire carrier between St. Louis and Chicago prompted 1,800 further applications for such service, the commission in 1971 announced its intention to allow competition in the provision of point-to-point intercity services.[7]

Thus in the space of about a quarter century the FCC reversed its policy from one of granting a near monopoly on intercity communications to AT&T to one of allowing limited competition. The commission gave the same reasons—efficiency and economy—for allowing competition as for granting monopoly.[8] The commission felt in the mid-1940s that microwave communications was a natural monopoly; yet by 1971 it felt that the natural monopoly had exhausted all economies of scale. This chapter addresses itself to whether this shift in policy has been justified by changes in the underlying parameters of cost and demand.

The "Natural" in Natural Monopoly

Traditional definitions of natural monopoly suggest that where one firm can supply the market at a lower per-unit cost than two or more firms, competition leads to the elimination of all firms but one—"the 'natural'

6. Ibid., *Cases*, vol. 5, pp. 639–72j; *Federal Communications Commission Reports*, vol. 17 (1952), p. 175.

7. Decisions cited in this paragraph are noted in *Federal Communications Commission Reports*, vol. 27 (1959), pp. 405–06; vol. 4, 2d series (1965), p. 415; vol. 18, 2d series (1969), p. 967; and FCC, First Report and Order, Docket 18920 (May 25, 1971).

8. Mid-1940s: "frequency economy requires that intercity television relaying be handled by the communications common carriers. . . ." (*Radio Regulation, Reports*, vol. 1, pt. 3, p. 91:58). 1971: "a general policy in favor of the entry of new carriers in the specialized communications field would serve the public interest, convenience, and necessity" (FCC, First Report and Order, Docket 18920 [May 25, 1971], p. 3315).

result of market forces is the development of a monopoly organization."[9] The problem of determining empirically whether a monopoly is justified by cost conditions—whether a natural monopoly exists—is difficult; attempting to do so by inference from the actions and cost data of a regulated utility is nearly impossible.

Neglecting for a moment the difficulties in measuring costs and capacities for a particular service, the problem can be restated as follows, and is illustrated in Figure 7-1. Suppose that technological conditions and level of demand in the past were as shown by the solid lines in the figure. Suppose further that both demand and technology have shifted as shown by the dashed lines. How can public policy prevent an "unnatural" monopoly— that is, a monopoly under cost and demand conditions that call for some degree of competition?

Figure 7-1. Shift of Natural Monopoly to Unnatural Monopoly

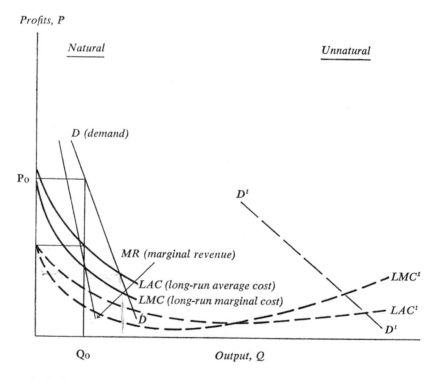

9. C. E. Ferguson, *Microeconomic Theory* (Richard D. Irwin, 1966), p. 223.

Assume that the cost and demand conditions shown in the figure represent a firm in an unregulated manufacturing industry. In time period one, the industry had all the characteristics of a natural monopoly, yet economists at the time would not have described production as having natural monopoly attributes. Instead, they would have suggested either that economies of scale acted as a barrier to entry or that insufficient demand in the short run led to supranormal profits.[10]

Now consider the long-run effects if the government had been convinced that the industry was a natural monopoly. Imposing regulation with marginal-cost pricing while cost curves were falling downward would necessitate price discrimination or subsidization for the firm to cover its total costs.[11] Instead of earning the monopoly profits from output Q_0, the firm would be constrained to earn only the regulated rate of return on its rate base. The natural monopoly would expand its rate base in order to earn the higher profits. In addition, the firm would tend to move into new ventures even where price was below marginal cost.[12] A detailed regulatory process would be developed to supervise the firm. More important, as time passed, the view that the industry is indeed a natural monopoly would be perpetuated. In fact, by period two (in Figure 7-1), who would know that the firm was no longer a natural monopoly, but one whose existence as a monopoly depended entirely on the regulatory process? The regulators would believe it, and their accounting data cannot prove the presence or absence of further scale economies. Constraints would be placed on both the existing firm and potential competitors so as to sustain the fiction. If a new firm wished to enter the market, the burden of proof would be on it to show that entry would be in the public interest—that is, to prove that the existing

10. For the first, see Joe S. Bain, *Barriers to New Competition* (Harvard University Press, 1956), chap. 3; for the second, Lester G. Telser, *Competition, Collusion, and Game Theory* (Macmillan, 1971), pp. 299–311.

11. William J. Baumol and David F. Bradford, "Optimal Departures from Marginal Cost Pricing," *American Economic Review*, vol. 60 (June 1970), pp. 265–83; Alfred E. Kahn, *The Economics of Regulation: Principles and Institutions*, vol. 2 (John Wiley, 1971); and Leland L. Johnson, "Communications Satellites and Telephone Rates: Problems of Government Regulation," Memorandum RM-2845-NASA (Santa Monica: RAND Corporation, 1961; processed).

12. Harvey Averch and Leland L. Johnson, "Behavior of the Firm under Regulatory Constraint," *American Economic Review*, vol. 52 (December 1962), pp. 1052–69; William J. Baumol and Alvin K. Klevorick, "Input Choices and Rate-of-Return Regulation: An Overview of the Discussion," *Bell Journal of Economics and Management Science*, vol. 1 (Autumn 1970), pp. 162–90; Milton Z. Kafoglis, "Output of the Restrained Firm," *American Economic Review*, vol. 59 (September 1969), p. 585.

firm has exhausted all scale economies. When cornered, regulators and regulated alike could point to the conditions that established the firm—efficiency dictates that there shall only be one firm.

In this way, the regulatory process itself creates a set of conditions that make it difficult, if not impossible, to break out of the regulatory circle when economies of scale are no longer a barrier to entry. These conditions can be subdivided into three sets: administrative red tape, the burden of proof falling on the innocent, and self-preservation by the monopolist.

The management of the regulated utility operating under the cost and demand conditions of period two is not likely to suggest that the utility be dissolved and competition allowed; a large but regulated empire is, after all, better than the possibility of no empire at all. Furthermore, personal prestige and salary may well be influenced by the absolute size of the firm. If the managers of the utility maximize not profits but sales revenue or other elements associated with revenue, a reduction in size of the firm will also reduce their welfare. For example, if management's salaries are determined in part by sales volume, or if management's utility function contains sales volume as a parameter, a reduction in size of the firm will decrease the utility of managers. It is also in the interests of the shareholders to fight any reduction in size.

It will therefore be in the self-interest of management to maintain the impression that the firm is still operating under natural monopoly conditions. The combination of this self-interest on the part of management with the impact of rate-of-return regulation means that it is nearly impossible for outsiders to determine whether the monopoly that has been granted by regulation is natural or not. That is, it is difficult to differentiate between true economies of scale and the spreading of existing overhead capital over an ever-larger output. Without adequate regulatory constraints on investment, there is little to prevent existing regulated firms from representing that incremental costs of expanding output are always lower than the total costs for a new system.

This simple model of the pattern of development in regulated industries has several implications. Most importantly, it shows that economies of scale cannot be analyzed solely by reference to the costs of the utility. The relevant cost data in a decision on whether a competitor should be permitted to enter are the full incremental costs for the utility *and* the prospective competitor. The utility's argument that the spreading of the existing capacity over incremental demand will result in scale economies is not of importance.[13] Unless policymakers can differentiate between true increasing returns and the case of an overextended excess-capacity system, the public will be at the mercy of the company with the foresight to over-build and then claim that competitors would "duplicate unnecessary facilities."[14] The only "unnecessary" part of such duplication may be the existing facilities.

The Communications Industry as a Natural Monopoly

In analyzing the intercity communications market, four types of potential scale economies must be considered. If there was, is, or will be a justification for a natural monopoly in this market, the exact specification of the particular scale economy present at each point in time is required. As will be shown, it is likely that all four of these potential scale effects were present in the early 1940s, justifying FCC rulings. It is also likely that several of these economies are no longer binding, so that some forms of competition are feasible today without increasing social costs.

The first constraint on the minimum efficient scale for an operator in the intercity communications market is the production economies at the *plant* level. In this market, production economies of scale will be defined as the internal scale economies present in joining two points by a communications plant providing a single output. These are the economies that are traditionally used as the justification for monopoly grants to utilities. The pertinent question here is do unit costs decrease substantially as the volume of intercity calls between two points increases?

13. The standard production-function definition of scale economies relates output Q to two factors K and L, which can be varied by some proportion λ: $Q\lambda^\alpha = Q(\lambda K, \lambda L)$. Increasing returns exist if $\alpha > 1$, decreasing returns if $\alpha < 1$. A definition of scale economies in terms of cost function is given below. For homogeneous production functions, the two definitions are equivalent. See W. E. Diewert, "An Application of the Shepherd Duality Theorem: A Generalized Leontief Production Function," *Journal of Political Economy*, vol. 79 (May–June 1971), pp. 481–507. This and all future discussions assume that the firm is a price taker in factor markets.

14. Compare this statement of Judge Learned Hand in the *Aluminum Company of America* case of the mid-forties (where Alcoa was convicted of reducing competition by building ahead of demand): "Nothing compelled it [Alcoa] to keep doubling and redoubling its capacity before others entered the field" (148 F.2d 416 [1945], p. 431) with the advertising slogan run by Bell Canada in March 1971: "We Plan to Stay Ahead of Your Demand For More, More, More."

The second scale economy to be considered is the grouping of a number of plants under one management to acquire *firm* economies of scale (again, where only one product is produced). This category normally includes the economies of management, finance, advertising, and research and development. In the intercity communications market, the firm economies of scale will be considered those economies resulting from system management—that is, the ability to use all plants simultaneously.

The third form of potential scale economy is the *multiproduct* economies, or the cost savings from integrating a number of products within the plant or the firm.

It is difficult to differentiate the fourth type of scale economy from firm economies. *Contracting* economies are the ability to reduce costs and risks by organizing activities within the firm. In other words, rather than negotiating a set of contracts, the firm is able to use internal rules that are more efficient.[15] Contracting economies will be analyzed in this industry as the efficiency of organizations other than a public utility in minimizing the transaction costs between firms.

The central issue of this chapter is that economies of scale on the plant or firm level—as traditionally measured in terms of average cost decrease as output increases—are largely irrelevant to determining the need for monopolies or the usefulness of competition in intercity communications. It is demonstrated below that such economies of scale have not been present in the industry for at least fifteen years. A comparison of scale economies present in a number of private microwave systems and in AT&T data indicates that a group of small systems will have average costs similar to those of one large system. The arguments that system economies, system integrity, and system maintenance produce scale economies are also shown to be faulty in a market the size of the United States. Likewise, little evidence is found of multiproduct economies, which invalidates the argument that competitive services in private line rental and data transmission will increase social costs.

It is the fourth type of scale economy, the contracting economies, that will be shown to provide the major justification for the perpetuation of a near monopoly in much of the intercity communications industry.

15. R. H. Coase, "The Nature of the Firm," *Economica*, n.s. vol. 4 (November 1937), pp. 386–405; Oliver E. Williamson, "The Vertical Integration of Production: Market Failure Considerations," in American Economic Association, *Papers and Proceedings of the Eighty-third Annual Meeting, 1970* (*American Economic Review*, vol. 61, May 1971), pp. 112–27.

The Communications "Product"

The product of the communications industry is communications ser-vices—providing the ability to send a message to a particular place at a particular time (with the purveyor of the service being uninterested in the content of the message and not altering its meaning in transmission).[16] A proper measure of the product flow must include some notion of the origin and destination of the message (two calls between equidistant points are not substitutes), the distance transmitted, the duration (one ten-minute call does not equal ten one-minute calls), and a measure of quality (static, interference, and, for data, the error rate).

Intercity communications services are provided by plants that transfer messages from one locality to another. The basic path of the message was by open wire pairs up to the early 1940s (as it still is within a city). Micro-wave radio and coaxial cable are the major transmission media in use today, and satellites, lasers, and waveguides are potential media. Besides providing the path for the message, an intercity system must be able to switch the messages among city-pair routes. To weigh the evidence on economies of scale, microwave technologies must be examined, since it is microwave systems that are the potential competitors to existing carriers.

Plant Economies of Scale

A microwave system consists of a number of stations, each within line of sight of another (twenty to forty miles), which receive a signal of a specific frequency, amplify it, and transmit it to the next station. Total fixed micro-wave costs can be segregated into three categories: real estate and buildings, outside equipment, and inside equipment. The first category consists of the land for the station, the easement or road to the station, and the station building. Outside equipment consists primarily of a tower, antennae, and reflectors. The inside equipment is composed of electronic equipment associated with transmittal, amplification and reception equipment used to channel the radio frequency, and generators, heaters, and air conditioners.[17]

16. Where the meaning of the message is altered, the data are processed rather than transmitted. For an analysis of the integrability of processing and communications, see Donald D. Cowan and Leonard Waverman, "The Interdependence of Communi-cations and Data Processing: Issues in Economies of Integration and Public Policy," *Bell Journal of Economics and Management Science*, vol. 2 (Autumn 1971), pp. 657–77.

17. This list has been simplified to the main cost components. For a remote sta-tion, the percentage distribution of the three types of cost are: real estate and build-

HYPOTHETICAL PREDICTIONS. In a study commissioned by AT&T,[18] Northrop Page Communications Engineers, Inc., analyzed two hypothetical microwave systems developed to meet a set of requirements provided by AT&T. For each actual site in these systems, Page estimated the minimum station and equipment costs necessary to meet the expected capacity. As Table 7-1 shows, the percentage of total cost assigned to each cost category is a function of the capacity of the system. As capacity increases, multiplex equipment represents a greater and greater share of total costs. Since, as will be shown, there are few economies in purchasing multiplex equipment, scale economies do diminish as capacity increases.[19]

Scale economies for a single microwave station depend on the indivisibility of certain items and on "engineering" economies. Whether the station can handle one circuit or a thousand, only one access road is needed. Similarly, the building needed to maintain the equipment can handle a large range of circuits, and the costs of constructing a building do not, over broad ranges, increase in proportion with the increase in volume. Firms can, however, overcome some of these indivisibilities. Land and roads that are available for other uses or used by other microwave stations can be used: "many station sites are already occupied by federal, state, common carrier, or industrial radio and microwave services. As a result, the arrival of a new station on top of a hill merely cuts the costs for everyone on that hill."[20] Towers can be erected on buildings used for other purposes. Even when none of these elements—land, road, or building—is already owned and used for other purposes, the firm can control its real estate and building costs in many other ways.[21]

There are also scale economies in the use of outside equipment. Larger antennae (in terms of beam) do not cost proportionately more than smaller antennae. However, larger antennae require stronger towers, and it is not clear that this trade-off between increased antenna capacity and increased tower strength leads to any appreciable scale economy. Two

ings, 33 percent; outside equipment, 20 percent; inside equipment, 47 percent. (Computed from data in Arthur D. Little, Inc., *The Cost of Acquiring and Owning a Private Microwave System* [Cambridge, Mass.: ADL, 1965].)

18. Page Communications Engineers, Inc., "Page Analysis of Microwave Systems 1 and 2," FCC Docket 18128, Bell Exhibit 10 (April 1, 1970), pp. 1–1, 2–1, 2–2.

19. The Page study estimates that multiplex equipment to channel 600 circuits costs $17,500; for 1,200 circuits, $35,160 (ibid., p. A-18).

20. Little, Inc., "Cost of Acquiring and Owning a Private Microwave System," p. 29.

21. One would therefore expect plant costs to vary greatly; the Little study found them to range between one-third and two-thirds of total cost (ibid., p. 43).

Table 7-1. Main Cost Components of Hypothetical Microwave Systems, by Number of Circuits

Number of circuits	Percent of total cost		
	Multiplex	Radio	Property
24	22	59	12
36	25	56	12
48	36	49	10
72	35	49	11
96	39	46	10
108	41	44	10
132	43	41	9
168	48	37	9
180	49	36	9
192	51	34	9
216	53	32	8
228	54	31	8
300	60	27	7
336	62	26	7
372	64	24	7
456	68	21	6
624	72	17	5
828	76	13	5
996	79	11	4

Source: Page Communications Engineers, Inc., "Page Analysis of Microwave Systems 1 and 2," FCC Docket 18128, Bell Exhibit 10 (April 1, 1970), pp. A-34, E-35.

elements of inside equipment—radio equipment and backup facilities—exhibit declining costs per operating circuit as capacity (in number of circuits) increases.[22]

Most systems include some form of backup facilities for the operating channels. The use of a backup radio channel (frequency diversity) has been called into serious question by the FCC.[23] The commission found that the accepted rules for backup facilities (one protection channel for five working channels in the 4-gigahertz (GHz) band, one for three in the 6-GHz band, and one for one in the 11-GHz band) are costly methods of achieving sys-

22. Radio equipment—the facilities that amplify and transmit the messages—can handle a number of channels (where each channel can be split into 600 to 2,400 voice circuits), depending on the multiplex equipment. Radio equipment can be the major cost item for very small systems (59 percent for the 24-circuit system in Table 7-1), while it is a minor share of the cost for large systems (11 percent for the 996-circuit system).

23. First Report and Order, Docket 18920 (May 25, 1971).

tem reliability. Frequency diversity uses up a large portion of the available frequency spectrum and therefore is a significant factor in the rising amount of frequency congestion. As a result, the commission ordered that the first two operating channels in the 4-GHz and 6-GHz bands not use a protection channel. Once a third operating channel is added in these two bands, a single protection channel can be added. In the 11-GHz band, the commission ordered a minimum of three working to one protection channel.

Another form of backup equipment is standby power equipment. Only one spare generator (or battery pack) is needed, no matter what the capacity in voice circuits of the microwave station. Thus, a station with a capacity of 3,000 circuits would have a lower fixed cost per operating circuit by 2–3 percent[24] because of the spreading of the costs of spare power equipment over a larger output.

Very large, nonseparable plants may generate diseconomies of scale, as, for example, where a breakdown in a single station destroys the ability to communicate between two points. Thus, even where scale economies dictate that a single plant should join two points, two smaller separate plants are often constructed so that a failure in one piece of equipment will affect only part of the traffic.[25]

Figure 7-2, based on data from the Page microwave study, plots the fixed costs per voice circuit for a hypothetical installation. It can be seen that total fixed cost per circuit rapidly approaches an asymptote as capacity increases, so that additional savings beyond a 1,000-circuit capacity are small. The shape of the total cost curve is highly dependent on the steep fall in average radio costs per circuit. Average property costs per circuit also exhibit a steep decline, but the economies in multiplex equipment flatten out in the capacity range of 250–300 circuits.

The economies of scale in operating (maintenance) costs are not so well documented. Estimates of their share of total costs vary from 33 percent to 23 percent,[26] and there is no obvious reason for assuming that variable costs per circuit should decrease as a function of the size of the system. In

24. Using estimates of the cost of standby power from the Page study.
25. See L. G. Abraham, "The Complexity of the Transmission Network," *Bell Laboratories Record*, vol. 38 (February 1960), p. 48. AT&T has used this argument to back up its application for additional submarine cable investment, as opposed to relying solely on the cheaper satellite technology, for intercountry transmission.
26. Thirty-three percent, Little, Inc., "Cost of Acquiring and Owning a Private Microwave System"; 23 percent, Rodney D. Chipp and Thomas Cosgrove, "Economic Analysis of Communication Systems" (paper delivered at the Seventh Communications Symposium of the Institute of Radio Engineers, October 1961; processed).

Figure 7-2. Costs per Voice Circuit, by Number of Circuits, Microwave Technology

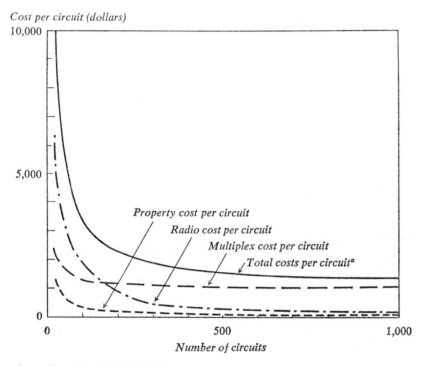

Cost per circuit (dollars)

Property cost per circuit
Radio cost per circuit
Multiplex cost per circuit
Total costs per circuit[a]

Number of circuits

Source: Page study cited in Table 7-1.
a. Includes terminal equipment costs in addition to the three cost groups plotted.

fact, the opposite may be true: "It is well known that systems with large cross sections, fully loaded, or nearly fully loaded, require greater and more careful attention although not necessarily more frequent attention than lightly loaded systems."[27]

Actually, voice circuits measure capital, not output; a more useful measure of output is the number of messages put through the system. The potential output of a communications system is the number of hundred call seconds of message time available. Table 7-2 shows the capacity of an installation in hundreds of call seconds as the number of circuits increases, for various grades of service *P*. The "marginal" columns show the increase in capacity caused by adding one open circuit to the existing system.

27. Little, Inc., "Cost of Acquiring and Owning a Private Microwave System," p. 51.

Table 7-2. Capacity of a Communications System by Number of Circuits and Grades of Service

Hundred call seconds per hour

Number of circuits	$P = 0.01$[a] Capacity	Marginal[b]	$P = 0.10$[a] Capacity	Marginal[b]
1	0.4	...	3.8	...
2	5.4	5.0	19.1	15.3
3	15.7	10.3	39.6	20.5
4	29.6	14.3	63.0	23.0
5	46.1	17.5	88.0	25.0
6	64.4	18.3	113.0	25.0
7	83.9	19.5	140.0	27.0
8	105.0	21.0	168.0	27.0
9	126.0	21.0	195.0	27.0
10	149.0	23.0	224.0	29.0
16	294.0	27.0	401.0	31.0
32	732.0	29.0	900.0	32.0
50	1,261.0	30.0	1,482.0	32.0
64	1,687.0	30.0	1,943.0	33.0
100	2,816.0	31.0	2,149.0	33.0
128	3,713.0	32.0	4,094.0	34.0
150	4,427.0	32.0	4,843.0	34.0

Source: AT&T, "Communications Engineering Manual" (July 1962; processed), sec. 81, pp. 9, 10, and author's calculations.
a. P = grade of service (see discussion in text).
b. Increase in capacity from adding one open circuit to the existing system.

For a probability of 0.99 that a call will be completed as dialed, the capacity of a single circuit is 40 call seconds. With the addition of another circuit, and under the assumption that the probability of incoming calls arriving at the same second can be approximated by a Poisson distribution, the capacity of the plant increases to 540 call seconds—an increase of over 1,000 percent. As the number of circuits increases, the probability that a caller will find an open line increases, and thus the capacity (in call seconds) of the system increases. For example, doubling the number of voice circuits from 64 to 128 at $P = 0.01$ increases usable capacity by 120 percent. The higher is the required quality of service (probability of receiving an open line), the greater is the increase in call-second capacity from adding an additional circuit. This is why, for example, doubling the number of voice circuits from 64 to 128 at a lower level of service, $P = 0.1$, increases usable capacity by only 111 percent. Measuring output in call seconds rather than voice circuits thus yields cost curves that fall much more sharply than those in Figure 7-2. As can be seen in Table 7-2, however, the increase in capacity from adding one more voice circuit rapidly approaches an asymptote.

The cost curve plotted in Figure 7-3 represents the hypothetical savings from increases in the size of private systems. This curve extends that in Figure 7-2 beyond the observed maximum capacity of 996 circuits; the slight drop in the curve beyond this capacity reflects the spreading of the overhead costs of backup facilities over increased operating radio channels. Also plotted in Figure 7-3 are three points indicating the costs of AT&T's microwave system at the same levels of output. At a capacity of 6,000 circuits, AT&T's fixed costs per circuit appear to be slightly lower than those of the hypothetical private system, but an extrapolation of AT&T data for capacities of 600 and 4,500 circuits suggests *higher* fixed costs for the carrier at these lower levels.[28] The limited evidence thus suggests there should be substantial scale economies in fixed costs up to a capacity of 1,000–1,200 voice circuits, and then a slight advantage (2–4 percent) for larger systems up to a capacity of 6,000 circuits.

EMPIRICAL EVIDENCE. In order to test the foregoing predictions about scale economies in microwave systems, investment and operating data were acquired for 141 private systems.[29] Of these, 80 meet AT&T reliability standards, and over 50 percent have a grade of service at least as great as AT&T's. The systems are classified into ten user types: petroleum and pipelines, power, business, forestry products, maritime, motor carriers, local government, police, highway maintenance, and railroads. The systems vary in distance from 15 miles to 2,262 miles, in operating channels from 3 to 960, and in ultimate channel capacity from 120 to 960.

Although a number of reasons have already been given why analyzing the costs of existing carriers would not provide good estimates of the advantages of size, these private microwave systems were built solely to minimize communication costs, so their investment and operating statistics should yield unbiased estimates of economies. Unfortunately, however, three important statistics are lacking—year of construction, location, and a measure of output. The absence of these data causes large error terms in the estimation of the determinants of system costs, but it need not bias the

28. It should be kept in mind that AT&T commissioned these studies of private microwave systems to prove to the FCC that its Tel-Pak rates were set to meet competition. It is not surprising that a system designed to carry 6,000 circuits has higher costs at 600 circuits than a system designed for the smaller capacity.

29. Data gathered by Microwave Services International and presented as FCC Staff Exhibit 47, Docket 16258 (Nov. 24, 1967), pp. 109–31.

Figure 7-3. Estimated and Actual Costs per Mile per Month per Voice Circuit, by Number of Circuits, Microwave Technology

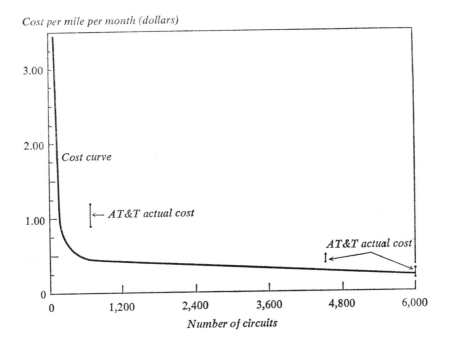

Sources: Figure 7-2; for AT&T actual costs, extrapolation from data in FCC Docket 14650, AT&T Exhibits, Witness Froggatt (1963). The AT&T data show fixed costs, which were translated into monthly charges by estimating the monthly annuity equal to the fixed cost at a 9 percent discount rate (the rate used in the Little study cited in note 17, above).

estimates of scale economies; that is, if there is no relationship between size, age, and location of systems, the lack of such data will not affect estimation of economies.

The lack of a measure of output is much more serious since scale economies are defined as output increasing more than proportionately to an increase in inputs. As a proxy for output, measures of capacity—the number of operating circuits U, the number of circuits available at full capacity S, and the number of hops H (the number of stations minus one)—have been used. The first is a measure of capacity utilized (the number of circuits *immediately* available), the second a measure of potential output, and the third is included to account for differences in fixed costs due to the length of the system (that is, doubling a system's length will increase fixed costs but does not mean that output has in any sense increased).[30]

The estimated cost functions are given in Table 7-3. Where the coefficients of S and U total significantly less than one, economies of scale are present.[31] Equation (1) indicates that there are economies of scale present

30. If the production is of a Cobb-Douglas form,

$$Z = b \prod_{i=1}^{n} X_i^{a_i},$$

where Z is output and X is a vector of inputs. Therefore, total cost C is

$$C = \sum_i p_i X_i = BZ^{(1/\Sigma a_i)} \prod p_i^{(a_i/\Sigma a_i)},$$

where p_i is the price of input i. Then

$$\log C = \log B + \sum_i \frac{a_i}{\Sigma a_i} \log p_i + \frac{1}{\Sigma a_i} \log Z.$$

A measure of output is represented by characteristics S, U, H, so that output is a Cobb-Douglas function of characteristics $Z = S^c U^d H^e$. With $c + d = 1$, if ultimate capacity and operating circuits are both doubled, output doubles:

$$\log C = \log B_0 + \sum_i \frac{a_i}{\Sigma a_i} \log p_i + \frac{1}{\Sigma a_i} (c \log S + d \log U + e \log H).$$

Data on p_i, the prices of inputs, were not available, but the omission of variables set p will not bias the estimate of a_i if p is uncorrelated with (S, U, H). Lack of correlation occurs if prices are constant or the production function is one of fixed proportions. Since the systems are of unequal (and uncertain) vintage, constancy of prices is unlikely. It is possible that input proportions are fixed, however. While such costs as land can be minimized, land cannot be substituted for radio equipment or radio equipment for multiplex equipment. The major source of variation in input proportions is thus between fixed costs and operating costs. If maintenance costs can be considered a substitute for fixed costs (backup equipment), they will be higher for nontoll grade systems.

Figure 7-2 shows that the proportions of various cost items vary with the scale of output, not that capital inputs are substitutes for each other. For input proportions to vary at any scale level would require that a change in the price of an item would cause shifts in factor proportions. For example, a reduction in the price of radio equipment will not cause radio to be substituted for land, but a decrease in antennae prices might lead to a substitution of antennae for land (in the form of stations placed farther apart). Input proportions are thus largely fixed, but with some trade-offs available, chiefly against land or operating expenses. To minimize possible bias, separate cost functions were run for nine components of fixed costs and for maintenance costs.

31. Returns to scale $= \dfrac{\text{percent change in average cost}}{\text{percent change in output}}$;

average cost $= C/Z = BZ^{(1/\Sigma a_i - 1)} \prod p_i^{(a_i/\Sigma a_i)}$;

returns to scale $= \dfrac{\delta (\log c/Z)}{\delta (\log Z)} = \dfrac{1}{\Sigma a_i} - 1.$

Table 7-3. Coefficients for Cost Functions for Private Microwave Systems[a]

Equation number	Cost function	Constant	Number of circuits available S_i	Number of operating circuits U_i	Number of hops H_i	Dummy G_i	$\bar{R}^2$
(1)	Total costs	−0.94* (−2.9)	0.23* (10.0)	0.45* (4.1)	0.83* (31.0)	0.43* (6.2)	0.9201
	Fixed costs						
(2a)	General	−3.22* (−6.0)	0.34* (3.4)	0.39* (5.3)	1.07* (20.0)	0.36* (2.9)	0.8116
(2b)	Land	0.14* (0.74)	−0.008 (−0.49)	−0.02 (−0.21)	1.14* (60.0)	0.08* (1.7)	0.9707
(2c)	Road	−0.26 (−1.1)	−0.03 (−0.55)	0.04 (0.96)	0.97* (41.0)	0.002 (0.03)	0.9387
(2d)	Building	−2.54* (−14.0)	0.53* (14.0)	0.05* (1.8)	1.00* (55.0)	0.003 (0.06)	0.9642
(2e)	Tower	−1.28* (−2.5)	0.45* (4.4)	−0.06 (−0.74)	1.12* (22.0)	0.48* (3.8)	0.8172
(2f)	Antenna	−0.95* (−5.5)	0.27* (7.9)	0.005 (0.03)	1.17 (67.0)	0.28* (6.6)	0.9766
(2g)	Radio	0.42* (2.3)	0.33* (8.9)	0.08* (2.6)	1.22* (66.0)	0.37* (8.2)	0.9769
(2h)	Multiplex equipment	0.37 (1.5)	0.24* (4.9)	0.65* (17.0)	0.56* (23.0)	0.25* (4.1)	0.9157
(2i)	Maintenance equipment	−0.06 (−0.18)	0.19* (2.8)	0.13* (2.4)	0.71* (20.0)	0.17* (1.9)	0.8082

Maintenance costs

(3a)	0.42*	0.08*	0.23*	0.74*	0.15*	0.9395
	(2.3)	(2.0)	(7.4)	(38.0)	(3.1)	
(3b)	2.49*	0.04	...	...	0.71*	0.1084
	(3.6)	(0.31)			(4.0)	

Source: Derived from investment and operating data for 141 private microwave systems compiled by Microwave Services International, and presented in FCC Docket 16258, Staff Exhibit 47 (Nov. 24, 1967), pp. 109–31.

a. The regression equation is:

$$\log C_i^k = aB + f \log S_i + g \log U_i + h \log H_i + j \log G_i,$$

where C_i^k = cost component k, installation

S_i = circuits at capacity, installation l

U_i = operating circuits, installation l

H_i = number of hops (number of stations minus one), installation l

G_i = dummy, with 1 for toll grade system, 0 otherwise

$f + g = 1/\Sigma a_i.$

See text for detailed discussion of the regressions.
The numbers in parentheses are t-statistics.
* Significant at the 99 percent level.

for total costs when the ultimate capacity of a microwave system ranges up to 996 circuits. This result corroborates the conclusion based on hypothetical systems, where the long-run average curve flattened out in the region of 1,000–1,200 circuits. For the specific components of cost, equation (2) indicates that economies of scale are present in all components except for general (2a) and multiplex equipment (2h), again, confirming earlier findings. Neither the ultimate nor operating capacity has any effect on the cost of land or road (2b), (2c). The building and antenna costs are not affected by the operating capacity of the system but do vary with ultimate circuit capacity.

Except for land, road, and building costs, a higher quality system increases fixed component cost ($j > 0$). Attempts to include dummies representing different types of companies suggested that there was no significant difference in costs for any component between types of companies.[32]

The coefficient h on variable H_i shows how cost components vary with increases in system length. As the number of stations doubles, general, road, and building costs double; land, tower, antenna, and radio costs more than double; while multiplex and maintenance costs increase by less than twice. This means that as the length of the microwave system increases, more radio equipment but less maintenance equipment is needed per unit of output.[33]

Maintenance costs are defined as the labor and parts necessary to maintain the quality level of the system. In equation (3b), maintenance costs are estimated as a function of ultimate capacity and the quality dummy. Only 11 percent of the variance in maintenance costs is explained and the coefficient for S_i is not significantly different from zero. In equation (3a), maintenance costs appear related mainly to the number of operating circuits and the length of the system. However, increases in either operating capacity or length raise maintenance costs less than proportionately.[34] The positive sign on coefficient G_i indicates that the higher-grade systems are

32. The quality dummy G_i may be masking company effects. Companies that should have lower costs—pipelines and electric utilities—have the highest quality systems. If quality affected land costs, company dummies would be insignificant, for the lower expected land costs would be offset by higher quality costs.

33. It is clear that land is a function only of the number of stations. It is not clear, however, why multiplex equipment should not increase as rapidly as the number of stations.

34. Since maintenance costs can be substituted for backup equipment, fixed coeffi-

more expensive to maintain; apparently low-grade systems do not trade off operating costs against fixed costs.

The results of the estimated cost functions thus confirm the existence of scale economies in fixed costs for microwave installations up to a capacity of 1,000 circuits. In addition, evidence of scale economies in maintenance costs are found up to this level.

ALTERNATIVE TECHNOLOGIES. Besides microwave radio, coaxial cable and satellites are currently available as means of communicating between two points, and several other media, including lasers and waveguides, are at the experimental stage. It is not necessarily in the public interest to allow competitive microwave carriers when alternative technologies are now or soon will be available with lower per-unit costs and higher scale economies.

At present, the major technological alternative to microwave radio is coaxial cable. A single coaxial cable has far larger ultimate capacity than the largest technically feasible microwave system (32,000 voice channels as compared to 12,000).[35] It is not clear, however, that coaxial cable is a lower-cost technology on either an installed or average cost basis. Table 7-4 shows the comparative costs for microwave and coaxial cable for small-capacity installations. In 1965, AT&T's TD2 radio system operating at full capacity (6,000 circuits) had a *lower* fixed cost per circuit route mile than a 12-tube coaxial system operating at 9,300 circuits. At equivalent utilization rates (80 percent), the fixed cost per circuit mile was $7.00 for coaxial and $5.00 for microwave radio. At a utilization rate of 50 percent, the costs were $6.50 per circuit mile for microwave and about $11.00 for coaxial. In 1968, the fixed costs per circuit mile were $2.75 for AT&T's TH radio system (capacity of 11,160 circuits), $5.35 for an L3 coaxial system (capacity of 16,740 circuits), and $2.50 for an L4 system (capacity 32,400).[36] In short, at small capacities, coaxial systems are far more expensive to maintain, but the largest coaxials are less costly to maintain.

---

cients in production cannot be assumed. With no input-price data, unknown bias may exist.

35. FCC Docket 16258, Bell Exhibit 24 (May 31, 1966). The figures in the following paragraphs are from this exhibit.

36. American Telephone and Telegraph Co., "Information on Economies of Scale" (April 11, 1968; processed). However, a comparison between large-scale microwave and coaxial installations based purely on these data exaggerates the competitive advantage (basically a new service offered at a lower investment cost) of a coaxial system operated by AT&T over an independent microwave firm.

Table 7-4. Basic Costs for Various Installed Communications Systems, 1960s

System	Basic installed cost per mile (dollars)	Number of channels	Installed cost per channel mile (dollars)	Annual operating cost per channel mile (dollars)	Operating cost per channel mile (dollars)
Coaxial cable	32,500	600	54	4,600	8
Microwave relay	10,000	600	17	2,652	4
Submarine cable	10,000	72	139	1,584	22
Tropospheric scatter	20,000	72	278	4,032	56

Source: Rodney D. Chipp and Thomas Cosgrove, "Economic Analysis of Communication Systems" (paper delivered at the Seventh Communications Symposium of the Institute of Radio Engineers, October 1961; processed).

The basic physical difference between microwave and coaxial as transmission media is the latter's far greater attenuation (loss of the signal as it passes over the medium).[37] Coaxial cables require repeaters every four miles, while for microwave radio, the repeaters are twenty-five to thirty miles apart. A coast-to-coast message would pass over about 800 amplifiers if it were transmitted by cable, but only 100 if by microwave. Naturally, the greater the number of repeaters that must be used for a message, the greater the possibility of noise and distortion. For transmitting television signals, however, for which high-quality amplification is needed, microwave is superior, as it is also for data transmission (unless digital methods are used to modulate the carrier signal, in which case coaxial transmission is as good).

The limited evidence available suggests that the most economical use of domestic satellites is *not* in point-to-point, two-way transmissions but in the transmittal of a signal to a number of dispersal points.[38] Thus, the

37. Attenuation for transmission through the air is an inverse function of distance; for a line medium, it is an exponential function of distance.

38 Leland L. Johnson argues that the best promise for satellites lies in "distribution of television programming from network centers to broadcasting stations scattered about the country as a substitute for present-day terrestrial microwave" ("Technological Advance and Market Structure in Domestic Telecommunications," in American Economic Association, *Papers and Proceedings of the Eighty-second Annual Meeting, 1969* [*American Economic Review*, vol. 60, May 1970], p. 204). The President's Task

satellite best at broadcasting would not be competitive with point-to-point microwave carriers established to mainly handle data transmission.[39]

Two other technological innovations are under way in the telecommunications field. A number of firms are working on the communications applications of the laser (light amplification by stimulated emission of radiation), by attempting to modulate the light frequency waves to act as a carrier of message frequencies just as microwave uses radio waves as a carrier. Experiments are being conducted through the air and through a pipe transmission, with the latter appearing to be more promising.[40] It has been estimated that a laser pipe one inch in diameter will carry upwards of 100 million voice channels.[41]

The waveguide is presently in use for very short distances, such as from the antenna to the station in a microwave complex. Long distance helical waveguide communication will be possible via circular tubes, where a fine wire is wound tightly around the inside of the tube in a helix. Coast-to-coast transmission of some 2 million circuits in one waveguide may be possible.[42]

The use of both waveguides and lasers may mean that economies of scale will increase substantially in the future. Both media contain in a single system a scale of output some 10 to 100,000 times that of the present systems. In addition, both technologies are well suited for data transmission.[43] If scale economies of this magnitude do occur, waveguides and lasers will be introduced as part or replacements of the whole public message

---

Force on Communications Policy is of a similar opinion (*Final Report* [U.S. Government Printing Office, 1969], pp. 8, 9). See also Kahn, *Economics of Regulation*, vol. 2, p. 138.

39. The fact that satellites are in some sense "movable capacity" able to handle peaks would not be an advantage because the times when they would be free of broadcast responsibilities (after midnight until 8:00 A.M., say) are the times when excess capacity would exist on point-to-point microwave systems and switched digital systems.

40. Roscoe L. Barrow and Daniel J. Manelli, "Communications Technology—A Forecast of Change (Part I)," *Law and Contemporary Problems* (Spring 1969), pp. 205–43.

41. Leland L. Johnson, "New Technology: Its Effect on Use and Management of the Radio Spectrum," *Washington University Law Quarterly*, vol. 1967 (Fall 1967), p. 537. James Martin suggests that the "laser communication links in the future may well carry 100,000 times as much information as today's microwave links" (*Telecommunications and the Computer* [Prentice-Hall, 1969], p. 160).

42. Martin, *Telecommunications*, pp. 10, 158.

43. Ibid., pp. 158, 161.

system in high-density areas, where the specialized common carriers are now operating.[44]

Existing carriers claim that allowing entry by other microwave carriers retards technical progress and "delay[s] the installation of large capacity facilities on high density routes—thereby jeopardizing the realization of declining unit costs. . . ."[45] But there is no reason for the presence of specialized systems to mitigate the desire of existing firms to introduce new technologies at lower costs. If lasers or waveguides provide scale economies so that costs per unit of output decline substantially, these technologies will eventually force firms using microwave out of business. Existing carriers contend on the one hand that entry should not be allowed today because the entrants use newer technology; on the other hand, they claim that this entry delays the introduction of new and superior equipment tomorrow.

An important but unanswerable problem is how a greater degree of competition would affect invention and innovation in the telecommunications market. One cannot make a simple comparison of the profit incentives to innovate in competitive versus monopoly markets; what is required is a comparison of the incentives in a regulated monopoly as opposed to a quasi-regulated competitive market. There has been little theoretical or empirical analysis of the effectiveness of innovation in regulated industries in general, or the communications industry in particular. Westfield has analyzed the incentives to innovate for monopolies regulated as to price, profit margin, or rate of return. He hypothesizes a firm, operating under production conditions involving constant returns to scale subject to Hicks-neutral or Harrod-neutral technical progress, on which the effects of regulation are complex, generally depending on elasticities of demand (and elasticities of marginal and average revenue curves) and parameters of the production function. He concludes that no single prediction is possible.[46]

To ask whether increased competition would increase or decrease innovation is to ask how the actual rate of innovation in the post-Second-World-War period might have been different if competition had been promoted. There is little evidence that AT&T and its subsidiary Bell Telephone Laboratories have been lax in research and development, although Shepherd

44. This is especially true for the system proposed by the Data Transmission Corporation.

45. FCC, First Report and Order, Docket 18920, Opinion of AT&T, p. 3270.

46. Fred M. Westfield, "Innovation and Monopoly Regulation," in William M. Capron (ed.), *Technological Change in Regulated Industries* (Brookings Institution, 1971), pp. 28–40.

argues that three instances—the slow introduction of microwave in the 1940s, the refusal to allow foreign attachments, and the Bell System's promotion of random-orbit satellites—suggest faulty innovative incentives.[47]

Of course, the mere existence of the proper incentives to innovate does not dictate the kind of invention made or its success. The Averch-Johnson effect and profit-maximizing behavior might produce incentives for capital-intensive technology, but not necessarily any reduction in innovative activity. The utility might still overspend on innovation, to protect the monopoly position through patent holdings or even to mitigate any possible social pressures for increased competition. What better way to convince the public and the regulators of the positive benefits of monopoly than to innovate consistently and conspicuously? The regulators would then tend to view competition as a threat to innovation.

So, again, a straightforward answer cannot be given to the question of how increased competition will affect both pure invention and the speed of introduction of new technology. But it is clear that existing carriers are trying to have it both ways: either there are substantial incentives to innovation in regulated monopolies, in which case new, specialized carriers are committing technological suicide in the long run by entering; or there are no advantages from the existing monopoly structure, so that competition would stimulate innovative activity in all market participants.

System Economies of Scale

The scale economies considered up to this point have resulted from the advantages of size inherent in transmitting messages from one point to another—economies analogous to economies of production at the plant level in the traditional process industries. Economies of scale at the system level are analogous to economies of the firm; they reflect the extent to which the joining of plants within a single decision-making apparatus leads to lower costs and the technical factors that tend to make decisions on the plant level interdependent.[48]

According to the carriers (AT&T in the United States, Bell Canada in Canada), the major advantages to the monopoly position of a single firm

47. William G. Shepherd, "The Competitive Margin in Communications," in Capron, *Technological Change in Regulated Industries*, pp. 86–122.
48. The arguments raised by Coase, Williamson, and others that rule by fiat, as opposed to rule by contract or market, limits the size of the firm are discussed in the last section of the chapter.

are: (1) Alternative routing and network management; (2) the interdependence of investment and capacity decisions; (3) integration and common standards; (4) administrative and accounting procedures; (5) design; and (6) emergency services. It is argued that these benefits of monopoly, in terms both of short-run operating criteria and long-run investment plans, require a single decision-making unit. This is because additional costs would be incurred if a large number of independent systems were joined. Decisions on such questions as the price for a call, the division of revenue, and how to record, account for, and transact intercompany payments would generate significant costs. Furthermore, for a call to pass easily over a number of systems, with only an acceptable loss in volume and an acceptable increase in noise and error rate, identical standards would have to be accepted by all companies involved so that the systems could integrate with one another; otherwise, the design of new equipment would be more difficult and expensive. Finally, the efficient operation of the entire network in an emergency would be a function of the degree to which each system accepted common design, integration, and standards. It is therefore conceivable that the national desiderata behind regulation—the availability of communications networks for emergency use and national defense routing—would be defeated if segments of the network were owned and operated by individual companies.

The carriers would suggest that if a large number of firms operated segments of the network, it would not be in their best interests to interconnect and accept common standards. However, a good case can be made that interconnection would not be difficult for companies to agree upon.[49]

Consider a call that would travel from point A to point C over the lines of two separate companies. Since the revenue of each depends on the ability

49. It is well known that AT&T and General Telephone and Electronics did not coordinate their systems or accept a common interface for quite a long period, apparently because both owned equipment manufacturing companies, and the standard finally accepted meant business for one manufacturer but high changeover costs for the other. This problem would not arise where intercity transmission links did not own such manufacturing facilities, and if it did, standards fair to both parties could be set by the government. It should be remembered also that the problem of standards and interconnection exist in many other industries, competitive and oligopolistic. Wheat farmers and typewriter producers, for example, are able to sell their output without resorting to monopoly; and the railroads found it in their best interests to decide on a common rail size (though not without costs to individual firms). The problems of standards and interface are now being discussed in the computer industry, but no one has seriously suggested that a monopoly here either in the production of computers or computer service bureaus is the answer.

of customers in city A to reach customers in city C and beyond (and vice versa), it would be in the self-interest of the firms to ensure compatibility and accept a common interface. It would not even be necessary for the companies to install exactly similar equipment for the intercity communications plant (microwave or other carrier system), since carriers on a fairly dense route can use a number of different systems of different vintages.[50] The systems are all compatible in that they have similar grade of service (though, of course, the quality of transmission for a particular call does vary with the equipment used). This makes it feasible to have a switching system that would connect a customer to any open circuit between two points. So it is clear that there is a strong incentive for the companies to interconnect, accept common standards, and generally interface with one another. Since the individual revenues and profits of each depend on their compatibility, the decision to interconnect should not be a difficult one.[51]

The available evidence suggests that this is in fact true. AT&T uses a complex system to allocate revenues among the twenty-four operating companies that control the intrastate plant and furnish interstate facilities in conjunction with the Long Lines Department of the holding company. AT&T refers to the operating companies and Long Lines as partners: "Each Partner determines, monthly, the amount of plant it furnished, the applicable reserves, the amounts it paid to connecting carriers not in the partnership, and the expenses (including taxes) it incurred in the partnership enterprise."[52] The principles by which the companies agree to divide revenue could also be used by "partners" not controlled by the same company. In addition, AT&T interconnects with some 1,700 other independent telephone companies. While some costs may increase because of this interconnection,[53] the problems are clearly not insurmountable.

50. For example, AT&T's present facilities between New York and Washington consist of three microwave systems (two of different designs), two coaxial systems, and an ancient cable system.

51. Ignored in this discussion is any reference to the difference in intensity of demand at A and C, which might allow one of the firms to collect side payments.

52. American Telephone and Telegraph Company, Long Lines Department, "The Twenty-four Partners" (AT&T, May 1969; processed), p. 2. Also described are the method by which each partner separates the plant used for interstate business from that used in intrastate transmission, how the shares of each in the partnership are determined (based on book value of interstate plant), and how transactions are made.

53. An example of increased cost is the slow response time of the electronic switching system (ESS 1) developed by Western Electric, which has to be compatible with every other switching device in the United States. When AT&T was forced to interface with L. M. Ericsson (California Supreme Court, 1969), a 1,000-word program had to be added to the system (based on discussions with a former Bell lab engineer).

International interconnections have also proved feasible. Calls can be made, often by direct distance dialing or telex, from points in the United States to other countries with very different telephone systems. For this to take place, agreements had to be made among independent firms on all the problems that AT&T suggests require monopoly decisions. Likewise, in Canada the intercity communications facilities are planned in common by eight independent firms, which have agreed on standards, investment policy, division of revenues, and so forth.[54] The operating standards of the Canadian system, among the best in the world, do not appear to have suffered from this arrangement. Another example of successful interconnection is the agreement between Canadian and American companies dividing revenues from calls made between the countries. The two countries also have an agreement whereby a call whose origin and destination are within one country, say, New York to Seattle, may go via Canada if all American lines between those two points are full. No revenue is exchanged for this set of calls.

The decisions involved in system routing and investment do present more complex problems for interconnected firms. The present system utilizes automated switching equipment that first tries the most direct route for a call between any two points. If this is full, the next most direct is tried, and so on until an open circuit is found. This automated system is complemented by a number of regional route managers, who can redirect traffic through or around their regions. This alternative routing is necessary because the capacity between two points cannot handle the peak traffic; network management allows the smoothing out of peaks by permitting capacity to be shared within the system. Even in a competitive system, such capacity sharing would be feasible where firms used contracts and the price mechanism instead of a network manager as the basis for individual decisions. Here again, system economies do not appear great.

Multiproduct Economies of Scale

Existing firms offer a wide range of services. For simplicity, the services can be divided into five areas: switched analogue voice, switched analogue data, switched hard copy, private line services, and switched digital services.

54. A. Rodney Dobell and others, "Telephone Communications in Canada: Demand, Production, and Investment Decisions," *Bell Journal of Economics and Management Science*, vol. 3 (Spring 1972), pp. 175–219.

Are there substantial scale economies involved in integrating a number of services within one plant or firm?

The conclusions reached in the previous two sections on the absence of scale economies on the point-to-point and system levels form the basis for evaluating the magnitude of multiproduct economies. Some competition in switched hard copy already exists between carriers, suggesting that scale economies are absent in this service. Pure digital systems have not as yet been constructed, so the question of integration economies between digital and analogue systems can be ignored for the moment.

Since it has been estimated that internal plant economies of scale are exhausted at the 1,000-circuit level, the addition of another point-to-point system of at least that size will not lead to higher transmission costs. It is also difficult to see how this additional capacity in independent hands could diminish the firm economies of system management.

There is one area where integration economies may exist. If voice, data, and private line services had different demand patterns over the day, the provision of the services within one plant rather than three would yield savings in fixed costs. It is not clear, however, that these differences in peak characteristics do exist. Voice communications tend to peak in the morning and at night, and, given the substantial off-peak charges for computer usage, the same peaks are likely for data transmission. Although the peaking characteristics of private line services cannot be verified, it can probably be assumed that the carrier operates as if the private line rental will be used twenty-four hours a day. Integration economies are thus absent.

There also seem to be few integration economies from combining a digital and an analogue system within one firm. An all-digital system using digital microwave equipment or coaxial cable and time-division multiplexing will be physically separate from an analogue microwave system. There can then, by definition, be no production economies of scale from jointly operating both systems between two points.

Contract Economies of Scale

It has now been demonstrated that plant, system, and multiproduct economies of scale are largely absent from the intercity telecommunications industry as presently constituted. In order to assess the wisdom of allowing greater competition, the fourth category of economies of scale—the contract economies—must be considered. In this section, contract economies of scale are discussed in connection with two possible radical restructurings of the industry. In the first, each link between a city pair is owned by a separate firm, so that competition between intercity firms exists only when there is more than one route between the cities. In the second case, each city pair is served by a number of intercity firms. Each city is assumed to remain a local monopoly for the distribution of calls, and economies of scale in switching calls are assumed to be negligible. All firms are assumed to maximize profits.

In general, there would be n nodes in the system (n local monopolies), with m arcs joining the nodes. For each node i, there is at least one node to which i is connected. Then, into any node i there exists at least one arc (ij) from another city j, and at most $K_i (K_i \leq m)$.[55]

A local monopoly i, wishing to place an intercity call to another local monopoly t, will then have available at least one route, and possibly a large number of routes. Each of these possible routes involves utilizing the facilities of a number of separate intercity firms ($\Sigma [K_i K_r \ldots]$, where $K_r \ldots$ is the number of arcs out of a node adjoining $i \ldots$; call this sum S_t). The first question is whether the local monopoly at i has to bargain with each of the S_t possible participants in a route from i to t. Since there are ($n - 1$) possible cities to call, a single local monopoly would have to then bargain with ($n - 1$)S_t firms. For the system as a whole, there would be $n(n - 1)S_t$ possible bargains or contracts. If all $n(n - 1)S_t$ contracts have to be made, it is assumed that transaction costs make the system infeasible.

If local monopoly i can obtain the facilities tied directly into it at the lowest price, then i should be unconcerned about the prices charged for routing the call through other facilities. Therefore, if any node i obtains the lowest prices for all K_i arcs directly connected to it, then for any call to any city, the utility at i obtains the lowest price for the complete call i to j. The number of possible negotiations or contracts is $K_i m$; if only $K_i m$ contracts have to be made, it is assumed that transaction costs are small. A competitive system would thus survive.

Assume that some node i has only one arc connecting it to the system. Utility i is faced by one intercity communications firm iA, which has a monopoly on intercity communications, but whose revenue depends on the number of calls from i to A and from A to i. Firm iA is thus a monopsonist providing intercity communications services, which are an input into monopoly i that demands these services. The solution to the bargaining

---

55. What follows is the sketch of a proof; a rigorous proof would utilize graph theory.

process between the local monopoly and the intercity transmission firm is the solution to a bilateral monopoly game. For any quantity of output, the local monopoly wants the lowest price possible for intercity communications services, while the intercity carrier wants the highest price possible. If the two collude, the output that maximizes their joint profits is the output that would be produced under competition.[56] But, in general, there is no guarantee that the local monopoly will exercise full power and the intercity firm no power in order to supply utility i with intercity services at the lowest price. No one local monopoly can assume that any indirect link over which it has no direct control is receiving the competitive or lowest possible price. Any local monopoly i will then be concerned with the entire set of bargains or contracts in the system.

Thus, given no real system economies, no advantages in planning or investing for the system as a whole, and no economies in utilizing spare capacity on indirect links, the problems of bilateral monopoly negotiations lead to a series of consolidations and vertical integration. There is a tendency for local distribution monopolies and direct linking intercity firms to join together both to avoid the costs of negotiation of the set of contracts that make up the system and to avoid being charged monopoly prices on some links.[57] A radical reorganization of the present industry into a number of local distribution firms and a number of intercity transmission firms, where each intercity firm has a monopoly on joining two cities, will not achieve the desired results, even where this dissolution does not reduce real scale economies.

An alternative method of reorganization would be to introduce a number of interconnecting carriers between all city pairs, so that on any route between two cities, a number of competing carriers would offer service. In this case, the monopoly buyer of the input, the local utility, would not be faced with the problems of bilateral monopoly negotiations; for any route between two cities, the intercity facilities would be purchased at the competitive price. As a result, each local utility would be unconcerned with the prices for indirect intercity links. No incentive for vertical integration would exist, since no additional monopoly profits could be earned by monopolizing the competitive input market.[58]

56. James M. Henderson and Richard E. Quandt, *Microeconomic Theory: A Mathematical Approach* (2nd ed., McGraw-Hill, 1971), p 247.
57. This is a reformulation of the Coase-Williamson arguments on the nature of the firm for the case of regional interacting monopolies.
58. Douglas Needham, *Economic Analysis and Industrial Structure* (Holt, Rinehart and Winston, 1969).

The conclusion to be drawn from these formulations is that full competition without reducing social welfare is possible in the communications
industry only if: (1) the economies of scale in joining two points are small,
so that a number of firms offer services between these points; (2) the economies of scale of managing the set of points that make up the network are
small; (3) the economies of scale in switching are small, or switching facilities can be designed to transmit messages over specific facilities; and
(4) the local monopolies of distribution facilities are regulated so as to prevent the earning of monopoly profits.

The Feasibility of Increased Competition

In the early 1940s, the volume of demand for intercity circuits was
fairly small by today's standards. AT&T's capacity was limited to 800
circuits on many major routes (New York–Philadelphia, for example).[59]
The cost curve estimated in this chapter for microwave installations in the
mid-1960s appears to flatten out in the range of 1,000–1,200 circuits; the
crucial level was probably in the range of 450–600 circuits in the mid-1950s
(an estimate based on the capacity of a single radio transmitter and multiplex equipment in this period). The early decisions of the FCC thus reflect
the true monopoly nature of the industry at the time, based on pure internal
production economies of scale at the plant level.

The introduction of network television necessitated a large increase in
capacity, because the transmittal of one television signal requires the same
capacity as 500 voice signals. To carry two programs between New York
and Philadelphia required that existing capacity be more than doubled.
So it was possible, based solely on the economies of scale in carrying signals
by microwave system between city pairs, for *two* intercity companies to
have existed in the late 1940s, a possibility attested to by the pressure of
independent firms to enter the market at that time.[60]

In the late 1960s, the number of interstate circuits available on direct
principal routes between the New York area (New York–Newark) and the
Philadelphia area (Lionville–Philadelphia) totaled 79,000 (including a line

59. *Federal Communications Commission Reports*, vol. 17 (1952), apps. 1–3, pp.
178–80.
60. Donald C. Beelar, "Cables in the Sky and the Struggle for Their Control,"
Federal Communications Bar Journal, vol. 21, no. 1 (1967), pp. 26–41.

from Colesville, N.J., to Lionville).[61] While this observation exaggerates the *average* number of circuits on principal routes, several independent carriers could probably offer microwave service on most routes without exhibiting higher average costs than the single firm. For example, routes across the northern United States from the East Coast to Chicago–St. Louis consist of eleven separate microwave and coaxial cable systems with a total capacity of 60,000 voice circuits. At a minimum, eleven separate companies or, at a maximum, fifty (60,000/1,200) companies could offer the service at nearly identical average cost.

In its historical First Report and Order, the FCC decided that the public would be benefited by a limited form of competition in intercity communications. Business users with a sufficiently large volume of traffic in various regions of the country will be offered a number of alternative services. New telecommunications firms will be able to compete with the existing carriers that use either microwave or coaxial transmission methods.

The benefits of such competition are numerous. A wider range of services, and greater reliability of service, will be offered. If the customers for these services are new to the communications industry, no existing consumers in any other market segment of the industry are hurt (assuming entrants have no scale disadvantages as compared to existing firms). If existing firms estimate demand as being relatively inelastic, when in fact it is elastic (as AT&T may be doing in the data communications market), competition may increase revenues for existing firms even when their prices actually fall.

Effect on Prices

Recent debate on the advisability of increased competition has centered on the effect of new entry on prices, not costs. It is argued that the costs of such services as toll messages or private wire differ markedly in various regions of the country, depending on density of population and the resulting level of demand. That is, the price of a call of given distance is the same in high-density as low-density areas, yet the costs of providing the service are higher in the latter than the former; on very low-density routes, price may even be less than the long-run or short-run marginal cost. Profits

61. These and the following figures are from an AT&T map of Long Lines major facilities, AT&T Application For Facilities Construction Approval (Blanket), 1970, Exhibit 9, examined at AT&T headquarters.

are thus high on high-density routes and low, negligible, or negative on low-density routes. It is possible that the existence of differing rates of return is simply evidence of price discrimination.

It has been suggested that business traffic is less price elastic than residential demand (Dobell and others, "Telephone Communications"). If business calls form a greater proportion of the traffic on high-density routes than on low-density routes, existing pricing patterns are consistent with rational price discrimination. Although no data on the relative weight of business and residential traffic could be found, it is certainly reasonable to expect demand between two major business centers such as Washington, D.C., and New York City to consist largely of business traffic. Likewise, a low-density route of the same length between two points in, say, North and South Dakota could be expected to carry a larger percentage of household calls.[62]

The evidence thus suggests that elasticities are indeed lower where net profitability is higher. The existence of markets where profit is negative may indicate the need to purchase the votes of special interest groups. A rule that prices be no less than long-run incremental costs would reduce this argument to one of maintaining the present discriminatory price structure.

Carriers argue that free entry would result in added service only on the high-density, high-profit routes and would force up the rates of existing carriers on the low-density routes. This would enable new competitors to earn high profits without having to use these profits to subsidize operations on low-cost routes. Existing carriers would also be faced with excess capacity on the high-density routes.[63]

To illustrate the carriers' case but also indicate the misallocative effects of internal subsidies, Figure 7-4 shows the effect of pricing above costs in a low-cost market. The firm prices above costs in low-cost market A, earning a total profit PC_1fg just sufficient to offset its total losses PC_2cd in the high-cost market B. The firm earns a normal rate of return on its investment. If competition is allowed, firms will enter market A, pushing the price down to marginal costs C_1. If the original firm maintained its price at level P in market B, it would incur losses; since price cannot be raised in market A because of the new competition, price must rise in market B. Allowing

62. Leland Johnson found that business calls are a larger proportion of long-haul traffic than short-haul traffic, and that the divergence between price and costs is greater for long-haul traffic ("Communications Satellites").

63. See FCC, Notice of Inquiry to Formulate Policy, Notice of Proposed Rule Making and Order, Docket 18920, p. 11, where AT&T states that its existing capacity is "more than adequate."

competition will then improve the welfare of consumers in the low-cost market A but decrease the welfare of consumers in the low-density, high-cost market B.[64]

Such a system of internal subsidies is a less efficient form of income redistribution than an external subsidy. Since the profits in market A (PC_1fg) exactly equal the loss in market B (PC_2cd), the firm earns no positive profits for the two markets together. But, if the firm charged a price equal to marginal costs in each market ($P_a = C_1$, $P_b = C_2$), output would rise to Q_2 in market A and fall to Y_2 in market B. As a result, consumers in market A would be better off by area PC_1fg (the savings on their previous purchases Q_1) plus area gfh (the gain in consumer surplus for the increased quantity consumed Q_1Q_2). Consumers in market B, on the other hand, would lose area C_2Pme (the increased price on the quantity Y_2 that they previously bought at the old price) and area emd (the decrease in consumer surplus on the reduction in output Y_1Y_2). Both markets would be better off if the gainers (market A) could compensate the losers (market B) for their entire loss ($C_2Pme + emd$); market A would still be better off (by area ecd in dollars and area gfh in consumer surplus).[65]

So, if the firm priced at marginal costs in market A, an external subsidy C_2Pdc could be offered to it for market B, and the community as a whole would be better off by area gfh (consumer surplus). In other words, charging above marginal costs on low-cost routes distorts demand by creating excess demand on high-cost, low-density routes and reducing demand on the low-cost routes; this distortion could be corrected by an external subsidy, which would have the additional advantage of showing the explicit cost of subsidizing the low-cost market, while with an internal price scheme the transfer costs are implicit.

This argument assumes that the external subsidy can be raised by means of nondistorting taxes, an assumption that the recent literature in optimal taxation suggests is not generally valid.[66] What is not clear, however, is whether the distortion created by internal subsidies is less than that created

---

64. This proof is similar to one of Ralph Turvey's *Optimal Pricing and Investment in Electricity Supply: An Essay in Applied Welfare Economics* (London: George Allen and Unwin, 1968), chap. 8.

65. Cf. Kahn (*Economics of Regulation*, vol. 1, p. 191): "This also means that the urban buyers could give the rural ones monetary compensation sufficient to offset the latter's loss of consumer surplus . . . and still remain better off themselves. . . ."

66. Peter A. Diamond and James A. Mirrlees, "Optimal Taxation and Public Production II: Tax Rules," *American Economic Review*, vol. 61 (June 1971), pp. 261–78; J. E. Stiglitz and P. Dasgupta, "Differential Taxation, Public Goods, and Economic Efficiency," *Review of Economic Studies*, vol. 28 (April 1971), pp. 151–74; and Baumol and Bradford, "Optimal Departures."

Figure 7-4. Effects of Internal versus External Subsidies for Firms in Low-Cost and High-Cost Markets

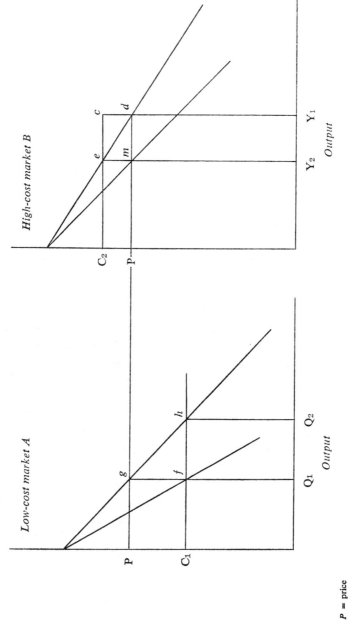

P = price
C_1, C_2 = marginal costs
gfh (emd) = increase (decrease) in consumer surplus when output rises to Q_2 in market A (falls to Y_1 in market B)
PC_1fg (PC_2cd) = profit (loss)
See text discussion.

by external subsidies. With the former, Pareto optimality conditions within the firm are destroyed, but the distortions of taxation are avoided. With the latter, taxes distort Pareto optimality, but relative prices for the firm are not distorted.

Politicians, regulators, and industry members dismiss such considerations as the Pareto optimality of subsidization schemes as politically naive. Not only would a scheme of grants tied to telephone costs be unworkable, but, they argue, it is too late to make such a change. Of course, it is easy to say that gainers should compensate losers, but unless they actually did so, high-cost (rural) areas would suffer. It is thus possible for new competition to have socially harmful effects on income distribution, even though the total costs of production might be the same or even lower when new firms enter. Since competition would create a market situation more efficient than a monopoly, but with different distributions of income, it will be political forces that will determine whether it is allowed—that is, whether the income redistribution it would effect is politically desirable.

The Regulatory Future

The new policies of the FCC will create competition in private line services and in switched digital transmission services. To extend this competition to other users would require a vast reorganization of the industry. The forces that caused the domination of a single firm in the late 1920s will be renewed unless a significant number of intercity firms operates between each city pair. However, there are many city pairs with low traffic volumes where such a multiplicity of intercity plants would not be efficient. Even if the industry were deregulated except for local areas and intercity loops that are natural monopolies, only a small portion of the regulatory process, bureaucracy, and costs could be dismantled—namely, the examination of many intercity charges. A continuous monitoring of new technologies and their costs would still be required. If the rates of return calculated for AT&T's services are correct, a form of deregulation would significantly change prices by increasing local rates and decreasing toll rates.[67] If toll calls constitute a larger proportion of the telephone bill for high-income groups than for low-income groups,[68] and if business shifts

67. In general, toll services appear to be discriminated against compared to local services, as long-haul service is compared to short-haul (Johnson, "Communications Satellites," pp. 49–51, 95).

68. Residential toll calls have been estimated to be income elastic in a time series analysis (Dobell and others, "Telephone Communications," p. 188); a cross-section analysis would probably give the same result.

any reduction in communications costs not onto customers but only onto shareholders,[69] then deregulation has perverse equity (income redistribution) effects.

The decision to deregulate the intercity telecommunications market where possible would lead to efficiency gains for society generally if it resulted in marginal cost pricing. These benefits would have to be weighed against certain costs. First, it is likely that a large regulatory authority would still be necessary, so the direct costs of maintaining the bureaucracy would continue. Second, it is possible that deregulation would redistribute income from rural to high-density urban areas. Finally, its effects on innovation are unknown. As a political decision, the costs of a substantial reorganization of the intercity communications market may exceed the benefits.

Conclusions

This chapter has attempted to lay a number of misconceptions to rest and raise some questions for further research. The "natural" in natural monopoly may well be the result of contracting costs rather than internal plant production economies. Drastic reorganization is not now planned; peripheral competition is being allowed. Entrants into the intercity business communications market are not increasing social production costs; any minor deleterious income redistribution effects they may have are a function of the past price discrimination of the carriers. While precise calculations cannot be made, increased competition is likely, in my view, to be in the public interest. Besides decreasing costs to business users, the impact of competition in the data market will tend to increase the range of services available, as well as increase speed and reliability.

The unfortunate aspect of the new competition is that it confirms the suspicion that the regulatory process tends to maintain monopolies when they are no longer justified, unless powerful interest groups would be better served by competition. The new competition in private line services, for instance, has come about because a number of powerful and vocal groups were dissatisfied with the services offered by existing firms.

The process of regulation creates a certain distribution of income. Where there are no great gains in efficiency from competition, or no power-

---

69. This is a simplifying assumption for illustrative purposes only; the question of corporate shifting is actually very complex.

ful interest groups that would gain from competition, those who are better off in the regulated income distribution will ensure that regulation continues. Where no clear comparisons can be drawn to suggest that society would be better off with a different structure (and, without competition, how can such a comparison be made?), the industry will continue to be regulated as a natural monopoly with, perhaps, peripheral competition in certain markets where competitive pressure is greatest.

The existence of specialized common carriers may, however, be transitory. If the new technologies, lasers and waveguides, prove efficient, the minimum efficient scale in intercity communications will vastly increase. Competition then will center on how to innovate most rapidly. The natural monopoly may return, for natural monopolies are time specific, dependent not on textbook analyses but on the actual technology and demand level. But let us hope that if a new, less costly media does evolve, FCC regulations will not deter its introduction in order to maintain the existing industry structure.

CHAPTER EIGHT

Competition, Regulation, and Product Quality in the Automobile Insurance Industry

DENNIS E. SMALLWOOD

THE AUTOMOBILE INSURANCE INDUSTRY has attracted considerable criticism in recent years, one result of which has been political pressure to replace the tort liability system of compensation with a "no-fault" plan.[1] The case for no-fault has been based primarily on evidence that most of premium revenue of a liability insurance company is allocated to company expenses, litigation costs, and minor "pain and suffering" claims of dubious merit—usually settled out of court—while victims of serious, costly accidents rarely receive full compensation even for tangible economic costs.[2] But it was a wide variety of publicly expressed grievances that generated the pressures for reform, only a few of which would clearly be resolved by no-fault. In numerous hearings and studies at the federal and state levels, particularly the extensive and continuing hearings before the Senate Antitrust and Monopoly Subcommittee,[3] the existence of dis-

---

1. As discussed below, "no-fault" is used to refer to a large number of proposals, among which there are significant differences.

2. Alfred F. Conard and others, *Automobile Accident Costs and Payments: Studies in the Economics of Injury Reparation* (University of Michigan Press, 1964); Robert E. Keeton and Jeffrey O'Connell, *Basic Protection for the Traffic Victim: A Blueprint for Reforming Automobile Insurance* (Little, Brown, 1966); U.S. Department of Transportation, Automobile Insurance and Compensation Study, *Economic Consequences of Automobile Accident Injuries*, vols. 1 and 2 (April 1970).

3. *The Insurance Industry*, Hearings before the Subcommittee on Antitrust and Monopoly of the Senate Committee on the Judiciary, pts. 1–19 (published periodically, 1958–72).

satisfaction with many dimensions of industry performance has been documented, including: the level and rate of increase of premiums; "unfair" differences in premium rates among drivers; the imposition of substantial surcharges after accidents; the slow reduction in accident surcharges causing cumulative surcharges that sometimes exceed the claim that generated them; refusals to renew policyholders after an accident claim, and sometimes for no obvious reason; difficulties encountered by those refused renewal in obtaining insurance from other companies; the inability of some applicants to obtain insurance from any "standard" insurer (as opposed to "substandard" firms that specialize in "high-risk" applicants, at correspondingly high rates); the limited coverage available through "assigned risk" plans; the unfairly low settlement of particular claims; delays in the settlement of both liability and first-party claims; and the generally uncooperative handling of claims by some companies.

Evidence on the actual extent of these problems is scant and unreliable, but the vigor of the political response indicates that they are significant indeed. For instance, a number of states have restricted companies' rights to cancel policies and now force them to give reasons for nonrenewal.[4] Also, a number of the reports commissioned by the Department of Transportation (DOT) in its Automobile Insurance and Compensation Study deal with policyholder complaints, assigned risk plans, the performance of the high-risk specialists, and similar topics not directly related to the no-fault question.

Some no-fault proponents suggest that their plan, in addition to producing more equitable and adequate compensation, also eliminates these other sources of dissatisfaction. But in fact, what effect no-fault or other reforms would have on industry performance in many of these dimensions has not been systematically analyzed. Industry spokesmen have attributed the problems of nonrenewals and underwriting stringency to "inadequate rates," maintaining that some insurance commissioners abused their power to regulate rates by not allowing a complete adjustment for spiraling claims costs. And in fact, the no-fault controversy has eclipsed another significant debate concerning the necessity for rate regulation and the appropriate criteria for "adequate" rates. New York and Florida recently discontinued active regulation in favor of "open competition," partly on the grounds

4. C. A. Kulp and John W. Hall, *Casualty Insurance* (4th ed., Ronald Press, 1968), pp. 438–39.

that allowing firms to file whatever rates they chose would eliminate some of these causes of consumer dissatisfaction.[5]

Although almost all the reports of the DOT study are concerned with some aspect of industry performance, none contains an explicit analysis of the industry in the "structure, conduct, and performance" mode, and neither does such an analysis exist in the extensive literature surrounding the no-fault and the rate regulation controversies.[6] A model that specifies the competitive mechanisms and structural elements distinctively character-istic of the automobile insurance industry is needed, and this chapter attempts to fill that gap.

Following a brief description of the industry and its regulation, a stylized model of the profit-maximizing automobile insurance firm is developed.[7] By explicitly introducing applicant characteristics, the profit-maximizing degree of underwriting stringency for a given premium rate and a particular rating class is derived. This yields a "supply" function for each rating class. On the assumption that the number of applicants is related to the premium level (the "applicant demand" curve), the optimal combination of premium rate and underwriting policy for each rating class is defined.

The relationship between acceptance criteria and accident records is then considered. "Equilibrium surcharge" patterns are derived; these represent relative premium surcharges, across different accident records, that would lead a firm to apply identical acceptance criteria in terms of all other applicant characteristics. The equilibrium pattern is shown to be steeper (that is, the surcharges are higher) the tighter the underwriting policy of the firm. By relating that finding to certain competitive and regulatory aspects of the industry, it can be concluded that firms will adopt surcharge patterns that are inadequate in the sense that some of the appli-cants who are acceptable with good accident records become unacceptable if they compile poor accident records.

5. State of New York Insurance Department, *The Public Interest Now in Property and Liability Insurance Regulation*, A Report to Governor Nelson A. Rockefeller (Insurance Department, January 1969).

6. Roy J. Hensley (*Competition, Regulation, and the Public Interest in Nonlife Insurance* [University of California Press, 1962]) organized his study along these lines but did not attempt to model the automobile insurance firm.

7. Although the majority of automobile insurance is written by nonprofit mutual firms, a nonprofit firm operating in an industry that has relatively low profit levels, as the automobile insurance industry has had in recent years, is forced to adopt profit-maximizing behavior, or at least an approximation of it, in order to survive. The industry is therefore treated as if all firms were explicit profit maximizers.

In the next section, the present industry equilibrium is interpreted in terms of the previously developed model. The effects of different types of rate regulation on statewide loss ratios are then analyzed. A significant regulatory effect is found in certain states, but the general deterioration in underwriting experience during 1967–69 was apparently not produced by regulatory stringency. An alternative explanation is suggested.

Following this is a brief explanation of the principal differences among the various no-fault plans. The implications of different plans for the competitive environment in the industry and for certain dimensions of industry performance are examined.

In the next section, the determination of product quality is considered in the extreme case in which buyers have no ability to judge quality before buying. The results of a Consumers Union survey are analyzed, and an empirical index of "product quality" across a number of large automobile insurance firms is developed. The firm differences thus determined are statistically highly significant. Firms that produce higher than average dissatisfaction on third-party claims also tend to produce higher than average dissatisfaction on first-party claims; this raises doubts about the ability of a no-fault plan to eliminate dissatisfaction with claims handling. There follows a summary of the frequency of complaints filed with the State of New York Insurance Department. These data suggest that a small proportion of automobile insurance firms are supplying a drastically inferior product, compared to the industry average, and are obviously exploiting buyer ignorance.

Finally, the last section summarizes the conclusions and comments on their policy implications.

Structure and Regulation of the Industry

The automobile insurance industry is characterized by moderate concentration and what appear to be low barriers to entry.[8] However, the

8. U.S. Federal Trade Commission, Bureau of Economics, *Structural Trends and Conditions in the Automobile Insurance Industry*, DOT, Automobile Insurance and Compensation Study (April 1970), pp. 1–20; Hensley, *Competition, Regulation, and the Public Interest*, chap. 4. For more detailed discussions of industry structure and regulation, see Frederick G. Crane, *Automobile Insurance Rate Regulation: The Public Control of Price Competition*, Bureau of Business Research Monograph 105 (Ohio State University Press, 1962); John G. Day, *Economic Regulation of Insurance in the United States*, DOT, Automobile Insurance and Compensation Study; Kulp and Hall, *Casualty Insurance;* and Jerome H. Zoffer, *The History of Automobile Liability Insurance Rating* (University of Pittsburgh Press, 1959).

industry differs from the competitive ideal in three critical ways. First, potential customers are not necessarily equally desirable to an insurer. Two applicants may be in the same rating class and therefore pay the same premium, but the insurer's (subjective) probability distribution of claims may predict different claims costs for each. A fundamental assumption of the model developed below is that the applicant characteristics that define the rating classes are not the only ones considered relevant by insurers, so that applicant selection occurs. This is an assumption that has been emphasized in the literature.[9] A model of the automobile insurance firm must explicitly include the applicant selection process if it is to be used to predict the effects of regulation or reform.

The second characteristic of the industry that falls short of the competitive ideal is the extreme difficulty of evaluating the quality of the product. The term "quality" is used here to refer primarily to the reasonableness of the firm's response to a sizable first-party claim (that is, a claim made against a policyholder's own insurer, as opposed to a third-party claim, which is made by another party against the policyholder's insurer, under a liability coverage). That significant differences exist among insurers is undeniable; a short perusal of the complaint files in the State of New York Insurance Department leaves the observer impressed at the imaginative methods of evasion, obfuscation, and stalling used by some firms. The problem is that judging the quality of an automobile insurance contract involves the prediction of the firm's actions in response to unknown contingencies, for which the firm's reputation may be an unreliable guide.

The third way in which the industry differs from the competitive model arises from the character of public regulation. In the past, the industry operated as a reasonably effective cartel. The bulk of automobile insurance was sold through the American Agency System, whereby independent agents, working on a commission basis, represented the various insurers. Premium rates were set jointly by rate bureaus. The common rates and the sanctions applied to enforce them were justified by the arguments that rates should be based on the widest possible experience, that insurer insolvencies inflict severe and highly inequitable welfare losses, and that competition inevitably leads to rate wars and inadequate rates. In this way, rates were kept comfortably high and few applicants were rejected. An at-

9. Kulp and Hall, *Casualty Insurance*, pp. 460–61, 479–80; see particularly the figures on pages 467–70 of Calvin H. Brainard, *Automobile Insurance* (Richard D. Irwin, 1961), which reflect assumptions similar to those made here.

tempt to select the better risks within each class was considered a destructive and unethical tactic; it was assumed that part of the insurer's function was to average losses over customers facing different degrees of hazard, within reasonable limits. The classification system was simple and did not include surcharges for accidents.

One difficulty faced by the cartel was the problem of keeping commission rates at a reasonable level. A company that raised its commission rate above the standard could gain a significant increase in market share. Since premium rates were comfortably high and most applicants attractive, there was a strong tendency for commission rates to rise; at one point in the 1940s they reached over 30 percent. The result was classic monopolistic competition at the retail level. Agreements were made to limit commissions or the number of agents in particular areas, but the low level of concentration and ease of entry weakened their effect.[10]

Two developments during the postwar period dramatically altered the structure of the industry. One was the rapid growth of direct writers—firms that sold automobile insurance directly, either through salesmen operating on a salary basis with a small commission, or through the mail. The cartel was vulnerable to the expansion of the direct writers both because of its high agent commissions and because agency firms were not fully exploiting differences in expected costs among applicants. From a minor position in the prewar period, the direct writers grew until, in 1968, they accounted for 41 percent of automobile liability premiums and 47 percent of physical damage premiums.[11]

The second development was rate regulation at the state level, following the *South-Eastern Underwriters Association* case in 1944.[12] In that decision, it was unexpectedly decided that insurance is commerce and thus subject to the antitrust laws. The resulting McCarran-Ferguson Act[13] exempted joint rate making in states that actively regulated the industry.

The state regulation that resulted falls into four categories. The system used by most states, although the details may vary, is called "file with approval." This means that premium rates must be filed with the insurance commissioner and must be approved before they can be used, but in most states this requirement is fulfilled if the commissioner does not reject the

10. See Simon N. Whitney, *Antitrust Policies: American Experience in Twenty Industries* (Twentieth Century Fund, 1958), vol. 2, pp. 360–61, 371–76.

11. *Structural Trends and Conditions*, DOT Study, p. 9.

12. *United States* v. *South-Eastern Underwriters Association*, 322 U.S. 533 (1944).

13. P.L. 15, 79 Cong. 1 sess. (1945) (59 Stat. 33).

submission within a specified time. The system in which the formal approval period is omitted but the right of the commissioner to reject rates is retained is called "file-and-use." It exists in Delaware, Maine, Massachusetts, Ohio, and Wyoming. Since a firm can use newly filed rates immediately, this is considered to produce looser regulation, although in theory a commissioner could be just as active as under the first system. A still looser system, in which rates are filed only to allow public access to them, or are not filed at all, is termed "open competition." An open competition law has been adopted in California, Idaho, Missouri, and Montana, and recently in Florida and Virginia. New York passed an open competition law that took effect January 1, 1970, but the no-fault plan that took effect February 1, 1974, brings back the system of file with approval. Finally, at the opposite extreme from open competition is the "mandatory bureau" system, in which all firms must use rates, submitted by a bureau, based on statewide loss experience. The mandatory bureau system is used in North Carolina and Texas, and, for minimum compulsory liability coverages only, in Massachusetts.

The universal criterion for acceptable premium rates is that they must not be "excessive, inadequate, or unfairly discriminatory"; this clearly leaves room for interpretation. One common interpretation is that charging different premium rates to two policy holders within the same rating class is discriminatory. Thus, in order to insure policyholders of different degrees of desirability at different rates, firms must create legally distinct subsidiaries. Many automobile insurance firms do include two or three subsidiaries, selling at successively higher rates to "preferred," "standard," and "substandard" applicants. For the purposes of the model, each subsidiary is treated as an independent firm, so that a "firm" is constrained to use a single premium rate in each rating class.

Until recently, rates were rarely rejected for being excessive, but since the mid-sixties several commissioners have disallowed proposed rate increases. During the forties and fifties, however, firms that attempted to file premium rates below those filed by the rate bureaus were frequently frustrated. While the right to file rates below bureau rates is now widely established except in the mandatory bureau states, several states still allow only "deviation filings," in which a firm's rates can differ from bureau rates only by a fixed percentage across rating classes. Where firms are allowed to file rates that are independent of bureau rates, they must often justify them as a "reasonable" markup over the firm's costs and "loss experience" (a term that refers to the firm's recent average claims cost in each rating class). In some states, a firm is allowed to use cost differences as a justification for rates below bureau rates but cannot justify lower rates on the basis of lower average claims.

Although joint rate making is exempt from antitrust law, other agreements, such as those with the purpose of controlling commissions, are not. And while the success of the direct writers has reduced agency commissions, a sizable differential persists; the "commission and brokerage" ratio averaged 16.2 percent in 1969 for the thirteen agency firms among the largest twenty firms in terms of automobile bodily injury liability premiums earned, and only 4.8 percent for the five direct writers in the group.[14] Since the premium rates of the direct writers are typically lower by 10 to 20 percent, this comparison understates the absolute difference.

Given this persistent cost difference, one may wonder why no agency firm has ever converted to direct writing. A major hurdle is that a converted firm would not legally be able to solicit its former policyholders in any way. The *National Fire Insurance* case of 1904[15] established an agent's property rights in the information related to his customers' expiration dates. The ruling not only allows an agent to sell his file of expirations (that is, to sell his agency) but also forecloses any actions by the insurer that might appear to be direct solicitation of its policyholders. Furthermore, since agents have active nationwide trade associations, an insurer that attempted to convert to direct writing in one part of the country would find its policyholders in other areas being transferred by its agents to other firms as their policies expired. An agency firm would thus have to convert to direct writing on a nationwide basis and without any direct attempt to retain its former policyholders. This barrier to conversion is strengthened by the fact that automobile insurance represents only a part (for some, only a small fraction) of the insurance written through agents by most of the agency firms, whereas the direct writers are typically more specialized. Some of the other types of insurance are less suitable for direct writing, so a firm that converted in some lines might find sanctions applied through business being withdrawn in others.

Agency firms are thus effectively locked into the agency system.[16] This

14. New York Insurance Department, *1969 Loss and Expense Ratios: Insurance Expense Exhibits* (The Department, n.d.), table 11. There were also two reciprocals— a type of cooperative direct writer that is clearly not comparable—among the top twenty.

15. *National Fire Insurance Company* v. *Sullard*, 89 N.Y.S. 934, 97 App. Div. 233.

16. Since the initial draft of this chapter was written, the Insurance Company of North America (INA), an agency writer, announced (in April 1972) a "limited experi-

has disadvantages in addition to the resulting high selling costs. It has already been mentioned that different applicants within a rating class are not equally desirable. But an application does not contain all relevant information, and, in any case, a firm cannot afford to review critically all applications submitted. Thus, an agency firm is concerned that an agent may not be allocating a proportionate share of the relatively good risks to it, but may instead be favoring other firms, whether because of commission levels, disguised payments in other forms, or advantages competitors may have in other lines. Since most agency firms have been minimally profitable in recent years, it might be concluded that commissions would fall because the agents' leverage, based on the threat of withholding business, has been eliminated. But their ability to control the mix of policies is still a source of some power, and when recent experience with a particular agent has been poor, the agency firm cannot be confident that it is not attributable to the ability or bias of the agent.

Furthermore, if an agency firm attempts to improve its portfolio by selectively refusing renewal, the agent's good will is jeopardized; a canceled or nonrenewed policyholder may withdraw other business from the agent and may broadcast his experience. But an agency firm cannot refuse renewal to a significant proportion of an agent's clients without risking the possibility that he will transfer the better risks elsewhere. Thus it is not uncommon for an agent to be dropped completely, which forces the firm to cancel or refuse renewal to all of his clients,[17] including some whom the firm might consider highly attractive risks.

Even with the handicaps of high commissions and vulnerability to agent favoritism, the large agency firms have held their own recently, in the midst of gradual rationalization: the thirteen agency firms among the twenty

_____

ment" to sell insurance by direct mail solicitation, through a subsidiary, in Indiana. Although INA had only 0.7 percent of the market in Indiana and the announced intention was only to supplement the agency efforts, the announcement prompted an emergency meeting of 350 agents from thirty-eight states, at which "although . . . counsel . . . cautioned against resolutions urging concerted action, many agents spoke of steps taken to cease writing new business for INA and/or not renew existing business" (*Best's Review*, vol. 73 [August 1972], pp. 2, 90, 91, and, for the quotation, p. 5). At the next meeting of the National Association of Insurance Agents, it was charged that the INA plan "is an attempt by the company to maintain, in its own name, its agency force for some business, and, at the same time under another name, become a direct writer for all practical purposes on the other business. One thing is certain, INA cannot have it both ways" (ibid., vol. 73 [June 1972], p. 5).

17. As discussed below, the heterogeneous and changing nature of rating territories is another cause of agency cancellations.

largest (in terms of total auto premiums in 1968) had 22.4 percent of the market in 1955 and 26.7 percent in 1968; the seven direct writers had 21.7 percent in 1955 and 29.8 percent in 1968.[18] This relative stalemate has evolved because most of the direct writers have adopted low premium rates and highly selective underwriting policies.

A Model of Selection and Firm Supply

The behavior of a profit-maximizing insurance firm differs from that of a firm producing an ordinary good or service. The cost and reliability of information concerning the degree of risk of applicants as well as the rational treatment of risk must be considered.[19]

Maximization Subject to a Selection Frontier Constraint

To analyze the behavior of a profit-maximizing insurance firm, three sets of information available to the underwriter must be distinguished. The first set is comprised of the characteristics embodied in the classification scheme used to set premium rates, and includes the age, sex, and marital status of the principal driver, the territory in which the car is garaged, use of the car to drive to work, and so forth. For simplicity, each applicant is assumed to represent a single "principal operator." Also, which is approximately true, each firm is assumed to use the same classification scheme. Although it is also reflected in rates, the driver's accident record[20] is distinguished as the second set of information. The third set includes all other characteristics of the driver or his car believed by the insurer to be relevant to his expected claims cost. Under the tort liability system, this third set includes the driver's occupation, personality traits, personal appearance, and poise, in addition to further details about the insured automobile and its use. For convenience, these three sets will be referred to as the *objective factors*, the *accident record*, and the *subjective factors*, respectively.

18. *Structural Trends and Conditions*, DOT Study, p. 22.
19. This section may be omitted by readers who are interested primarily in the policy implications of the model for regulatory purposes, which are presented in the next two sections.
20. Since underwriters appear to consider conviction for a major traffic violation to be equivalent to an accident as an indicator of riskiness, the term "accident" is used to refer to either in the model.

The following analysis refers to the population of applicants who share the same objective factors and accident record. The basic assumption is that drivers are of two types—good and bad; while good drivers have accidents, bad drivers have them more often. If a driver can have 0 or 1 accident per period, then in each period

(1)   prob [accident | good driver] = u, $0 < u < 1$.

prob [accident | bad driver] = $u(1 + d)$, $d > 0, u(1 + d) \leq 1$.

One period is assumed to be the duration of all insurance policies; in fact, most policies are written for six months. Obviously the assumption that accidents occur according to a binomial probability law is not completely appropriate, and is made here for the sake of simplicity.

The parameters u and d may differ for drivers with different objective characteristics—that is, for drivers in different rating classes. Accidents in different periods are assumed to be independent stochastic events for each driver. These highly stylized assumptions about the risk characteristics of drivers in each rating class are made primarily to simplify the exposition; the model can easily be generalized.

It is assumed further that the cost of each accident is the same. Ignoring the randomness of accident costs is merely a formality in the analysis, since only expected values are relevant. When the effect of different accident records is considered, it becomes a restrictive assumption, since both differences in expected accident costs and differences in frequency become relevant. In fact, the evidence does not suggest that there is a substantial difference in the average severity of accidents between drivers who are frequently involved in accidents and those who are infrequently involved. Assigning different accident severity distributions to good and bad drivers would complicate the analyses of accident records slightly, but it would not alter the conclusions.

The costs related to particular policies are then: c = the cost of a claim, assumed to be equal for all claims; and w = the cost of writing a policy. Loss-adjustment expenses, which are the direct costs of settling claims other than payments to the claimants, are assumed to be included in c; both administrative costs and agent commissions are included in w. That for some (but not all) firms the cost of renewing a policy is substantially less than the cost of writing a new one is ignored.

The expected cost of writing a good driver is thus $(w + cu)$, while the expected cost of writing a bad driver is $(w + cu + cud)$. The premium rate is written R. If $R < (w + cu)$, the firm that attempts to maximize expected profits would be unwilling to write anyone. If $R > (w + cu + cud)$, the firm would be willing to accept all applicants in the class. If $(w + cu) < R < (w + cu + cud)$, the firm would prefer to accept all good drivers and reject all bad drivers.

These statements ignore the effect of discounting. Since premiums are paid at the beginning of the period while claims occur during or after the period, the firm earns investment income as well as underwriting income. But as long as the claims of good and bad drivers are distributed the same with respect to time, the inclusion of investment income does not affect the analysis. Suppose that the timing of claims, measured from the beginning of the period, occurs according to the distribution $x(t)$, $t \geq 0$, and that the relevant (continuous) discount rate is r. Then it can be shown that a firm that maximizes expected discounted profits will make exactly the same decisions as if claims of size C^* were paid at the beginning of the period, where:

$$C^* = c\left[\int_0^\infty e^{-rt}x(t)dt\right].$$

Thus, if it is assumed that the cost of a claim, c, has been corrected as above, it is valid to treat the firm as if it were maximizing underwriting income alone or, equivalently, as if it were operating with a discount rate of 0. Henceforth c will represent the corrected cost of a claim.

The basic premise of the model is that the insurer cannot distinguish with certainty the good and bad drivers. This is not to say that all applicants look alike to him, but that the applicants' subjective factors are not distributed independently of the quality of being a good or bad driver. It is immaterial, in modeling insurer behavior, whether such characteristics are in fact related to driver quality; the operative factor is that the insurer *believes* that they are. The underwriting function in this context is to decide which combinations of the subjective factors define acceptable applicants and which unacceptable.

Figure 8-1 shows the case of a single subjective characteristic x, with respect to which the population of good drivers in this class has probability density $f_g(x)$, and the population of bad drivers has a probability density $f_b(x)$. Figure 8-2 represents the case of two characteristics, x and y. Level curves (along which the probability density is constant) of the two joint probability densities are drawn. Also indicated are two points in Figure 8-1 and three lines in Figure 8-2 that represent possible selection rules (for

Figure 8-1. Probability Densities for Automobile Insurance Applicants, Based on a Single Subjective Characteristic, x

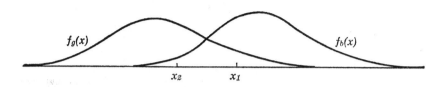

f_g, f_b = probability density of good and bad drivers, respectively
x_1, x_2 = selection rule points

Source: See discussion in the text.

example, drivers whose characteristic x falls to the left of x_1 or to the left of line *1* should be accepted, those to the right should be rejected).

The choice of different rules involves a trade-off between two goods: the probability that a good driver (randomly generated from the population of good drivers) is accepted and the probability that a randomly generated bad driver is rejected. Let p = the probability that a good driver is accepted, and q = the probability that a bad driver is rejected. The relationship between p and q is particularly easy to see in the one-characteristic case: if the selection rule is to accept all applicants with $x \leq x_1$, then p is the proportion of the density $f_g(x)$ to the left of x_1, while q is the proportion of the density $f_b(x)$ to the right of x_1. As the point x_1 moves along the x-axis (or as the selection line shifts across the x—y plane in the two-characteristic case), a function $p = h(q)$ is defined that has the characteristics of a production possibilities frontier. This function will be referred to as the *selection frontier*.

Such a frontier is shown in Figure 8-3. There, points *1*, *2*, and *3* could correspond to lines *1*, *2*, and *3* in Figure 8-2. The selection rule represented by line *3* would be inefficient, while within the set of efficient selection rules, line *1* would represent a tighter underwriting policy than line *2*. Point C in Figure 8-3 represents completely indiscriminate acceptance; point E represents complete rejection; and point D represents perfect discrimina-

Figure 8-2. Probability Densities for Automobile Insurance Applicants, Based on Two Subjective Characteristics, x and y

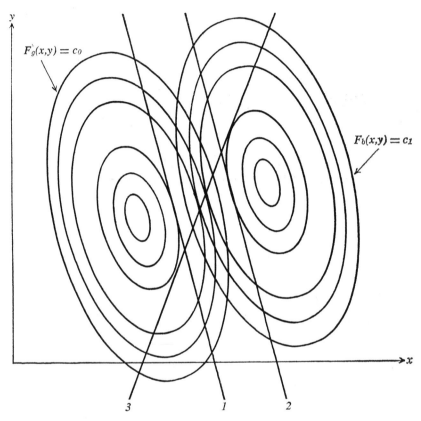

F_g, F_b = probability density of good and bad drivers, respectively
1, 2, 3 = selection rule lines

Source: See discussion in the text.

tion between the two populations. If two points in the p—q plane are attainable, then any point on the line segment between them is attainable by applying the selection rule that produces the first point a proportion α of the time and the other point $(1 - \alpha)$ of the time. Thus the curve $p = h(q)$ is always concave, and is assumed to be strictly concave. Note that the selection frontier is defined for a particular class of applicants; its shape may differ across classes. Although the number of subjective factors that firms consider may be great, it does not follow that the selection frontier is

Figure 8-3. The Selection Frontier for the Automobile Insurance Firm's Acceptance or Rejection of Applicants

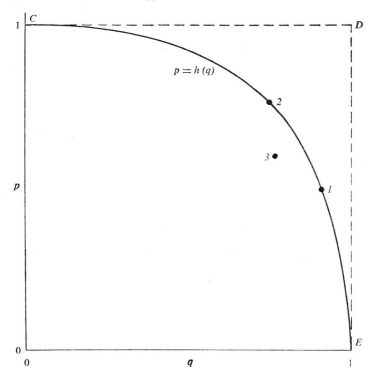

p, q = probability that a good (bad) driver is accepted (rejected)
1, 2, 3 = selection rule points
C, E, D = completely indiscriminate acceptance, complete rejection, perfect discrimination between the two populations, respectively

Source: See discussion in the text.

close to point D. The literature suggests that the explanations of the causes of accidents and accident proneness are extremely crude, with a poor statistical foundation.[21] On the other hand, the careful screening of applicants by insurance firms demonstrates that they believe their selection frontiers do differ significantly from a straight line.

The auto insurance firm is assumed to maximize expected profits while

21. See David Klein and Julian A. Waller, *Causation, Culpability and Deterrence in Highway Crashes*, DOT, Automobile Insurance and Compensation Study, and DOT, *Driver Behavior and Accident Involvement: Implications for Tort Liability*, Automobile Insurance and Compensation Study.

constrained by a selection frontier and by either a given premium rate or a demand curve that relates the number of applicants to the premium rate.

Suppose that the firm chooses to operate with premium rate R for the class under consideration and at point $(q, h[q])$ on the selection frontier. Then the relevant quantities are as follows:

Item	Good drivers	Bad drivers
Expected total applicants	$(1 - k)A(R)$	$kA(R)$
Expected total acceptances	$h(q)(1 - k)A(R)$	$(1 - q)kA(R)$
Revenue per acceptance	R	R
Expected cost per acceptance	$w + cu$	$w + cu + cud$

where $A(R) =$ the number of applicants per period within the class, and $k =$ the proportion of bad drivers in the population of possible applicants.

Thus, at premium rate R and underwriting policy q, the firm's expected profits are

(2) $\quad E\pi(R, q) = h(q)(1 - k)A(R)(R - w - cu)$
$$+ (1 - q)kA(R)(R - w - cu - cud).$$

Direct computation produces the following first-order conditions:

(3) $\qquad \dfrac{\partial E\pi}{\partial q} = 0 \qquad \dfrac{1 - k}{k} h'(q) = \dfrac{R - (w + cu + cud)}{R - (w + cu)}$

(4) $\qquad\qquad\qquad R = w + cu + cud\left[\dfrac{k}{k - (1 - k)h'(q)}\right]$

(5) $\qquad \dfrac{\partial E\pi}{\partial R} = 0 \qquad -\dfrac{A(R)}{A'(R)} = R - w - cu$

$$- cud\left[\dfrac{(1 - q)k}{(1 - q)k + (1 - k)h(q)}\right].$$

If ϵ is the point elasticity of the demand curve $A(R)$, then the equations $-A(R)/A'(R) = R/\epsilon$ and $MPR = R(1 - 1/\epsilon)$ are both identities, where MPR is defined as "marginal potential revenue"; that is, where MPR is equal to marginal revenue in the case where all applicants are accepted. Using these identities, equation (5) can be rewritten:

(6) $\qquad MPR = w + cu + cud\left[\dfrac{(1 - q)k}{(1 - q)k + (1 - k)h(q)}\right].$

From above, the expected number of bad drivers accepted, B, and expected total acceptances, T, are defined

(7) $\quad B = (1 - q)kA(R), \qquad T = (1 - q)kA(R) + h(q)(1 - k)A(R).$

If s is defined as B/T, it can be loosely interpreted as the expected ratio of bad drivers to drivers accepted. From (7),

(8) $$s = B/T = (1 - q)k/\{(1 - q)k + h(q)(1 - k)\}.$$

Since

(9) $$\frac{\partial B}{\partial q} = -kA(R) \quad \text{and} \quad \frac{\partial T}{\partial q} = -kA(R) + (1 - k)A(R)h'(q),$$

then

(10) $$t = \frac{\partial B}{\partial T} = \frac{\partial B}{\partial q} \bigg/ \frac{\partial T}{\partial q} = \frac{k}{k - (1 - k)h'(q)},$$

where t is the probability that a "threshold" applicant, whose characteristics are precisely on the borderline between the acceptance and rejection regions, is a bad driver. In terms of the parameters t and s, the first-order conditions can be rewritten as

(11) $$R = w + cu + (cud)t$$

(12) $$MPR = w + cu + (cud)s.$$

Equations (11) and (12) are capable of direct interpretation. With the premium rate fixed, (11) implies that underwriting standards should be adjusted so that the expected cost of a threshold applicant is equal to the premium rate. Suppose, alternatively, that underwriting standards are fixed at a point where the firm accepts a proportion μ of all applicants. Since s is the proportion of accepted applicants who are bad drivers, the expected marginal cost of one extra applicant is $\mu[w + cu + (cud)s]$. A reduction in R sufficient to attract one extra applicant will result in an expected loss in revenue equal to

$$\mu \left[\frac{A(R)}{A'(R)} \right] = \mu MPR,$$

so that (12) represents the equality of expected marginal cost and expected marginal revenue. The assumption that $h(q)$ is strictly concave implies that both $t(q)$ and $s(q)$ are strictly decreasing functions. The value of s is thus uniquely related to the value of t:

(13) $$s = \psi(t) \qquad t* \leq t \leq t**,$$

where

(14) $$t* = \frac{k}{k - (1 - k)h'(1)} \quad \text{and} \quad t** = \frac{k}{k - (1 - k)h'(0)},$$

representing the probabilities that a threshold applicant is a bad driver under the tightest and loosest possible underwriting standards. The function ψ relates the proportion of bad drivers among the population of acceptable applicants to the probability that a threshold applicant is a bad driver. Combining (13) and (11), a function called the *selective marginal cost* curve (*SMC*) can be defined as follows:

(15) $SMC =$

$$
\begin{cases}
w + cu + cudt_* & R(A) < w + cu + cudt_* \\
w + cu + cud\ \psi\{[R(A) - w - cu]/cud\} & \begin{array}{l} w + cu + cudt_* \leq R(A) \\ \leq w + cu + cudt_{**} \end{array} \\
w + cu + cudt_{**} & R(A) > w + cu + cudt_{**}
\end{cases}.
$$

The selective marginal cost curve indicates the expected cost of an additional (randomly generated) acceptance when underwriting standards have been adjusted to the premium rate $R(A)$. Combining (11), (12), (13), and (15), the joint equilibrium with respect to both R and q can be written

(16) $MPR = SMC,$

and can be depicted as in Figure 8-4.

The figure can be used to illustrate some comparative static results. Consider the effect of a change in the elasticity of the applicant demand curve, as in Figure 8-5. Since the *SMC* curve depends on the applicant demand curve, consider a rotation of the demand curve in a small interval such as (A_1, A_2) around the equilibrium point. If the elasticity of the demand curve is increased, the *MPR* curve is shifted up while the *SMC* curve is rotated slightly around the old equilibrium. Since the *SMC* curve is monotonically decreasing, the new equilibrium must occur at a lower R and at a point on the *SMC* curve corresponding to a higher q. This means that in response to an increase in the elasticity of the applicant demand curve at the equilibrium point, the profit-maximizing insurance firm will lower the premium rate and adopt a more highly selective underwriting policy.

Since the direct cost of writing a policy differs significantly across firms, the response of R and q to a change in w is also of interest. The differentiation of (16) with respect to w, after some manipulation, yields

(17) $\dfrac{\partial R}{\partial w} = (\Delta_D - \Delta_{SMC})/(\Delta_{MPR} - \Delta_{SMC})$ and

$$\frac{\partial(R - w)}{\partial w} = (\Delta_D - \Delta_{MPR})/(\Delta_{MPR} - \Delta_{SMC}),$$

where Δ_D, Δ_{SMC}, and Δ_{MPR} are the (absolute) slopes of the applicant demand curve, the selective marginal cost curve, and the marginal potential

Figure 8-4. Applicant Demand, Marginal Potential Revenue, and Selective Marginal Cost Curves for an Automobile Insurance Firm

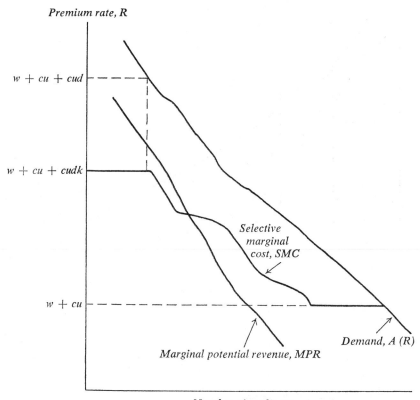

$w + cu$ and $w + cu + cud$ = cost of writing a good and bad driver, respectively
k = proportion of bad drivers in the population

Source: See text equations (1) to (16).

revenue curve, respectively. The condition $\Delta_{MPR} > \Delta_{SMC}$, implying that the MPR curve cuts the SMC curve from above, is a necessary condition for the equilibrium point to represent a maximum. Both denominators in (17) must therefore be positive. From (11), $\partial t/\partial w$ has the same sign as $\partial(R - w)/\partial w$. Thus, three possibilities exist:

(I)	(II)	(III)
$\Delta_D < \Delta_{SMC} < \Delta_{MPR}$	$\Delta_{SMC} < \Delta_D < \Delta_{MPR}$	$\Delta_{SMC} < \Delta_{MPR} < \Delta_D$
$\dfrac{\partial R}{\partial w} < 0, \dfrac{\partial t}{\partial w} < 0$	$\dfrac{\partial R}{\partial w} > 0, \dfrac{\partial t}{\partial w} < 0$	$\dfrac{\partial R}{\partial w} > 0, \dfrac{\partial t}{\partial w} > 0.$

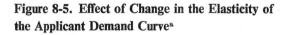

**Figure 8-5. Effect of Change in the Elasticity of
the Applicant Demand Curve**[a]

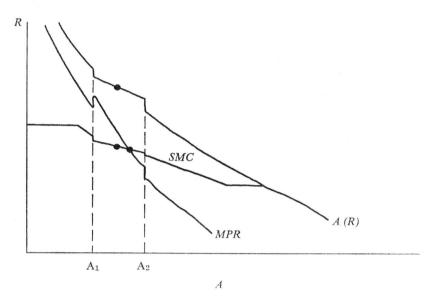

a. The symbols are as defined in Figure 8-4. See the text for further explanation.

In case (II), an increase in w leads to an increase in R and tighter underwriting standards (a lower t). This is the normally expected response; but
case (I) can arise if the selection frontier has a small curvature at the
related point, while case (III) arises if the elasticity of the applicant demand
curve is rapidly increasing in $A(\Delta_D > \Delta_{MPR})$ (that is, if the elasticity with
respect to A of the *slope* of the curve $R(A)$ is greater than 1).

The Effect of Different Accident Records

The profit-maximizing premium rate and underwriting policy has now
been derived for a subset of applicants who share the same objective
factors, which determine their rating class, and the same accident record.
Next is a consideration of a subset of applicants within a particular rating
class and an analysis of the relevance of their different accident records.

Suppose that information on N periods is available for a driver, and that
within those N periods he had M accidents. By assumption, a driver can
have at most one accident per period, so that $M \leq N$. The subset of applicants under consideration are all those in the given rating class who have

M/N accident records. The subscript M/N is thus appended to the premium rate and to the threshold probability t, so that the equilibrium condition for drivers with an M/N accident record becomes

(18) $$R_{M/N} = w + cu + cud\, t_{M/N}.$$

The probability $t_{M/N}$ is based on both the subjective factors and the applicant's accident record; for two applicants with identical subjective characteristics, a poorer driving record will imply a higher $t_{M/N}$. The two sources of information are combined by Bayes theorem on conditional probabilities, which in this context can be written

(19) $$P[b \mid (M/N)] = P_b[M/N] \cdot P_* + P_g[M/N] \cdot (1 - P_*),$$

where $P[b \mid (M/N)]$ is the inferred probability that a driver is bad, based on *both* his driving record and his subjective characteristics; $P_g[M/N]$ and $P_b[M/N]$ are the probabilities that good and bad drivers, respectively, will compile (M/N) accident records; and P_* is the probability that a driver is good or bad based *solely* on his subjective characteristics.

The parameters u and d and the selection frontier $h(q)$ are constant across the population of applicants within a particular rating class. The difference between two populations of applicants who have the same subjective characteristics but different accident records is reflected entirely in a different k, the proportion of bad drivers in the population. From (1), the assumptions about accident probabilities for good and bad drivers imply that:

(20) $$P_g[M/N] = \binom{N}{M} u^M (1 - u)^{N-M}$$

(21) $$P_b[M/N] = \binom{N}{M} [u(1 + d)]^M [1 - u(1 + d)]^{N-M}.$$

If $r_{M/N}$ is defined as

(22) $$\begin{aligned} r_{M/N} &= P_b[M/N]/P_g[M/N] \\ &= (1 + d)^M \{(1 - u(1 + d))/(1 - u)\}^{N-M}, \end{aligned}$$

then (19) can be rewritten:

(23) $$P[b \mid (M/N)] = \frac{r_{M/N} \cdot P_*}{r_{M/N} \cdot P_* + (1 - P_*)}.$$

The equilibrium condition (18) can be expressed thus:

(24)
$$\frac{R - (w + cu)}{cud} = t_{M/N} = P[b \mid (M/N)] = \frac{r_{M/N} P_*(M/N)}{r_{M/N} P_*(M/N) + 1 - P_*(M/N)},$$

where $P*(M/N)$ is the probability that a threshold applicant is a bad driver, based entirely on the applicant's subjective characteristics. If the $R_{M/N}$ is independent of the accident record, then (24) implies that the profit-maximizing firm will set $P*(M/N)$ lower, the poorer the accident record (that is, the higher is $r_{M/N}$). In other words, in the absence of accident surcharges, the firm will impose tighter underwriting standards—in terms of the subjective factors—the poorer the accident record. Some applicants who are acceptable when they have good accident records thus become unacceptable if they compile poorer records.

If the $P*(M/N)$ is held constant across accident records, (24) defines an "equilibrium surcharge pattern"—that is, a schedule for the $R_{M/N}$ that will provide the same underwriting standards for all applicants (including renewals) in the rating class, independent of their accident record. Solving (24) for $R_{M/N}$ and using $R_{0/0}$ as a numeraire (note that $r_{0/0} = 1$) produces

$$(25) \quad \frac{R_{M/N} - R_{0/0}}{R_{0/0}} = \left\{ \frac{\bar{P}*(1 - \bar{P}*)(r_{M/N} - 1)}{r_{M/N} \cdot \bar{P}* + 1 - \bar{P}*} \right\} \left\{ \frac{1}{\bar{P}* + \left(\dfrac{w + cu}{cud} \right)} \right\},$$

where $\bar{P}*$ is the common probability that a threshold applicant is a bad driver on the basis of his subjective characteristics alone. The equilibrium surcharge pattern thus depends on both the severity of the underwriting standards and the parameters of the model. Equilibrium percentage surcharges were computed for different values of $\bar{P}*$ and for all combinations of the following choices for each parameter:

$u = 0.05, 0.10 \qquad d = 4, 5 \qquad w = 0.15, 0.20 \qquad cu = 0.40, 0.50.$

Table 8-1 shows the percentage surcharges for the combinations of the parameters that produced the steepest and the flattest patterns. The most significant observation is that the equilibrium surcharge pattern is much steeper for firms that are highly selective (a low $\bar{P}*$) than for less selective ones.

The firm is not constrained, however, to apply the same underwriting standards to policyholders with different accident records. In fact, both competitive and regulatory pressures may lead firms to adopt accident surcharge plans that are not consistent with (25). Competitive pressures arise because the schedule of accident surcharges, as well as the basic premium rate, is a factor in the attractiveness of a policy. The maximizing firm for which a tight underwriting policy is optimal—either because it has relatively high costs or because it is using a low premium rate to attract applicants—must choose either to use a surcharge schedule significantly

Table 8-1. Equilibrium Percentage Surcharge Patterns for Automobile Insurance Applicants with Different Accident Records, for Two Sets of Parameters[a]

Percent

Number of accidents and number of periods	Probability of bad driving quality based solely on subjective characteristics, $\bar{P}_*$			
	0.20	0.40	0.60	0.80
$d = 5, u = 0.05, w = 0.15, cu = 0.50$				
0:4	−29	−36	−34	−24
0:3	−24	−29	−26	−17
0:2	−18	−20	−18	−11
0:1	−10	−11	−9	−5
0:0	0	0	0	0
1:4	38	33	21	10
1:3	54	43	27	12
1:2	71	53	31	14
1:1	87	61	35	15
2:4	137	80	43	18
2:3	145	83	44	18
2:2	152	85	44	18
3:4	169	89	46	19
3:3	170	90	46	19
4:4	173	91	46	19
$d = 4, u = 0.10, w = 0.20, cu = 0.40$				
0:4	−31	−44	−49	−45
0:3	−28	−38	−41	−33
0:2	−22	−30	−29	−21
0:1	−14	−17	−15	−9
0:0	0	0	0	0
1:4	−4	−5	−4	−2
1:3	14	14	10	5
1:2	36	32	21	10
1:1	62	48	29	13
2:4	80	56	33	14
2:3	100	65	36	16
2:2	115	70	38	16
3:4	130	75	40	17
3:3	134	76	40	17
4:4	138	77	41	17

Source: Derived from equation (25).
a. u = prob [accident | good driver]
$u(1 + d)$ = prob [accident | bad driver]
w = cost of writing a policy
c = cost of a claim.

more severe than that of other firms or to use a typical surcharge schedule and refuse to renew marginal policyholders who compile poor accident records. The choice will depend on how thoroughly premium rate information can be disseminated compared to how rapidly and thoroughly the knowledge of nonrenewals spreads. But firms can advertise premium rates, while information on the extent of nonrenewals seems to be almost non-existent, much less publicized. Furthermore, a policyholder who was hit with a very large surcharge after an accident may complain as loudly as one who was refused renewal. Thus, a highly selective firm will probably be discouraged from adopting a steep surcharge schedule.

Regulatory pressures may be direct, as where an insurance commissioner in a state with a file with approval or file-and-use system disallows a pro-posed surcharge plan. Behind the rejection could be the belief, based on a lack of understanding of the probabilistic basis for surcharges, that the policyholder should not be forced to "repay" an accident claim, or the belief, possibly justified, that a low basic premium rate combined with a steep surcharge schedule may create the illusion that policyholders are obtaining better terms than they actually are. More pervasive is an indirect regulatory effect that relates to the requirement in most states that premium rate differentials be justified by differences in loss experience within the firm, at least, and, in some states, across all firms operating in the state.

Equilibrium surcharge patterns, as defined by (25), reflect the relation-ship between expected claims cost and (M/N) for a threshold policyholder in a particular rating class. Thus, loss experience data would be consistent, on average, with (25) only if they were for a single rating class and only if all policyholders within the class had subjective characteristics that implied the same $P*$. In fact, to the author's knowledge, all existing surcharge plans are applied uniformly across rating classes. This procedure obviously reduces administrative costs and may simplify promotional efforts. In any case, a plan involving different surcharge patterns for each class would probably face heavy opposition from many commissioners, who retain the traditional presumption that innovations in the rate structure should be justified by extensive evidence from previous loss experience.

From (25), the equilibrium surcharge pattern for a particular rating class depends upon u, d, and $\bar{P}*$. The parameters u and d may differ substantially across rating classes. Furthermore, there is no reason to expect that the optimal degree of underwriting stringency will be the same across all classes. Equilibrium surcharge patterns for different rating classes will thus differ, and may in fact be much steeper for some classes than for others. If uniform surcharges are related to *combined* loss experience and applied across rating classes, the resulting surcharge pattern will be flatter than an equilibrium pattern for some classes and steeper for others. As a crude generalization, it can be said that the uniform surcharges will tend to be inadequate for classes in which the risk difference between good and bad drivers is large (a high d) relative to other classes, and in which the firm is more highly selective (a low $\bar{P}*$) than in the typical class. The surcharges will tend to be more than adequate for rating classes with a lower than average d and in which the firm has a relatively loose underwriting policy.

This effect is compounded in states where firms must justify premium differentials on the basis of the loss experience of all firms operating in the state. The industry-wide surcharge schedule will then represent the average policyholder, and the percentage surcharges will be too low to be equilibrium surcharges for highly selective firms and too high for less selective firms. In states where commissioners restrict rate schedules to bureau filings or to uniform percentage deviations from the bureau rates, the surcharge schedules imposed on all firms will reflect the experience of bureau firms, which generally tend to use high premium rates and relatively loose underwriting standards. In these states the surcharge schedule will be inadequate for any firm that uses a tighter underwriting policy than the typical bureau firm.

Thus, pressures of both competition and regulation tend in many states to promote the adoption of inadequate surcharge schedules by some firms, usually those with a tighter than average underwriting policy. The profit-maximizing strategy for such firms is to accept some applicants who will be refused renewal if they compile poor accident records. This would not be a serious problem if the cost to a policyholder of being refused renewal were merely the search cost of finding an insurer with slightly less strict underwriting standards and a slightly higher premium. But other insurers will not know the precise reason for the nonrenewal; it might be due to the company's persistently poor experience with a particular agent or in a particular section of a territory, or to the discovery of prejudicial information about the policyholder (that he is a heavy drinker or has family problems, for instance) during an accident investigation. All victims of nonrenewal thus become suspect, and the fact that an applicant has been refused renewal becomes, itself, a subjective characteristic.

Therefore, the lowest premium obtainable by a nonrenewed policyholder will often represent what seems to be an unfairly large increase. More importantly, the nonrenewal will shift some marginal applicants into the category of those who cannot obtain automobile insurance from the standard insurers and so must obtain coverage from either an assigned risk plan or a nonstandard insurer. Thus, a discontinuity not predicted by theory appears to exist in practice. Furthermore, assigned risk plans offer limited coverages, often only the minimal liability coverage, and their rates are typically set on the basis of the loss experience of the assigned risk population, which includes the very worst drivers in the population. Serious inequities might still be avoided if the nonstandard market operated in a manner approximating the competitive ideal. But the selection process in the nonstandard market seems exceedingly crude; it appears that many firms simply set huge premium rates (such as three times the bureau rate) and accept all applicants. Furthermore, the complaints records of the State of New York Insurance Department indicate that a disproportionate number of the firms selling a "low-quality" product, as defined in the section on product quality in automobile insurance, are nonstandard firms. Thus, many nonrenewals produce significant inequities.

Effects of Regulation

Consider an automobile insurance industry in which firms operated according to constant returns to scale, an infinite supply of firms able to operate at minimum cost levels w and c existed, and consumers had perfect knowledge about the premium rates and acceptance criteria of all firms. If entry were free, a perfectly competitive equilibrium would result. Such an equilibrium would involve not simply one premium rate for each rating class and accident record, however, but a premium rate for each set of equivalent subjective characteristics. Each policyholder would pay precisely his expected costs, $(w + cu + cud\, t_{M/N})$, based upon all of his objective and subjective characteristics. Each accident surcharge would precisely compensate for the effect of the accident record on $t_{M/N}$, and thus no policyholder would be refused renewal.

Premium rates would still reflect imperfect inferences about applicants' true expected costs, and would not necessarily be equitable. Good drivers who happened to share observable characteristics with most bad drivers would pay high rates, and vice versa. One can argue that this inequity— really, guilt by association—would gradually disappear as the inferences about a particular driver's quality reflect his accident record more completely and his subjective characteristics less. But insurers seem to limit the extent to which they rely on accident records, both because most state motor vehicle departments maintain accident and citation records for only three years and because of the possibility that good drivers may become bad drivers, and vice versa, as time passes. Competitive rates would perfectly reflect differences in accident proneness only if the selection frontier allowed perfect discrimination.

This perfectly competitive equilibrium is not an accurate representation of the present structure of the automobile insurance industry. First, a large number of the firms file rates jointly through two rating bureaus, the Insurance Rating Board and the Mutual Insurance Rating Bureau. Since it is costly to file and justify statistically an entire set of rates, only large firms can afford to file independently. Second, the major independent firms have significant shares of the market in most states. Third, entry into the industry may be easy for an agency firm, but a direct writer that uses salesmen must generate enough business to support its sales staff. The result is oligopoly, although market shares and regulatory practices produce considerably more competition in some states than in others. The oligopolistic interconnections are complicated by the fact that a competitive equilibrium would include an entire spectrum of premium rates.

The competitive assumption of perfect consumer knowledge seems particularly inappropriate in the automobile insurance case, since the typical classification scheme involves several thousand different rates in each state. A typical policyholder will have friends who are paying considerably more and friends who are paying less for automobile insurance. However, he can make a valid comparison between his premium rate and a friend's only when the other is in the same age bracket and of the same sex; has the same number and type of secondary operators in his household; is buying the same coverages (liability, property damage, medical payments, uninsured motorist, and so on) with the same limits and deductibles; lives in the same territory; has an equivalent driving record; and owns a car or cars of equal value. Even when a policyholder does encounter a perfectly matched friend who is paying a lower premium rate, he will not know whether he meets the underwriting criteria of the friend's insurer.

In such circumstances, small reductions in premium rates are unlikely to generate dramatic increases in the number of applicants. There is probably a significant threshold effect, in the sense that a small percentage premium decrease might have little effect but a larger one could have a substantial effect. Of course, this argument depends upon the assumption that it is more than a trivial effort for an applicant to obtain many premium quotations and make many applications.

Consider an auto insurer operating in an industry in which most insurance is sold at or near bureau rates and where a sizable premium differential below premium rates is needed to attract a significant proportion of all applicants. Such a situation for a particular class is depicted in Figure 8-6. With such a threshold effect, the elasticity of the applicant demand curve facing the firm would significantly increase over some interval below R_B, the bureau rate. Thus, the MPR curve would flatten out and could rise over some range. Possible selective marginal cost curves, as defined in (15), are drawn corresponding to different levels of w, the cost of writing a policy. The equilibrium for a bureau firm would then be at point A, corresponding to premium rate R_B. For firms with slightly lower writing costs, such as large agency firms that have to compete with comparable commission rates but may enjoy small economies of scale in distribution, the equilibrium might be at C. But a firm with much lower writing costs could have two possible local maxima, such as at E and at F, or, if writing costs are sufficiently small, just one at, say, G. The definition of the selective marginal cost curve indicates that a point such as F or G represents a much tighter underwriting policy than points such as A, C, or E.

Although the scale of Figure 8-6 is not necessarily realistic,[22] it appears valid to conceptualize the present equilibrium in the automobile insurance industry as involving: small agency firms writing at bureau rates, in equilibrium at a point like A; larger agency firms at a point like C, with fairly small rate deviations and a loose underwriting policy; and most large direct writers (except those that write only first-party insurance and are affiliated with a finance company), with considerably lower writing costs, in equilibrium at a point like F or G related to a tight underwriting policy. Note that entry is easy only to a point like A; to obtain writing costs corresponding to F or G requires a large sales- and claims-processing network. To say that the industry is unconcentrated may also be misleading, since in 1968 the two largest direct writers accounted for 63 percent of earned premiums among the largest twenty firms that write all automobile lines.[23]

Certainly it is highly misleading to say that a firm operating at point G

22. The suggested explanation for the shape of the demand curve in the figure depends on the assumption that all other firms are writing at, or near, bureau rates. To suggest that the implied partial equilibrium provides an explanation of overall industry equilibrium is, obviously, to ignore various complications involving both unrecognized interaction and oligopolistic interdependence.

23. *Structural Trends and Conditions*, DOT Study, p. 22.

Figure 8-6. An Applicant Demand Curve, with Firm Equilibria Corresponding to Different Selective Marginal Cost Curves[a]

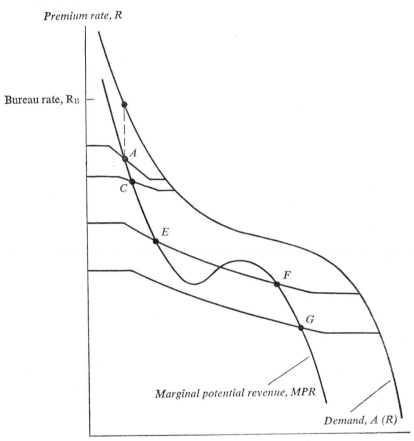

Premium rate, R

Bureau rate, R_B

A

C

E

F

G

Marginal potential revenue, MPR

Demand, A (R)

Number of applicants, A

a. See text for explanation of points *A*, *C*, *E*, *F*, and *G*.

is selling at a much lower *price* than a firm operating at point *A*, for the former sells its product to only a proportion, possibly a small proportion, of those to whom the latter sells. That is, firms with different premium rates can reasonably be said to be selling the same product at different prices only if they have identical underwriting standards.

For an individual, the price can be measured in units of risk the insurer agrees to cover per dollar premium. That is, if L represents losses covered under the policy, the price to the holder is $R/E(L)$, where $E(L)$ is the expected value of losses and R is the premium paid. If this actuarial price is averaged across the policyholders of a company, relying on the law of large numbers to assume that total claims represent a reliable approximation to total expected claims ex ante, the reciprocal of the loss ratio for the firm, $(1/l)$,[24] is obtained as an index of the price paid by policyholders. On average, policyholders pay one dollar in premiums to get l dollars of losses paid; $(1/l)$ is thus the average actuarial price.

One explanation for the apparent tightening of underwriting standards during the late sixties is that regulation produced inadequate rates. Insurers bitterly maintained that some commissioners were not willing to pass on exogenous cost increases to policyholders and held rates below those implying a normal profit. Direct writers maintained that, after having gradually won the right to file lower, independent rates, some commissioners were preventing them from adjusting freely to changing costs. Agency firms charged that, to the contrary, commissioners were giving a freer hand to the direct writers, allowing them to adjust their rates as long as they were lower than bureau rates.

Without attempting to judge the validity of the specific charges, there follow some simple analyses of the average actuarial price in recent years across forty-eight states (excluding Hawaii and Alaska). To summarize the typical experience of the leading firms, the loss ratio of the top thirty-six firms in each state, where available, is computed for the three principal lines (bodily injury liability, property damage liability, and collision) for 1967, 1968, and 1969.[25] When each observation is weighted by premiums written, so that the larger states have proportionately greater weight, ordinary least squares produce the following fit:[26]

$$(26) \quad l = 0.6502 + 0.0719(PDL) + 0.0756(COLL)$$
$$ (460.5) \qquad (26.3) \qquad\quad (40.7)$$
$$ -0.0390(1968) - 0.0693(1967),$$
$$ (20.6) \qquad\qquad (34.6)$$
$$ R^2 = 0.18 \qquad N = 15{,}471$$

where (PDL), $(COLL)$, (1968), and (1967) are zero-one variables representing property damage liability, collision, and the two years, respectively.

24. Net of loss adjustment expenses; thus, l is simply total claim payments divided by total premiums.

25. The data are from *Best's Executive Data Service*, 1968 and 1969 editions. The A. M. Best Company does not guarantee the accuracy of the data.

26. Regressions using either l or $(1/l)$ as the dependent variable were computed; those involving l produced uniformly better fits, so only those are reported. The numbers in parentheses below the coefficients are t-statistics.

When each observation is weighted by premiums written as a proportion of total state premiums in that line, giving each state approximately equal weight, the ordinary least squares regression becomes

$$(27) \quad l = 0.6582 + 0.1202(PDL) + 0.0551(COLL)$$
$$\quad\quad\quad (304.5) \quad\quad (50.1) \quad\quad\quad (22.6)$$
$$\quad\quad\quad\quad\quad\quad\quad\quad\quad\quad\quad\quad -0.0482(1968) - 0.0887(1967).$$
$$\quad\quad\quad\quad\quad\quad\quad\quad\quad\quad\quad\quad\quad (19.9) \quad\quad\quad (36.3)$$

$$R^2 = 0.20 \quad\quad N = 15,471$$

The 1967–1968–1969 time effects seem to explain insurers' protests about their deteriorating position. Although rating procedures include a credibility factor to reduce the impact on rates of fluctuations in experience, such a large and significant increase in l suggests the influence of regulation.

To investigate the possible effects of different regulatory structures, overall statewide loss ratios and several of their components (again for the forty-eight states and for 1967, 1968, and 1969) were regressed on a time trend, T (with 1968 as $T = 0$), while allowing different time trends for the file and use $(F + U)$, open competition $(OPEN)$, and mandatory bureau $(MAND)$ states. A different time trend was also allowed for five states that had a recent record of regulatory stringency according to an ad hoc criterion: a state was classified as stringent $(STRIN)$ if the commissioner had disapproved a rate filing as excessive or had otherwise intervened in a case significant enough to generate prominent discussion in the trade press. Table 8-2 gives the regressions on these variables of the overall loss ratios for all firms within the state (l_S), for the major (those classified by Best's as nationwide) agency firms (l_A), for all direct writers (l_D), for all firms for just their third-party lines (l_{3RD}), and for all firms for just their first-party lines (l_{1ST}). For the regression involving l_S, the successive addition of certain variable groups produced the following F-ratios, which are representative of all the equations:

Added variables	F-ratio relevant to the significance of the added variables
T	88.4
$(F + U)\cdot T, (OPEN)\cdot T, (MAND)\cdot T$	0.3
$(F + U), (OPEN), (MAND)$	0.1
$(STRIN), (STRIN)\cdot T$	134.5

It can be seen that the basic time trend and the differential effect of stringent regulation (which is primarily a difference in the level of l rather than its

Table 8-2. Loss Ratios l^a for Automobile Insurance Firms, 1967–69[b]

Variable or summary statistic	All firms l_S	Major agency firms l_A	Direct writers l_D	Third-party lines l_{3RD}	First-party lines l_{1ST}
Variable					
Constant	0.6336	0.6096	0.6675	0.6382	0.6285
	(158.6)	(127.6)	(149.1)	(121.5)	(123.2)
Time trend T	0.0431	0.0427	0.0424	0.0240	0.0736
	(8.8)	(7.3)	(7.7)	(3.7)	(11.8)
File and use states					
$(F + U)$	0.0042	0.0006	0.0074	0.0062	0.0033
	(0.4)	(0.1)	(0.6)	(0.5)	(0.3)
$(F + U) \cdot T$	−0.0108	−0.0185	0.0049	−0.0110	−0.0140
	(0.1)	(1.2)	(0.4)	(0.7)	(0.9)
Open competition					
states $(OPEN)$	−0.0017	−0.0069	−0.0080	−0.0053	0.0062
	(0.2)	(0.6)	(0.7)	(0.4)	(0.5)
$(OPEN) \cdot T$	−0.0013	0.0089	−0.0042	−0.0011	−0.0051
	(0.1)	(0.6)	(0.3)	(0.1)	(0.3)
Mandatory bureau rates states					
$(MAND)$	−0.0040	0.0031	−0.0200	−0.0159	0.0157
	(0.3)	(0.2)	(1.4)	(0.9)	(0.8)
$(MAND) \cdot T$	−0.0166	−0.0152	−0.0098	−0.0124	−0.0184
	(1.0)	(0.8)	(0.6)	(0.6)	(0.9)
Regulatory stringency					
states $(STRIN)$	0.0502	0.0505	0.0542	0.0641	0.0216
	(5.6)	(4.7)	(5.4)	(5.5)	(1.9)
$(STRIN) \cdot T$	−0.0157	−0.0160	−0.0102	−0.0158	−0.0106
	(1.4)	(1.2)	(0.8)	(1.1)	(0.8)
Summary statistic					
N	144	144	144	144	144
R^2	0.52	0.43	0.49	0.28	0.62
F	16.0	11.4	14.5	5.8	23.8

Source: Based on equations (26) and (27), using data from A. M. Best Company, *Best's Executive Data Service*, 1968 and 1969 editions.

a. Loss ratio = total claim payments divided by total premiums.

b. The regressions are based on data for the top thirty-six firms in each of forty-eight states (excluding Alaska and Hawaii), where available, for bodily injury and property damage liability insurance and collision insurance for 1967–69. See the text for detailed explanation of the variables and results.

The numbers in parentheses are *t*-statistics.

rate of change) are highly significant, but otherwise the mode of regulation appears to have no significant effect.

The regressions on the various subratios are revealing. The effect of stringency is primarily on the third-party lines. It is plausible to infer that commissioners feel a greater obligation to keep automobile liability rates low, since some liability insurance is compulsory, or essentially compulsory under the financial responsibility laws, in all states. Stringent regulation appears to have a similar effect on the direct writers as on the agency firms; if there is a systematic bias, it is small. The general upward trend in loss ratios is seen to be primarily confined to the first-party lines, which are largely collision insurance. This is consistent with the hypothesis, offered by several industry executives, that the principal cause of sharply increasing costs in the late sixties was the appearance of several American cars so highly and delicately styled, particularly the grillwork and front fenders, that minor collisions produced heavy repair bills. Undoubtedly, the trend in both first- and third-party lines also reflects the accelerating inflation in labor costs during the period, specifically in repair costs and medical costs.

Thus it appears valid to conclude that in a few states regulation was the cause for subnormal rates, but that the general deterioration in loss ratios experienced by automobile insurers was not significantly related to either regulatory structure or type of firm.

A plausible cause of the general upward trend in l is a possible increase in the elasticity of the applicant demand curve. Infinite elasticity for those curves was dismissed as unrealistic because of the problems buyers have in comparing rates, the considerable effort involved in obtaining quotations, and other reasons. But as automobile insurance costs grow as a proportion of family budgets (caused by the positive income elasticity of automobile demand as well as higher rates per automobile), one would expect buyers to search more diligently for the firms with low premium rates. This will increase the elasticity of the applicant demand curves, particularly for the firms with relatively high premium rates. But, as was demonstrated in Figure 8-5, an increase in elasticity at the point of equilibrium will move the optimal premium rate/underwriting policy combination toward a lower premium rate and a tighter underwriting policy, which tends to reduce l.

Unfortunately, it is not possible to translate either the general upward trend in l or its increase due to regulatory stringency directly into a quantitative effect on underwriting stringency. The model of selection and firm supply implies that a smaller proportion of all applicants will be acceptable if l is higher, ceteris paribus; there was, in fact, no comparable fall in other expenses during the period. But the model does not determine the elasticity of supply (that is, the proportion of all applicants who are acceptable). An attempt was made to do so empirically by estimating the relationship between statewide premiums written and the statewide level of l. Again, the thirty-six largest automobile insurers in each state for the years 1967, 1968, and 1969 constituted the sample, using a specification consistent with (11). That the resulting estimated elasticity was negligible and insignificant is not surprising, though, since a number of serious compromises were involved. In particular, a change in premiums written can represent either a change in applicants accepted or a change in premium rates, or both. Having no information on the latter, it was necessary to assume that premium increases were uniform across firms—clearly a questionable and possibly a critical assumption.

State rate regulation produced an actuarial price in 1968 that was a statistically significant 8 percent lower, but otherwise regulatory structures appear to have little differential effect. Of course, the historical rationale for rate regulation was not to control high rates but to keep firms from using the inadequate rates, generated by ruinous competition, that would cause insolvencies. If premium rates are kept high, it is asserted, the public will be protected from the risk of having a claim against an insolvent insurer.

This reasoning involves two major fallacies. First, with entry easy, at least for a small agency firm, industry equilibrium will be of the monopolistic competition type, with marginal firms earning only a competitive profit rate and being just as susceptible to insolvency as a firm of the same size and competence in an environment where rates are competitively determined. Second, high rates do not insure that all firms will be competently managed; in fact, the temptation for inefficient firms to enter will clearly be greater. One way to conceptualize varying degrees of managerial competence or, alternatively, agent favoritism, is to think of firms as operating with different selection frontiers. It is clear that relatively minor differences in the ability to select applicants efficiently override the risk due to the variance in competence for even modestly sized firms.

The automobile insurance business is risky, but the risk is primarily a result of competitive selection. In these circumstances, neither rate regulation nor requirements for reserve accounts seem appropriate or adequate. A direct solution to the insolvency problem, such as a corporation analogous to the Federal Deposit Insurance Corporation, as suggested by Senator Philip A. Hart,[27] makes more sense.

27. *Federal Insurance Guaranty Corporation,* Hearings before the Senate Committee on Commerce, 91 Cong. 1 sess. (1970).

Selection Criteria and No-Fault Plans

Subjective characteristics were defined as any attributes of an applicant, other than those explicitly appearing in the rate classification scheme, that an insurer or his agent believes are not distributed independently of expected claims costs. Their effect is to alter an underwriter's belief about the probabilities of three contingencies: (1) that the applicant will be involved in an accident; (2) that if he is involved, the circumstances will raise questions of his negligence; (3) that if the applicant were the defendant in a liability suit with a *given* set of circumstances, a randomly selected jury would find him negligent.

One of the subjective characteristics that affect the first belief is the exact area of a rating territory within which an applicant lives and works. The rating territories typically are large, relative to an average daily trip, and are not homogeneous with respect to driving environment or crime rate, which is relevant to the comprehensive coverage. Furthermore, although driving conditions within different areas and over particular routes can change rapidly, it is expensive and time-consuming for large insurers or the bureaus to justify statistically a change in the territorial definitions (and possibly politically hazardous in many cases). Since many agents write insurance primarily in their immediate neighborhoods, these considerations provide another explanation for the practice of dropping agents.

Both contingencies (1) and (2) may be affected by virtually any personality trait or personal circumstance that suggests, at least to an underwriter, a higher propensity for driving while preoccupied with a problem, for working out tensions behind the wheel, or for indulging in alcohol or drugs. Thus recent divorcées and others with marital problems are considered particularly poor risks, and any evidence of reckless behavior is carefully scrutinized. This interest in applicants' personal lives has not helped the industry's image.

The effects of such factors on availability and price are not obviously inequitable. But an underwriter must also consider *any* characteristic of an applicant that he believes would tend to bias a jury deciding a liability claim toward a finding of negligence or toward a larger award. This consideration probably contributes to the high rates paid by young drivers; it is unnecessary to belabor its significance for applicants from unpopular minorities. Some insurers have been known to instruct agents to be cautious about applicants who have a "swarthy" complexion, who have scars, blemishes, or an otherwise unattractive appearance, or who have an un-appealing personality. Clearly, underwriters have considered jury bias to be a serious problem.[28]

The enactment of a no-fault plan changes the nature and relative impor-tance of the subjective characteristics for two reasons. First, when the prob-lem of jury bias becomes less relevant, a significant inequity is reduced. The impact of the subjective characteristics is not simply a premium differential that just compensates for the extent of perceived jury bias; it also means that the greater the number of "unfavorable" subjective charac-teristics an applicant possesses, the fewer will be the firms willing to write him. Since ghetto dwellers usually have unfavorable characteristics with respect to both accident proneness and jury bias, it is not surprising that they are more likely to be forced into assigned risk plans for minimal coverages and to substandard specialists for wider coverage.[29]

Second, the more important are the subjective characteristics (in terms of the variance of expected claims costs across applicants within a rating class), the more likely that industry performance will reflect competition in terms of applicant selection rather than in terms of expense reduction or actuarial price. That is, if there were no significant subjective character-istics, all applicants within a class would be equally attractive to an under-writer. Premium differences across firms would be tenable only to the extent that they represented perceived differences in services or quality. The differences across firms in equilibrium accident surcharge schedules would disappear. The source of much of the independent agents' market power—the ability to allocate applicants of varying desirability—would be gone, and the competitive position of agency firms would therefore im-prove. Additionally, homogeneous classes would promote the spread of group insurance plans in automobile insurance, since self-selection would not create complications.

Plans for replacing or modifying the tort liability system of compensat-ing automobile accident victims have proliferated in recent years.[30] Al-though not the first, the "basic protection plan" developed by Keeton and

28. See particularly Jeffrey O'Connell, *The Injury Industry and the Remedy of No-Fault Insurance* (University of Illinois Press, 1971), chap. 8.

29. Douglas G. Olson, *The Price and Availability of Automobile Liability Insurance in the Nonstandard Market*, DOT, Automobile Insurance and Compensation Study (1971).

30. Numerous surveys and critiques of the different plans have appeared; see, for instance, Willis P. Rokes, *No-Fault Insurance* (Santa Monica: Insurors Press, 1972), in which different plans and proposals are discussed.

O'Connell appears to have catalyzed the pressures for reform.[31] The plans that have been adopted in a few states or are under serious consideration in others are generally similar to the Keeton-O'Connell plan, with one important variation. A common feature of these plans is a requirement that automobile owners carry first-party insurance under which they would be compensated, without regard to negligence, for economic losses incurred as a result of automobile accidents. The proposed coverage differs across plans with respect to the limits per person or per accident, the limit on compensation for income losses, the deduction of compensation from other sources, and other details.

A more fundamental difference involves the extent to which the right to recover through a tort liability action is retained, either by the injured party for "pain and suffering" damages and economic losses in excess of the no-fault coverage, or by the insurer for the cost of a claim. The plan proposed in 1972 by Senators Hart and Warren G. Magnuson and the plan adopted in Oregon represent the extremes in this dimension. The Hart-Magnuson plan virtually eliminates recovery on the basis of negligence (except for those who are neither automobile owners nor spouses or dependents of owners), whereas the Oregon plan retains the right to recovery under all circumstances. Except for the imposition of binding arbitration on insurers who attempt to recover the cost of a claim, the Oregon plan is essentially compulsory medical-disability insurance. Plans that combine compulsory first-party coverage with no significant restriction on tort liability recovery have thus been termed "pseudo no-fault" plans.[32] Intermediate plans, such as the one adopted in Florida, eliminate double recovery and the right to make small pain and suffering claims, but otherwise retain tort liability. Such plans eliminate nuisance claims but do not assure adequate compensation in the most serious cases. No attempt is made here to evaluate alternative plans, however, although the possible effect of various plans on the importance of selection criteria and thus on competitive performance is recognized as a relevant consideration.

Under a plan such as the Hart-Magnuson proposal, in which the role of liability insurance is practically eliminated, the relevance of the subjective characteristics related to negligence findings and jury bias would be eliminated; with a plan in which the right to recovery on the basis of fault is not significantly restricted, their importance is maintained. However,

31. See Keeton and O'Connell, *Basic Protection for the Traffic Victim.*
32. Rokes, *No-Fault Insurance*, p. 4.

the imposition of binding arbitration for some claims should reduce the importance of factors related to jury bias.

On the other hand, the relative importance of the factors related to accident proneness would increase, even with a pseudo no-fault plan, since a much larger proportion of the cost of the typical automobile insurance package would be for first-party coverage. The importance of non-homogeneous territories for selection would also increase. There is, however, no obvious reason to expect that subjective characteristics as a whole would diminish in importance; industry performance would continue to reflect competition in terms of selection. Modifications that tend to diminish the variation in expected costs within rating classes would improve competitive performance. For instance, under the typical plan income losses are covered up to particular limits, so that two otherwise identical individuals who have different incomes, both of which fall below the maximum level of compensation, will have different expected claims costs. At least in terms of the effect on selection, it would be preferable to cover income losses separately, so that proportional premiums could more accurately reflect expected claims costs. This might also allow deductible alternative sources, such as workmen's compensation, to be explicitly treated as a rating factor, instead of being implicitly treated by underwriters as a subjective characteristic. In short, while a no-fault plan would not eliminate the underlying causes of some of the unpopular aspects of competitive performance, the details of the particular plan adopted could have a significant effect on the nature of competition in the industry.

A Polar Model of Product Quality

The traditional analysis of how product quality is determined in a competitive market begins with the premise that buyers can perfectly evaluate the quality of the product and concludes that equilibrium will involve the sale of a variety of qualities that reflect the different value put on quality by different consumers. If the quality of the automobile insurance product can be considered to be the degree to which the company handles a first-party claim (particularly a large claim) with fairness and candor, as opposed to relying heavily on stalling, bargaining ploys, misleading statements, and so forth, the traditional analysis seems at best of doubtful relevance. How, then, can insurance quality be evaluated?

As a point of departure, a model is considered that adopts a polar assumption about the ability of buyers to evaluate product quality before buying—namely, that they have none at all. In the Appendix to this chapter, the behavior of firms and the nature of industry equilibrium are analyzed under the following assumptions:

(a) The product in question lasts one period.

(b) There is a nonzero probability that the product will "break down" during the period, an event that is left otherwise undefined.

(c) The only difference among brands is the probability b that they will break down; thus, brands differ only in quality, and higher quality is reflected in a lower b (or higher $-b$).

(d) A customer cannot evaluate b and has no independent source of information.

(e) The customer buys the same brand he purchased during the previous period as long as it did not break down.

(f) If his brand broke down, the customer chooses another brand. He chooses the new brand either:

(f1) by randomly selecting a different brand, with all other brands having equal probabilities of being selected; or

(f2) by soliciting a recommendation, which consists simply of the statement "I am using Brand X," from a randomly selected friend.

(g) For simplicity, the customer is considered not to retain a memory or record of experience beyond that of the previous period.

(h) The higher the quality of the product (and, thus, the lower is b), the more it is assumed to cost to produce.

These assumptions are consistent with either a situation in which the prices of all brands are the same or a situation in which prices are different but buyers do not consider price to be an indicator of quality.

Under these assumptions, the firm trades the cost of producing a high-quality product for an increased likelihood of repeat sales. Of this period's customers, a fraction $(1 - b)$ repeat next period, a fraction $(1 - b)^2$ the next period, and so forth. New customers, who are disgruntled customers from other firms, are not related to the firm's choice of b. Since product quality is determined purely by the mechanism of repeat sales, it is not surprising to find that the firm's choice of its product's quality $(-b)$ is positively related to profit per unit and negatively related to the firm's discount rate and its production costs. Thus, the more effective competition is, the lower product quality is, since it is negatively related to unit profit margin.[33]

The more striking facets of firm behavior concern equilibrium market shares. This behavior is independent of how different firms actually choose the quality of their products; they are implied by assumptions (a) through (g) alone. Suppose there are I firms in the industry, that the ith firm produces a product with a probability of breaking down, b_i, and has market share m_i. Under assumption (f1), in which a disgruntled customer randomly chooses another brand and all brands are equally likely to be chosen,[34] the resulting market shares are shown in the Appendix to be in equilibrium if and only if

$$(28) \qquad m_i b_i = m_j b_j \qquad i, j = 1, I,$$

which are equivalent to the condition that

$$(29) \qquad m_i = \frac{(1/b_i)}{\sum\limits_{j=1}^{I} (1/b_j)} .$$

Under assumption (f2), according to which disgruntled customers solicit a random recommendation, new brands are chosen with probabilities that are proportional to market shares. The equilibrium conditions then become

$$(30) \qquad \frac{b_i}{1 - m_i} = \frac{b_j}{1 - m_j} .$$

From (29), it is clear that for every possible vector $(b_1, b_2, \ldots, b_I)$, industry equilibrium implies a positive market share for each firm as long as $0 < b_i < 1$ for each i. But not every vector of b_is represents a possible equilibrium, according to (30). A necessary requirement is that

$$(31) \qquad b_i < \left(\frac{1}{I - 2}\right) \sum_{j \neq i} b_j$$

must hold for all i if all the m_i are to be positive. Under assumption (f2), firms whose product is significantly worse than average will not survive.

---

33. These conclusions are analytically derived in the Appendix.

34. This would be a reasonable assumption where advertising plays a major role and where it operates with a low threshold effect and little cumulative effect (that is, where it pays everyone to advertise but added doses have little marginal effect). It could also reflect a world in which all brands are stocked in a typical store and advertising has little effect.

For instance, suppose that only two qualities are being produced, with k_1 firms producing a b_1 product and k_2 firms producing a b_2 product. If $b_1 < b_2$, then the condition necessary for the survival of firms producing the poorer product is $(k_1 - 1)b_2 < k_1 b_1$. The disparity between the quality of products produced cannot be too great, and the bound is more narrow the greater the number of firms producing the good product. Yet, given that one firm producing a b_2 product can survive, it follows that any number of such firms can survive, so that the addition of more such firms decreases the market shares of the firms producing the better product.

Table 8-3 shows the equilibrium market shares for various vectors of b_is. Although assumption (f1) implies that every firm survives, while (f2) implies that surviving firms produce reasonably similar qualities, the table shows that the difference in average quality produced in equilibrium is quite small. It thus appears that very crude responses are sufficient to drive poor-quality firms out of business, or at least to keep their market shares small. The act of soliciting information is a kind of public good in this context, in that, when done by a single individual, it does not decrease the probability that his choice will break down in the next period. But if *all* consumers solicit recommendations, the long-run probability that each will experience breakdowns decreases. However, there is no assurance that the average product quality is high, or that the marginal cost of increasing it bears any relation to the disutility consumers experience due to a breakdown.

Beyond the need to consider the possibility of price differences, the conclusions about market equilibrium have limited relevance because the effect of entry is ignored. An interesting implication of this model is that it is rational for buyers to inquire about how long a firm has been in business. The conclusions arrived at about firm behavior might well be changed by taking advertising into account. Casual empiricism suggests a significantly negative correlation between the index of product quality for automobile insurers derived in the next section and the extent to which firms advertise nationally. The inclusion of advertising could thus invalidate the simple correlation derived here between profit rate and product quality.

Product Quality in Automobile Insurance

How should the "quality" of an automobile insurance contract be quantified? Given a quantified index of quality, can one find systematic differ-

Table 8-3. Market Shares of Firms with Equal Prices and Different Product Qualities

Probability of brand breaking down b_i	Equilibrium market shares	
	Assumption (f1): buyers change with equal probabilities	Assumption (f2): buyers change with probabilities proportional to market shares
.05, .10	2/3, 1/3	2/3, 1/3
.05, .20	4/5, 1/5	4/5, 1/5
.05, .40	8/9, 1/9	8/9, 1/9
.05, .05, .10	2/5, 2/5, 1/5	1/2, 1/2, 0
.05, .05, .40	8/17, 8/17, 1/17	1/2, 1/2, 0
.05, .05, .05, .10	2/7, 2/7, 2/7, 1/7	1/3, 1/3, 1/3, 0
.05, .10, .10	1/2, 1/4, 1/4	3/5, 1/5, 1/5
.05, .10, .10, .10	2/5, 1/5, 1/5, 1/5	4/7, 1/7, 1/7, 1/7
.05, .05, .10, .10	1/3, 1/3, 1/6, 1/6	1/2, 1/2, 0, 0
.04, .05	5/9, 4/9	5/9, 4/9
.04, .05, .05	5/13, 4/13, 4/13	3/7, 2/7, 2/7
.04, .05, .05, .05	5/17, 4/17, 4/17, 4/17	7/19, 4/19, 4/19, 4/19
.04, .04, .05	5/14, 5/14, 4/14	5/13, 5/13, 3/13
.04, .04, .05, .05	5/18, 5/18, 4/18, 4/18	1/3, 1/3, 1/6, 1/6
.04, .04, .04, .05	5/19, 5/19, 5/19, 4/19	5/17, 5/17, 5/17, 2/17
.04, .04, .04, .04, .05	5/24, 5/24, 5/24, 5/24, 4/24	5/21, 5/21, 5/21, 5/21, 1/21
.04, .04, .04, .04, .04, .05	5/29, 5/29, 5/29, 5/29, 5/29, 4/29	1/5, 1/5, 1/5, 1/5, 1/5, 0

Source: Derived from equations (28)–(30). See also Appendix equations.

ences in quality across automobile insurance firms? This section attempts to develop an index of product quality.

Claims Handling and Firm Incentives

Consider the quality of the (first-party) automobile insurance product to be the quality of the response the firm makes to a reasonably large claim: whether it is processed without delay, whether the firm negotiates fairly and candidly, whether it attempts to exploit the policyholder's ignorance or poor understanding of his coverage, and so forth. Judging product quality thus involves predicting a firm's response to a possible claim sometime in the future. Previous experience and reputation are the only guides.

But large claims are infrequent. An indication of how well consumers are informed is the common belief that a severely injured plaintiff in a liability case is almost assured of a gold mine; a series of studies have shown just how mistaken that view is. The development of firm reputations is limited by the generally low concentration in most areas and is also hindered by the proliferation of groups and affiliates with similar names.[35]

The automobile insurance industry thus conforms rather well to the extreme assumptions in the polar model of product quality about the inability of buyers to judge quality. But even the mechanisms that tend to keep quality high in that model—the value to the firm of repeat sales and the long-run effect of disgruntled customers switching brands—are particularly weak in the case of automobile insurance.

First, the cost of generosity is likely to dominate the value of discounted profits on repeat policies for even moderately large claims, particularly if profits are chronically poor for most firms. Second, policyholders who have recently had a serious accident apparently feel locked in to their insurance company. *Consumer Reports* advised its readers to consider switching insurers only if they did not have a recently poor accident or claims record.[36] Possibly, this advice is not justified; the model of selection and firm supply does not imply any such locking-in effect. One factor not considered in the model, however, that would tend to produce a partial locking-in effect is the fact that the direct cost of writing a new applicant

35. For instance, the American Fidelity Company is part of the American International Group, but American Fidelity Fire Insurance Company is part of the American Plan group; American Fire and Indemnity Company is in the American Indemnity group, while the American National Fire Insurance Company is part of the Great American National General group.

36. *Consumer Reports*, vol. 35 (June 1970), p. 339.

is higher than the direct cost of renewing a policyholder. Since firms usually investigate an applicant's background, this differential always exists. In addition, the commission rate on renewals is often lower, sometimes considerably so, than on new policies; this differential is typically greater for direct writers. So a surcharge may be adequate to cover the higher expected costs of most renewals but not most new applicants, since it reflects only the increase in expected claims costs. Another factor could be that agents make less than totally rational decisions about accepting "bad" drivers, giving more weight to their higher expected claims costs than to their increased premiums. The suggestion in *Consumer Reports* may also be based on the belief that people tend to give a biased account of their accident and citation record. Since companies have a 60-day grace period in which a new applicant can be investigated and canceled at will (even in states with an anticancellation law),[37] those who shop around and tell less than the truth could be accepted and then canceled.

It is apparent, particularly when advertising and firm entry are also considered, that competitive sanctions on firms that give poor claims service are weak if not negligible. It is possible that firms whose primary strength is their ability to exploit the ignorance of buyers can survive in the present market structure.

The Consumers Union Survey

During 1969, Consumers Union sent a questionnaire to all subscribers to *Consumer Reports*.[38] Of the 300,000 who responded, 230,871 answered the section on automobile insurance. Of those, 81,000 reported an experience involving a first-party claim within the previous five years and 56,000 reported an experience involving third-party claims. Respondents to the first-party section were asked to name the insurance company against whom the claim was made, the state they resided in at the time, the provisions of the policy (collision, comprehensive, medical payments, uninsured motorists, other) under which compensation was sought, and how much was paid (or if the claim had not yet been settled or had been rejected). They were also asked to indicate whether they felt this payment had been "too little," "about right," "exactly right," "overly generous," or if they didn't

---

37. Kulp and Hall, *Casualty Insurance*, p. 439.

38. Consumers Union has not participated in the analysis presented here and accepts no responsibility for the conclusions drawn; in fact, however, the inferences made here are consistent with their conclusions.

know or were unsure. In addition, they were asked to indicate whether the time it took (or had thus far taken) to settle the claim was "quite short," "reasonable," "too long," "far too long," or if they didn't know.[39]

Respondents to the third-party section were asked the name of the other person's insurance company, the type or types of loss for which compensation was sought (property damage, medical or hospital costs, pain and suffering, loss of earnings, deductibles not payable by one's own insurance company, other), how much was paid or if the claim was rejected, whether the insurance firm made any preliminary payments, whether a lawyer was hired and the size of his fee, and the questions described above about size of payment and promptness.

Defining

$$Y_1 = \begin{cases} 1 & \text{if the respondent checked "too small"} \\ 0 & \text{otherwise} \end{cases}$$

$$Y_2 = \begin{cases} 1 & \text{if the respondent checked "far too long"} \\ 0 & \text{otherwise} \end{cases}$$

$$Y_3 = \begin{cases} 1 & \text{if the respondent checked either "too long"} \\ & \text{or "far too long"} \\ 0 & \text{otherwise} \end{cases},$$

regressions were computed using Y as dependent variable, with independent variables representing payment size, claim type, and firm effects. Observations in which "don't know" was checked were omitted.

The effect of payment size is modeled as a piecewise linear continuous curve by including both S (payment size in hundreds of dollars) and variables of the type $S \cdot D_{>150}$, where

$$D_{>150} = \begin{cases} S - 1.50 & \text{if the payment exceeded \$150} \\ 0 & \text{otherwise} \end{cases}.$$

The coefficient on the variable $S \cdot D_{>150}$ is an estimate of the change in the slope of the relationship, given the type of claim and the firm, between average dissatisfaction and payment size, at the point \$150.

The effects of claim type and different firms are also modeled as zero-one variables, so that

$$D_{COLL} = \begin{cases} 1 & \text{if the claim was made under the collision} \\ & \text{coverage} \\ 0 & \text{otherwise} \end{cases},$$

39. *Consumer Reports*, vol. 35 (June 1970), pp. 332–38.

and so forth. Interaction effects between payment size and uninsured motorist claims in first-party claims and between payment size and pain and suffering claims in third-party claims were also allowed.

Firm variables were added in three sets. Two firms that together account for over one-third of the observations were added first. Since they were almost certain to cause a significant reduction in explained variance simply because of the large number of observations represented, they were added separately so that the possible significance of the firm effects as a group could be distinguished from the possible significance of these two firms. Other frequently appearing firms (200 or more first-party observations or 100 or more third-party observations), totaling twenty-six, including one exclusive first-party insurer, were then added. Exclusive first-party insurers are typically associated with finance companies, which require collision and comprehensive insurance to qualify for an automobile loan. Finally, all firms that appeared often (100 first-party observations or 50 third-party observations) were added; this set contained seventeen firms, including two exclusive first-party insurers.

Table 8-4. Effects of Payment Size and Claim Type on Automobile Insurance Claimants' Dissatisfaction

	First-party claims[a]		Third-party claims[a]	
Independent variable or summary statistic	*Too small,* Y_1	*Too slow,* Y_3	*Too small,* Y_1	*Too slow,* Y_3
Variable				
Intercept	5.423	6.350	8.301	29.527
	(8.2)	(8.0)	(4.7)	(13.4)
Size of payment, S	−1.389	1.222	0.267	4.069
	(3.9)	(2.9)	(0.5)	(5.8)
Difference between S and \$150,				
$S \cdot D_{>150}$	1.897	−0.147	...	...
	(3.9)	(0.3)		
$S \cdot D_{>200}$	...	...	0.268	−3.402
			(0.3)	(3.3)
$S \cdot D_{>400}$	−0.499	−0.788	...	...
	(1.6)	(2.1)		
$S \cdot D_{>500}$	...	...	0.187	−0.491
			(0.4)	(0.8)
$S \cdot D_{>800}$	0.808	0.227	...	...
	(3.3)	(0.8)		

Table 8-4. Continued

Independent variable or summary statistic	First-party claims[a]		Third-party claims[a]	
	Too small, Y_1	Too slow, Y_3	Too small, Y_1	Too slow, Y_3
$S \cdot D_{>1,500}$	−0.773	−0.520	−0.688	0.523
	(5.0)	(2.8)	(2.3)	(1.4)
$S \cdot D_{>3,000}$	...	...	0.710	−0.971
			(0.1)	(3.1)
$S \cdot D_{>4,000}$	−0.095	−0.041	...	...
	(1.5)	(0.6)		
$S \cdot D_{>6,000}$	...	...	−0.092	0.251
			(0.8)	(1.8)
Uninsured motorist, $S \cdot D_{UNIN}$	0.085	0.172	...	...
	(3.6)	(6.1)		
Pain and suffering, $S \cdot D_{P\&S}$	...	...	0.073	0.093
			(3.6)	(3.7)
Type of claim				
Comprehensive, D_{COMP}	−1.170	−2.964	...	...
	(3.0)	(6.4)		
Property damage, D_{PROP}	...	...	−3.114	−1.365
			(2.4)	(0.9)
Collision, D_{COLL}	0.870	0.614	...	...
	(2.2)	(1.3)		
Medical, D_{MED}	1.432	2.503	4.692	0.735
	(3.3)	(4.8)	(5.0)	(0.6)
Pain and suffering, $D_{P\&S}$	...	...	10.690	4.605
			(9.2)	(3.2)
Uninsured motorist, D_{UNIN}	7.666	4.233	...	...
	(13.0)	(6.0)		
Loss of earnings, D_{EARN}	...	...	7.503	3.300
			(6.0)	(2.1)
Deductibles, D_{DEDUC}	...	...	9.123	15.872
			(6.0)	(8.4)
Other, D_{OTHER}	−0.891	−0.866	8.457	8.413
	(1.1)	(1.0)	(2.9)	(2.3)
Summary statistic				
Number in sample	47,553	47,553	20,333	20,333
F	31.4	44.0	45.2	24.3
R^2	0.026[b]	0.036	0.082	0.046
Mean	7.4	15.3	18.5	50.7

Source: Regressions using data collected by Consumers Union in a 1969 survey. See text for a description of the sample.

a. "Too small" and "too slow" refer to respondents' evaluations of claims settlements on questionnaire. Only frequently appearing firms (those having 200 or more first-party observations and 100 or more third-party observations) are included in the regressions. The period covered is the five years previous to 1969. The numbers in parentheses are t-statistics.

b. Not an appropriate measure of fit in this context.

Table 8-5. Firm Effects on Evaluation of Automobile Insurance Settlements, Measured around the Group Mean

Firm	First-party claims[a]		Third-party claims[a]	
	Too small	*Too slow*	*Too small*	*Too slow*
1	1.315 (1.6)	−2.705 (2.7)	−5.052 (2.9)	−6.118 (2.8)
2	1.058 (1.5)	1.181 (1.4)	6.779 (4.4)	2.643 (1.4)
3	4.283 (7.8)	5.474 (8.4)	8.708 (7.2)	7.753 (5.1)
4	2.203 (1.7)	2.501 (1.6)	−5.218 (1.7)	−0.324 (0.1)
5	−4.113 (3.8)	−5.861 (4.6)	−3.874 (1.5)	−11.552 (3.6)
6	−2.337 (1.6)	−2.212 (1.2)	−3.633 (1.3)	−1.291 (0.4)
7	−3.663 (2.6)	−3.762 (2.3)	−3.747 (0.9)	−7.341 (1.4)
8	1.489 (1.0)	0.611 (0.4)	2.152 (0.8)	1.009 (0.3)
9	21.857 (10.9)	34.226 (14.4)	33.206 (10.2)	33.582 (8.6)
10	−0.506 (0.7)	−1.008 (1.1)	0.078 (0.1)	−4.389 (2.4)
11	0.700 (0.6)	−1.122 (0.8)	−0.827 (0.4)	1.649 (0.6)
12	8.134 (5.3)	11.952 (6.5)	. . .	. . .
13	4.369 (3.1)	0.669 (0.4)	5.700 (1.3)	9.090 (1.7)
14	0.217 (0.4)	0.737 (1.1)	0.200 (0.1)	−1.919 (1.0)
15	1.099 (1.3)	2.475 (2.5)	−3.011 (1.7)	1.037 (0.5)
16	4.249 (3.7)	7.756 (5.6)	1.359 (0.4)	8.406 (2.2)
17	−2.445 (2.4)	0.885 (0.7)	−3.140 (1.2)	5.255 (1.7)
18	2.043 (1.2)	4.597 (2.3)	2.484 (0.8)	5.382 (1.4)
19	−0.259 (0.4)	−0.037 (0.1)	7.994 (4.5)	8.138 (3.7)
20	−1.817 (1.4)	−0.821 (0.5)	−2.596 (0.8)	4.408 (1.1)
21	−0.033 (0.0)	2.265 (1.1)	2.142 (0.6)	−0.827 (0.2)
22	−1.077 (1.4)	−2.751 (3.0)	1.082 (0.7)	−6.433 (3.2)
23	1.306 (0.9)	1.544 (0.9)	−0.748 (0.3)	8.342 (0.3)
24	−0.863 (0.8)	−0.499 (0.4)	−0.386 (0.1)	−0.143 (0.0)
25	−1.152 (2.2)	−2.254 (3.7)	1.014 (0.8)	−3.849 (2.5)
26	0.272 (0.4)	1.689 (1.9)	−2.795 (1.8)	4.147 (2.2)
27	−4.096 (6.7)	−6.317 (8.6)	−4.784 (1.6)	−17.301 (4.7)
28	−2.232 (2.0)	−3.032 (2.3)	0.129 (0.0)	−5.784 (1.5)

Source: Same as Table 8-4.

a. "Too small" and "too slow" refer to respondents' evaluations of claims settlements on questionnaire. The numbers in parentheses are the ratios of the differences to their estimated standard deviations.

Table 8-4 shows the estimated effects of payment size and claim type on the regressions in which all the frequently appearing firms occurred. The regressions using Y_2 and Y_3 produced similar results, but the coefficients were typically more significant with Y_3, so only those results are reported. Table 8-5 shows the deviations between the estimated firm coefficients and the (simple) average of the coefficients, together with the t-ratios on the significance of the deviation. Almost half the firm deviations are significant at the 5 percent level, and most of the poorer-than-average firms are significant at the 1 percent level.

In Table 8-6, the F-ratios related to the progressive addition of each set of variables are listed. With this many observations, critical F-values at the 0.1 percent level are roughly 6.9, 4.1, 3.5, 2.5, and 2.1 for the addition of two, five, seven, fifteen, and twenty-five variables, respectively. These groups of variables, even the effects of the less frequently appearing firms, appear to be highly significant. Since the dependent variable in these regressions is a binary variable, the error term cannot be normally distributed and the use of the F-statistic cannot be rigorously justified. However, the estimated covariance matrix for the coefficients is still an unbiased estimator, and the comparison of the firm coefficients to their standard errors indicates that very significant firm effects can be safely inferred.

The regressions indicate significant differences among firms in the extent of claimant dissatisfaction. The question that arises is whether the results reflect a single dimension of firm behavior or a number of different tendencies, such as that some firms are generous but slow, others pay quickly but are stingy, some treat their own policyholders well but fight all liability claims, and the like. If the data do reflect a single dimension of firm behavior, the firm effects from the different regressions would be expected to be highly intercorrelated and to reduce, at least approximately, to a

Table 8-6. F-Ratios on the Progressive Addition to the Automobile Insurance Settlements Equation of Five Sets of Variables

Type of variable added	First-party claims[a]		Third-party claims[a]	
	Too small	Too slow	Too small	Too slow
Size	60.4 (6)	100.8 (6)	130.5 (6)	65.0 (6)
Kind of claim	53.7 (5)	42.2 (5)	69.1 (6)	22.4 (6)
Two largest firms	102.7 (2)	131.9 (2)	87.2 (2)	67.9 (2)
Firms appearing frequently[b]	13.4 (26)	21.4 (26)	10.3 (25)	9.3 (25)
Firms appearing less frequently[b]	2.2 (17)	1.6 (17)	3.4 (15)	3.3 (15)

Source: Same as Table 8-4.

a. The number of added variables in each set is given in parentheses.

b. Frequently appearing firms are those in the sample with 200 or more first-party observations and 100 or more third-party observations; less frequently appearing firms are those with 100 first-party and 50 third-party observations.

single index of claims behavior. Such an index can best be derived by computing the first principal component of the four estimated firm effects.

After normalizing the four vectors of firm effect coefficients (by dividing by the standard deviation, across firms, of each coefficient), the first principal component of the coefficients of the twenty-six firms that appear frequently in both first-party and third-party cases was computed. The weights on the four vectors of coefficients and the proportion of total variance explained are as follows:

Weights

Sample	First-party claims		Third-party claims		Percent of variance exhausted
	Too small	*Too slow*	*Too small*	*Too slow*	
With firm 9	0.51	0.51	0.49	0.49	90.8
Without firm 9	0.52	0.53	0.41	0.52	73.8

Of the total variance of the estimated firm coefficients, 74 percent can be explained by a single variable, which can thus be interpreted as an index of claims behavior. Since estimation error will tend to make the inferred proportion smaller than its counterpart in the population, this is a striking result indeed. The derivation of this index, based only on frequencies, involves an implicit assumption that all responses of "payment too small" and "delay too long" should be given the same weight. Since no information was available as to how much too small respondents felt the payments were or how much too long settlements took, it was not possible to discriminate further.

There are two possible explanations for the existence of products of different quality in the automobile insurance market. One view is that information about firm practices spreads rapidly and is not unreasonably difficult to obtain. Quality differences can then persist only if compensating premium differentials exist. Firms selling high-quality automobile insurance will be those that give good service on first-party claims but energetically fight third-party claims. Informed buyers will thus seek out such firms in the expectation that their claims will be treated fairly while their premium rates are kept low by stringency on third-party claims. This suggests that the first principal component of the implied pattern of firm differences would have weights on the first-party dissatisfaction variables with signs opposite to those on the third-party variables. Another implication of this point of view is that a no-fault insurance plan will lead to the virtual disappearance of dissatisfaction with claims handling, since almost all claims would be first-party and policyholders would receive the quality of service they had consciously paid for and thus expected.

An alternative view is that firms are always either aggressive and stringent on all claims, first- and third-party, or seem reasonable and prompt to the claimant on both. Such a situation would result if claims handling were determined by corporate philosophy rather than profit maximization, if information on claims experience diffuses so poorly that its effect on profits is negligible, or if stringency on first- and third-party claims does not affect firm reputation differently because people do not keep the distinction in mind. In this case, firms that showed better than average first-party satisfaction would also show better than average third-party satisfaction. The first principal component would have weights on the four dissatisfaction variables that all had the same sign. This view implies that while a no-fault plan would eliminate much of the consumer dissatisfaction that arises because of the tort liability system, there is little reason to believe that the quality of claims handling would correspond to what people expected or had chosen to pay for.

The correlations among the four measures of dissatisfaction, the demonstration that 75 percent of their joint variance can be attributed to a common variable, and the fact that this index attributes almost equal weights with the same sign to the four measures of dissatisfaction are all evidence in support of the second view. Whatever the explanation, the data strongly support the contention that firms producing better than average first-party claim satisfaction also produce better than average third-party claim satisfaction. It should be emphasized that no implicit judgment is made here that those who register dissatisfaction are necessarily justified; the contention is merely that the proportion of claimants who register dissatisfaction is highly correlated with the proportion who *should* feel dissatisfied according to some appropriate standard. Support for this contention is found in the analysis of complaints in the next section: the proportion of complaints that the State of New York Insurance Department ultimately upholds, across firms, appears to be completely independent of the degree to which different firms generate complaints.

As a test of the robustness of these conclusions, the first principal component of various sets of variables was computed, where each variable represents the proportion dissatisfied, across firms, for some subset of claim types and some interval of payment sizes. The results suggest that firm effects are adequately specified as a zero-one variable and that the conclusions do not reflect primarily dissatisfaction within some sub-category, such as small claims or large claims.

New York State Complaint Experience

The State of New York Department of Insurance does an admirably thorough job of processing complaints submitted to it. A complainant, who usually requests that the department intervene on his behalf, must describe his grievance either in a letter or by a personal visit to a department office. If the complaint appears to have possible justification, the department writes to the firm involved, describing the complaint and requesting an explanation.

If the department ultimately concludes that the complaint is valid and uses its influence to attempt to force the firm to change its position, the complaint is said to be upheld. The department cannot order compliance, and has at its disposal only the implicit threat of regulatory harassment, plus the more unlikely threat of a fine or even a license revocation. If during the correspondence the parties reach a compromise in which the firm has at least altered its position, the complaint is said to be adjusted. The department will close the file if the complainant does not respond to an inquiry or if the nature of the dispute is found to be a question of fact (for instance, the firm states that the market value of a car was $2,000 while the complainant maintains the market value was $3,000), which can be settled only in a court of law. Of course, some of the complaints that are neither upheld nor adjusted are those which the department decides have no justification. But a firm that disputes the facts far more than average may well be providing an inferior product, even though the department is not able to uphold the resulting complaints.

Lists were obtained that include the number of complaints involving automobile insurance, the number upheld, the number adjusted, and total automobile insurance premiums (lagged one year) for almost all firms writing auto insurance in New York State for the years 1962 through 1969. Only firms that had ten or more complaints in each year were listed. The number of firms or affiliates with similar names, the fact that affiliates are sometimes aggregated into their groups or fleets and sometimes not, the fairly common name changes of firms or affiliates, and the not uncommon mergers or consolidations often made it impossible to trace with confidence the same company through all eight years. Only firms that met two criteria were considered: they must be clearly identifiable in at least five years, and it must be unlikely that their (possible) absence in the other years is due to their having fewer than ten complaints.[40] There are sixty-one such firms, of which thirty-seven were identifiable in all eight years.

In Figure 8-7, the average $(A + U)/P$ ratios are graphed against the average C/P ratios for sixty of those firms, where C/P is the ratio of the number of complaints to total automobile insurance premiums in the previous year (in millions of dollars), and $(A + U)/P$ is the ratio of the number of complaints adjusted plus the number of complaints upheld to premiums in the previous year. As the figure shows, the proportion of complaints upheld or adjusted is similar for all the firms; the correlation between C/P and $(A + U)/P$ for those firms represented is 0.98. Thus, the much higher proportion of complaints per premium dollar for some firms does not represent simply a tendency for the policyholders of some firms to complain more frequently without cause.

The impressive attribute of Figure 8-7 is the distribution of firms with respect to either (C/P) or $(A + U)/P$. Within a small area near the origin, there are forty-three firms tightly clustered, for which (C/P) averages between two and eight. There are then seventeen firms scattered over the rest of the graph; in addition, one of the firms has ratios that are too large to fit on the diagram. The upper ranges of the diagram are more sparse than would apparently be the case with more data. Among the firms missing due to incomplete data are six with a (C/P) ratio of over 100 in one or more years, three more with a (C/P) ratio of over 50, and nine others with a (C/P) ratio of over 30. One firm managed to produce one hundred one complaints in one year, with premiums the past year of $173,000, to produce a (C/P) ratio of 584; furthermore, eighty-four of the one hundred one were upheld or adjusted.

While differences in the (C/P) ratios among firms within the dense area in the figure are statistically significant, it seems reasonable to consider that region as defining a high-quality product, while firms falling outside it are producing a lower-quality product, although the lower quality may

40. The decision was based on the following procedure. Premiums, P_t, were regressed on a time trend. A low estimate, $\hat{P}_t$, was obtained for each missing period by taking predicted premiums for the period minus two standard deviations. If the ratio $(10/\hat{P}_t)$ is then more than two standard deviations below the mean of the ratios (C_t/P_t), where C_t is complaints in period t, it is highly unlikely that the reason the firm is not on the list for the period is that it had fewer than ten complaints. If all the missing periods passed this test, the firm was retained.

Figure 8-7. Ratio of Number of Automobile Insurance Complaints Adjusted (*A*) and Upheld (*U*) to Premiums (*P*), by Ratio of Number of Complaints (*C*) to Premiums, New York State, 1962–69

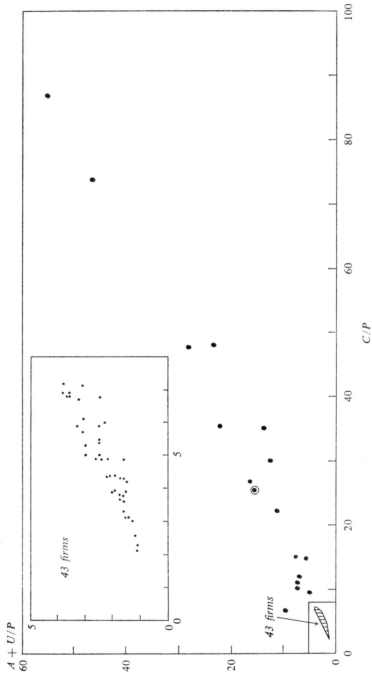

Source: Computed by the author from data in the files of the State of New York Department of Insurance.

range from slightly lower to ridiculously low. The lower-quality firms are relatively small, except for that represented by the circled point in Figure 8-7; this corresponds to firm 9 in the Consumers Union survey. On the basis of its continuing accomplishments on the complaint ratio "hit parade," the claims practices of this firm were investigated in the summer of 1971, resulting in the imposition of a fine of $15,000.[41]

A Policy Suggestion

A claimant may have difficulty understanding and defending his rights when confronted with an insurer who intends to exploit the claimant's ignorance. The case for active, extensive regulation with the purpose of eliminating unfair claims handling is thus strong.[42] But only a handful of states pursue complaints as thoroughly as New York, and many have minimal regulation. Since a specialized professional background is needed to understand the limits and implications of the various automobile coverages, processing complaints through general consumer protection agencies seems obviously inadequate.

Yet even the commendably thorough activity of the New York Insurance Department may have minimal effect. It cannot intervene on behalf of a complainant except to advise the insurer that it considers a complaint valid and to hold out the unlikely threat of an eventual license revocation or a fine. Even if it had a mandate to do so, the department could hardly regulate the settlement of individual claims without introducing the substantial costs of bureaucracy.

But one dimension of the claims handling problem could be directly mitigated. In the Consumers Union data, a strong correlation was found between the proportion of claimants who felt a settlement was much too small and the proportion who felt that it took too long, for both first-party and third-party claims. The firm has every incentive to stall, except in a few cases where prompt payment may encourage smaller total claim costs. Stalling can be a particularly effective tactic to use against a claimant who has been in a costly accident and whose financial resources are dwindling. The New York complaint files reveal that a few firms even adopt the simple strategy of totally ignoring some claims.

An effective and administratively simple response to the problem would

41. *Best's Review*, vol. 72 (January 1972), p. 89.
42. As, of course, is the case for imposing serious penalties for consciously misrepresenting the facts of a claim.

be passage of a law that imposed an interest charge, computed at a healthy rate (for instance, the Baa corporate bond rate plus 5 percent), to be added to all benefits and awards other than those for pain and suffering. Interest would be computed from the date the company was informed of the incurred loss until the date reimbursement was paid. For third-party claims, the interest charge could stop accumulating at the time a claim went to court. However, it would be preferable to reduce the incentives to use legal ploys to stall and to place powerful firms in a position to benefit from reduced court schedules. Such a law would obviously raise premiums, ceteris paribus. The direction of the implied income transfers, from policyholders in general to those who are slowly reimbursed, seems easily justified. The significant effect would be to improve the competitive position of firms that settle claims promptly.

Conclusions

The present analysis of the automobile insurance firm's underwriting decision was based on a highly stylized model of the population of drivers in each rating class. But the assumption that drivers are either good or bad could easily be replaced with a general specification. For instance, the distribution of accident costs could be assumed to be a function of an accident-proneness parameter λ, which is an unobservable characteristic of drivers.[43] By also assuming that the distribution of λ across drivers is statistically related to a vector of observable variables, a general, plausible model is obtained of the environment within which the automobile insurer operates. The model of selection and firm supply developed here is a special case of that general specification, in which λ is restricted to two values. Allowing λ to vary continuously would have greatly complicated the exposition of the model and obscured the basis of the inferences drawn from it without adding anything substantive to it. The conclusions, however, would be unaffected.

The model indicates the complicated nature of industry equilibrium. If the automobile insurance industry were purely competitive, a continuum

43. Joseph Ferreira, Jr. (*Quantitative Models for Automobile Accidents and Insurance*, DOT, Automobile Insurance and Compensation Study), adopts such a model, but then discusses its implications for policy while apparently assuming that there are *no* observable characteristics of drivers that are correlated with λ. That assumption is obviously inconsistent with the continuing statistical justification of the rate classification system.

of rates would exist, firms with expense levels greater than the minimum could not survive, and all those charging the same premium rate would have the same expected claims costs. Regulatory pressure on premium rates will certainly produce more restrictive underwriting standards and larger assigned risk populations, but attempts by agency firms to retain their position while locked into an inefficient distribution system or adjustments by all firms to higher demand elasticities will have the same effect.

In any case, none of these factors is the crucial one in arbitrary non-renewal behavior. It was demonstrated that equilibrium surcharge patterns, for which a firm would find the same applicants acceptable whatever their accident records, will differ across rating classes for a given firm and will differ between loose and tight underwriters for a given rating class. Furthermore, surcharges computed by averaging over rating classes for a given firm will be inadequate for marginal policyholders in some of the classes. It is concluded that both the method of computing surcharges and the pressures of competition produce an incentive to accept some applicants who will not be renewed if they compile poor accident records. Imperfections in information cause a policyholder who has been refused renewal to be less attractive to other insurers, and may make it difficult for him to obtain insurance from a standard insurer at all. Because of the limited coverages available from assigned risk plans, the manner in which assigned risk premiums are determined, and the unsatisfactory nature of the alternative nonstandard market, nonrenewal may result in significant inequities.

Restrictive underwriting is a result of competition in the industry, and would disappear only if the industry were cartelized. The cause is the existence of subjective characteristics that carry information about expected claims costs but are not reflected in the rating classifications. They will not disappear with the enactment of a no-fault plan, however sweeping it might be. It is argued, however, that the more completely a no-fault plan eliminates the right to recover on the basis of fault, the better industry performance will be in terms of selection behavior. Subjective characteristics will not only tend to be less important, but will also be less objectionable in terms of equity.

Empirical evidence was provided that supports the contentions that there are significant differences in the quality of claims handling across companies, and that companies with a below-average record on first-party claims tend to be below average on third-party claims, and vice versa. Since the level of dissatisfaction is considerably higher on third-party claims, no-fault will clearly reduce dissatisfaction, but the evidence indicates that no-fault will not eliminate it, nor will it eliminate the opportunity for some firms to exploit buyer ignorance. That some firms do so is demonstrated by the complaint data of the State of New York Insurance Department.[44] Finally, it is suggested that since close regulation of claims practices is infeasible, the imposition on firms of an interest charge, computed from the claim notification date to the date of reimbursement, would be beneficial.

Appendix

Let the per-unit cost of producing a product that has a probability b of breaking down be $F(b)$, with

$$(32) \qquad F'(b) < 0, 0 < b < 1; \quad F'(b) = 0; \quad \lim_{b \to 0} F(b) = +\infty.$$

If the price is P, then profit per unit each period is $P - F(b)$. Given the assumption that a customer whose product breaks down will change brands, a proportion $(1 - b)$ of these customers will buy the same brand next period. Thus, expected profit per unit next period is $(P - F(b))(1 - b)$, and so forth. If the firm's discount rate is r, it thus wishes to maximize

$$(33) \qquad \sum_{i=1}^{\infty} (P - F(b))(1 - b)^i/(1 + r)^i,$$

which implies the condition

$$(34) \qquad P = F(b) - (r + b)F'(b).$$

Since exactly the same calculation applies to the new customers who appear each period (they can be treated as a function of the bs chosen by other firms and their market shares only as long as the market share of the firm in question is small), this provides a stationary equilibrium.

Let the product quality of the ith firm be b_i and its market share m_i, for $i = 1, I$. Then each period a proportion $b_i m_i$ of all customers leave the ith firm. Suppose that they randomly choose one of the other I-1 firms with equal probabilities. Then market shares are in equilibrium if and only if

---

44. Since the data do not distinguish first- and third-party complaints, the conclusion, drawn from the analysis of the Consumers Union survey, that there is a strong correlation across firms between dissatisfaction on first-party and third-party claims is crucial.

$$(35) \qquad b_i m_i = \sum_{i \neq j} \left(\frac{1}{I-1} \right) b_j m_j \qquad i = 1, I,$$

from which is derived the condition that

$$(36) \qquad b_i m_i = b_j m_j \qquad i, j = 1, I.$$

This implies that

$$(37) \qquad m_j = (1/b_j) \Big/ \left[\sum_{i=1}^{I} (1/b_i) \right].$$

Alternatively, suppose that when a customer experiences a breakdown, he randomly asks for a recommendation from a neighbor. In that case, of the customers who leave the first firm, a fraction $m_2/(1 - m_1)$ will go to the second firm, a fraction $m_3/(1 - m_1)$ to the third firm, and so forth. Market shares then will be in equilibrium if

$$m_1 b_1 = (m_2 b_2)(m_1/(1 - m_2)) + \cdots + (m_I b_I)(m_1/(1 - m_I))$$

$$(38) \qquad \begin{matrix} \cdot & & \cdot & & \cdot \\ \cdot & & \cdot & & \cdot \\ \cdot & & \cdot & & \cdot \end{matrix}$$

$$m_I b_I = (m_1 b_1)(m_I/(1 - m_1)) + \cdots + (m_{I-1} b_{I-1})(m_I/(1 - m_{I-1})),$$

from which is deduced

$$(39) \qquad \frac{b_i}{1 - m_i} = \frac{b_j}{1 - m_j} \qquad i, j = 1, I.$$

Using (39) to solve for $m_2, \ldots, m_I$ in terms of m_1 and using the condition $\Sigma m_i = 1$, it follows that

$$(40) \qquad m_1 = 1 - (I - 1)\left(\frac{b_1}{B} \right),$$

where

$$B = \sum_{i=1}^{I} b_i.$$

Thus a particular choice of $b_1, \ldots, b_I$ is consistent with positive market shares for all firms only if

$$(41) \qquad b_i < \frac{B}{(I-1)} \qquad i = 1, I,$$

which is equivalent to the condition

$$(42) \qquad b_i < \left(\frac{1}{I-2} \right) \sum_{j=1}^{I} b_j \qquad i = 1, I.$$

CHAPTER NINE

The New York Stock Exchange: A Cartel at the End of Its Reign

H. MICHAEL MANN

THE MINIMUM COMMISSION RATES charged to nonmembers of the New York Stock Exchange (NYSE) for the purchase and sale of securities remained virtually unchallenged for 176 years. Then, early in 1968, the Securities and Exchange Commission (SEC) announced its intention to investigate certain aspects of the commission rate structure on all exchanges and invited responses from interested parties. The investigation opened formal hearings in mid-1968; it was the beginning of an assault on the exclusive right of members of the exchanges to determine commission rates. By April 1972, an end had been put to fixed commission rates on portions of orders in excess of $300,000, and a recently proposed rule change would eliminate fixed rates on orders of any size by May 1, 1975.[1]

The NYSE offered a vigorous defense for the minimum commission rate structure in the 1968 and 1969 hearings before the SEC.[2] The essence of

1. Securities and Exchange Commission, "Proposal to Adopt Securities Act Rules 19b-3 and 10b-22," Securities Exchange Act of 1934, Release no. 11073 (Oct. 24, 1974).

2. James J. Needham, chairman of the NYSE, and some in the brokerage community had, by 1973, begun to advocate the abolition of fixed rates. The financial difficulties of 1974, however, caused a reexamination of this position and reinvigorated the opposition to negotiated rates ("Big Board's Needham Hints Exchange May Drop Support of Negotiated Rates," *Wall Street Journal*, Aug. 2, 1974).

the argument was that price regulation insured a strong, centralized trading market with continuity, depth, and liquidity, avoided the consequences of destructive competition, and promoted good performance in areas where active price competition would not. Persuasive rebuttals of some of the propositions underlying these contentions, particularly the first two, have been put forth.[3]

This chapter is concerned with the theory of competition and its applicability to the brokerage business, in an attempt to discover whether negotiated rates would actually cause destructive competition. First is a description of the NYSE's commission rate structure, which can be considered representative of the other exchanges in all important respects. Next, the conditions favorable to destructive competition and their applicability to the brokerage industry are explored. The final section investigates the connection between fixed rates and market performance in the areas of price, service, and technological progress.

Minimum Commission Rates

The NYSE's rate structure regulates the commission paid to a broker for transacting the sale and purchase of securities. A transaction by a broker has two parts: one is execution—the process of using the exchange's facilities to find a seller or buyer for consummation of a trade; the second is clearance—the making of arrangements for the actual transfer of the securities bought and sold.[4] There are essentially two classes of rates, one for nonmembers and another for members. It is the former that has created controversy and is treated in this section. Rates for members are substantially lower than for nonmembers, and are separated into the

3. See William F. Baxter, "NYSE Fixed Commission Rates: A Private Cartel Goes Public," *Stanford Law Review*, vol. 22 (April 1970), pp. 675 ff.; Alfred E. Kahn, *The Economics of Regulation: Principles and Institutions* (John Wiley, 1971), vol. 2, pp. 193–209; Richard R. West and Seha M. Tinic, "Minimum Commission Rates on New York Stock Exchange Transactions," *Bell Journal of Economics and Management Science*, vol. 2 (Autumn 1971), pp. 577–605; Irwin Friend and Marshall E. Blume, *The Consequences of Competitive Commissions on the New York Stock Exchange* (University of Pennsylvania, Wharton School, Rodney L. White Center for Financial Research, 1972).

4. A broker, of course, does more than simply execute and clear; he is also a salesman for his firm and offers the investor current information about the quality of potential investments. The rates more than cover, as shown below, the costs of salesmanship and other services.

**Table 9-1. Minimum Commission Schedule for Nonmembers,
New York Stock Exchange, Effective March 24, 1972**

Type and value of order (dollars)	Minimum commission[a]
Single round-lot orders	
Under 100	As mutually agreed
100–799	2.0% + $6.40
800–2,499	1.3% + $12.00
2,500 and above	0.9% + $22.00
Multiple round-lot orders	
Under 100	As mutually agreed
100–2,499	1.3% + $12.00 ⎱ plus, per lot:
2,500–19,999	0.9% + $22.00 ⎱ 1st to 10th lots, $6.00;
20,000–29,999	0.6% + $82.00 ⎰ 11th lot and
30,000–300,000	0.4% + $142.00 ⎰ above, $4.00
Above 300,000	As mutually agreed[b]

Source: New York Stock Exchange, *1973 Fact Book* (NYSE, 1973), p. 56.
a. The minimum commission on single round-lot orders may not exceed $65; for multiple orders, the commission per lot may not exceed the single round-lot commission.
b. Effective April 24, 1972.

functions of execution and clearance, execution only, and clearance only, rather than being unitary.[5]

The schedule of commissions for nonmembers effective March 24, 1972, is presented in Table 9-1. The table reflects the rates applicable to all orders up to $300,000, which constitute the bulk of the business transacted on the NYSE.[6] Since April 1972, the commission on the part of an order in excess of $300,000 is negotiated, not fixed. The computation of the commission for a particular transaction is straightforward. For a single round-lot order—100 shares of a stock priced at, say, $20 per share—the commission is the round-lot value times the appropriate percentage plus the fixed charge: in this case, $2,000 × 1.3% + $12 = $38. For a multiple round-lot order, the procedure is identical except that another fixed charge is added, whose amount depends upon whether the order contains up to or more than 10 round lots. To illustrate: an order for 800 shares of a $20 stock has a total value of $16,000; the commission is $16,000 × 0.9% + $22 + ($6 per round lot × 8 round lots) = $214.

5. *Report of Special Study of Securities Markets of the Securities and Exchange Commission*, H. Doc. 95, pt. 2, 88 Cong. 1 sess. (1963), p. 297.
6. The commissions earned from fixed rates account for more than 75 percent of total commission income (Testimony of William C. Freund, in *Stock Exchange Commission Rates*, Hearings before the Subcommittee on Securities of the Senate Committee on Banking, Housing and Urban Affairs, 92 Cong. 2 sess. [1972], p. 123).

Until December 1968, the commission schedule was entirely based on a sliding scale of money involved per round lot; that is, the rate on a larger order was a multiple (the number of round lots in the order) of the rate paid on a single round-lot order. A volume discount was introduced at the end of 1968, followed by negotiated rates on portions of orders in excess of $500,000 in April 1971, and then in excess of $300,000 in April 1972.

Three important characteristics of the rate schedule gave rise to certain means of transacting business that, in effect, bypass the established minimum rates. These are: (1) the minimum rates apply uniformly to all nonmembers;[7] (2) the rates cover the brokerage function, execution and clearance, and ancillary services; (3) there is no provision for volume discounts (except, recently, on portions of orders exceeding $300,000). These features led to the "give-up," reciprocal arrangements, and the development of an over-the-counter (OTC) market in listed securities.

The give-up, banned by the NYSE in late 1968, is a practice in which a customer directs an NYSE member who is executing a transaction for him to pay to another NYSE member that part of the commission not attributable to execution and clearance. The give-up is thus a transfer of cash among members that can amount to as much as 60 percent of the nonmember commission.[8] It typically occurs when a mutual fund directs an NYSE member with which it has placed an order to pay part of the commission to another member as a favor for services—such as research, quotations and wire facilities, or sales of mutual fund shares—rendered to the fund. Sometimes the give-up is directed toward a member who performs services for a nonmember; in such a case the give-up benefits the nonmember who cannot directly receive the cash payment involved.

The second practice that has arisen from the minimum commission rate schedule involves reciprocity. Reciprocal arrangements occur because a nonmember firm has some business, either for a customer or for its own account, that is best transacted through the NYSE. If the trans-

7. The schedule shown in Table 9-1 did provide for a discount to certain non-member brokers for their orders executed through the NYSE. In 1973, the directors of the NYSE recommended that the discount arrangement be made permanent and that the eligibility requirements be liberalized ("NYSE Asks to Eliminate Fixed Rates," *Washington Post*, March 2, 1973).

8. *Special Study of Securities Market*, pt. 2, pp. 316–17. See also Memorandum of the United States Department of Justice on the Fixed Minimum Commission Rate Structure, SEC File 4-144 (Jan. 17, 1969), pp. 88–89. It is questionable whether give-ups have actually been eliminated, since the fixed minimum commissions that gave rise to the practice still exist (see Kahn, *Economics of Regulation*, vol. 2, p. 198).

action is for a customer, the nonmember firm cannot charge more than the NYSE minimum rate or the customer would switch to a NYSE member. The minimum, however, covers only the transaction cost and none of the other costs of attracting and executing orders. If the transaction is for the nonmember's own account, the rate, particularly if the order is large, may be excessive, but the member is not permitted to rebate any part of the commission to the nonmember who originated the order.

Since nonmember business is important to NYSE members,[9] business is directed to nonmembers according to some reciprocal ratio that always favors members.[10] Typical instances of reciprocity involve an NYSE member, also a member of a regional exchange, who places business with a member of a regional exchange when the NYSE member could have transacted the business directly; who buys or sells a security in a regional exchange when the security is dually listed and therefore could have been bought or sold directly on the NYSE; who places business involving nonlisted securities with a nonmember even though the member has a trading department capable of dealing through the OTC market.[11] The key feature of reciprocal deals is that "the NYSE member is generally able to handle directly, and at least as effectively, the business he places with his reciprocal partner."[12] Reciprocity thus avoids the NYSE's constitutional provision against rebates.[13]

The third effect of the rate structure is the growth of an OTC market (the "third market") in securities listed on the NYSE and the American

9. In 1969, nonmember brokers' orders accounted for 7.4 percent of the total share volume processed for the accounts of institutions and intermediaries, which, in turn, accounted for 42.4 percent of the exchange's total volume (NYSE, Research Department, *Public Transaction Study—1969* [NYSE, 1970], pp. 8, 15).

10. A ratio of two to one means that $1 of commissions will be directed to a nonmember for every $2 of commissions received from him. One survey found extensive participation in reciprocal arrangements in the four largest regional exchanges that produced significant income for the nonmembers (*Special Study of Securities Markets*, pt. 2, pp. 303–04).

11. The OTC market differs from an auction market, such as that provided by the NYSE, in that it does not bring buyers and sellers together in one physical location. Securities unlisted on any of the organized exchanges are traded in the OTC market; these are generally small, less well known companies, with such exceptions as Anheuser-Busch, Inc., and BankAmerica ("Huge Firms Stay Unlisted," *Boston Globe*, Dec. 8, 1970).

12. *Special Study of Securities Market*, pt. 2, p. 303.

13. The antirebate rule was challenged in *Thill Securities Corporation* v. *New York Stock Exchange*, CCH Fed. Sec. L. Rep. ¶92,479 (E.D. Wisc. 1969). On appeal, the case was remanded to the district court, which had disclaimed jurisdiction in the matter (433 F.2d 264 [C.A. 7, 1970]). The NYSE was denied certiorari from the Supreme Court on the appeals court decision (401 U.S. 994 [1971]).

Stock Exchange. This market permits trades, particularly in large blocks, at commissions that are negotiated rather than fixed. The third market accounted for 2.7 percent of share volume and 3.4 percent of the value of shares traded on the NYSE in 1965; in 1971 the respective figures were 7.0 percent and 8.4 percent.[14] The basis for this growth was suggested in the finding that price and cost considerations motivated three-quarters of the institutional respondents to a survey to purchase or sell NYSE-listed securities on regional exchanges or the third market.[15]

The common element of the give-up, reciprocal arrangements, and the increasing resort to the third market is that they sidestep the minimum commission rate structure. As long as there are fixed rates, these practices are to be expected. What, then, is the reason for regulated prices at all? And what accounts for the fact that the power to set commission rates has long rested in the hands of a private cartel composed of the members of the NYSE?[16] The answer, as advanced in the 1968 and 1969 hearings before the SEC, is that unfettered price competition would be ruinous and lead to less satisfactory market performance than orderly competition. The next section examines whether competition is likely to be destructive in the brokerage industry.

Destructive Competition: Theory and Practice

The chief effect of destructive competition is that most, or all, of the firms in an industry sustain losses for a prolonged period. According to economic theory, the conditions that promote this situation are a high ratio of fixed to total costs and the persistent excess capacity. These, in association with a large number of sellers or a few sellers with ineffective collusion, force prices below average costs for a long time. Demand inelasticity aggravates the problem, since the excess capacity cannot be absorbed by increased demand.

The primary adverse effect of destructive competition is "the loss or

14. New York Stock Exchange, *1972 Fact Book* (NYSE, 1972), p. 15.
15. *Special Study of Securities Market*, pt. 2, p. 857.
16. The SEC has the power under section 19(b) of the Securities Exchange Act of 1934 to ensure that commission rates are "reasonable" (48 Stat. 899). The criteria for reasonableness were never spelled out, however, either in the legislative history of the exchange act or by the SEC in its rate change decisions since 1934 (*Special Study of Securities Markets*, pt. 2, pp. 300, 328–33).

Table 9-2. Distribution of Selected Operating Expenses of Member Firms,[a] New York Stock Exchange, 1969–71

Percent

Operating expense[b]	1969	1970	1971
Registered representatives' compensation	20.3	18.5	22.6
Other variable costs	9.3	9.0	8.9
Clerical and administration	29.5	29.1	29.3
Communication	9.6	9.9	9.1
Occupancy and equipment	7.4	9.1	8.3
Interest	11.3	12.1	9.4
Promotional	4.0	3.6	3.2
Other fixed costs	8.6	8.7	9.2
Total	100.0	100.0	100.0

Source: New York Stock Exchange, *1972 Fact Book* (NYSE, 1972), p. 64.
a. Member firms doing a public business.
b. Excludes expenses for partners' compensation, federal income taxes, and interest on partners' capital.

deterioration of capacity needed when demand recovers";[17] that is, the cost of restoration of the capacity when demand recovers may well exceed the cost of maintenance during the slump.[18] In the brokerage industry, the costs of excess capacity could be more substantial. Widespread bankruptcy would shake investors' confidence in the ability of capital markets to provide liquidity, the repercussions of which could threaten the stability of the financial system. Whether fear of these consequences is legitimate depends on how closely the brokerage business meets the conditions necessary for destructive competition.

Fixed Costs

The evidence suggests that the brokerage industry is one in which fixed costs are a small proportion of total costs, a finding not consistent with the NYSE's fears of destructive competition. Table 9-2 gives a breakdown of NYSE operating expenses (except for partners' compensation, federal income taxes, and interest on partners' capital) for 1969–71. The distributions suggest a high ratio of fixed to total costs if the

17. F. M. Scherer, *Industrial Market Structure and Economic Performance* (Rand McNally, 1970), p. 200. The NYSE puts the argument this way: "unless rates are established so as to permit the maintenance of excess capacity during some periods, peak needs will remain unmet" (NYSE, *Economic Effects of Negotiated Commission Rates on the Brokerage Industry, the Market for Corporate Securities, and the Investing Public* [NYSE, 1968], p. 92).
18. Kahn, *Economics of Regulation*, p. 175.

NYSE's classification of only the first two items as variable costs is accepted. However, by the conventional definition of fixed costs—those that remain invariant as output changes—the proportion of fixed to total costs is actually relatively small. For example, clerical and administration costs—compensation paid to personnel who carry out the myriad of tasks necessary for the execution, recording, and consummation of orders—are clearly variable; they are reducible by laying off personnel as demand declines.[19] Promotional costs are variable in the same sense. The sum of the first three categories in Table 9-2 plus promotional costs accounts for more than 60 percent of total operating costs. Furthermore, although the communication and occupancy and equipment categories are probably truly fixed, the facilities themselves are not highly specialized. That is, the brokerage business does not involve large-scale investment in complex, durable assets, but rather chiefly office equipment such as desks, chairs, and office supplies, which are readily transferable to other uses. In short, nearly two-thirds of the operating expenses of brokerage firms are variable,[20] and those that are fixed do not entail the kind of commitment that encourages persistent utilization of assets in the face of depressed conditions rather than their transfer to other uses.

The experience of the industry in the 1960s further suggests the improbability of prolonged excess capacity. That decade saw two slumps: one in 1962, following an upswing in the volume and value of trading activity in 1961; and one in 1969–70, following an increase of approximately 250 percent in volume and value from 1963 to 1968. Was the industry able to adapt its capacity to changed demand conditions during these periods? Although there is no direct measure of capacity in the brokerage industry, number of personnel is a reasonable touchstone, given the large share of labor costs in the provision of services (as shown in Table 9-2). These data show that the number of total personnel in 1962 was about 5 percent less than in 1961. The number immediately rose again when demand picked up in 1963, rising steadily through the period of increasing demand (1963–68), and the 1969–70 decline in activity produced a 12 percent drop from the 1968 total.[21]

19. Bache and Company's cost-cutting drive reduced its number of employees by more than 20 percent in the lean period of 1969 through early 1970 (Carol J. Loomis, "Wall Street on the Ropes," *Fortune*, vol. 82 [December 1970], p. 63).

20. Friend and Blume ("Consequences of Competitive Commissions," p. 28) give an even higher proportion.

21. The figures in this paragraph are from NYSE, *1972 Fact Book*, pp. 75, 81. Total personnel did increase from 1968 to 1969, but very modestly compared to the

Although the number of member firms of the NYSE has fallen annually from a high of 681 in 1961,[22] the number of offices follows a pattern suggesting the same kind of flexibility. In 1962, the number of offices rose, but at a rate only a fraction of that between 1960 and 1961. The pace quickened during 1963–68, the total being nearly one-third higher at the end of this period than at the beginning. After 1968, the number of offices fell sharply; by 1970, there were 15 percent fewer than in 1968.[23]

The responsiveness to changes in demand of the NYSE's labor force and number of offices serving investors thus suggests that supply is highly elastic, a condition that is inconsistent with the possibility of a protracted period of excess capacity.

Market Structure

Transactions on the NYSE are funneled through its members, who own seats on the exchange. Since 1953, the membership has numbered 1,366, most of whom are affiliated with one of the 577 member firms.[24] For a brokerage firm to become a member, "at least one member of the Exchange must be a general partner or a director holding voting stock."[25] Many members belong to firms whose essential function is to handle transactions that are beyond the immediate capacity of another member firm's floor broker, to trade in odd lots (less than 100 shares), or to provide for an orderly market. Such firms, or firms that concentrate on activities such as the flotation of new securities, do not transact public commission business. One estimate indicates that more than two-thirds of the member firms are engaged in public business.[26]

Among this group of over 400 firms, there is noticeable, though not

---

previous two years. The delay in cutbacks might have reflected a view that the demand decline was temporary and additional capacity would be justified soon.

22. From 1968 to mid-1970, ninety NYSE members, including some prominent ones, went under. That some 14 percent of the NYSE's members could be driven into liquidation in the space of eighteen months suggests that revenue can quickly dip below variable costs in times of decreased demand ("Making Brokers Toe the Mark," *Business Week*, July 18, 1970).

23. NYSE, *1972 Fact Book*, p. 81.

24. As of the end of 1971 (ibid., pp. 58, 59).

25. *Special Study of Securities Markets*, pt. 2, p. 45.

26. Memorandum on the Fixed Minimum Commission Rate Structure, pp. 96–97; see also *Special Study of Securities Markets*, pt. 1, p. 16. Public business as used here means the sum of business provided by individual investors, institutions, and intermediaries, and excludes the transactions of members for their own accounts.

substantial, concentration. The 4 largest firms account for some 20 percent of the public commission business, the 20 largest, 46 percent, and as many as 175, 90 percent.[27] The combination of large numbers and a relatively mild level of concentration suggests a market structure approximating atomistic competition. Further, it appears that entry into the brokerage business is quite easy, although direct access to an exchange is blocked by the limit on the number of memberships.[28] This limit, although consistent with an atomistic market structure, will not guarantee the long-run equilibrium of price equal to long-run average and marginal costs.

Apart from purposeful limitation, however, there do not appear to be any forces in the industry that might limit the number of sellers to a few. Economies of scale seem to be present but disappear at a level that permits a large number of efficient-sized firms.[29] Product differentiation is present, but it is at least partly caused by the emphasis on service competition forced by fixed prices. It seems clear that the absence of minimum brokerage commissions, given the number of firms involved, would create more price competition than now exists.[30] There are no patents with respect to technology; and the brokerage industry "is essentially a service business requiring relatively small capital investment. . . ."[31]

To summarize, the brokerage industry's market structure with respect to the number of firms suggests that price, if not fixed, would fall below average costs in a slump and, given a high ratio of variable to total costs,

27. Memorandum on the Fixed Minimum Commission Rate Structure, p. 98. Another estimate, picturing a modest level of concentration, indicates that one-half "of all the commission business done on the NYSE in 1961 was accomplished by not more than 5 percent of the firms" (*Special Study of Securities Markets*, pt. 1, pp. 18–19); see also *Economic Effects of Negotiated Commission Rates*, table 8, p. 70. The 5 percent figure represents 33 firms.

28. The NYSE first limited membership in 1817 (*Special Study of Securities Markets*, pt. 1, p. 75).

29. A statistical estimate of the long-run total cost function, which corrects for heteroscedasticity, indicates that economies of scale will not dictate small numbers. For a presentation of the issues involved in the debate concerning heteroscedasticity in the estimations of the NYSE and Department of Justice, see the Appendix to this chapter and Friend and Blume, "Consequences of Competitive Commissions," pp. 36–57.

30. It should be noted that instances of price competition in the form of the give-up and various reciprocal arrangements are frequently nothing more than payments for manifestations of service competition.

31. *Special Study of Securities Markets*, pt. 2, p. 329.

lead quickly to the exit of capacity. But the ease of entry suggests that a market recovery would create new capacity to serve increased demand.

Demand Inelasticity

No studies have estimated the coefficients of price elasticity for trading securities. Some contend that a decrease in commission rates would have little impact on the volume of securities traded.[32] This argument has two parts. First, investors will primarily be concerned with the quality of their investment, in terms of expected profitability and the degree of certainty with which the expected return will be realized. It is this consideration, rather than a change in the rate paid to transact a purchase or sale, that will motivate investors to buy or sell. Second, if a significant amount of trading activity reflects expectations of returns on the order of, say, 20 percent, a rate decrease is not likely to influence the decision to trade since the cost relative to the capital gain would not be very large. For example, a 20 percent return on a $400 transaction would yield $80, on which the commission would be $14.40, given a round-lot transaction (see Table 9-1). A decrease in the commission rate from 2 percent to 1 percent would cut the commission to $10.40, thereby increasing profit by 5 percent, a relatively modest proportion.

A counterargument to the second proposition is that an investor's expected profitability on a transaction can never be considered certain. If, therefore, an investor demands some minimum return--say, 5 percent, or $20 on a $400 transaction—before entering the market at all, a drop in the commission rate could positively influence the decision to trade by making a transaction profitable at the investor's required minimum return.[33] Furthermore, a drop in rates might encourage certain kinds of trading activity that are not now profitable.

It is difficult to assess the opposing contentions about the effect of commission rates on trading activity. It is probably reasonable to say that a decline in stock market activity primarily reflects pessimistic judgments about expected profitability, and that decreases in commission rates during slumps are not likely to be a significant factor in investors'

32. See Memorandum on the Fixed Minimum Commission Rate Structure, pp. 137–38.

33. See Henry C. Wallich, In the Matter of Securities and Exchange Commission Rate Structure Investigation of National Securities Exchanges, Official Transcript of Proceedings, SEC File 4-144 (Oct. 31, 1968), pp. 3773–75.

willingness to trade.[34] It is thus unlikely that the financial difficulties of brokerage firms in depressed periods would be relieved by commission rate cuts.

Conclusion

The brokerage industry, although characterized by conditions that could aggravate destructive competition—many sellers and demand inelasticity—does not have the key prerequisite, a high ratio of fixed to total costs. Without this condition, supply is likely to be quite elastic, which precludes prolonged periods of excess capacity or inadequate capacity in peak demand times.

However, the rapid exit of brokerage firms in a slump, even if consistent with a supply response that avoids destructive competition, could have untoward consequences if the stability of the financial system is shaken. One safeguard against this possibility has been established as a result of the anguished attempt by the NYSE to protect investors during the crisis period of 1968–70: it is the Securities Investor Protection Act of 1970, which provides "insurance for customer accounts of all registered broker-dealers with a limitation of $50,000 for each customer, of which up to $20,000 may be in cash."[35] This, in addition to strict enforcement of financial regulations, should provide adequate protection for investors.

Fixed Commission Rates and Market Performance

Having defined the characteristics of the brokerage industry with respect to the possibility of destructive competition, it now remains to determine whether customers receive lower prices, better services, and greater technological progress with regulation than without.

Price Levels

The theory that regulation produces a lower price for the customer than competition rests on the proposition that an industry with widely

34. Another piece of evidence that the total demand is inelastic is the testimony of William Freund that "the loss of industry commission revenues as a result of negotiated rates at $500,000 has been approximately $64 million per year, or 2.1 percent of commission revenues" (*Stock Exchange Commission Rates*, Hearings, p. 122).

35. *Securities Industry Study*, Report of the Subcommittee on Commerce and Finance of the House Committee on Interstate and Foreign Commerce, H. Rept. 92-1519, 92 Cong. 2 sess. (1972), p. 12.

fluctuating prices appears more risky than one with stable prices. The reason is that the bankruptcy of firms during periods of depression causes the industry subject to cyclical swings in demand to have to pay a higher rate of return to attract the same amount of capital than an industry with more stable demand. The higher cost of capital will then necessitate a higher price for the good or service.[36]

Two conditions promote marked price instability: unstable demand and inelasticity of supply.[37] There is no doubt that the first condition is met: there are large swings in the daily volume of securities sold on the NYSE. In 1970, there were 254 trading days: on 4 of these, 6 to 7 million shares were traded; on 23, in excess of 16 million shares were traded. The mode was 9 to 10 million shares, occurring on 48 days. The same pattern characterized other years: a distribution in which a small percentage of the total trading days represents volumes of radically different magnitudes, but a typical volume accounts for a significant fraction of the total trading days.[38] However, the variation around the typical volume is marked. In 1970, the mean volume (on 27 of the 254 trading days) was 11,564,000 shares. The volume on 48 of the trading days was 9 to 10 million shares; on 42 days, 10 to 11 million shares; and on 29 days, 12 to 13 million shares. Thus, on 119 of the 254 trading days, the variation in volume ranged from about 10 to 20 percent of the mean. For the rest of the trading days, the variation was much greater, reaching almost 90 percent of the mean on the highest day and about 58 percent on the lowest.[39]

These fluctuations, however, are an inevitable characteristic of the stock market and have been documented for at least seventy years.[40] It is unlikely that commission rates would gyrate in reaction to these day-to-day volume changes or that the survival of any brokerage firm is at

36. See Scherer, *Industrial Market Structure*, pp. 201–02. He goes on to demonstrate, however, that the avoidance of price fluctuations by collusive price fixing may not lead to a lower price (pp. 202–06).

37. William C. Freund, vice-president and chief economist of the NYSE, maintains that demand volatility in the securities business exceeds that in other highly cyclical industries such as autos, steel, and housing starts. See "Demand Instability in the Securities Industry" (paper delivered before the American Finance Association, Detroit, Dec. 28, 1970; processed).

38. NYSE, *1971 Fact Book* (1971), p. 6. Wide swings in the number of transactions are also evident. In 1970, the high day recorded 58,780 round-lot trades; the average day, 29,786; and the low day, 17,347 (letter to the author from William C. Freund, March 23, 1971).

39. NYSE, *1971 Fact Book*, p. 6.

40. Ibid., p. 72. They have probably existed throughout the exchange's history, but data are recorded only back to 1900 in the current *Fact Book*.

stake on a low-volume day. It is also unlikely that price would vary much in reaction to annual demand changes.

Thus, there seems little reason to expect demand volatility, if freed from NYSE control, to increase the level of commission rates. Rather, the evidence suggests that rates, except possibly for small trades, would fall substantially with unregulated price competition. Consider the following facts. First, the price of a seat on the NYSE is high and is correlated with the intensity of trading activity.[41] Such a relationship strongly suggests the existence of monopoly rents, which are captured in the present value of a seat in times of strong demand. Second, the commission rate was, until the most recent schedule, directly tied to the value of the round lot regardless of the size of the transaction. This means that the commission on an order larger than 100 shares was a multiple of the number of round lots in the order. The present schedule reduces the multiple considerably, but it still seems improbable that the costs of executing and clearing large transactions rise in the same proportion as the commission fees. In fact, there are two strong indications that they do not. First, it is clear that give-ups and reciprocal arrangements are, in effect, price concessions. The explicit discount for nonmember brokers offered by the NYSE in early 1972 is an open acknowledgment that these arrangements were indirectly bringing the minimum commissions more closely in line with costs. Second, the growth of the third market and the trading of NYSE-listed stocks on regional exchanges indicate the substantial divergence of prices from costs. These markets accounted for 26.1 percent of the dollar volume of NYSE-listed trades in 1971, as opposed to about 7.4 percent immediately following the Second World War.[42] The substantial growth of these alternatives indicates the magnitude of savings in off-board trading. Friend and Blume estimate that $60 million annually were saved from the freeing of rates on the part of orders over $500,000, and that additional savings of $150 million could have been realized in 1971 with competitive rates on all trades.[43] Institutions will certainly continue to do an increasing amount of trading away from the NYSE until rates more closely conform to costs.

The last indication that commission rates are substantially in excess

41. The high price in 1971 was $300,000; the low was $145,000 (NYSE, *1972 Fact Book*, p. 59). See also Harold Demsetz, "Perfect Competition, Regulation, and the Stock Market," in Henry G. Manne and others (eds.), *Symposium on Economic Policy and the Regulation of Corporate Securities, Proceedings* (American Enterprise Institute for Public Policy Research, 1967), p. 19.

42. Leonard Silk, "The Big Board's Erosion," *New York Times*, Oct. 18, 1972.

43. "Consequences of Competitive Commissions," p. 133.

of costs is that brokerage firms offer many services to customers without explicitly charging for them. The obvious implication is that the difference between the commission rate and the unit cost of executing and clearing a transaction is large enough to cover these services. The NYSE has argued that the abandonment of fixed rates will lead to severe price discrimination, particularly in slack times—that is, that rates will be lower for large, institutional investors and higher for small investors, whose demand is likely to be highly inelastic.[44] All the evidence indicates, however, that the price charged for the brokerage service is, except possibly for small trades, considerably above costs, the divergence increasing with the size of the transaction. Thus it is doubtful that customers, except those dealing in small transactions, will face higher prices with the abolition of fixed rates.

Service Competition

Brokerage firms offer a wide variety of services to their customers besides the execution and clearance of a transaction. Services that precede the transaction are provision of research and investment advice, obtaining of quotations, and provision of a "customers' room" where customers can watch the tape. Those that follow the transaction are safekeeping of customers' securities and collection and delivery of dividends, rights, and warrants on customers' securities left in street name with the broker.[45] Since these services are covered by the commission rate and not priced separately, they "constitute the most significant area of competition among members of the Exchange."[46] Many other services have arisen especially to attract the volume investor, including special studies done solely for a customer, installation of direct wires on a customer's premises, and pricing and computation of the asset value of mutual fund customers' portfolios several times each day.[47] No separate price is charged for any of these services, either.

44. Memorandum on the Fixed Commission Rate Structure, pp. 79–88. As Kahn points out, "this is a somewhat ironic defense of a system that has, heretofore, discriminated *against* the large transaction" (*Economics of Regulation*, p. 204). Even more ironic is that it was a small investors' group, the Independent Investor Protective League, that filed suit against the SEC to force negotiated rates for all transactions, not just those in excess of $300,000 ("SEC Faces Suit over New Rates for Big Board," *Wall Street Journal*, Sept. 24, 1971).
45. *Special Study of Securities Markets*, pt. 2, p. 321.
46. Ibid.
47. Ibid., pp. 312–13.

If product competition "tends to improve the scope, depth, and quality of those services which are useful to the public, this would appear to be a desirable characteristic of the rate schedule."[48] At issue here is the assumption that customers would be deprived of services they desire in the environment of price competition that would be generated by negotiated rates.[49] To evaluate this assumption, the following question must be answered: are the increments to buyer satisfaction greater than or equal to the increments in the costs of providing the services? In the judgment of one scholar, this question cannot be satisfactorily answered because the requisite information is lacking.[50] In general, empirical studies have not been able to draw any solid conclusions about the effect of observed patterns of product competition on buyer welfare. The same problem is encountered here, as well, although both economic theory and some evidence concerning the quality of investment advice cast some doubt on the benefits of nonprice competition.

Consider the evidence first. A case documented by the Special Study[51] suggests that investment advice, one of the major services provided by brokerage houses, is not always as sound as it should be, and that customers are not getting uniform quality in the product they are buying at a fixed price. Dunn Engineering Corporation, which began business in Massachusetts in 1951, made its only public offering in July 1959. The stock did well, but by the summer of 1961, Dunn was in financial difficulties. After six months of obvious morbidity, a petition in bankruptcy was filed against the firm in April 1962. The Special Study comments: "While management's published statements during the last 6 months of Dunn's history are unusually lacking in candor, their translation into recommendations to buy Dunn stock was facilitated by superficial and irresponsible securities research practices, of which the Dunn case is by no means an isolated example."[52]

A case study, even if not an "isolated example," does not permit generalization. However, a recent survey of users of investment advice tends to confirm the quality of research found in the Dunn case. Among

48. Ibid., p. 321.

49. Kahn has pointed out the contradiction between the NYSE's concern that investors would, without fixed rates, be deprived of services and its insistence that investors want (and presumably would demand) the services offered by brokers. (*Economics of Regulation*, p. 205, note 95.)

50. Joe S. Bain, *Industrial Organization* (2nd ed., John Wiley, 1968), pp. 421–25.

51. In *Special Study of Securities Markets*, pt. 1, pp. 334–44.

52. Ibid., p. 336.

the comments were: "Many institutional investors rate the general level of broker research as satisfactory at best and sometimes only fair . . . There is also frequent criticism of the short-term market orientation of many broker reports, often keyed to 'buy' recommendations . . . In summary, investors' views about broker research may appear ambivalent. Over-all, there may be too much of it . . ."[53]

"Too much" research is not, according to economic theory, an unexpected result of a system of fixed rates. "The customer who wants to buy execution of orders plus salesmanship, advice, and research pays the same price as the customer that wants only the first of these. The consequence is an inherent tendency to what might be termed service inflation, in which an equilibrium of cost and price is achieved not by reducing price to marginal cost but raising marginal cost to price."[54] In other words, this rate structure does not allow customers to choose freely among those services they wish to pay for and those they do not. Without separate pricing of the product and its associated services, or alternative mixes of product plus service with different prices, there is no direct market test of the value customers attach to the offered services. The result is not only the existence of more service than a price-competitive market would probably sustain, but, to the extent that the Dunn incident is representative, inferior service as well.

Technological Progress

The fundamental difficulty in evaluating this dimension of market performance is that the observed record cannot be compared to what could have been. That is, the relevant question—have brokerage firms exploited every technological opportunity that would reduce costs of providing service over time and forgone those opportunities that would raise costs?—is unanswerable because the kind of information necessary to evaluate performance is lacking. The requisite information would include ". . . not only the long-run cost-reducing impact of each technological change adopted (a *relatively* easy thing to learn), but also the identities of all available opportunities for technological change which were rejected, and the estimated effect on cost of each rejected opportu-

53. Eileen Shanahan, "At Market Hearings: Worries on Research," *New York Times*, Nov. 14, 1971.

54. Kahn, *Economics of Regulation*, p. 207.

nity. Only then could we tell if the observed innovation record reached or reasonably approximated the ideal."[55]

This statement of the requirements for evaluating an industry's progressiveness cannot be applied to the brokerage industry because the data are not available. Yet, one cannot help wondering whether, to choose one example, the industry has done all it could to solve its "fails" problems. Fails refer to the "failure of a broker-dealer to deliver a certificate in proper form at the agreed settlement date to another broker-dealer."[56] The Special Study, written over ten years ago, warned that "the rise in fails to deliver in periods of heightened market activity suggests the danger that present securities handling, clearing, and delivery methods would prove inadequate to meet any sustained increase in volume. A 'fails' situation such as that which arose in the spring of 1961 should not again be allowed to occur."[57]

The volume of the fails that concerned the Special Study was $1.5 billion as of April 28, 1961, calculated on the basis of a questionnaire sent to members of the National Association of Securities Dealers, to which more than one-half of the membership responded.[58] When the NYSE began keeping fail statistics in April 1968, the dollar amount fluctuated between $2.7 billion and $3.8 billion from April to November 1968, reaching $4.1 billion in December.[59] Although the largest proportion of fails occurs in the OTC markets, most of the business in these markets is transacted by NYSE members, and so OTC fails would be included in the exchange's data.[60]

In April 1969, eight years after the Special Study's express warning, fails reached at least $1 billion *more* than the level that had elicited the concern. Two fundamental causes of fails are errors in the accounting system and the unavailability of stock certificates to deliver. The first of these imposes substantial costs in the industry: "Errors in orders are costing brokerage firms an estimated $100 million per year to correct.

55. Bain, *Industrial Organization*, p. 421.

56. *Special Study of Securities Markets*, pt. 1, p. 416.

57. Ibid., p. 427.

58. Ibid., p. 417. The dollar amount represents the contract value of transactions that selling brokers have not been able to deliver to buying brokers by the fifth day after the transaction.

59. *Securities Markets Agencies*, Hearings before the Subcommittee on Commerce and Finance of the House Committee on Interstate and Foreign Commerce, 91 Cong. 1 sess. (1969), p. 140.

60. Ibid., p. 141.

Added to this are the costs of the clerical forces required to track down each mistake. Then when the error is found it must be corrected in each of the multitude of records into which it has propagated itself. The cost and effort required to find and correct an error increase dramatically as time passes."[61]

The second cause of fails adversely affects brokerage houses' cash flow in two ways. First, a broker-dealer has to pay the customer who delivers his securities for sale on the settlement date even if he fails to deliver the securities to the broker-dealer purchaser. If the broker-dealer accumulates many fails, especially relative to payments for securities he receives on the settlement date from broker-dealer purchases, a financial drain on the firm occurs. Such drains, occurring in the context of record fails at the end of 1968, forced many brokerage houses to seek additional capital, and eventually contributed to the liquidation of some. The second adverse influence on cash flow is the growth of "short differences"—securities that are supposed to be in a firm's inventory but are not. Short differences, like fails, negatively influence a broker's financial situation in that they must be made up, usually by buying the stock in the open market in order to replenish the inventory.

It is clear that the stock certificate plays a key role in the problems of accounting errors and the unavailability of securities. Donald T. Regan, chairman of Merrill Lynch, Pierce, Fenner, and Smith, Inc., has stated that "unless our markets do away with stock certificates, we're going to choke again."[62] The chief difficulties with the stock certificate are that it has to be physically moved from one location to another and cannot be transmitted electronically; information from it is transcribed manually, giving rise to errors; and it is a negotiable instrument and therefore liable to loss, theft, destruction, and counterfeiting.[63] To overcome the shortcomings of the stock certificate and its propensity to disrupt, rather than facilitate, an orderly market process in high-volume times, it has been proposed that certificates be taken out of circulation and placed in depositories, and that the accounting system be automated.[64]

61. North American Rockwell Information Systems Company, *Securities Industry Overview Study* (American Stock Exchange, 1969), p. 5.

62. Quoted in Terry Robards, "Stocks: Dam is Holding," *New York Times*, Feb. 14, 1971.

63. North American Rockwell, *Securities Industry Overview*, p. 65. Apparently the loss from theft can reach sizable amounts (George Lardner, Jr., "Stock Thefts Hit $400 Million in 2 Years, Mitchell Testifies," *Washington Post*, June 9, 1971).

64. North American Rockwell, *Securities Industry Overview*, p. 39.

The question now is whether implementation of this solution, proposed in September 1969 and still to be fully adopted, has been delayed too long. Could the NYSE have brought the fails problem, still very much on the minds of the brokerage community, under control by now, especially in view of the Special Study's warning of several years ago? No confident answer can be given, but the following example suggests that the brokerage industry's record might have been better than it was. The Midwest Stock Exchange Service Corporation has automated its accounting system for its ninety-two member firms. The service permits firms to ". . . transmit their information on cash and securities movement over the communications system [which links the brokerage firms with a central data processing facility in Chicago]. After this information is processed in Chicago, confirmations are printed on terminals located in brokerage offices and linked directly to Chicago computers.

"Confirmations are returned to the broker on the same day the transaction takes place so they can promptly be mailed to customers."[65] A regional exchange, then, organizing its service firm in 1961, has led the way toward implementing one of the proposed solutions for the industry's fails problems, automated bookkeeping. There is one consideration, however, to be examined before concluding that the technological performance of the NYSE has been inferior.

It is claimed that since there is a serious shortage of personnel in the brokerage industry trained to operate automatic data processing equipment,[66] rapid conversion to automation might increase errors and lengthen the time required for processing, thereby raising costs over time. This point does not seem very telling, however. If personnel shortages exist, they did not stop the Midwest Exchange from innovating. Furthermore, the costs of *not* automating are substantial: the estimate cited above that errors in orders are costing $100 million annually does not even include an estimated $100 million in dividend suspense accounts—accounts that arise because dividends continue to be paid to persons who have since sold the stock to which the dividends belong. The cost of processing the movement of dividends to the rightful parties alone runs into millions.[67]

65. William D. Smith, "Midwest Stock Exchange Automates Paperwork," *New York Times*, Feb. 14, 1971.

66. *Securities Markets Agencies*, Hearings, p. 90, note 7.

67. North American Rockwell, *Securities Industry Overview*, p. 58.

It is difficult to imagine that the costs of more speedy automation in the 1960s would have exceeded these figures.[68]

It must be remembered, though, that both the Midwest Exchange and NYSE operate under fixed commission rates, so comparison between them may permit only a negative conclusion: if fixed rates are supposed to encourage technological progress, they have clearly not done so for NYSE members.

Conclusions

The substitution of negotiated for fixed commission rates in the broker-age industry implies neither destructive competition nor deterioration in market performance in the dimensions of price, service, or technological progress. This judgment is similar to that arrived at by others who have examined the strong defense of regulated rates offered by the NYSE in 1968 and 1969, although the studies have differed in emphasis and in arguments covered.

It now appears that the NYSE minimum commission schedule will be abandoned. The primary reason for this step is the rapid growth in the importance of institutional trading and the consequent unhappiness of institutions with commissions well in excess of the costs of executing their trades. The increase in the proportion of institutional trading on the NYSE is reflected in the decrease in individual trading: in 1960, indi-viduals dominated the volume and dollar value of trading, accounting for 69 percent and 61 percent, respectively; ten years later, the respective percentages were 44 percent and 38 percent.[69] This reversal was associated with the acquisition of memberships by institutions through their broker-age subsidiaries on regional exchanges, with the purpose of recapturing some of the overcharge through reciprocal deals; resort to the third

68. It has been claimed that the net cost of fails could be reduced by $89 million measured against a benchmark figure of $125 million that represents the cost of fails under the present system with a 20-million-share day. This saving is arrived at after estimating the costs of implementing "minimum structural change" that would involve banks and brokers and not going to "... certificate depositories and nationwide clearing for OTC stocks." See R. L. Petruschell and others, *Reducing Costs of Stock Trans-actions: A Study of Alternative Completion Systems* (Rand Corporation, 1970), vol. 1, p. 8.

69. NYSE, *1971 Fact Book*, p. 53.

market where commissions are negotiated;[70] and use of a "fourth market" —trades effected directly among institutions themselves.

The effect of all this has been to accelerate off-board trading of NYSE-listed securities and thereby force the realization that retention of fixed rates, at least on orders of the size commonly transacted by institutions, would hasten the decline of the NYSE's position of dominance in the trading of securities. The role of the institutions in the rapid change in the pricing of brokerage services since 1968 has thus been crucial. The lesson of this experience may be that a regulatory agency will be unlikely to worry about the price-cost relationship for a good or service under its jurisdiction unless important customers find it not in their interest to pay the price charged and can bring pressures to bear, as the financial institutions did.

For investors in general, it is critical that changes not be limited to those that would satisfy institutions.[71] It should be kept in mind that a monopolist never gives up its position easily and will, if allowed, try to control, if not blunt, any change that portends an increase in competition.

Appendix. Statistical Estimation of Long-run Costs in the Brokerage Industry

Three functional forms have been fitted to cross-section cost data for 369 firms in 1966: a polynomial, an exponential, and a split polynomial. The firms vary considerably in size and all are used in all regressions unless otherwise noted. The figures in parentheses throughout are *t*-statistics.

Polynomial Function

In running a regression on a polynomial in which the independent variable is positive for all observations, it is necessary first to start with

70. Trading in the third market has been facilitated by the introduction in February 1971 of the National Association of Securities Dealers Automated Quotation System. This system provides subscribers with continuous and current net bid-and-asked-price quotations for securities traded in the OTC markets.

71. In early 1973, the chairman and chief executive of Prudential Insurance Company of America expressed the view that Prudential receives fair treatment under the present schedule, which permits negotiated rates on orders in excess of $300,000. Nonetheless, Prudential favors continuation of the third market, despite James Needham's proposal to abolish it in return for deregulation of the rate schedule ("Prudential Indicates It Opposes Ending Big Board Fixed Fees," *Wall Street Journal*, March 6, 1973).

NOTE. This appendix was prepared by Glen Ramsay, assistant professor of economics, University of Rhode Island.

a Kth-degree polynomial such that K is larger than any reasonable a priori expectation, then to "step out" X^K, X^{K-1}, X^{K-2}, and so on. To do otherwise could be to violate the Gauss-Markov assumptions. For example, suppose that the true mechanism for determining cost is

$$Y = \alpha + \beta X + \gamma X^2 + \delta X^3 + \epsilon,$$

where Y is cost, X is output, and ϵ is the error term. The model is then specified thus:

$$Y = \alpha' + \beta' X + \gamma' X^2 + n,$$

where, to avoid confusion, n is the disturbance term of the model. In fact, n is really $(X^3 + \epsilon)$; thus, it can be seen that the disturbance term has a mean of δX^3 and not zero. Furthermore, the disturbance term is no longer independent of the independent variables, so that $\hat{\beta}$, the estimate of β, will be biased.

Hence, there is the problem of determining how far the polynomial should be extended. Consider the model

$$Y = \beta_0 + \beta_1 X + \beta_2 X^2 + \cdots + \beta_K X^K + \epsilon.$$

In addition to estimating the coefficients, the unknown degree of the polynomial, K, must also be estimated.[72] A polynomial is estimated with a K sufficiently high so that it is reasonably certain that β_K is zero and, thus, that $\beta_{K+1} X^{K+1}$ has a mean of zero; this assures that ϵ has a zero mean. From this regression, the sum of squared residuals (SSE) is recorded, and the order of the polynomial is lowered by 1:

$$Y = \beta_0 + \beta_1 X + \beta_2 X^2 + \cdots \beta_{K-1} X^{K-1},$$

which again gives the sum of squared residuals. If S_K is the difference between the sum of squared residuals for $(K - 1)$ and K, then

$$F = (T - K - 1)S_K/SSE_K \text{ is distributed as}$$
$$F \text{ with 1 and } (T - K - 1) \text{ degrees of freedom}$$

if and only if β_K is zero.

By repeating this test for polynomials of increasingly lower orders until the first significant F is reached, an estimation of K can be made. The results are:

K	SSE	F
3	2.623×10^{15}	2.24
2	2.639×10^{15}	42.7
1	2.948×10^{15}	. . .

72. The method for deriving an estimate of K can be found in Roger L. Plackett, *Principles of Regression Analysis* (Oxford: The Clarendon Press, 1960).

Thus, it can be seen that $K = 2$, yielding the regression

(1) $Y = (4.76 \times 10^5) + 31.348X - (1.083 \times 10^{-6})X^2.$
             (2.98)   (40.39)   (−6.54)
                            $R^2 = 0.934$

This equation was originally presented by the NYSE. The statistically significant coefficient of X^2 indicates the presence of economies of scale throughout the observable range. It is interesting to note, however, that the largest firm (three times larger than the second largest firm) is chiefly responsible for the significance of X^2. With this observation omitted, the results are:

$$Y = (3.93 \times 10^5) + 32.8X - (2.3 \times 10^{-6})X^2.$$
$$(2.21) \qquad (2.06) \quad (-1.95)$$
$$R^2 = 0.897$$

When this equation is corrected for heteroscedasticity (with any deflation), the X^2 coefficient has a t-ratio of less than one. This suggests that the large observation is an anomaly and that there are, in fact, no important economies of scale. Further, although the costs of the largest firm fall below the fitted total cost function of the other firms, its presence in the equation does not, as indicated below, make an impressive argument for the existence of economies of scale.

The Antitrust Division of the U.S. Department of Justice argues that equation (1) is heteroscedastic and assumes, as suggested by Johnston and Goldberger,[73] that the disturbance is proportional to X. The division deflated the equation by X, obtaining

(2) $Y = (3.42 \times 10^5) + 25.57X + (4.34 \times 10^{-6})X^2,$
             (32.3)   (7.07)   (0.503)

where the coefficient of X^2 has changed sign and become insignificant.

However, the NYSE argued that the assumption of a constant proportion is not valid. The exchange claims that "there is a second, economic, influence on this relationship, namely, that small firms tend to have expected (or average) levels of profit similar to large firms but with much greater variance."[74] Guth explored the problem in some detail by esti-

73. See J. Johnston, *Statistical Cost Analysis* (McGraw-Hill, 1960), and Arthur S. Goldberger, *Econometric Theory* (John Wiley, 1964).
74. "Testimony of Louis A. Guth," In the Matter of S.E.C. Rate Structure Investigation (see p. 311, note 33), p. 34.

mating a relation between the residuals and X, using ordinary least squares. His best-fitting equation is:

$$\text{var}(e_i) = 4.85 + X^{1.45}.$$

This agrees qualitatively with the analysis of Gerald Glasser, another witness for the NYSE, who obtained 1.2 for the exponent of X.[75] This result implies that equations (1) and (2) are both heteroscedastic; that is, the division of the original equation by X has overcorrected, causing the ϵs associated with small xs to have a larger variance than the ϵs associated with large Xs. Therefore, the Ys and Xs should be deflated not by X, but by a root of X somewhere between $X^{0.65}$ and $X^{0.75}$.

Thus, it is necessary both to deflate (to eliminate heteroscedasticity) and to estimate the Kth-order polynomial (to avoid specification error). This was done for two different deflations, $X^{.75}$ and $X^{.70}$. For $X^{.75}$,

$$\frac{Y}{X^{.75}} = \frac{\beta_0}{X^{.75}} + \frac{\beta_1 X}{X^{.75}} + \frac{\beta_2 X^2}{X^{.75}} + \cdots + \frac{\beta_K X^K}{X^{.75}}.$$

The results of this estimation of K are:

K	SSE	F
3	6.569×10^7	...
2	6.585×10^7	0.891
1	6.631×10^7	2.54

Both F-statistics are insignificant at the 95 percent level. It may be concluded that, when deflating by $X^{.75}$, the total cost function of the brokerage industry is

(3) $$Y = 2.24 \times 10^5 + 34.13X,$$
$$(17.2) \qquad (24.4)$$

a linear function that exhibits no economies of scale. With the X^2 term included, deflation by $X^{.75}$ yields

(4) $$Y = 2.22 \times 10^5 + 35.16X - (2.31 \times 10^{-6})X^2.$$
$$(16.68) \qquad (22.78) \quad (-1.60)$$

The X^2 term here is not significant at the 95 percent level.

For deflation by $X^{.7}$,

K	SSE	F
3	1.559×10^8	...
2	1.567×10^8	1.87
1	1.587×10^8	4.68

75. "Testimony of Gerald J. Glasser," in ibid., pp. 15–16.

In this case, the F-statistic when $K = 2$ is significant at the 95 percent but not the 99 percent level. Guth's estimation with this deflation is:

$$(5) \qquad Y = 2.17 \times 10^5 + 35.25X - (2.27 \times 10^{-6})X^2.$$
$$\qquad\quad (14.45) \qquad\quad (26.27) \quad (-2.14)$$

The t-ratio for the X^2 term exhibits the same significance that the F-statistic did—significant at the 95 percent but not the 99 percent level. Thus, the results are inconclusive at this deflation level.

Exponential Function

Guth also estimated an exponential cost function of the form:[76]

$$Y = \alpha X^\beta.$$

He found that

$$(6) \qquad\qquad \log Y = 2.53 + 0.802 \log X.$$
$$\qquad\qquad (29.96)\ (44.17)$$
$$\qquad\qquad \bar{R}^2 = 0.841$$

The coefficient of $\log X$ is significantly less than one, the relevant t-ratio being -9.5, not 44.17, as reported. However, this specification has two shortcomings. First, it permits no possibility that the long-run average cost curve could be U-shaped; in fact, if the true curve has a positive intercept, any results other than Guth's would be surprising. Second, the restriction to a zero intercept is inconsistent with the results of the polynomials, and Guth admits that a positive intercept is not inconsistent with the estimation of a long-run cost curve.[77]

Split Function

A function was tried that supposes economies of scale to be present up to a certain output, after which constant returns to scale obtain. Based on this supposition, a Quandt test was performed; the maximum likelihood function peaks at the 160th firm. Thus, X was partitioned into firms 1 to 160 and firms 161 to 369, where X was sorted by size. The results for undeflated equations are presented, since the deflation causes

76. "Testimony of Guth," p. 30.
77. Ibid., pp. 30–31. See also John R. Meyer and others, *The Economics of Competition in the Transportation Industries* (Harvard University Press, 1959), p. 22.

the same loss of significance as it did in the polynomial regressions. For small firms,

$$Y = (1.97 \times 10^5) + 27.2X + (4.07 \times 10^{-4})X^2;$$
$$(1.81) \qquad (1.74) \quad (0.866)$$

for large firms,

$$Y = (7.25 \times 10^5) + 30.8X - (9.96 \times 10^{-7})X^2.$$
$$(2.37) \qquad (27.5) \quad (-4.31)$$

The results are precisely the opposite of the original assumption: that is, there are constant returns to scale among small firms and economies of scale among larger firms. Although the Chow test does not indicate that the break is significant, the change in sign and the sharp difference in t-ratios suggest that the large firms have a very different production function from the small firms.

Conclusion

The econometric results leave much doubt about the existence of economies of scale. It is clear that the undeflated data are heteroscedastic, but the significance, and even the sign, of the X^2 coefficient is very sensitive to the deflator, which makes a clear interpretation impossible. The equations are also ambiguous because the omission of one observation renders the X^2 coefficient statistically insignificant. If the intercept of $200,000 found in the polynomials is a threshold cost, the exponential specification must be rejected a priori. The results of the split polynomial are interesting but ambiguous for the same reasons the polynomial regressions are: namely, the sensitivity to deflation and the reaction to the elimination of the largest firm.

It seems clear that the massive amount of statistical analysis done by the NYSE and the Antitrust Division has shed very little light on the true shape of the long-run cost function. However, even assuming that long-run average cost continues to decline beyond the point established by equation (5) as exhausting significant economies—300,000 transactions—the returns to scale are not very impressive. A firm operating at a level of 300,000 transactions will have an average cost per transaction of $35.29; a firm twice as large (600,000 transactions) has an average cost per transaction of $34.25. Thus, the saving achieved by doubling the output is $1.04 per transaction, or a 3 percent reduction.

CHAPTER TEN

Competitive Policy for Depository Financial Institutions

ALMARIN PHILLIPS

I HAVE EXPRESSED THE VIEW elsewhere that regulatory reform constitutes the most effective means of increasing competition among commercial banks.[1] This is because, I argued, regulation of the behavior of banks and the structure of banking markets is the principal source of monopoly power among banks. In addition, "private regulation," in the form of accepted patterns of behavior reinforced by the formal and informal associations of bankers, also inhibits the operation of competitive forces. This argument suggests, as I then noted, that efforts at the federal level to improve the performance of banking markets by control of bank mergers and holding companies are but tilting at windmills. That is, the regulatory framework seems to dominate the other determinants of market performance to the extent that policies aimed at maintaining a competitive structure and preventing collusion can have only minor effect, at best.

This chapter attempts, first, to extend this argument to depository institutions other than commercial banks. An examination of the effects of regulation on the degree of actual and potential *inter*industry competition is in some ways more fruitful than consideration of *intra*industry effects alone. Second, the dynamic interrelations between market structure, behavior, and performance at various times and the growth and development of public regulation are explored in some detail. In this connection,

---

1. Almarin Phillips, "Competition, Confusion, and Commercial Banking," *Journal of Finance*, vol. 19 (March 1964), pp. 32–45.

a descriptive model of regulated markets is developed, which, despite its generality, may clarify the arguments concerning the nature of regulation and the possibility of increasing the role of competition in financial markets. Third, the impact of new technologies on inter- and intra-industry competition and on the nature and effectiveness of regulation is examined. Finally, some fundamental changes in public policies are proposed such that technological opportunities could be realized without disruption of the financial system and competition could play a more positive role in the future. There is little cause for optimism, however, that these changes are likely to be instituted.

The Regulation of Depository Financial Institutions

The regulated depository financial institutions of the United States are commercial banks, savings and loan associations (S&Ls), mutual savings banks (MSBs), and credit unions.[2] At the end of 1970, there were 13,705 commercial banks in the country, with a total of 35,585 offices. Savings and loan associations numbered 5,738, with 10,075 offices, and there were 494 mutual savings banks, with 1,581 offices.[3] Data on concentration in banking are easily available and need not be repeated here. Suffice it to say that it is not uncommon for small communities to have no more than one or two institutions of any single type and for two- or three-bank deposit concentration ratios to be well over 50 percent even in large metropolitan areas.[4]

The regulatory framework governing these institutions is relatively complex. Commercial banks and mutual savings and loan associations may be either state or federally chartered. State charters are available to mutual savings banks in eighteen states; there is no provision for federal

2. No attention is given here to the last, but see *The Report of the President's Commission on Financial Structure & Regulation* (Government Printing Office, 1972), pp. 54–58, 63–64 (cited hereafter as *Report on Financial Structure*), for a discussion of their peculiar problems.

3. National Association of Mutual Savings Banks, *National Fact Book of Mutual Savings Banking, 1971* (NAMSB, 1971), p. 13.

4. See Bernard Shull, "Concentration in Banking in the United States," in H. Arndt (ed.), *Die Konzentration und der Wirtschaft* (German Economic Association, forthcoming), and Benjamin J. Klebaner, "Recent Changes in the Structure of Banking," *Proceedings of a Conference on Bank Structure and Competition* (Federal Reserve Bank of Chicago, 1970), pp. 36–57.

chartering. Charters for stock savings and loan associations were granted by twenty-one states in 1971.

Each state has at least one bank regulatory agency, and some have separate agencies for each type of institution. On the federal level, the Office of the Comptroller of the Currency charters, examines, and supervises national banks, including the approval or disapproval of branches and, under the Bank Merger Act of 1960, amended in 1966, bank merger applications where the resulting institution would be a national bank. The Federal Deposit Insurance Corporation (FDIC) examines and supervises insured, state-chartered commercial banks that are not members of the Federal Reserve System, as well as insured mutual savings banks. Under the Bank Merger Act, it approves or disapproves bank merger applications where the resulting bank would be an insured, state-chartered nonmember bank. The Board of Governors of the Federal Reserve System examines and supervises state-chartered member banks, approves or disapproves of mergers where the resulting bank would be a state-chartered member bank, and is responsible for administration of the Bank Holding Company Act of 1956, amended 1970, and the Edge Act.[5] The Board of Governors and the FDIC set the maximum interest rates that may be paid on time and savings deposits and certificates of deposit by commercial banks and federally insured mutual savings banks.

The Federal Home Loan Bank Board (FHLBB) charters, examines, and supervises federally chartered savings and loan associations; it also examines and supervises state-chartered savings and loan associations that are insured by its subsidiary, the Federal Savings and Loan Insurance Corporation, or that are members of the Federal Home Loan Bank System. The FHLBB in cooperation with the Board of Governors and the FDIC sets the maximum interest rates that may be paid on deposits of savings and loan associations.

Under the National Banking Act of 1863 and under most state statutes, commercial banks are allowed to offer a full array of personal and business, secured and unsecured short-term loans, mortgage loans, and construction loans. The National Banking Act, reflecting the "real bills doctrine" of banking, originally prohibited all real estate loans by national banks, and such loans are still restricted by the many regulations affecting

5. The Edge Act of 1919 permits U.S. banks to charter corporations to engage in foreign banking and other foreign operations. Problems relating to foreign operations of U.S. banks and the operations of foreign banks in the United States are not treated here, but they are likely to become increasingly important.

the type of collateral, loan-to-value ratios, loan maturities, and repayment methods.[6] The original prohibition and subsequent regulation of such loans was, in fact, a major factor in the rapid growth of savings and loan (or, as they were then called, building and loan) associations in the late nineteenth century. Commercial banks are generally empowered to invest in a broad list of "investment securities" in the form of bonds, notes, and debentures, including some types of state and local revenue bonds. They are the only institutions universally to offer demand deposit and checking account services. Time and savings deposits, certificates of deposit, and, with some limitations, subordinated capital notes and debentures also may be offered. So, too, may trust department services, including management of pension funds.[7]

Mutual savings banks and savings and loan associations have far more restricted powers. S&Ls can ordinarily make property improvement and equipment loans, government-guaranteed or insured loans, personal loans secured by time or savings accounts of the borrower held at the same association, loans on some types of mobile homes, and a full complement of real estate loans, excepting loans on unimproved lands and forest tracts and for industrial and commercial properties. Investment powers are broad, but usually exclude stocks and bonds of private corporations and financial institutions, revenue bonds, and public utility bonds. Deposits are restricted to time and savings accounts and certificates of deposit.[8] MSBs have somewhat broader powers than savings and loan associations. They can make loans to other financial institutions, educational loans, loans secured by savings accounts held in other institutions, loans secured by private and public equity and debt securities, multiunit residential mortgage loans, real estate loans on raw lands and forest tracts, and investments in a variety of private and public equity and debt securities. Mutual savings banks may issue debt instruments, but sometimes these are not regarded as capital for regulatory purposes.[9]

6. For additional details, see Comptroller of the Currency, *Comptroller's Manual for National Banks: Regulations* (1971), pts. 1, 3, 6 (hereafter cited as *Comptroller's Manual*).

7. For additional details, see *Report on Financial Structure*, pp. 41–54, and *Comptroller's Manual*, pt. 9.

8. See *Report on Financial Structure*, pp. 34–41.

9. MSBs may offer demand deposits in six states. In Massachusetts and New Hampshire they are allowed to offer interest-bearing "negotiable orders of withdrawal" (N.O.W.) accounts; these utilize checklike negotiable orders for payment from interest-bearing savings accounts, which, while technically not payable on demand, are in fact paid through a commercial bank when presented. Such accounts were prohibited

The McFadden Act of 1927, as amended, extended to national banks the same powers to branch within home office areas as applied to the state-chartered banks of the states in which the national banks were located. State laws governing branching are typically classified into those permitting statewide branching, limited geographic area branching, and unit banking only, but there are many variations within these classifications. It is not unusual, for example, for states permitting statewide or limited area branching to place restrictions on branch locations on the basis of proximity to the head office or to branches of other institutions or on population density.[10] Other forms of home-office protection or differences in the treatment of de novo branching and branching by merger also exist.[11] The combined effect of the McFadden Act and state laws is to prohibit interstate branching by either national or state-chartered commercial banks. The McFadden Act does not apply to federally chartered savings and loan associations. The FHLBB has the power to permit federal associations to branch in contravention to the laws governing state-chartered associations, but in practice the board has historically observed state laws. Since 1973, however, the board has shown more freedom in exercising its right to grant branches to federal associations despite state laws. As mutual savings banks are not federally chartered, only the laws of the chartering states apply to them.

State laws governing branching often give different treatment to the different classes of financial institutions. In Texas, for example, branching by commercial banks is prohibited, while savings and loan associations may branch statewide. In New York, on the other hand, commercial

---

in other states by 1973 federal legislation. In 1974, MSBs in New York instituted noninterest-bearing N.O.W. accounts.

10. For illustrations, see Almarin Phillips, "Structural and Regulatory Reform for Commercial Banking," in Giulio Pontecorvo and others (eds.), *Issues in Banking and Monetary Analysis* (Holt, Rinehart, and Winston, 1967).

11. In Virginia, for example, de novo branching is not restricted in the county of a bank's home office, but only one de novo branch is allowed in other counties. Branching by merger is unrestricted in all counties. For the situation in Pennsylvania, where a number of home-office protection clauses exist in the law, see Almarin Phillips, "Bank Mergers, Branch Banking and Bank Holding Companies in Pennsylvania," *University of Pennsylvania Law Review*, vol. 115 (February 1967), pp. 560–88. For an analysis of the effects of such laws, see Paul M. Horvitz and Bernard Shull, "The Impact of Branch Banking on Bank Performance," *National Banking Review*, vol. 2 (December 1964); and Bernard Shull, "The Effects of Recent Changes in Banking Law on Banking Markets in New York and Virginia" (paper submitted to the President's Commission on Financial Structure and Regulation, n.d.; processed).

banks until 1971 had broader branching powers than either savings and loan associations or mutual savings banks.

The Bank Holding Company Act of 1956, as amended in 1970, requires all bank holding companies—defined as any corporation holding 25 percent or more of the voting stock or otherwise controlling one or more insured banks—to register with the Board of Governors of the Federal Reserve System. Acquisitions of additional banks must be approved by the board. The act applies to state-chartered as well as national banks, and, except in the few states with more restrictive holding company legislation than that of the act, is the controlling legislation. The act also provides criteria and procedures for approving and regulating the types of finance-related services that the subsidiaries of bank holding companies may offer. The nonbank subsidiaries of bank holding companies may have an interstate system of offices; but, except for holding companies with banks in more than one state before 1956, interstate ownerships of bank subsidiaries is prohibited.[12]

Because of the nature of their ownership, holding companies for mutual S&Ls and MSBs cannot be formed. Holding companies for stock S&Ls do exist, and, again with the exception of holding companies formed prior to the legislation, the permissible functions for their subsidiaries are governed by the Savings and Loan Holding Company Amendments of 1967.[13] That act is administered by the FHLBB, although all of the involved associations are state chartered.

12. The literature on bank holding companies is vast. For a historical survey, see Gerald C. Fischer, *Bank Holding Companies* (Columbia University Press, 1961). See also Herbert V. Prochnow (ed.), *The One-Bank Holding Company* (Rand McNally, 1969); John R. Bunting, Jr., "One-Bank Holding Companies: A Banker's View," *Harvard Business Review*, vol. 47 (May–June 1969), pp. 99–106; Samuel B. Chase, Jr., "The Bank Holding Company: A Superior Device for Expanding Activities?" in *Policies for a More Competitive Financial System*, Conference Series 8 (Federal Reserve Bank of Boston, 1972); G. R. Hall, "Anticompetitive Impacts of Expanded Bank Service Lines" (paper submitted to the President's Commission on Financial Structure and Regulation, n.d.; processed); David G. Hayes, "Permissible Bank Holding Company Activities" (Office of the Comptroller of the Currency, Department of Banking and Economic Research, 1971; processed); Larry R. Mote, "The One-Bank Holding Company: History, Issues, and Pending Legislation," *Business Conditions* (Federal Reserve Bank of Chicago, July 1970), pp. 2–16; and "The Future of Registered Bank Holding Companies: Operation, Regulation, and Potential in a Changing Environment," prepared by Carter H. Golembe and Associates, Inc. (Washington: Association of Registered Bank Holding Companies, 1971; processed).

13. Enacted February 1968 (82 Stat. 5).

Market Structure, Conduct, Regulation, and Performance, 1924–70

The triad of structure, conduct, and performance traditional in industrial organization studies has been used primarily for the analysis of unregulated markets. Thus, in an unregulated market defined in terms of cross-demand and cross-supply relationships, there are a priori as well as empirical reasons to argue that

$$(1) \qquad P_{kt} = P(S_{it}, C_{jt}, D_t),$$

where P_{kt} ($k = 1, 2, \ldots, p$) is a set of performance variables, S_{it} ($i = 1, 2, \ldots, s$) is a set of structural variables, C_{jt} ($j = 1, 2, \ldots, c$) is a set of conduct variables, and D_t represents the conditions of demand, input factor supply, and other exogenous influences on market performance. All variables are set at a given time, t.

In this model, market structure variables usually include the number of sellers and buyers, their size distributions, their geographic locations, the cost structure of sellers, cross-elasticity of supply conditions among existing sellers and between them and potential entrants, and cross-elasticity of demand conditions among firms in the market and between them and firms in other markets. Conduct variables include price, advertising, research, and innovative behavior, all of which may be determined by firms independently or with various degrees of collusion. Together with D_t, the structure and conduct variables are seen as determining performance, as measured by market prices (and hence allocative efficiency), rates of return, growth of sales, technological progressiveness, and, conceivably, other similar factors. While these relationships are not fully specified, allocative efficiency is generally believed to be adversely affected by decreases in the number of firms, by increases in the degree of positive skewness in their size distribution, by decreases in supply cross-elasticities among sellers and between them and potential entrants, and by decreases in demand cross-elasticities among sellers. Similarly, independently determined price behavior is regarded as socially preferable to collusive behavior. Although there are numerous hypotheses concerning advertising, research, and innovative behavior, none seems to be received as conventional wisdom, nor are relations between the structural and conduct variables and the performance variables other than price well defined.[14]

For regulated industries, an appropriate extension of equation (1) would be

$$(2) \qquad P_{kt} = P(S_{it}, C_{jt}, D_t, R_t),$$

where R_t is the set of regulatory constraints on prices, advertising, product quality, entry, rates of return, and so forth. Some of these constraints may be essentially structural (for example, charter requirements and locational restrictions) and some may be influences on conduct (for example, interest rate regulations and restrictions on product offerings). I have argued in the past that as R_t becomes a more comprehensive set, the effects of S_{it} and C_{jt} on P_{kt} tend to diminish.[15] If, for example, R_t is defined with respect to the products that may be sold and their prices, to nonprice competitive behavior, and to entry, there are few aspects of performance left for S_{it} and C_{jt} to effect. For financial markets, however, R_t represents not a single regulatory agency but rather the influence of many federal and state bodies with differing controls both at a single point in time and over time.

With equation (2) in mind, let us review the history of market structure, conduct, regulation, and performance in financial markets, beginning, somewhat arbitrarily, in the mid-1920s.

1924–30

As Table 10-1 shows, there were 27,223 commercial banks, 12,403 savings and loan associations, and 611 mutual savings banks in operation at the end of 1925. Of the commercial banks, 720 were branch banks, with a total of 2,525 branch offices.[16] Thus, the financial structure was essentially one of unit institutions. Branching, however, was becoming more prevalent; in 1900, only 87 commercial banks operated branches, with a total of only 119 branch offices.[17] There is little detailed evidence on the extent of interlocking ownership and control of banks, but chain and group banking sys-

14. For an excellent survey of the theoretical and empirical literature, see F. M. Scherer, *Industrial Market Structure and Economic Performance* (Rand McNally, 1970).

15. Phillips, "Competition, Confusion, and Commercial Banking," pp. 32–33.

16. Gerald C. Fischer, *American Banking Structure* (Columbia University Press, 1968), p. 31. This is by far the best recent work on the development of the banking structure.

17. Ibid.

tems were certainly fairly common. These systems tended to concentrate in particular cities or limited areas around cities, with at least one exception—the empire of banker Amadeo Giannini, who established branch systems in California, New York, and other states.[18] Thus, despite the relatively large number of institutions, local market concentration was high, entry via branching was uncommon, and cross-demand elasticities were probably lower than today.

Market conduct in the mid-twenties was openly collusive. No antitrust case charging conspiracy among financial institutions had ever been successfully brought, and it was generally believed that banks were immune from the Sherman Act because of their regulated character and because their services were not commodities in interstate commerce. In cities where the number of banks was large enough to require them, clearing-house associations prescribed banking hours, rates of interest on loans and deposits, and rates of exchange and collection charges for check and bank-note clearings. In smaller towns, and as a supplement to clearing-house agreements in the larger cities, private agreements and custom produced similar results. Whatever the structure of markets, privately and collusively determined conduct worked to mitigate substantially any incentives to compete on the basis of price, banking hours, or other nonprice variables that might seriously influence market results for individual firms.[19]

By the mid-1920s, the National Banking Act had been in effect for six decades and the Federal Reserve Act for one decade. Under administrative and judicial interpretations of the former, national banks were permitted only one full-service office, regardless of state laws. In 1925, eighteen states had legislation expressly prohibiting branching and another twelve had de facto prohibitions. Nine states had legislation permitting statewide branching and two others permitted statewide branching without express legislative direction. Limited branching was permitted by law in seven states and two others allowed limited branching de facto.[20]

In contrast to the comparatively strict branching laws for national banks and in most states, the public regulation of banking practices was in other ways less strict than today. Commercial banks were permitted

18. Ibid., pp. 72–82.

19. Ibid., pp. 246–55. See also James G. Cannon, "Clearing-House Methods and Practices," in Clearing Houses and Credit Instruments, Publications of National Monetary Commission, vol. 6 (Washington: NMC, 1911).

20. Fischer, American Banking Structure, pp. 62–63. Alaska, Hawaii, and the District of Columbia are included in these statistics.

Table 10-1. Number of U.S. Depository Financial Institutions, 1924–35

Year	At beginning of year	Began operations			Ceased operations				Other changes	Net change during year	At end of year
		New	Reopened	Total	Absorbed	Suspended	Voluntarily liquidated	Total			
					Commercial banks						
1924	28,396	383	108	491	373	738	80	1,191	28	−672	27,724
1925	27,724	403	81	484	363	579	59	1,001	16	−501	27,223
1926	27,223	345	160	505	462	924	75	1,461	13	−943	26,280
1927	26,280	296	127	423	567	636	57	1,260	25	−812	25,468
1928	25,468	252	53	305	534	479	71	1,084	14	−765	24,703
1929	24,703	235	69	304	636	628	57	1,321	9	−1,008	23,695
1930	23,695	153	155	308	769	1,292	68	2,129	3	−1,818	21,877
1931	21,877	105	275	380	798	2,213	99	3,110	2	−2,728	19,149
1932	19,149	93	279	372	433	1,416	101	1,950	7	−1,571	17,578
1933	17,578	323	697	1,020	322	3,891	89	4,302	56	−3,226	14,352
1934	14,352	511	752	1,263	231	44	104	379	7	891	15,243
1935	15,243	101	87	188	160	34	91	285	15	−82	15,161
					Savings and loan associations						
1924	10,744	…	…	…	…	…	…	…	…	1,100[a]	11,844
1925	11,844	…	…	…	…	…	…	…	…	559[a]	12,403
1926	12,403	…	…	…	…	…	…	…	…	223[a]	12,626
1927	12,626	…	…	…	…	…	…	…	…	178[a]	12,804
1928	12,804	…	…	…	…	…	…	…	…	−138[a]	12,666
1929	12,666	…	…	…	…	…	…	…	…	−324[a]	12,342
1930	12,342	…	…	…	…	190[b]	…	…	…	−565[a]	11,777
1931	11,777	…	…	…	…	126[b]	…	…	…	−335[a]	11,442
1932	11,442	…	…	…	…	122[b]	…	…	…	−527[a]	10,915
1933	10,915	…	…	…	…	88[b]	…	…	…	−319[a]	10,596

1934	10,596	...	...	...	68[b]	...	...	148[a]	10,744
1935	10,744	...	...	...	239[b]	...	...	−478[a]	10,266

Mutual savings banks

1924	618	...	...	...	...	...	...	−5	613
1925	613	...	...	...	...	...	...	−2	611
1926	611	...	...	...	...	...	...	9	620
1927	620	...	...	...	...	...	...	−2	618
1928	618	...	...	...	...	...	...	−2	616
1929	616	...	...	...	...	...	...	−5	611
1930	611	...	...	...	...	...	...	−5	606
1931	606	...	...	...	...	...	...	−6	600
1932	600	...	...	...	...	...	...	−6	594[c]
1933	594[b]	...	...	...	...	...	...	−18	576[c]
1934	576[b]	...	...	...	...	...	...	2	578[c]
1935	578[b]	...	...	...	...	...	...	−7	571[c]

Sources: Commercial banks, data adapted from Board of Governors of the Federal Reserve System, *Federal Reserve Bulletin* (November 1937), p. 1087; savings and loan associations, number of associations from unpublished data of Federal Home Loan Bank Board, number of failures, Leon T. Kendall, *The Savings and Loan Business: Its Purposes, Functions, and Economic Justification, A Monograph Prepared for the Commission on Money and Credit* (Prentice-Hall, 1962), p. 142; mutual savings banks, *Annual Report of the Comptroller of the Currency, 1933*, p. 118, and *1936*, p. 125.
a. Includes data not available separately.
b. Failures.
c. Includes one stock savings bank.

to underwrite private and public equity and debt issues and to invest in the securities of private corporations. Bank trust departments were essentially unsupervised. State-chartered banks typically had broad powers to make real estate loans. No federal laws restricted the payment of interest on either demand or time deposits, though a few states did impose legal maxima on these rates. Savings and loan associations and mutual savings banks were restricted to time and savings accounts and, generally, to residential real estate loans and investment grade debt issues, but, because of their broader loan and investment powers and their less direct association with real estate, MSBs have historically had a smaller percentage of their assets in residential mortgages than have S&Ls.[21] Nonetheless, both were specialized in contrast to commercial banks. Since commercial banks had only restricted authority to make mortgage loans, and since the thrift institutions could not make the other types of loans made by commercial banks, the thrift institutions and the commercial banks could legally compete only in the market for time deposits. Regulations, in other words, kept their markets largely separate.

It is with respect to chartering, however, that the regulatory framework of the late nineteenth and early twentieth centuries was especially procompetitive. State-chartered banks usually had less stringent capital requirements, lower reserve requirements, and broader lending powers than national banks. Until checking accounts were widely recognized as a substitute for bank notes, the state banks were somewhat disadvantaged by the Act of March 3, 1865, which imposed a 10 percent tax on their notes; but after 1880, this disadvantage largely disappeared and the number of state banks increased rapidly.[22] Overt chartering rivalry developed between the comptrollers of the currency and the state banking agencies. State bank charters allowed greater operating freedom and, in states where it was permitted, greater freedom to branch. In 1900, there were 12,427 commercial banks in the country; in 1920, there were 30,291; in 1925, 27,223. From 1900 through 1920, there were net increases of 4,293 national banks and 13,571 state banks.[23] Between 1910 and 1925, the comptrollers received 4,422 applications for charters, acted on 3,634

21. See *Savings and Loan Fact Book, 1971* (Chicago: United States Savings and Loan League, 1971), table 80, p. 96; and John Lintner, *Mutual Savings Banks in the Savings and Mortgage Markets* (Harvard University, Graduate School of Business Administration, 1948), app. table VIII-2, pp. 488–89.

22. Fischer, *American Banking Structure*, pp. 177–78.

23. Ibid., p. 192.

of these, and approved 3,107.[24] Yet even with this high approval rate for charters and, as shown below, a lower bank failure rate, the number of national banks declined relative to the number of state banks.

Savings and loan associations also grew in number during this period. In 1900, there were 5,356 S&Ls in the country; by 1927, the number had increased to a historic peak of 12,804. Mutual savings banks, on the other hand, did not increase in number. There were 652 in existence in 1900 and only 611 in 1925.[25] Although confined to only eighteen states in the northeast, MSBs accounted for nearly 46 percent of all savings in banks, savings and loan associations, and life insurance policies in 1900. By 1925, the figure had fallen to less than 23 percent. Commercial banks, which had 12 percent of all savings in 1900, had nearly 38 percent in 1925. Savings and loan associations' share rose from 8 percent to 12 percent, while insurance companies' share fell from 34 to 28 percent. In the states where savings banks competed with the other institutions, the figures are even more telling, with gains being made by insurance companies as well as depository institutions other than the MSBs.[26]

By the 1920s, the freedom of chartering that had existed during the previous decades, together with depressed economic conditions in agricultural areas and the lack of deposit insurance, were exerting obvious effects on market performance. The entry of new financial institutions had increased numbers to the point where the combination of patterns of conduct, regulations on conduct and structure, and demand conditions had created at least localized instability, in the form of an uncommonly high number of failures. The banks, the public, and the regulators were all pressing for changes in the character of banking, but the resulting proposals were anything but uniform, either within or among these groups.

Pressures for Change

Equation (2) is inadequate to describe the pressure for change: other relationships among structure, conduct, regulation, and performance are involved. To indicate what these are, U_t^1 is defined as a vector denoting levels of satisfaction of the decision makers in banks. Then, for example, it can be hypothesized that

$$(3) \qquad U_t^1 = U^1(P_{kt}^1, P_{k\,t-1}^1, \ldots, P_{k\,t-T}^1),$$

24. Ibid., p. 196.
25. See Table 10-1.
26. Lintner, *Mutual Savings Banks*, app. tables II-1 through II-7, pp. 463–70.

where P^1_{kt}, a subset of P_{kt}, contains the performance variables that measure the achievements of these decision makers, and T is a number of years so far in the past that events earlier than T no longer affect decisions at time t.

What can be said of U^1_t in the mid-1920s? Bankers were upset by the apparent effects of new banks on failure rates. From 1910 through 1925, there were suspensions of 520 incorporated national banks and 3,028 incorporated state banks, with more than 80 percent of these failures occurring during 1920–25. In comparison, only 31 national banks and 141 state banks failed in the 1907–08 years of panic.[27] There are no data that indicate how many of the failures were of rural banks and thus related to the depressed conditions of agriculture, but this—expressed in D_t of equation (2)—probably accounts for many of the suspensions. More specifically, many bankers with national charters were displeased by the chartering practices of state banking agencies, since national banks were unable to operate full-service branches even where permitted by state law, had more restrictive mortgage lending requirements and, often, higher reserve requirements than state banks. Some bankers, national and state alike, were troubled by the trend toward more branches, while others believed branching to be the answer to poor performance and instability in the system. And a number, whether or not they favored branching, recognized that the growing number of failures was likely to result in more relaxed branching laws. Since the owners and managers of failing and failed banks naturally did not wish to be denied the opportunity to merge with other banks and continue operations as a branch, the antibranching faction held that deposit insurance should be added to the regulatory framework; that is, they believed that to the extent that insurance would reduce the failure rate, the pressure for broader branching powers would be reduced.[28] Furthermore, as interest rates rose in the late 1920s, banks were dissatisfied with the growing tendency to compete for deposits by the offering of higher rates. This competition, it was argued, also contributed to bank failures, and regulations on deposit interest rate maxima were urged as the remedy.[29]

Decision makers in the banks were not the only ones whose satis-

27. *Banking Studies*, by Members of the Staff of the Board of Governors of the Federal Reserve System (Waverly Press, 1941), p. 419.

28. Fischer, *American Banking Structure*, pp. 50–52.

29. Ibid., pp. 247–53.

faction was being affected by performance. From equation (3), it can be further hypothesized that

(4) $$U_t^2 = U^2(P_{k\,t}^2, P_{k\,t-1}^2, \ldots, P_{k\,t-T}^2)$$

and

(5) $$U_t^3 = U^3(P_{k\,t}^3, P_{k\,t-1}^3, \ldots, P_{k\,t-T}^3).$$

Equation (4) expresses the levels of satisfaction with the industry's performance of consumers and the general public, and, to incorporate the regulation case, equation (5) depicts the satisfactions of the regulating agencies. As shown below, there is interdependence among U_t^1, U_t^2, and U_t^3, since in some cases the same performance variables enter the various functions (often, however, with different signs for the first-order partials). In equation (5), performance is expressed in terms of the regulatory objectives—interest rate levels, price levels, unemployment rate, credit flows, earnings, failure rates, and so forth.

The market performance of the 1920s accentuated the public mistrust and criticism of banking that have characterized its history in this country. Agricultural interests, with incentives sharpened by depressed agricultural demands, decried rising interest rates, inadequate farm credit, and the proclivity of banks to foreclose mortgages. In areas where banks failed, depositors and borrowers alike suffered losses from structural instability. There were a few who saw the dangers of financial control of business arising from the participation of banks in holding companies engaged in other branches of commerce. Echoing complaints of the past, some saw bank mergers and the trend toward branch banking as warnings of the development of greater "money power" in the economy.

Bank regulators had related worries. There was concern about the "quality" of bank credit. It was argued that competition among financial institutions for deposits led to asset portfolios with higher yields but higher risks. Bank speculation in equity and real estate investments also increased risks. As noted above, there were differences in views among the state agencies and between them and the comptroller regarding chartering and branching. And, as explained below, many of the complaints expressed by banks and the public were reflected in the views of the regulatory agencies.

From equations (3), (4), and (5), an adaptive response model can be posited. More specifically, the general hypothesis is that

(6)
$$\frac{d(S^1_{it})}{d(t)} = S^1(U^1_t)$$

and

(7)
$$\frac{d(C^1_{jt})}{d(t)} = C^1(U^1_t),$$

where the superscripts of S_{it} and C_{jt} denote the subsets of structural and conduct variables over which the firms' decision makers have some direct control. Thus, structure changed as new banks entered markets, as banks failed, as bank mergers occurred, as new branches were built, and as bank holding companies were formed. Similarly, conduct changed with respect to loan and investment portfolios, interest rates, and, probably, efforts to regulate through private agreements those aspects of bank behavior seen as causing poor performance.[30]

The influence of the regulatory agencies is less direct. To define it, assume that

(8)
$$E^1_t = E^1(U^1_t)$$

and

(9)
$$E^2_t = E^2(U^2_t),$$

with E^1_t and E^2_t representing, respectively, expressions of displeasure by banks and by the public about regulatory performance. Then, to close the system, the argument is that

(10)
$$\frac{d(R_t)}{d(t)} = R_t(E^1_t, E^2_t, U^3_t).$$

From equation (2), performance at any point in time depends on, in addition to the D_t factors, industry structure, privately determined business conduct, and the constraints imposed by the regulatory agencies. From equations (6) and (7), structure and conduct change over time because of private decisions by firms and, from equation (10), because of changes in the character of the regulation. The latter effect, however, is itself related to the performance of the industry as reflected by reactions of the firms, the public, and the regulators.

Relevance of the Model

In reality, the system is hardly as neat as the equations may suggest. Neither the direct relationships depicted in equation (2) nor the feedback

30. Ibid., pp. 248–55. Fischer, it should be noted, does not draw this conclusion as to cause and effect.

mechanisms of the remaining equations are specified; indeed, full specification may be impossible. But a number of points about the operation of the system should be stressed.

First, it is a human rather than a mechanical system. In consequence, behavioral and organizational factors underlie all the indicated relationships. Thus, except for individuals or institutions whose own positions are threatened, little impulse toward change can be expected. In the 1920s, most members of the public, most banks, and probably most of the regulatory agencies did not perceive strong threats to achievements. There were some "squeaking wheels," to be sure, but a need for drastic overhaul of the system was not widely felt.

Second, the system is characterized by conflicting objectives and conflicting proposals for change. Improved performance from the view of the public is likely to be regarded as poorer performance from the view of the banks. For example, higher deposit rates of interest were advantageous to bank customers but hardly seemed so to the banks or to those regulators who saw the higher rates as a cause of bank failures. In the 1920s, then, there was no broad consensus on the major weakness in the system, so it is to be expected that the pressures for change would be localized in those parts of the system in which difficulties appeared.[31]

Finally, and akin to theoretical problems of model specification, there are problems associated with the limited knowledge and "bounded rationality" of participants in the system. That is, the possible effects, direct and indirect, of a change in one part of the system are not fully known. Since the certainty of an existing situation has positive value compared with the uncertainties of change, there are inertial elements in the system, and extensive change is likely to occur only when there are major failures in achievements throughout.[32]

These considerations help to explain the behavior of the system in the twenties. As Table 10-1 shows, the feedback effects did not operate quickly enough for a new and stable structure to emerge soon after the systemic weaknesses were recognized. Suspensions and mergers continued at a high rate even before the Great Depression: by the end of 1930, there

31. For the behavioral principles involved, see Richard M. Cyert and James G. March, *A Behavioral Theory of the Firm* (Prentice-Hall, 1963), chaps. 3–6, especially chap. 6, which summarizes the concepts. If the behavioral theory were fully reflected here, equations (3), (4), and (5) would be expressed in terms of differences between actual and desired performance, with the latter subject to change in response to the size and sign of the difference.

32. Ibid., pp. 118–25.

were only 21,877 commercial banks, 11,777 savings and loan associations, and 606 mutual savings banks. Yet some changes other than the obvious structural ones had occurred, specifically in the pattern of regulations.

At the federal level, the criteria for chartering were raised. While the number of applications for national bank charters between the beginning of 1926 and the end of 1930 were roughly the same as those between 1921 and 1925, the approval rate dropped from 76 percent in the earlier period to 54 percent in the later.[33] By 1932, many of the state supervisory authorities had also tightened their standards for new charters.[34] The imbalance between the branching powers of national and state-chartered banks was largely corrected by the McFadden Act of 1927, which was essentially a localized solution for a set of local problems. This legislation was of considerable importance in allowing the alternative of merger rather than suspension and liquidation for failing national banks in states where branching was permitted. From 1928 through 1930, an estimated 4,534 banks ceased operations. Of this number, 1,939 were absorbed by other banks before suspension, and an unknown number was taken over by other banks following suspension.[35] Many of these amalgamations would have been impossible without the McFadden Act. Still, there were many failing banks that had no alternative to suspension and liquidation because of the unit banking laws of some states that barred mergers.

Overall, however, most of the change during this period in financial market performance was due to privately determined structural and behavioral response and little to regulatory change. More severe restrictions on chartering were suggested, yet only modest changes were made. Federal deposit insurance was urged, yet no act was passed. There were proposals for more strict portfolio supervision, yet no major regulation was passed.

Regulatory Response, 1931–34

What really altered the regulatory framework was the depression. The D_t factor in equation (2) fell, and performance deteriorated rapidly from the point of view of bankers, the public, and the regulators. From the beginning of 1930 to the end of 1933, 11,491 commercial banks ceased operations. There was a net decrease of 1,746 savings and loan

33. Fischer, *American Banking Structure*, p. 196.
34. Ibid., pp. 190, 203–07.
35. Ibid., p. 204.

associations and of 35 mutual savings banks in the same period. As Table 10-1 shows, only 14,352 commercial banks, 10,596 savings and loan associations, and 576 mutual savings banks remained in operation as of December 31, 1933. And it was this avalanche of structural change, with the resulting recognition of achievement failures by all the major participants in the system, that prompted some radical changes in state and federal regulations on structure and conduct.

The Banking Act of 1933 amended the McFadden Act by permitting a national bank to merge with another bank located outside the city, town, or village of its home office. The purpose of the legislation was not to promote competition, but rather to expand the capability of strong banks to absorb weak ones in order to lessen the structural instability of the system.[36] Fifteen states also expanded the branching powers of banks under their jurisdiction, with the same primary purpose. The Banking Act of 1933 established the FDIC, with initial coverage of $2,500 per deposit. The insurance was designed in part to provide safety for depositors and liquidity in the general payments mechanism, thus serving the objectives of both the public and the regulators. In addition, however, unit banks saw deposit insurance as a safeguard against extended branching. In this respect, the objectives of many banks—in many cases, politically powerful though small ones—were also served, and this could well have been the critical force in the adoption of the insurance section of the act.[37]

The Banking Act of 1935 ended much of the rivalry between federal and state chartering agencies. The comptroller of the currency was given new criteria to be employed in granting charters to national banks, and the same criteria were given to the Board of Governors and the FDIC for their certification for the insurance of state-chartered member banks and insured, state-chartered nonmember banks, respectively. This meant that only noninsured state-chartered banks could escape the de facto chartering standards set by Congress.[38] State chartering agencies also tightened their chartering regulations, with the overall result that fewer banks applied for charters, a smaller proportion of the applications was approved and relatively few new banks were formed after 1935.[39]

A number of important controls on conduct were instituted in the thirties. The Banking Acts of 1933 and 1935 prohibited interest payments

36. *Comptroller's Manual*, pt. 5.
37. Fischer, *American Banking Structure*, pp. 51–52.
38. *Comptroller's Manual*, pt. 5.
39. Fischer, *American Banking Structure*, pp. 207–17.

on demand deposits and gave regulatory powers over the maximum
rates on time and savings accounts at commercial banks to the Board of
Governors and the FDIC. The stated purpose behind these measures was
to prevent undue competition among banks. The Glass-Steagall Act of
1932 largely separated the investment banking business from commercial
banking by prohibiting national banks from underwriting anything other
than direct U.S. government obligations, a few indirect federal government obligations, and general obligations of states and municipalities.[40]
Section 21 of the Banking Act of 1933 went further, making it illegal for
any firm engaged in the securities business to engage also in the business
of receiving deposits. The Securities Exchange Act of 1934 authorized
the Board of Governors to set margin requirements for loans made by any
bank for the purchase of securities registered on national exchanges. And
the supervision by federal agencies of investment portfolios, begun under
the McFadden Act in 1927, was generally tightened after 1933, mainly
with regard to "investment grade" securities.[41]

By 1935, then, commercial banks were far more regulated, both as to
structure and conduct, than they had been in the 1920s. Entry was controlled, branching was controlled, loan portfolios were more restricted
and more closely examined, deposit interest rate competition was controlled, and the banks were more isolated from investment banking and
security dealing.

Only a small part of the banking legislation of the 1930s extended to
the thrift institutions. As Table 10-1 shows, 526 savings and loan associations failed between the end of 1929 and the end of 1933. It was to aid
both the failing associations and homeowners whose mortgages were
foreclosed that the Federal Home Loan Bank Act of 1932 was passed.
The act created the Federal Home Loan Bank Board (FHLBB), with
powers to grant emergency loans to savings and loan associations. The
Home Owners' Loan Act of 1933 gave the FHLBB power to grant federal
charters to mutual associations and to make loans and advances to all
member associations. The National Housing Act of 1934 created the
Federal Savings and Loan Insurance Corporation to insure accounts of
all federal S&Ls and those state-chartered S&Ls that applied and qualified
for insurance, as well as to supervise and examine federally chartered

40. *Comptroller's Manual*, pt. 1, § 1.3(c).
41. Ibid., pt. 1, § 1.3(b). See also George J. Benston, "Bank Examination" (paper
prepared for the President's Commission on Financial Structure and Regulation, 1971;
processed), for a discussion of the examination process as a regulatory device.

associations and those insured state-chartered associations that requested insurance.

Mutual savings banks, unlike commercial banks and savings and loan associations, did not experience a rash of failures during the depression. Indeed, they have never had a period of structural instability since the first savings bank was established in 1816.[42] The reasons for this record are not clear, but several factors seem to be involved. First, the savings banks have historically appealed to low- and middle-income families, who viewed their accounts as rainy-day accumulations rather than liquid balances for transaction purposes. Second, mutual savings banks have been less intimately associated with real estate than savings and loan associations. In 1930, for example, only about 55 percent of the assets of savings banks was invested in mortgages, in contrast with nearly 89 percent for savings and loan associations.[43] The savings banks were thus somewhat more sheltered from the collapse of the real estate market after 1929. Finally, it is possible that differences in examination and supervision favored the savings banks during the early thirties. It appears that their cash positions permitted defaulted mortgages simply to be extended and carried at face rather than market values. As a consequence, the mutual savings banks at no time showed significant losses on their portfolios, thus avoiding the conditions that encourage runs on deposits.[44] The only federal measure affecting them directly was their inclusion on a voluntary basis in FDIC insurance.

The Postwar Period

A full cycle in the model has now been reviewed. By 1935, economic conditions were improving and regulations on structure and conduct had reestablished a period of structural stability within and among the depository institutions. In the terms of the model used here, the next several years were ones of dynamic equilibrium, with little feedback from

42. Lintner, *Mutual Savings Banks*, pp. 20–21; American Bankers Association, Savings Division, *Response to Change: A Century of Commercial Bank Activity in the Savings Field* (ABA, 1965), p. 12.

43. National Association of Mutual Savings Banks, *National Fact Book of Mutual Savings Banking, 1970* (NAMSB, 1970), p. 2; *Savings and Loan Fact Book, 1971*, p. 96.

44. For data on Massachusetts savings banks during this period, see Lintner, *Mutual Savings Banks*, pp. 497–501. Operating income and dividends actually rose after 1928. Retained earnings remained about stable. Losses on assets occurred in only 1929. It is impossible to determine the extent to which this is attributable to face value rather than market value accounting.

performance to structure, conduct, and regulation. Yet by the mid-1950s it was clear that new forces were at work that would create new relationships among the variables. These were the postwar market environment and new technologies.

The outstanding structural changes relate to mergers, de novo branching, and holding companies. Bank merger activity declined after 1933 and remained low during the war, but picked up again in the early 1950s. During 1952–60, 1,467 commercial banks ceased operations through mergers, absorptions, and consolidations. During the same period, 4,227 branches began operations, approximately doubling the number that existed at the end of 1951.[45] By the end of 1970, the number of branches of commercial banks had again doubled, reaching a total of 21,424. Of these, 10,744 were in the same county or a county contiguous to that of the home office of the bank. However, the combined effect of new charters, mergers, and absorptions and suspensions on the total number of banks was not great: by the end of 1970, there were still 13,688 commercial banks.[46]

Effects at the state and local levels were more pronounced. Since mergers, consolidations, and de novo branching are governed by state laws, their occurrence and effect on structure within states vary according to state laws. While no general pattern by state can be discerned, some states and some metropolitan and local areas have had significant structural changes due to mergers.[47]

Accompanying the bank merger movement was an expansion in holding company activities. Bank holding companies have existed in the United States for many decades, and their number increased significantly in the late twenties for much the same reasons behind the wave of bank mergers.[48] After 1930, the number of holding companies fell, until by 1950 there were only 28 registered with the Board of Governors. Each company controlled two or more banks (then the requirement for registration), and they had a total of 1,386 offices and $18.5 billion in deposits. In that year, the deposits of registered bank holding companies amounted

45. Fischer, *American Banking Structure*, pp. 130, 133.

46. *Federal Reserve Bulletin*, vol. 57 (April 1971), pp. A 94, A 95.

47. For the example of a state with general increases in concentration, see Phillips, "Bank Mergers, Branch Banking and Bank Holding Companies." For a more general review, see Shull, "Concentration in Banking in the United States," and Klebaner, "Recent Changes in the Structure of Banking."

48. For an excellent history, see Fischer, *Bank Holding Companies.*

to about 12 percent of total commercial bank deposits.[49] By 1970, there were 121 multibank holding companies, with 4,155 offices and $78.1 billion in deposits, accounting for roughly 20 percent of total bank deposits.[50] The states with the largest relative expansion in deposits controlled by holding companies from 1956 to 1969 were Colorado, Florida, Maine, New York, Ohio, Virginia, and Wisconsin;[51] all of these save Maine prohibited (or, in the case of Virginia, restricted) statewide branching.

In the late 1960s, a novel movement toward "one-bank holding companies" (OBHCs) emerged.[52] The new OBHCs, unlike many previous kinds of holding companies, were formed by banks to buy interests in or form firms doing types of business not permitted to banks themselves or to affiliates of registered multibank holding companies. In 1965, there were 550 OBHCs, with only $15 billion in deposits; by the end of 1970, there were 1,352 OBHCs, with about $160 billion in deposits.[53] This represents a growth of from 5 percent to 38 percent of total bank deposits in just five years. Total holding company deposits—multibank and OBHC —were 57 percent of the total in 1970.[54]

The reasons why banks chose to merge, enter holding companies, or form OBHCs after the Second World War are different from those of the late twenties and early thirties, when imminent failure was the impetus. According to surveys, the major reasons given by acquired banks for mergers are management problems, attractive offer price, common ownership with the acquiring bank, weak earnings, retirements, community need for larger banks, and desire to achieve a more competitive position. Banks entered holding companies primarily to increase liquidity or capital gains for controlling stockholders, although management problems and needs

49. Fischer, *American Banking Structure*, p. 97.

50. *Federal Reserve Bulletin*, vol. 57 (August 1971), p. A 98.

51. Association of Registered Bank Holding Companies, "The Future of Registered Bank Holding Companies," pp. 7–8.

52. Before December 1970, bank holding companies were required to register only if, among other things, the holding company held or controlled 25 percent or more of the stock of each of two or more banks. Hence, one-bank holding companies were neither required to register nor subject to the control of the Board of Governors.

53. ARBHC, "The Future of Registered Bank Holding Companies," p. 140; "One-Bank Holding Companies Before the 1970 Amendments," *Federal Reserve Bulletin*, vol. 58 (December 1972), pp. 999–1008.

54. Total bank deposit data used in these calculations are demand and time deposits plus currency (M_2) as reported in the *Economic Report of the President, January 1973*, p. 254. It is not clear whether holding company figures include large certificates of deposit or not.

for more and improved services are also important.[55] Formation of an OBHC, on the other hand, represented privately determined structural change aimed almost solely at circumventing the existing regulatory mechanisms; it was a device to permit a bank to engage in product lines and market areas otherwise prohibited by federal or state laws or regulations.[56]

The reasons given by bankers, however, fail to place proper emphasis on the underlying factors behind mergers or holding company formations. That there are economies of scale in banking and that many banks are of less than the minimum efficient scale is well documented.[57] Whether there are economies involved in branching is less easily determined, but the tendency for banks to merge where permissible suggests that, at least for some types and sizes of branches, branch operations are less costly than unit banking.[58] Consideration of economies, by themselves, would thus tend to encourage branching.

The use of new technologies has also been important in the postwar market.[59] The computer, in particular, has had a major impact. It may have increased the minimum efficient scale of operation; it surely has made

55. Fischer, *American Banking Structure*, pp. 134–36.

56. For additional detail, see ARBHC, "The Future of Registered Bank Holding Companies," pp. 141–47, and the congressional hearings and reports cited throughout the book. Some banks even saw OBHCs as a device for full conglomeration, with product extensions far outside bank-related areas (see Bunting, "One-Bank Holding Companies: A Banker's View").

57. See George J. Benston, "A Statistical Study of the Cost of Banking Operations" (Ph.D. thesis, University of Chicago, 1963); idem, "Branch Banking and Economies of Scale," *Journal of Finance*, vol. 20 (May 1965), pp. 312–31; idem, "Economies of Scale and Marginal Costs in Banking Operations," *National Banking Review*, vol. 2 (June 1965), pp. 507–49; Horvitz and Shull, "The Impact of Branch Banking on Bank Performance"; Frederick W. Bell and Neil B. Murphy, "Economies of Scale in Commercial Banking" (Federal Reserve Bank of Boston, 1967; processed).

58. Phillips, "Bank Mergers, Branch Banking and Bank Holding Companies."

59. See Mark J. Flannery and Dwight M. Jaffee, *The Economic Implications of an Electronic Monetary Transfer* (Lexington Books, 1973); Eugene M. Lerner, Joseph S. Moag, and Donald P. Jacobs, "A Report on the Effect of an Electronic Payments System on Bank Structure" (paper submitted to the MAPS Committee of the American Bankers Association, n.d.; processed); Donald P. Jacobs and others, *The Impact of Electronic Money Transfers on the Savings and Loan Business* (U.S. Savings and Loan League, 1972); "Evolution of the Payments Mechanism," *Federal Reserve Bulletin*, vol. 58 (December 1972), pp. 1009–12; George W. Cloos, "A New Banking System," *Business Conditions*, Federal Reserve Bank of Chicago (November 1967), pp. 10–16; Norman E. Douglas, "A Step Toward Electronic Funds Transfer," *Burroughs Clearing House*, vol. 55 (December 1970), pp. 25ff.; Aubrey N. Snellings, "The Evolving Payments System," *Monthly Review*, Federal Reserve Bank of Richmond (May 1970), pp. 2–6; Richard E. Towey, "An Evaluation of the Payments Mechanism in California, 1946–1975," in Hyman P. Minsky (ed.), *California Banking in a Growing Economy: 1946–1975* (University of California, Berkeley, Institute of Business and Economic

feasible the production of the information necessary to administer a complex organization. It has reduced the importance of geographic distance between head office and branches. It has also made it feasible, and, from their point of view, desirable, for financial institutions to engage in product lines not permitted under existing laws. In short, the new technologies have spurred both mergers and holding company formations.[60]

It is possible, however, that regulations themselves have been an even more important factor in branching than costs and technologies. Since regulations have prevented banks from using interest rates to attract deposits, the institutions have resorted to nonprice competition of many kinds. One kind has been the locational convenience for customers provided by branching. That is, customers have been paid for their deposits through lower transportation and time costs rather than through higher deposit rates of interest.

The effects of bank mergers and holding company affiliations on the public interests in performance are also fairly well documented. When increases in market concentration do not result from such moves, the public appears to benefit: facilities tend to improve, new services are offered, and, except for checking account charges, costs to the public seem, if anything, to fall.[61] But when mergers result in higher concentration, particularly in markets already highly concentrated and with little opportunity for entry, the public tends to suffer through somewhat less favorable loan terms and lower interest rates on deposits.[62]

Research, 1965); and Hubert D. White, "Credit Transfer: An Element of the Coming Payment Mechanism," *The Magazine of Bank Administration*, vol. 45 (March 1969), pp. 26ff.

60. *Report on Financial Structure*, pp. 14–15, 46.

61. New York State Banking Department, "Branch Banking, Bank Mergers and the Public Interest" (NYSBD, 1964; processed); ARBHC, "The Future of Registered Bank Holding Companies," pp. 40–72.

62. Franklin R. Edwards, "Concentration in Banking and Its Effect on Business Loan Rates," *Review of Economics and Statistics*, vol. 46 (August 1964), pp. 294–300; Theodore G. Flechsig, "The Effect of Concentration on Bank Loan Rates," *Journal of Finance*, vol. 20 (May 1965), pp. 298–311; George G. Kaufman, "Bank Market Structure and Performance: The Evidence from Iowa," *Southern Economic Journal*, vol. 32 (April 1966), pp. 429–39; Almarin Phillips, "Evidence on Concentration in Banking Markets and Interest Rates," *Federal Reserve Bulletin*, vol. 53 (June 1967), pp. 916–26; Richard C. Aspinwall, "Market Structure and Commercial Bank Mortgage Interest Rates," *Southern Economic Journal*, vol. 36 (April 1970), pp. 376–84; and Jack M. Guttentag and Edward S. Herman, *Banking Structure and Performance* (The *Bulletin*, New York University, Graduate School of Business Administration, Institute of Finance, No. 41/43, February 1967).

Like the desire of banks to move into new geographic areas, their desire to enter new product lines may tend to increase actual and potential competition. Computer services, credit card services, life insurance, and travel agencies may or may not be regarded as bank related; what is clear is that those engaged in supplying these services see the entry of banks as potentially threatening to their own positions.[63]

Other interindustry market changes in structure and conduct have been less noted but of possibly greater consequence. From the end of the Second World War until the mid-1960s, the term structure of interest rates was positively sloped:[64] long-term debt bore considerably higher rates of interest than did short-term. This enabled the thrift institutions to pay attractive dividends on savings accounts, to lend funds in the long-term market—primarily mortgages—and to maintain relatively high rates of return. Commercial banks, with their predominantly short-term assets, were in a less favorable position. Between 1945 and 1965, the total assets of savings and loan associations grew at a compound rate of 14 percent per year, assets of mutual savings at a rate of over 6 percent, and commercial bank assets at only a 4 percent rate.[65] One consequence of these developments was that commercial banks began to pay more attention to attracting funds through savings and time deposit accounts from individuals; the proliferation of de novo branches into suburban areas was predicated in part on this objective. While the rates of interest on savings and time accounts at commercial banks were generally lower than those at thrift institutions, the convenience of branches and the attraction of full-service banking helped the banks to attract savings funds. Individual savings and time deposit accounts at commercial banks rose from $29.9 billion in 1945 to $134.2 billion in 1965, an increase of almost 350 percent.[66] In the same period, the increase in demand deposits was only about 100 percent.[67]

63. See, for example, National Association of Insurance Agents, Inc., "Position Paper Presented to the President's Commission on Financial Structure and Regulation" (1971; processed), in which the NAIA expressed its opposition to the entrance of banks into the insurance agency business. For the public policy aspects of the problem, see Memorandum of the United States Department of Justice, "Before the Board of Governors of the Federal Reserve System, In the Matter of Proposed Amendment of Section 222.4 of Regulation Y—Interests in Nonbanking Activities and Related Matters" (Feb. 26, 1971).

64. *Report on Financial Structure*, p. 36.

65. Ibid., pp. 34–35.

66. *Savings and Loan Fact Book, 1971*, p. 15.

67. The 1945 base is somewhat misleading since special conditions relating to the end of the war caused federal government demand deposits to total $23.7 billion.

After 1965, monetary developments were more favorable to the commercial banks and less so to the thrift institutions. Interest rates rose generally and short-term rates increased relative to long-term, at times even exceeding them.[68] The thrift institutions, with their long-maturity assets, did not have the earning power to pay premium deposit rates, and the interest ceilings on deposits that were intended to protect them from commercial bank competition were not wholly effective. Commercial banks' time and savings accounts rose from a total of $134.2 billion in 1965 to $216.4 billion in 1970. Savings and loan accounts increased from $110.4 billion to $146.7 billion, and accounts in mutual savings banks from $52.4 billion to $71.5 billion in the same period.[69] The commercial banks were not only better protected from the risks of high and changing interest rates, but they continued to have branching advantages in many states, they had the attraction of full-service banking, and much of their funds came from interest-free demand deposits.

This sequence of events fits into the theoretical view of the regulatory process presented above. Technological change, growing scale economies, and what might be called a "growth syndrome" among some American businessmen in the postwar period caused many executives of financial firms to seek larger firms and larger markets. That is, the performance of their firms fell short of the levels that appeared possible and led them to private decisions that altered market conduct and structures. Among the changes were those resulting from interest rate patterns that caused the thrift institutions to grow relative to commercial banks and far more intensive interindustry competition for savings to emerge.

There were, of course, "squeaking wheels" in the system, and much conflict about what, if anything, should be done. Those unfavorably affected by the changes complained to the regulators and the legislatures. The growth of branching, both de novo and by merger, and the development of holding companies were again seen as a threat to small banks. Ignoring the anticompetitive effects of the regulations sheltering small banks and the possible procompetitive effects of certain types of mergers,

Other demand deposits of insured banks, excluding interbank deposits, amounted to $80.3 billion in that year; on December 31, 1965, they totaled $159.7 billion (*Federal Reserve Bulletin*, vol. 57 [August 1971], p. A 22).

68. For 1969, the rates on prime commercial paper, prime bankers' acceptances, federal funds, and three-month Treasury bills averaged 7.83 percent, 7.61 percent, 8.22 percent, and 6.677 percent, respectively. In the same year, yields on Aaa corporate bonds averaged 7.03 percent, all corporate industrial bonds averaged 7.22 percent, and long-term U.S. government bonds averaged 6.10 percent.

69. *Savings and Loan Fact Book, 1971*, p. 15.

some equated the preservation of large numbers of small banks with the maintenance of competition.[70] In general, large banks in unit-banking states wanted the laws amended to permit branching, while the more numerous smaller banks, often located in nonurban areas, opposed branching amendments, as they did proposals to broaden branching powers in states where limited branching was already permitted.[71] The public was little involved in this controversy, and the desirability of promoting market competition—in contrast to preserving particular classes of competitors—was seldom invoked. Indeed, the tendency for holding companies to grow where branching was prohibited seems not to have been well recognized by even those bankers who objected to more liberal branching laws. Thus, opposition to a procompetitive branching policy actually fostered the growth of holding companies.

At the federal level, the Bank Holding Company Act of 1956 and the Bank Merger Act of 1960 were passed primarily in response to the pleas of the smaller banks. The competitive tests required by these statutes discouraged dominance of local, regional, or statewide markets by single companies, but the regulatory agencies were also influenced by other industry conditions and by the constraints imposed by state laws.[72] The competitive test gained primacy only after the *Philadelphia National Bank* case,[73] in which the Department of Justice prevailed in upsetting a merger that had been approved by the Comptroller of the Currency, which had primary jurisdiction. Such activity of the Justice Department in banking matters and the decision that the Clayton Act was fully applicable to the industry led to the 1966 amendments to the Bank Merger Act.

The loudest squeaks of the wheel came from the thrift institutions during and after the 1966 and 1969–70 periods of high interest rates. Most of the complaints were directed at an alleged imbalance between monetary and fiscal policies during times of high levels of aggregate demand, and not at the effects of portfolio regulations. In fact, most

70. Independent Bankers Association of America, *Independent Banking: An American Ideal* (Sauk Centre, Minn: IBAA, 1973).

71. To its credit, the Antitrust Division was not among those seeking to inhibit all types of branching. See "Research Paper and Policy Statement of the United States Department of Justice Regarding State Legislation Affecting the Structure of Banking Markets" (U.S. Department of Justice, 1971; processed).

72. For an early analysis of the factors used by the regulatory agencies in deciding bank merger cases, see George R. Hall and Charles F. Phillips, Jr., "Bank Mergers and the Regulatory Agencies" (Board of Governors of the Federal Reserve System, 1964; processed).

73. *United States* v. *Philadelphia National Bank*, 374 U.S. 321 (1963).

spokesmen for the institutions argued that regulations on deposit interest rates be extended to the thrift institutions and that rates be set well below those prevailing in the other money markets.[74] These regulations were expanded in 1966, and the thrift institutions were permitted maximum rates slightly above those applicable to commercial banks. This prevented significant disintermediation among the deposit institutions, but by 1970 the regulations were becoming ineffective in preventing disintermediation between the deposit institutions and the unregulated market. Borrowers and savers alike learned how to bypass the regulated markets, in which prices were low and supplies short, in favor of markets in which prices were performing their allocative function.[75]

A growing number saw the removal of regulation on portfolios and expanded operating powers as the appropriate solution for the thrift institutions.[76] Such a move would both improve the ability of the firms

74. For additional details, see David I. Fand, "The Viability of Thrift Intermediaries as Financial Institutions" (paper submitted to the President's Commission on Financial Structure and Regulation, 1971; processed); Leo Grebler, *The Future of Thrift Institutions: A Study of Diversification versus Specialization* (Interstate, 1971); Richard T. Pratt and others, "Savings and Loan Viability and Deposit Rate Ceilings," Working Paper 14 (Federal Home Loan Bank Board, n.d.; processed); Robert Lindsay, *The Economics of Interest Rate Ceilings* (*The Bulletin*, New York University, Graduate School of Business Administration, Institute of Finance, nos. 68–69, December 1970); Clifton B. Luttrell, "Interest Rate Controls: Perspectives, Purposes, and Problems," Federal Reserve Bank of St. Louis, *Review*, vol. 50 (September 1968), pp. 6–14; Preston Martin, "A Case for Regulation Q," *Journal of the Federal Home Loan Bank Board*, vol. 3 (October 1970), pp. 1–6; Lawrence S. Ritter, "Regulation Q: Issues and Alternatives" (Chicago: Association of Reserve City Bankers, 1965; processed); Charlotte E. Ruebling, "The Administration of Regulation Q," *Review*, Federal Reserve Bank of St. Louis, vol. 52 (February 1970), pp. 29–40; and Paul A. Samuelson, "An Analytic Evaluation of Interest Rate Ceilings for Savings and Loan Associations and Competitive Institutions," in Irwin Friend (director), *Study of the Savings and Loan Industry*, vol. 4, Prepared for the Federal Home Loan Bank Board (U.S. Government Printing Office, 1970).

75. See *Report on Financial Structure*, pp. 13–15, 46–48. The rapid growth of one-bank holding companies in this period was also influenced by these and related regulations. Banks could buy and sell funds through nonbank subsidiaries in ways and at rates prohibited for the banking entity itself. This is another illustration of the sort of adaptive response pictured in the model.

76. See *Report on Financial Structure*, pp. 31–58; Grebler, *The Future of Thrift Institutions;* Irwin Friend, "Changes in the Asset and Liability Structure of the Savings and Loan Industry," in *Study of the Savings and Loan Industry*, vol. 3; Arnold W. Sametz, "Thrift Institutions and Demand Deposits," Research Paper 6 (American Bankers Association, October 1970); and William L. Silber, "Removing Asset and Liability Restrictions on Financial Institutions: Short-Run and Long-Run Implications" (paper submitted to the President's Commission on Financial Structure and Regulation, 1970; processed). Other remedies were also proposed, particularly expanded use of variable rate mortgages (see *Report on Financial Structure*, pp. 77–86).

to adapt to the interest rates that characterize an inflationary environment and promote more effective competition. Most, however, simply hoped that the high interest rates would pass, never to occur again, and the crisis did not reach such proportions that a strong consensus emerged for prompt and radical change. The same hope reemerged in 1973 and 1974 when even higher interest rates caused even worse problems of disintermediation.

Proposals for Regulatory Reform

Let us suppose that, God-like, we can control equation (10) as we please. As criteria for change in R_t, we take the values implicit in U_t^3 as guides; that is, the changes sought should be those that most would agree are in the public interest and not necessarily those compatible with the interests of the industry and the regulators. The following reforms are suggested.[77]

1. *Eliminate laws and regulations that force specialization and restrict competition with and among institutional types.* This measure applies primarily to the thrift institutions. It would, for example, allow savings and loan associations and mutual savings banks to make mortgage loans on all types of property, residential and nonresidential, and to make construction, consumer, and commercial loans related to real estate activities. It would also allow them to invest in investment grade debt instruments. On the liability side, it would allow them to offer demand deposit services, credit card services, and other forms of third-party payment arrangements. These reforms would include abolition of geographic restrictions on areas in which loans may be made and an extension of the nonfinancial services institutions may provide, subject to the antitrust protections and civil remedies for damages explained below. The statutory restrictions on real estate loans embodied in the National Banking Act should be removed. In addition, the Glass-Steagall Act should be amended to permit banks to operate collective investment funds for managed agency accounts and, again subject to antitrust protection and new forms of civil remedy, to supply nonfinancial services.

77. In addition to the changes recommended in *Report on Financial Structure*, see Department of the Treasury, *Recommendations for Change in the U.S. Financial System* (Washington, Aug. 3, 1973), and S. 2591, a bill considered in the Ninety-third Congress, for less radical reform proposals.

The primary rationale for these changes is that they permit existing institutions to enter new financial and nonfinancial markets. Whether the degree of institutional and geographic specialization would in fact be decreased, monopoly power would certainly be reduced by the increase in potential competition, and cross-supply elasticities would be increased, even if no new competitors actually entered. In addition to the pro-competitive rationale, the greater freedom in asset selection that the changes would allow is a necessary predicate to the abolition of interest rate controls and other subsidization techniques now used to protect deposit intermediaries during periods of rising and high rates of interest. Such controls, or their subsidy alternatives, themselves constitute regulatory restrictions on competition.

2. *Eliminate interest rate ceilings on time and savings deposits and certificates of deposit.* These regulations were instituted to restrain interest rate competition among banks, and they still have that effect. Now, however, the restraints extend to competition among institutional types and between deposit institutions and the remainder of the money market. The controls have encouraged many varieties of nonprice competition, including locational convenience and the provision of services with no explicit prices attached. Moreover, because the cross-interest rate elasticity of savers between the deposit institutions and the rest of the market is higher for large savers than for small, the regulations have become highly discriminatory.[78] Finally, the regulations have had the effect of increasing the cyclical sensitivity of supplies of credit to certain classes of borrowers. Small mortgage borrowers and small businesses—often with few, if any, alternative sources of credit outside the deposit institutions—find funds unavailable during times of high interest rates.

3. *Eliminate the prohibition of interest payments on demand deposits.* This prohibition was also instituted to restrain competition, and, as with ceilings on time deposits, it has encouraged the development of various forms of nonprice competition. In addition, large customers of commercial banks, often with the cooperation of the banks, have found means to invest transactions balances in interest-bearing assets, the incidental costs of which might be largely eliminated if the prohibition were lifted.[79] Thrift institutions and credit unions have been encouraged to enter limited

78. See Edward J. Kane, "Short-Changing the Small Saver: Federal Government Discrimination against Small Savers During the Vietnam War: A Comment," *Journal of Money, Credit and Banking*, vol. 2 (November 1970), pp. 513–22.

79. See *Report on Financial Structure*, pp. 27–29.

forms of third-party payment services that provide interest on the savings account balances used for customer payments orders. The innovation and growth of negotiable orders of withdrawal accounts is illustrative of techniques used to circumvent the prohibition. Further improvements in computerized payments systems should increase the ability of financial institutions other than banks to generalize these payment methods. Thus, without a removal of the prohibition, demand deposits as currently defined will tend to disappear as the principal deposit liability used in the funds transfer mechanism. If interest were allowed on demand deposits, the funds transfer mechanism could be adapted to new technology in the most efficient possible manner, with probably more use of demand deposits than with the alternatives under the interest prohibition.

4. *Eliminate anticompetitive geographic restrictions on branching and holding companies.* Geographic restrictions on branching operate to protect the markets of individual institutions and, often, to prevent the achievement of scale economies and branching economies except at the expense of greater market concentration. Intermarket branching, both de novo and by merger, should be permissible in the absence of anticompetitive effects; and holding companies should be permitted to acquire banks under the same conditions. This would require repeal of the McFadden Act and permission for federally chartered banks, savings and loan associations, and mutual savings banks to branch irrespective of the state laws. Interstate branching would also have to be allowed if full adaptation to the economic characteristics of markets is to be achieved. The Bank Holding Company Act would have to be amended to permit interstate holding company acquisitions. Unless state-chartered institutions are to be severely disadvantaged, parallel changes in state laws would be necessary, and would probably be rapidly forthcoming.

5. *Eliminate anticompetitive restrictions on chartering.* At present, both federal and state chartering provisions make it possible for the authorities to refuse charters even when the applicants have adequate initial capital and all the necessary safeguards for investors have been met. Some test based on "adequacy of existing services" or "convenience and needs of the community" can be invoked as a barrier to entry.[80] However, the desired performance results of competition are impossible to achieve when regulations, such as those affecting chartering, are used to protect

80. See David A. Alhadeff, "A Reconsideration of Restrictions on Bank Entry," *Quarterly Journal of Economics*, vol. 76 (May 1962), pp. 246–63.

the structure of existing institutions. Competition necessarily implies that some competitors will fail, owing to both management errors and market factors. If applicants for a new charter meet nondiscriminatory minimum capital requirements and "blue sky" investor protection requirements, entry should be permitted. Similarly, firms of one institutional type should be able to convert their charters to other institutional types. The mere potential of entry should operate to create market performance such that the rate of entry will in fact be low. Firms existing in today's protected markets may suffer losses in profits and market shares due to new entry, but this is precisely the effect necessary to prevent the exploitation of monopoly power.[81]

It is true that periods of relatively free entry into financial markets have also historically been periods when failure rates were high. Depositors and those relying on the institutions for sources of credit, along with bank stockholders, suffered from the failures. But the market and regulatory characteristics of such periods were quite different from those that would be created by the present proposals. The period of "free banking" between 1838 and 1863 was so different that it needs no comment. Between, say, 1890 and 1930, differences in the regulation of state- and federally chartered banks gave rise to a chartering rivalry that did produce an "over-banked" situation. Over-banking, in the sense of the model given here, implies a regulatory system that promises noncompetitive rates of return, on the one hand, and relatively free entry, on the other—clearly incompatible goals. Free entry without regulatory promises of quasi-monopolistic returns, however, need not, and should not, result in over-banked financial markets with concomitant high failure rates. Furthermore, deposit insurance has largely dissipated the earlier threat of systemic bank runs.

6. *Provide for risk-related deposit insurance premiums.* Deposit insurance is necessary to prevent systemic collapses in the payments mechanism and to prevent individual depositors from losses, the probability of which they are incapable of judging. The current system of uniform premiums regardless of the asset portfolios of the insured institutions discriminates

---

81. The seminal work on this subject is Joe S. Bain, *Barriers to New Competition: Their Character and Consequences in Manufacturing Industries* (Harvard University Press, 1956). For an illuminating analysis of the factors creating entry barriers, see Franco Modigliani, "New Developments on the Oligopoly Front," *Journal of Political Economy*, vol. 66 (June 1958), pp. 215–32.

against conservatively managed firms. At the same time, and for related reasons, it encourages the insuring agency to supervise portfolios to minimize the likelihood of claims against the fund.

Competition would be encouraged by permitting greater freedom in portfolio choices. But greater competition, as it reduces monopolistic quasi rents, directly increases the probability of failures. The probability of failures will be further increased to the extent that institutions react to the greater freedom by adopting portfolios involving higher-risk assets. Assessments of the adequacy of the present rates suggest that premiums at an average equal to those now prevailing would suffice even with greater competition. Rate differences based on portfolio risk differentials are necessary, however, to end the discrimination inherent in uniform premiums. Given the nonrandom character of failure risks, implementation of a precise, actuarially based system is unlikely, but improvements on the present arrangements seem clearly possible.[82]

7. *Eliminate discriminatory reserve requirements and taxes.* Reserve requirements for commercial banks are different for members and non-members of the Federal Reserve System and state requirements for non-members vary widely. Requirements for members vary depending on the type of deposit, the size and location of the bank, and, in terms of marginal and average reserves, the size of the bank's deposits.[83] Reserve requirements for savings and loan associations are less formally established; they are computed in terms of the ratios of liquid assets and of capital and surplus to deposit liabilities. Reserves of insured S&Ls are set through examination by the Federal Savings and Loan Insurance Corporation, while noninsured associations are governed by state law and examination. The FDIC establishes de facto requirements for insured mutual savings banks, and all such banks must also conform to applicable state laws.

From the point of view of the institutions, reserve requirements for commercial banks operate much as taxes. Higher reserves mean that a higher proportion of assets are nonearning assets, or, alternatively, that there is a higher proportion of assets on which there is a 100 percent "tax" on income. Thus, differential reserve requirements provide taxlike advantages to particular classes of institutions, generally to the smaller commercial banks, to commercial banks outside of major metropolitan

---

82. For additional detail, see Thomas Mayer and Kenneth E. Scott, "Risk and Regulation in Banking: Some Proposals for Federal Deposit Insurance Reform," *Stanford Law Review*, vol. 23 (May 1971), pp. 857–902.

83. *Federal Reserve Bulletin*, vol. 58 (December 1972), p. A 10.

areas, and to the thrift institutions, as contrasted with commercial banks. If reserves are required at all—and it is arguable that formal reserve requirements are unnecessary for monetary policy purposes—a procompetitive policy would have identical requirements for the same type of deposits irrespective of the size, location, or class of the institution. In view of the fading distinction between savings and demand deposits, it is probable that a continuation of higher requirements for the latter would serve only to hasten the development of third-party payments from time deposits. High reserves for all classes of deposit institutions would also encourage the use of other institutions for savings purposes and the development of payments mechanisms that minimize the deposit balances required for funds transfers. And, in any case, full equalization of the burden of reserves may be impossible because of different requirements for maintaining correspondent balances.

Tax differences are even more complicated and can be only briefly mentioned here. They vary by institutional type and, within types, by class of assets. The Tax Reform Act of 1969 reduced the interinstitutional disparities, but some authorities feel that there are remaining tax differences that affect the competitive status of the institutional types.[84] These, too, should be removed if a procompetitive policy is to be fully pursued.

8. *Full application of the antitrust laws to financial institutions.* Under current legislation, special laws, involving some degree of regulation by financial regulatory agencies, pertain to bank mergers, bank holding companies, savings and loan holding companies, and interlocking directorates among banks. While the Sherman Act presumably applies in full force to all financial institutions, its use to prevent anticompetitive tying agreements, exclusive dealing contracts, and discriminatory pricing is largely unexplored. A strong antitrust policy would place competitive matters with the Antitrust Division of the Department of Justice, excluding the regulatory agencies and, with them, consideration of the so-called banking factors in individual cases. The special statutes would be rescinded, and mergers and holding companies made subject to the Clayton Act without qualification. Full enforcement of the conspiracy and collusion provisions of section 1 of the Sherman Act should, of course, also prevail.[85]

---

84. Daniel I. Halperin, "Federal Income Taxation of Banks," in National Tax Association, *1971 Proceedings of the Sixty-fourth Annual Conference on Taxation* (1972), pp. 307–32.

85. Although this need not involve strict application of the per se rule to all collective activities. See *United States* v. *Morgan*, 118 F. Supp. 621 (1953).

The interlocking directorate provisions of section 8 of the Clayton Act should also be amended to provide that no officer, director, or employee of one firm may serve as an officer, director, or employee of another (whether or not the firms are financial) where a price-fixing agreement, a merger, or another type of contract between the firms would violate any antitrust law. Section 3 of the Clayton Act, which covers tying agreements, could be amended to include services as well as commodities and to make explicit its applicability to financial institutions. While it may be true that Sherman Act standards for tying arrangements and exclusive dealing have been reduced to those of the Clayton Act, and that the Sherman Act is already applicable to financial services, express legislation would clarify any doubts.[86] Moreover, if financial institutions are permitted to engage in a wide variety of services, prohibition of anti-competitive practices in this area is all the more necessary.

Finally, the price discrimination prohibitions of section 2 of the Clayton Act should be repealed and replaced by new language with the degree of generality of that of section 7. The present language of the statute is ambiguous, particularly as it defines permissible defenses for price discrimination and as it relates to the provision of services. The case law that has developed under the statute is at best confusing and in some respects contradictory. The prevalence of nonprice competition among financial institutions and some classes of nonfinancial institutions makes it particularly important that they be subject to a broad law prohibiting discrimination where the effects may be substantially to lessen competition.

9. *Clarify by legislation the rules pertaining to the "piercing of the corporate veil" in order to facilitate private actions for damages and to preserve the safety and soundness of deposit institutions.* The diversification of financial institutions by means of holding company arrangements and corporate subsidiaries raises fundamental legal questions concerning, on the one hand, private actions for damages and, on the other, the safety and soundness of the institutions themselves. At present, intrasystem assets can be arranged so that, where the courts are not fairly free to "pierce the corporate veil" of affiliated corporations, there are few assets for damaged parties to proceed against. For example, if a commercial bank acquired exceptionally risky assets from an affiliated, nonbank corporation and subsequently failed, neither individual depositors nor the insuring agency would be able to rely on the assets of the affiliated

---

86. A recent case extending the Sherman Act to tying arrangements is *Fortner Enterprises, Inc.* v. *United States Steel*, 394 U.S. 495 (1969).

firms unless piercing were permitted. This suggests that legislative guidelines should be developed to facilitate such piercing where relationships between the bank and its nonbank affiliates, or the directors, officers, and employees of such affiliates, are a proximate cause of losses to third parties who are creditors of the bank.

There is a lack of full symmetry in the opposite case, however. If a subsidiary were to fail and the assets of the banking organization were made available to creditors, the end result could be that the insuring agency and, to the extent their deposits were uninsured, the depositors would ultimately pay for the liabilities of the bankrupt affiliate. Since the insuring agency, in particular, can hardly assess premiums for deposit insurance on such risks, some limitations are necessary. A possibility is that the piercing be limited by capital adequacy tests on financial institutions in order to preserve their basic safety and soundness and the integrity of the deposit insurance system.

Both matters, however, are legally complex and are mentioned here more as they relate to other problems than as capable of ready solutions.

Some Implications of Reform

Since the market model developed above has strong endogenous elements, the implementation of these regulatory changes would not be the end of the story. First, there would be structural reactions. Mergers might occur that were motivated by the desire to re-create the monopoly power dissipated by the regulatory changes. To prevent this, an active antitrust effort would be necessary. Other mergers, and some bankruptcies, might occur because of the pressure placed by competition on inefficient institutions. Given the possibility of economies of scale and economies of branching, such mergers—some based on assets revalued through bankruptcy proceedings—could result in real economies. To distinguish these from the anticompetitive mergers, especially in a situation where the number of disappearing institutions would exceed the number of new entrants, would require a very sagacious merger policy.

Increased tendencies toward private regulation could also be expected, placing a heavy burden on strict enforcement of section 1 of the Sherman Act. Again, sagacity would be necessary, since a variety of conduct changes could be anticipated. Some of these would relate only to individual enterprises and so would raise no difficulties. Others, however, might be

of an interfirm character and involve real economies arising from contractual relationships rather than from mergers. New methods for extended
loan participations and the sharing of credit card services and general
computer facilities are possible illustrations of interfirm contractual
arrangements that mean the realization of lower resource costs.

What is advocated here is the reverse of the policy actions of the 1930s.
Then the aim was to mitigate competitive forces in order to preserve the
structure of financial markets; here the aim is to increase competitive
forces by deregulation and antitrust policy, letting the structure adapt
as efficiency requires. While economies of scale and branching do appear
to exist, they are not so extensive as to suggest that structure itself makes
competition impossible. But it may be impossible anyway. A pervasive
and fundamental reorganization of social institutions is involved. The
public at large is unlikely to perceive the possible gains, and the few who
do can easily be dismissed as theorists with no real understanding of the
practical world.

The industries and the regulators would both perceive a common
threat in such drastic changes, and they would undoubtedly prevail in a
fight against them. It must be recognized that the strong homeostatic
properties built into the institutional response mechanisms of the system
may indeed make competition impossible.

CHAPTER ELEVEN

The Legal Framework of Competitive Policies toward Regulated Industries

EDWIN M. ZIMMERMAN

THE WRITERS REPRESENTED in this book have in common the conviction that it is desirable to upgrade the role of competition in regulated industries. New legislation that would wholly or partially deregulate the industries examined in this volume is proposed by all the authors save Waverman. New or more energetic application of the antitrust laws to ocean shipping, securities exchanges, electricity generation, and financial institutions is explicitly called for by Larner, Mann, Weiss, and Phillips, respectively. In the chapters concerning domestic airlines and surface freight transportation, Eads and Moore recommend greater reliance upon competition, with the implicit need for additional use of the antitrust laws. In addition, new principles, emphasizing competition, by which the administration of existing regulatory legislation may be guided are urged by Eads, Larner, Smallwood, Mann, Primeaux, Weiss, and Phillips.

However, although most proposals involve a larger role for competitive principles, at least vestiges and sometimes major portions of the existing regulatory system would be retained. Eads, for example, does not suggest the elimination of regulations governing aircraft certification and safety. Larner sees little possibility of fully deregulating shipping rates. Weiss acknowledges that the structures of the transmission and distribution phases of the electricity industry do not lend themselves to reliance on competition. Primeaux's argument for competition among distributors of electricity is limited to small utilities, and even for those, notes of caution are sounded. The uncertain results of rate deregulation in intercity communications lead Waverman to reject the idea. And Phillips, while suggesting the elimination of many controls on the structure and conduct of financial institutions, recognizes the continuing need for basic "safety and soundness" regulation.

Still, taken as a whole, this volume proposes a brave new competitive world for the regulated industries. This chapter reviews some of the legal issues that surround the implementation of these policy proposals for regulated industries.

Criticisms of Regulation

Criticism of the neglected role of competition in the regulated sector has not been confined to economists, and is hardly new. The burst of reliance on regulation that characterized the New Deal eventually generated second thoughts. For example, in 1954, Louis B. Schwartz contended that competition received short shrift in regulatory agency proceedings because the judiciary had abdicated its responsibilities in deference to the supposed expertise of the agencies. Schwartz urged the courts to assume responsibility for defining the general national economic policy within which the regulators must function. He proposed that "free enterprise ought to prevail to the maximum extent consistent with the . . . objectives of the applicable legislation" and that any curtailment of competition should require a demonstration that it was either explicitly authorized by statute or "was necessary in order to achieve some paramount objective of administrative regulation."[1]

In addition to such general expressions of discontent with the subordination of competition by the regulatory process, a mass of specific criticisms have come from many sources.[2] In the recent past, both the Nixon and Johnson task forces on antitrust policy stressed the need to

1. Louis B. Schwartz, "Legal Restriction of Competition in the Regulated Industries: An Abdication of Judicial Responsibility," *Harvard Law Review*, vol. 67 (January 1954), pp. 456–60; quotation from p. 475.

2. For example, see Lucile Sheppard Keyes, "Reconsideration of Federal Control of Entry into Air Transportation," *Journal of Air Law and Commerce*, vol. 22 (Spring 1955); Walter Adams, "The Role of Competition in the Regulated Industries," in American Economic Association, *Papers and Proceedings of the Seventieth Annual Meeting, 1957 (American Economic Review*, vol. 48, May 1958), pp. 527–43; Ronald H. Coase, "The Federal Communications Commission," *Journal of Law and Economics*, vol. 2 (October 1959); John R. Meyer and others, *The Economics of Competition in the Transportation Industries* (Harvard University Press, 1959); Richard N. Farmer, "The Case for Unregulated Truck Transportation," *Journal of Farm Economics*, vol. 46 (May 1964), pp. 398–409; Michael E. Levine, "Is Regulation Necessary? California

give competitive principles greater weight in regulated areas.[3] The Johnson report complained of a massive regulatory bias against competition and urged further study of regulated industries to determine the extent to which competition and competitive standards could be substituted for some aspects of regulation. The Nixon report urged a major reorientation of regulatory policy to encourage the entry of new firms wherever an absolute contradiction of regulatory goals was not involved, as well as the abandonment of minimum price regulation. It proposed that the merits of competition be "impressed" upon the regulatory commissions; that each agency have at least one economist as a commissioner; and that there be periodic reviews of the functioning of the agency, presumably to detect and inhibit anticompetitive policies.

The growing criticism of the extent to which competition has been neglected by the regulatory agencies has been accompanied by increasingly skeptical assessments of the "actual" purpose of regulation and regulatory agencies.[4] The frequent accusation that regulatory agencies tend to fall under the influence of the industries being regulated has been followed by theories of "political economics" that suggest that even a well-motivated agency will inevitably pursue policies inconsistent with consumer welfare.[5] The recent flourishing of consumer advocacy has added to the literature in which the regulatory agencies are charged with ineptitude and neglect of competitive principles.[6] Moreover, as this book illustrates,

---

Air Transportation and National Regulatory Policy," *Yale Law Journal*, vol. 74 (July 1965), pp. 1416–47; James R. Nelson, "The Role of Competition in the Regulated Industries," *Antitrust Bulletin*, vol. 11 (January–April 1966), pp. 1–36; Harold Demsetz, "Why Regulate Utilities?" *Journal of Law and Economics*, vol. 11 (April 1968), pp. 55–65; Richard A. Posner, "Natural Monopoly and Its Regulation," *Stanford Law Review*, vol. 21 (February 1969), pp. 548–643; Ann F. Friedlaender, *The Dilemma of Freight Transport Regulation* (Brookings Institution, 1969).

3. "Report of the White House Task Force on Antitrust Policy" (The Task Force, 1968; processed), printed in *Congressional Record*, vol. 115, pt. 11, 91 Cong. 1 sess. (1969), pp. 13890–907; "Report of the Task Force on Productivity and Competition" (The Task Force, 1969; processed), partially printed in *Congressional Record*, vol. 115, pt. 12, 91 Cong. 1 sess. (1969), pp. 15652–661.

4. See, for example, George J. Stigler, "The Theory of Economic Regulation," *Bell Journal of Economics and Management Science*, vol. 2 (Spring 1971); Richard A. Posner, *Economic Analysis of Law* (Little, Brown, 1973), pp. 153, 329–32.

5. See, for example, Roger G. Noll, *Reforming Regulation: An Evaluation of the Ash Council Proposals* (Brookings Institution, 1971), pp. 40–46.

6. See, for example, Robert C. Fellmeth (project director of Ralph's Nader's study group), *The Interstate Commerce Omission: The Public Interest and the ICC*, the Ralph Nader Study Group Report on the Interstate Commerce Commission and Transportation (Grossman, 1970); Mark J. Green (ed.), *The Monopoly Makers*, the Ralph Nader Study Group Report on Regulation and Competition (Grossman, 1973).

scholars have begun to produce detailed studies of specific regulatory areas which analyze and evaluate the adverse consequences of inadequate utilization of competition. The economic losses attributable to deficiencies of regulation are beginning to be quantified, and, however rough the estimates, they serve to confirm the idea of substantial cost.[7] The older criticism that regulation is often ineffective is being displaced by a harsher indictment of its extraordinary burdensomeness and waste. It is now frequently suggested that the regulatory process, however well run, is incapable of achieving even an approximation of the desirable results of competition in such vital areas as innovation.[8] And, with continued study of the regulatory experience, there is increasing suspicion that certain problems are too complex and subtle to be capable of regulatory solution.[9]

The criticism of regulatory policy—as, once again, this volume illustrates—is typically substantive in nature. Procedural reform, exemplified by the proposals of the 1971 Ash Council,[10] is regarded as unresponsive to the important shortcomings;[11] the more significant problem is thought to be how to effectuate a change at the policy level.

The Feasibility of Increased Competition

Despite the abundance of interest in upgrading the role of competition reflected in this volume, doubts about the feasibility of such upgrading exist. As far back as 1954, Schwartz was pessimistic about the likelihood of his suggestions being followed: "There may be small reason for thinking that today's Congress or today's Court will be alert to preserve a competi-

7. See, for example, Chapter 3.

8. See, for example, Noll, *Reforming Regulation*, pp. 25–27; William M. Capron (ed.), *Technological Change in Regulated Industries* (Brookings Institution, 1971).

9. In informal discussions, Roger G. Noll has classified such criticisms of regulation into four types: (1) the "complaint" theory, where regulators respond only to "squeaking wheels"; (2) the "captive" theory, where regulators act to maximize the objectives of the regulated; (3) the "Parkinsonian" theory, where regulators act to maximize the organizational objectives of the regulating agency; and (4) the "muddle-through" theory, where the situation is too complex and subtle for the regulatory agency to be capable of achieving its ostensible goals. See also Phillips's pessimistic appraisal in Chapter 10.

10. *A New Regulatory Framework: Report on Selected Independent Regulatory Agencies* (U.S. Government Printing Office, 1971).

11. See the conclusions of a Brookings conference of experts on government regulation reported in Noll, *Reforming Regulation*, pp. 110–11.

tive economy."[12] And today, Phillips balefully predicts the futility of efforts to increase competitive forces in banking by deregulation and antitrust policy.[13]

Such pessimism does not appear irrational. The recommendations regarding regulated industries made by the two presidential task forces mentioned above languish in total obscurity. There is reason to suppose that the recommendations of the President's Commission on Financial Structure and Regulation may not enjoy a better fate.[14] Congress has not demonstrated a greater commitment to competitive principles in recent years; on the contrary, the record suggests that Congress is apt to pass limiting legislation when antitrust laws are applied too effectively. For example, within the past decade, victories by the Justice Department in antitrust suits against bank mergers and newspaper joint ventures have been followed by legislation—the Bank Merger Act Amendment of 1966 and the Newspaper Preservation Act of 1970—intended, in part, to undo or limit the effects of the suits. Outside government, solutions such as those advocated in this volume are often rapidly rejected by industry groups, even where self-interest might indicate support. It would seem that theories that predict that the policies of regulatory agencies will inevitably be at odds with the economist's goal of allocative efficiency are equally applicable in predicting policies prescribed by legislative action. In short, the obstacles to the translation of ideas into practice appear to be greater than the difficulties of defining the ideas in the first place and securing an expert consensus on them.[15]

Although pessimism about the prospects of increased competition in the regulated area is well founded, the fact remains that there is at present an unusual vitality in the discussion of the problem. Proposals for reform are not confined to academic journals and have, in fact, been cast as legislative proposals. There also appears to be a broad consensus among economists, and to some extent among a wider group of activist reformers also, that it is appropriate, at least as a first approximation, to measure the

12. "Legal Restriction of Competition," p. 475.

13. See Chapter 10. Phillips's reasoning is somewhat different from Schwartz's, however. He depicts a dynamic model of regulation that comes close to making competition an unstable condition, in the terms of economic theory.

14. *The Report of the President's Commission on Financial Structure and Regulation* (U.S. Government Printing Office, 1972).

15. The difficulties of consensus should not be minimized, however. Even among economists and lawyers who advocate increased reliance on competition, there is disagreement about what constitutes adequate competition and the means necessary to achieve it.

adequacy of regulatory performance against the standard of allocative efficiency.[16] This increases the likelihood that pressures for reform will move in roughly the same direction. Moreover, there have been developments of some consequence in the recent past that may facilitate further change. The courts have tended to strengthen the role of antitrust policy in regulatory decisions; and, for the past eight years or so, the Antitrust Division of the Department of Justice has, with some success, advocated competitive policy in various regulatory issues with far more energy and sophistication than before.[17] However, past experience with the difficulties of implementation of procompetitive policies indicates that a closer look at the problems and methods of implementation is warranted.

Means of Increasing Competition

Other writers in this volume identified some devices for implementing the recommended upgrading of competitive principles in the regulated area. Five of these, some of them interrelated, will receive some attention here. First, and most obvious, is new legislation. Second, even without new legislation, the courts may have interpretative leeway under existing legislation that enables them to upgrade the role of competition through their supervision of administrative agency determinations. Third, the agencies themselves may possess substantial discretion under their legislative mandates and can, regardless of judicial direction, place greater stress on competitive policies than they now do. Fourth, further enforcement of the antitrust laws can serve to establish and advance competitive principles in the regulated area. Finally, as a device for promoting competitive principles in the courts and agencies, the Department of Justice or other entities with a procompetitive commitment may participate in agency proceedings in order to furnish the facts and arguments to support an otherwise unrepresented consumer welfare interest.

16. See, for example, Mark Green and Ralph Nader, "Economic Regulation vs. Competition: Uncle Sam the Monopoly Man," *Yale Law Journal*, vol. 82 (April 1973), pp. 871–902. For a review of various regulatory goals, see Alfred E. Kahn, *The Economics of Regulation: Principles and Institutions* (Wiley, 1970), vol. 1, pp. 1–14.

17. A number of these efforts are reviewed in Donald I. Baker (of the Antitrust Division, Department of Justice), "The Role of Competition in Regulated Industries," *Boston College Industrial and Commercial Law Review*, vol. 11 (May 1970), pp. 571ff.

Legislation

Most of the more ambitious recommendations for implementing competitive policy toward an industry require new legislation that deregulates wholly or in part. It is the certain difficulties in obtaining this type of legislation that have given rise to much of the pessimism about the prospects for substantial change.

Before examining those difficulties, it should be noted that less drastic legislative remedies have been proposed, based on the premise that the anticompetitive bias of regulatory agencies has been facilitated by their broad mandate to operate "in the public interest," with little, if any, specification of what that meant. It is argued that this discretion, combined with the predictable tendency of agencies to adjust to the more immediate demands of organized industry groups, causes the competitive component of the public interest to be slighted. The legislative solution indicated by such an analysis is one of clarification of the goals of regulation in each case, with a specification of the relative importance of competition or allocative efficiency where a possible conflict among goals exists.

The Bank Merger Act Amendment of 1966 is a version of this type of legislation. Enacted to provide some relief to banks from the rigors of ordinary merger law, it requires that a competitive test for determining the permissibility of mergers—might the merger substantially lessen competition?—be the controlling factor unless anticompetitive effects are "clearly outweighed" by the probable effect of the merger in meeting the needs and convenience of the community. The litigation that has occurred under the act indicates that, while the hope of merging banks springs eternal, the "needs and convenience" justification for anticompetitive mergers has not as yet proven to be effective. The legislation has thus retained primary emphasis on the competitive considerations.

However, the experience under the Bank Merger Act does not necessarily mean that regulatory legislation with a similar presumption in favor of competition would be equally effective. The act has the advantage of being confined to a particular industry, focusing on a particular type of conduct—mergers—and incorporating a competitive test that has acquired a predictable content because it has already been extensively litigated in other industries. It is primarily an antitrust act with the potentiality of modification for broad regulatory purposes rather than a regulatory act that accords special weight to competition. Questions as to the existence and content of the "competitive" policies to be favored in other regulatory contexts, particularly where specific regulatory goals are stated, could generate confusion about when the presumption of competition is operative and when it is overcome.

The enactment of a "competitive presumption" type of legislation might be somewhat more feasible than passage of legislation that deregulates precisely because its consequences are less predictable. Such legislation will have some virtue in instructing the agencies how to array conflicting considerations[18] and will no doubt result in some shift in regulatory results where clearly identifiable anticompetitive conduct is involved. But it will not serve the same broad purposes as deregulation.

The difficulties in the path of broadscale legislative deregulation include possible opposition from the presumed beneficiaries of regulation, from the regulatory agency, and from those who fear the power of the unleashed industry. One can imagine that the countervailing influence of members of the American Economic Association and others committed to the goal of allocative efficiency would not much impress congressmen counting noses.[19] But the obstacles to deregulation do not arise solely from the relative strength of special interests. There are genuine problems posed by broad deregulation that might well cause even a Congress fervently committed to competition to hesitate. Proponents of deregulation usually (though not always) urge that competitive market processes can be relied upon in lieu of regulation and that the antitrust laws will assure their effectiveness. However, there is also a large body of criticism that complains of the lack of competition in the large segments of unregulated markets that are oligopolistic. It is also often argued that the antitrust laws are unable to assure that competitive processes govern in such markets. Moreover, it is debatable that enforcement of the antitrust laws reflects a policy primarily concerned with allocative efficiency, as proponents of deregulation tend to assume. A prudent congressman, lacking the certitude of some economists that no regulation is always preferable to some regulation, might well be reluctant to deregulate any industry that does not have an obviously unconcentrated structure.

Other considerations undoubtedly help make legislators wary of deregu-

18. This is considered desirable on a variety of grounds. See Henry J. Friendly, *The Federal Administrative Agencies: The Need for Better Definition of Standards* (Harvard University Press, 1962).

19. For a discussion of why legislative regulation of the economy does not result in optimal resource allocation, see Posner, *Economic Analysis of Law*, pp. 329–32.

lation. Dislocation of the existing commitments and expectations based on present regulation would be costly to those affected.[20] Deregulation would also disturb the cross-subsidization and the redistribution of income that often accompany regulation.[21] It may appropriately be argued that such functions are incidental to the legitimate purpose of regulation, and that, if desirable, they should be separately articulated and evaluated by the legislature. Nevertheless, since the decision to deregulate may in fact affect such functions, those consequences make the decision that much harder to reach.

An alternative to legislating near-complete deregulation would be new legislation that narrows the scope of present regulation. For example, substantial leeway for price competition could be allowed, limiting agency intervention to exceptional situations. This approach is exemplified by the Canadian railroad legislation, which confines maximum rate regulation narrowly and uses variable costs as a basis for determining the low end of a reasonable rate. Although such a second-best solution may have un-intended consequences, it should be remembered that existing regulation may itself be an accumulation of sui generis responses to disparate problems rather than a logical whole. Hence, it is at least conceivable that changes involving significant partial deregulation might introduce no new mischief while avoiding some of the political difficulties inherent in major deregulation. Whether this is in fact possible remains to be seen.

The Courts

Even in the absence of new legislation, the courts undoubtedly have the power to upgrade the role of competitive principles in the regulated area, both when settling jurisdictional conflicts between regulatory and antitrust statutes and when reviewing the work of regulatory agencies. They have already done so to some extent in resolving issues concerning the con-

20. The reaction to recommendations of the President's Commission on Financial Structure and Regulation to deregulate barriers to entry in the financial field is illustrative. Segments of the financial community welcomed opportunities to compete in markets previously closed to them but were opposed to allowing other segments to compete in markets currently occupied only by themselves.

21. On cross-subsidization, see Richard A. Posner, "Taxation by Regulation," *Bell Journal of Economics and Management Science*, vol. 2 (Spring 1971), pp. 22–50; on redistribution of income, see Stephen Breyer and Paul W. MacAvoy, "The Natural Gas Shortage and the Regulation of Natural Gas Producers," *Harvard Law Review*, vol. 86 (April 1973), pp. 941–87.

current role of antitrust and regulatory laws.[22] For example, the courts purport to construe exemption from the antitrust laws strictly and to find an implied repeal of antitrust only when such repeal is "necessary" to make a regulatory statute work.[23] The Supreme Court recently construed the scope of an agency's jurisdiction narrowly, in part because that jurisdiction could be exercised to confer antitrust immunity.[24] Such decisions have served to help keep the antitrust laws applicable in regulated areas, though in any particular case the courts might decide that the regulatory scheme preempts the antitrust laws.

In addition to determination of questions of the applicability of antitrust laws, the courts also have the function of reviewing the work of regulatory agencies against the standards of the regulatory legislation. In doing so, they probably could adopt procompetitive presumptions analogous to those they have developed in determining whether the antitrust laws have been displaced. For example, where the agency operates under a broadly stated "public interest" mandate, it is probably open to the courts to follow the Schwartz suggestion and hold that competitive considerations should prevail in the absence of powerful justifications for a different course. In fact, the courts have not staked out such a position.[25] But they have supported the more modest proposition that an agency must ordinarily weigh competitive effects in determining whether a transaction should be approved as in the public interest.[26] And the Supreme Court upheld an agency's right to develop a policy of refusing to approve, under a public interest mandate, actions contrary to antitrust principles unless a powerful demonstration of necessity was made.[27]

Even where legislation provides a detailed statement of regulatory goals and not merely a public interest mandate, courts may still have the leeway to develop a procompetitive presumption. The Justice Department so argued with regard to the Transportation Acts of 1920 and 1940 in the *Northern Lines* merger cases,[28] urging the Supreme Court to find that the Interstate Commerce Commission erroneously approved the merger in

22. See Phillip E. Areeda, "Antitrust Laws and Public Utility Regulation," *Bell Journal of Economics and Management Science*, vol. 3 (Spring 1972), pp. 42–57.
23. See, for example, *United States* v. *McKesson & Robbins, Inc.*, 351 U.S. 305, 316 (1956); and *Silver* v. *New York Stock Exchange*, 373 U.S. 341 (1963).
24. *Federal Maritime Commission* v. *Seatrain Lines, Inc.*, 411 U.S. 726 (1973).
25. *McLean Trucking Co.* v. *United States*, 321 U.S. 67 (1944).
26. See *Gulf States Utilities Co.* v. *Federal Power Commission*, 411 U.S. 747 (1973).
27. *Federal Maritime Commission* v. *Swedish American Line*, 390 U.S. 238 (1968).
28. *United States* v. *Interstate Commerce Commission*, 396 U.S. 491 (1969).

question because the elimination of competition between two healthy railroads required an extraordinary justification and none existed. The Transportation Act of 1920 did favor consolidation, but the Justice Department argued that the legislative intent was confined to cases involving a "sick" railroad. The Court, however, declined to construct a presumption against the merger of healthy competitors, and found usual merger economies to be sufficient justification for the agency's approval.

This suggests limits to the willingness or ability of courts to make procompetitive interpretations of congressional legislation, particularly where some contrary legislative intention may be implied. Thus, the Supreme Court has recently declared that since Congress provided for "just and reasonable" rates and for the regulation of the price of natural gas, the courts could not permit an agency to "regulate" rates by placing exclusive reliance on market prices.[29]

It is conceivable that, in situations where there is no contrary indication of legislative intent, the courts could exercise their review powers to require agencies affirmatively to promote competition in their exercise of jurisdiction—for instance, by requiring that agencies pursue a policy permitting new entry into a market in the absence of clear proof that the applicant is in some generally accepted way unsound. But the courts have not in fact attempted to impose this kind of procompetitive obligation on the work of the regulatory agencies, and it is unlikely that they will. They are probably more apt to interfere with an agency's tolerance of conduct that is recognizably anticompetitive under the antitrust laws, with which courts are familiar, than to interfere with agency regulatory determinations on the basis of their inappropriateness as measured by standards of allocative efficiency.

Agencies

Even without new legislation and without the stimulus of reviewing courts, administrative agencies have substantial discretion to place a greater premium on competition in their exercise of jurisdiction. For example, they can be restrictive or liberal in the execution of their authority to pass on applications for new entry. In passing on mergers, they can be sensitive or insensitive to competitive considerations. In their control of prices, they can, within limits, keep a tight or loose rein. In their approach to problems

29. *Federal Power Commission* v. *Texaco, Inc., U.S. Law Week*, vol. 42 (June 11, 1974), p. 4873.

of alleged discrimination or predatory pricing or related questions of relative efficiency, they can be protectionist or not. In their assessment of the extent to which competition must be displaced to assure achievement of regulatory goals, they can be strict or generous. When given a broad public interest mandate, and even when given a narrower but neutral one, they may, of their own volition, adopt a presumption in favor of competition.[30] The much vaunted expertness of the agencies, resulting from their continued access to industry facts and problems, could be used to explore with objectivity and depth the claims that departures from competitive policy are justified by efficiencies, destructive competition, and so forth.

Of course, the very existence of a regulatory scheme and the agency that implements it limits the role of competition. But, given the variety of decisions that can be made in a manner consistent with competitive assumptions, "enlightened" regulation can have significant consequences. The crucial question is how remote the likelihood of such agency self-reform is. Those who regard the regulatory process as unalterably involving an anticompetitive bias will hold little hope for this kind of change. Certainly some pessimism is warranted. But regulatory agencies have been known to change their position on some key issues—the SEC's changing attitude on fixed commission rates is an example—and it is worth remarking that in some cases regulatory policy that seems perverse to economists may be so not because of any deliberate bias or because it conforms to some theory of political economics, but for want of an articulate, energetic, and documented expression of the procompetitive position. However remote the prospect for substantial reform from within the regulatory agency, it may be more feasible than major reform through legislation or competitive activism in the courts.

Antitrust Litigation

Litigation under the antitrust laws has an obvious role in advancing competitive principles in the regulated area. For instance, although bank mergers were once thought to be immune from application of section 7 of the Clayton Act, aggressive Justice Department action in the *Philadelphia National Bank* case successfully asserted the section's applicability, and since then antitrust law enforcement has undoubtedly had an impact in

---

30. See especially the behavior of the Federal Maritime Commission in the *Swedish American Line* case cited above.

inhibiting increases in market concentration in commercial banking.[31] There may well be a number of areas where the fact of regulation has little or no bearing on the considerations that ordinarily justify antitrust litigation.

The relatively recent initiation of antitrust actions in the electric power and securities industries illustrates the fact that the scope of permissible application of the antitrust laws is still surprisingly undefined. Weiss suggests[32] that a formidable plan of antitrust enforcement can be constructed as part of an overall program of enhancing competition in the electric power industry. In addition, the very possibility of the application of antitrust can have a significant impact on conduct within an industry, and can generate procompetitive action by the regulatory agency.

There are, however, substantial problems associated with the increased use of antitrust law enforcement as a major means of promoting competition in the regulated area. First, such suits invariably raise highly complex and time-consuming procedural and jurisdictional issues that the courts must resolve to accommodate the roles of the regulatory agency and the courts.[33] Second, while antitrust litigation may serve to bar certain anticompetitive conduct or structure, it does not necessarily provide a vehicle for enforcing procompetitive policies; this is important where the problem is not volitional restrictive conduct by the regulated entities but constraints imposed by the agencies acting under the law. Third, conventional antitrust analysis, with its per se rules and assumptions about a free market, may require substantial reformulation for actual applicability to a regulated entity.[34] Fourth, the antitrust lawsuit is a device available to complainants seeking treble damages as well as to federal enforcement agencies; and even if the antitrust enforcement agencies were unqualifiedly committed to a view of antitrust as concerned principally with allocative efficiency (and they are not), it is fair to say that private claimants seeking trebled damages do not have so pure a commitment. Nor can the courts be relied on to validate only competitively desirable claims. In summary, the antitrust lawsuit is a device that is sometimes useful but one that can lead to

31. Note, however, Phillips's argument in Chapter 10 that regulatory constraints make the performance of banks noncompetitive even if concentrated market structures are avoided through a vigorous antitrust policy.

32. See Chapter 5.

33. See, for example, *Ricci* v. *Chicago Mercantile Exchange*, 409 U.S. 289 (1973).

34. For example, in *Otter Tail Power Company* v. *United States*, the Court, after having found that the antitrust laws apply and were violated, made relief subject to regulatory approvals and anticipated implementation of policies in the Federal Power Act (410 U.S. 366).

Draconian results. Major reform of the kind called for in this volume probably requires other and finer tools.

Competitive Advocacy

Vital to the performance of the agencies and courts in upgrading competition is the advocacy on the basis of which their decisions are made. The Department of Justice in recent years has played an expanded role within the councils of government and before the agencies as an advocate of competitive policies.[35] It has on occasion performed this function on an analytical level that surpasses the standard of its performance as an antitrust litigator and law enforcer. In part, this is because the Antitrust Division can be more selective in deciding to intervene in agency proceedings than in carrying out its law enforcement obligation; perhaps it is also because the complexity of the issues and the need for persuasion forces the division to develop new analyses and arguments for the agencies. For certain issues, such as stock exchange commission rate fixing, the division aggregated a substantial volume of current academic economic thinking for presentation to the agency involved.

These activities have been conducted with relatively little legal and economic manpower, considering the magnitude and importance of the problems addressed—though this commitment of effort has been sufficient to arouse complaints from those who believe that traditional antitrust enforcement in the nonregulated area has suffered from a diversion of resources. Inevitably, there are gaps in the issues selected for the division's attention, some scantiness in the substance of some interventions, and some tendency to utilize indiscriminatingly, the same all-purpose litany on the virtues of competition. And the division is not without its own limitations in its view of the competitive consensus. But its contributions have been considerable. While consumer-oriented public-interest law firms or a new Consumer Protection Agency might be expected to complement the department's activities in the representation of specific consumer interests in regulatory problems, it is unlikely that such entities can be as oriented toward a competitive goal of allocative efficiency as the Justice Department. Experience thus far suggests that the burden of accomplishment will, for the most part, remain with the division.

35. See Baker, "Role of Competition."

Prospects for Change

A rough appraisal can be made of the relative prospects for success the various means of increasing the role of competitive principles are likely to have.

As to the prospects of legislation, one must guess that extensive deregulation in any particular area is still improbable, however meritorious it may be. Gradual deregulation over an extended period of time would not have the same dislocating effects, but it might still lack the needed support. Somewhat more probable is partial deregulation in certain areas in the form of narrowing the scope and changing the tools of regulation. Perhaps, to minimize disruption of functions and expectations, it might be accompanied by compensation in subsidy or other forms, in the hope that an amalgam of changes might attract support from several sources, including the regulators, the regulated, and the consuming public.

In the absence of new legislation, there is no compelling reason to suppose that the courts will encourage and supervise a national policy of upgrading competition (as distinguished from preserving a role for the antitrust laws) in the regulatory field. Perhaps greater judicial awareness of economic principles and of an "economic consensus," if such there be, could be developed through persuasive scholarly analyses of industry problems; this volume is an effort in that direction. But different judges will have but glancing encounters with these problems and there is little basis for predicting significant change. Establishment of a specialized administrative court to review agency decisions could, theoretically, produce greater awareness of and responsiveness to an economic consensus (if, in fact, a consensus on the "best" competitive solution could be reached); but specialized bodies and procedural solutions have often disappointed expectations in the past, and could well do so in this case.

Increased agency responsiveness to competitive principles, of its own volition, is possible to some extent. The widespread skepticism about such a development is probably exaggerated. It is conceivable that, with quantification of the costs of certain anticompetitive regulatory policies and with further analyses such as those in this volume, there may well be critical changes in the way agencies use their discretionary powers. The suggestion of the Nixon Task Force on Productivity and Competition that economists be appointed as commissioners, if ever adopted, would probably be a step in this direction, but its significance should not be overestimated.[36]

Expansion of the role of the Department of Justice (or the Federal Trade Commission) as a self-appointed proponent of competitive policy in the regulatory areas is without obvious inherent limitations other than budgetary ones. Although increased commitment of resources does not guarantee that the department will significantly and persistently influence results, otherwise unrepresented positions will at least be presented. If the arguments are lucid and firmly based on fact, it will be difficult for the regulatory agencies to ignore them. Some improvement in regulatory performance may thus occur, at least in those cases where the regulatory malfunctioning is due to lack of expert argument.

The tool of antitrust litigation can be of occasional important use. In some cases in the regulatory area, there is absolutely no basis for deflecting the ordinary application of the antitrust laws. Moreover, the threat of the use of this blunt instrument can on occasion stimulate substantial adjustments by a regulatory agency. But for many purposes litigation may not be the ideal means for gaining the economic goal. Such considerations as untoward consequences in treble damages and limits on the nature of the relief a court may give circumscribe the potential of litigation.

This survey suggests that the prospects for rapid change are remote. The extensive deregulatory legislation that would be required for such change is unlikely to be passed. Partial deregulation in some areas is more possible of achievement and, combined with court surveillance, competitive advo-

36. For the purpose of historical perspective, it is worth noting Schwartz's observation in 1954 on the contribution of economists:

"We have only to look about at the social science experts and the real role they play in community life to see that expertness is not wisdom and that the relative ordering of values in a society—the ultimate problem of choosing between alternative courses of action—is something we do after the expert has completed his task of collecting data, describing, and, to a limited extent, predicting. This should be sufficiently clear from the field of economics, which is closest to the immediate concern of this paper. The most contradictory policies are constantly buttressed by economic experts of unquestionable authority. How can anyone believe in policy by experts when he finds men of unexceptional scholarly qualifications serving as economists and voices of policy for the CIO and the NAM, the Antitrust Division and the ICC, the Federal Reserve Board and the Treasury Department. In the *Cement Institute* case one battery of economic experts testified that uniform delivered prices for cement demonstrated that here at last perfect competition had been discovered in real life, while other experts testified as convincingly that this price behavior was self-evidently monopolistic" ("Legal Restriction of Competition," p. 472).

cacy, antitrust litigation, and agency discretion, makes some continued movement toward more competition both feasible and probable.

There is throughout this discussion an assumption that a broad consensus exists on the changes that are needed in the regulated sector, and it is this assumption that provokes impatience with institutional and other obstacles to prompt and major reform. For the sake of perspective, it is worth recollecting that while there may be some such consensus on the part of many—but hardly all—academic economists, it does not extend to most noneconomists. The resource allocation standard is hard to discern in the legislative history of the various regulatory statutes. Further, the tools of economic reasoning used to demonstrate competitive shortcomings, though conventionally accepted by those in the profession, may be neither impressive nor convincing to those outside it. Similarly, statistical samples may be regarded as unpersuasive. The preference expressed in this volume for an unregulated market with reliance on antitrust action to check abuses may be unacceptable to those who emphasize the more popular concept of the present abuses of the unregulated market and the ineffectiveness of the antitrust laws. It should not, therefore, be surprising that the valid contributions of economic analysis and data may be only slowly incorporated into government policy. Awareness of that fact, at least, suggests the need for patience and persistence rather than despair.

Conference Participants

MORRIS A. ADELMAN *Massachusetts Institute of Technology*

W. BRUCE ALLEN *University of Pennsylvania*

DONALD I. BAKER *Department of Justice*

WILLIAM F. BAXTER *Stanford Law School*

RICHARD S. BOWER *Dartmouth College*

STEPHEN G. BREYER *Harvard Law School*

WILLIAM M. CAPRON *Harvard University*

SAMUEL B. CHASE, JR. *Board of Governors of the Federal Reserve System*

ROGER C. CRAMTON *Cornell Law School*

GEORGE W. DOUGLAS *University of Texas*

GEORGE C. EADS *George Washington University*

ALLEN R. FERGUSON *Public Interest Economics Center and Foundation*

GENE L. FINN *Securities and Exchange Commission*

GEORGE W. HILTON *University of California at Los Angeles*

ALFRED E. KAHN *Cornell University*

ROBERT J. LARNER *Brandeis University*

SIMON LAZARUS III *Arnold and Porter*

PAUL W. MACAVOY *Massachusetts Institute of Technology*

H. MICHAEL MANN *Boston College*

EDWARD MARGOLIN *University of Pennsylvania*

JAMES C. MILLER III *Council of Economic Advisers*

THOMAS GALE MOORE *Michigan State University*

EDWIN S. MILLS *Princeton University*

NEIL B. MURPHY *University of Maine at Orono*

JAMES R. NELSON *Amherst College*

ROGER G. NOLL *California Institute of Technology*

WILLIAM D. NORDHAUS *Yale University*

BRUCE M. OWEN *Stanford University*

JACK PEARCE *Pearce and Brand*

JOSEPH A. PECHMAN *Brookings Institution*

MERTON J. PECK *Yale University*

ALMARIN PHILLIPS *University of Pennsylvania*

LEE E. PRESTON *State University of New York at Buffalo*

WALTER J. PRIMEAUX, JR. *University of Illinois*

GLEN RAMSEY *University of Rhode Island*

LEONARD SILK *New York Times*

DENNIS E. SMALLWOOD *University of California at San Diego*

HASKELL P. WALD *Federal Power Commission*

LEONARD WAVERMAN *University of Toronto*

LEONARD W. WEISS *University of Wisconsin*

LAWRENCE J. WHITE *Princeton University*

OLIVER E. WILLIAMSON *University of Pennsylvania*

EDWIN M. ZIMMERMAN *Covington and Burling*

Index

Abbott, Lawrence, 52
Abraham, L. G., 212n
Adams, Henry C., 176n
Adams, Walter, 55n, 175n, 368n
Adelman, Morris A., 123n
Advertising, 2, 335, 336
Agricultural commodities, transport of, 59, 69–70, 75
Air California, 49
Air carriers, European, 43–45
Air carriers, U.S., 8; capacity, 16, 31–33, 41–42; charter versus scheduled, 15; city-pair markets for, 13, 15, 16, 31, 41, 51; competition, 13, 15, 16, 27, 31–34, 39–40, 43, 45–46, 47–48, 52–53; effect of deregulation on, 52–53; entry into market by, 13, 48, 49, 52n–53n; intrastate, 33n, 48–52; load factor, 15, 20, 21–22, 24, 25–27, 30, 31–34, 37, 38, 44, 46, 48, 49; monopoly route, 26, 27, 30, 34; as natural monopoly, 15; regulation of, 13–15, 39–42; schedule delay, 20–21. *See also* Costs, airline; Fares; Service quality
Air Line Pilots Association (ALPA), 50, 51
Airlines. *See* Air carriers
Alexander, Joshua N., 101
Alexander Report, 101–04, 131
Alhadreff, David A., 360n
Allocative effect, of regulation, 5, 11–12, 56, 72, 85, 90, 123, 335, 380
ALPA. *See* Air Line Pilots Association
American Agency System, 245
American Airlines, 22n, 41, 46
American Economic Association, 374
American Electric Power System, 165, 166n, 167
American Telephone and Telegraph Company (AT&T), 10, 210, 215, 224; facilities of, 227; microwave transmission monopoly of, 202–03
Annable, James E., Jr., 62n
Antitrust Division, Department of Justice, 371, 372, 380, 382; depository fi-

nancial institutions and, 356, 363, 378; electric power industry and, 9, 135, 161, 162, 164, 165, 166; ocean freight industry and, 100, 125; railroads and, 88, 376–77
Antitrust policy: and automobile insurance industry, 246; conference system violation of, 100–02; and depository financial institutions, 337, 363–64, 366; and electric power industry, 160–65, 168, 379; and railroads, 88, 376–77; task force on, 368–69, 371
Areeda, Phillip E., 376n
Ash Council Report. *See* President's Advisory Council on Executive Organization
Aspinwall, Richard C., 353n
Atlantic Container Line consortium, 117, 118n
Atomic Energy Act of *1954*, 164
AT&T. *See* American Telephone and Telegraph Company
Australia, deregulation of trucking industry, 74
Automobile insurance: assigned risk, 242, 276; basic protection plan for, 276–77; commission rates, 246, 249, 284; Consumers Union survey of, 284–90, 295; direct writers of, 246, 248, 258; elasticity of demand for, 260; handling of claims, 242, 283, 291, 296, 297; New York State complaint experience with, 245, 291, 292–95, 298; no-fault, 241, 244, 276–78, 290, 298; problems relating to renewal of, 242, 249, 265–66, 297; quality of contract for, 245, 278–84, 290; selection process for applicants for, 243, 245, 252–60, 275–76. *See also* Automobile insurance industry; Premium rates
Automobile insurance industry, 10; competition in, 242, 244, 245, 247, 297; competitive equilibrium in, 266–68; criticism of, 241–42; entry of firms into, 244, 267, 268; joint rates by, 246, 248, 267; profit

387